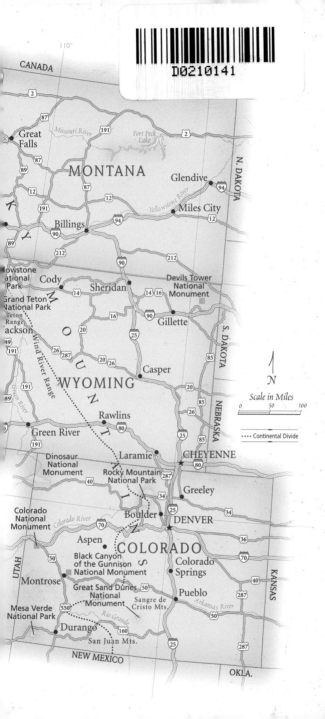

CANADA

110°

MONTANA

Great
Falls

Missouri River

Fort Peck
Lake

Glendive

N. DAKOTA

Miles City

Yellowstone River

Billings

Devils Tower
National
Monument

Yellowstone
National
Park

Cody

Sheridan

Gillette

S. DAKOTA

Grand Teton
National Park

Teton
Range

Jackson

Wind River Range

WYOMING

Casper

M O U N T A I N S

Rawlins

Green River

Laramie

CHEYENNE

Dinosaur
National
Monument

Rocky Mountain
National Park

Greeley

Colorado
National
Monument

Colorado River

Boulder

DENVER

Aspen

COLORADO

Black Canyon
of the Gunnison
National Monument

Colorado
Springs

Montrose

KANSAS

Great Sand Dunes
National
Monument

Sangre de
Cristo Mts.

Pueblo

Arkansas River

Mesa Verde
National Park

Rio Grande

Durango

San Juan Mts.

NEW MEXICO

OKLA.

UTAH

NEBRASKA

Scale in Miles

0   50   100

······ Continental Divide

N

D0210141

NATIONAL
AUDUBON
SOCIETY®
FIELD GUIDE TO THE
Rocky Mountain
STATES

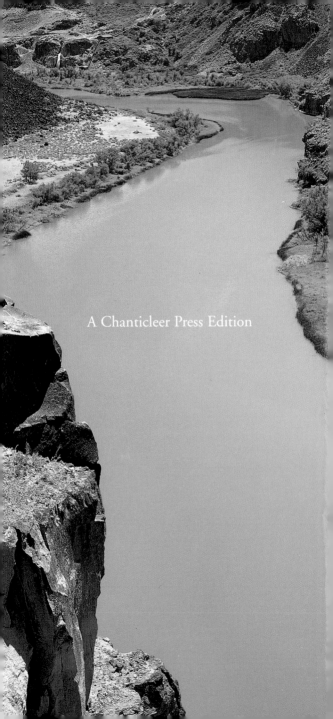
A Chanticleer Press Edition

NATIONAL AUDUBON SOCIETY
FIELD GUIDE TO THE
Rocky Mountain STATES

Peter Alden

Brian Cassie   John Grassy

Jonathan D. W. Kahl   Amy Leventer

Daniel Mathews   Wendy B. Zomlefer

Alfred A. Knopf, New York

This is a Borzoi Book.
Published by Alfred A. Knopf, Inc.

Copyright © 1998 by Chanticleer Press, Inc.
All rights reserved under International and Pan-American Copyright Conventions. Published in the United States by Alfred A. Knopf, Inc., New York, and simultaneously in Canada by Random House of Canada Limited, Toronto. Distributed by Random House, Inc., New York.

www.randomhouse.com

Knopf, Borzoi Books, and the colophon are registered trademarks of Random House, Inc.

Prepared and produced by
Chanticleer Press, Inc., New York.

Printed and bound by
Dai Nippon Printing Co., Ltd., Korea.

First Edition
Published April 1999
Fourth Printing, January 2005

Library of Congress Cataloging-in-Publication Data

National Audubon Society field guide to the Rocky Mountain states /
   Peter Alden . . . [et al.] — 1st ed.
      p.   cm.
   Includes index.
   ISBN 0-679-44681-8
   1. Natural history—Rocky Mountains Region—Guidebooks.
2. Natural areas—Rocky Mountains Region—Guidebooks. 3. Parks—
Rocky Mountains Region—Guidebooks.   I. Alden, Peter.
II. National Audubon Society.
QH104.5.R6N38   1999
508.78—dc21   98-38192

National Audubon Society

The mission of NATIONAL AUDUBON SOCIETY *is to conserve and restore natural ecosystems, focusing on birds, other wildlife, and their habitats, for the benefit of humanity and the earth's biological diversity.*

One of the largest, most effective environmental organizations, Audubon has 550,000 members, 100 sanctuaries, state offices, and nature centers, and over 500 chapters in the Americas, plus a professional staff of scientists, educators, and policy analysts.

The award-winning *Audubon* magazine, published six times a year and sent to all members, carries outstanding articles and color photography on wildlife and nature, presenting in-depth reports on critical environmental issues, as well as conservation news and commentary. Audubon also publishes *Audubon Adventures,* a children's newspaper reaching 450,000 students in grades four through six. Through Audubon ecology camps and workshops in Maine, Connecticut, and Wyoming, Audubon offers nature education for teachers, families, and children; through Audubon Expedition Institute in Belfast, Maine, the Society offers unique, traveling undergraduate and graduate degree programs in Environmental Education.

National Audubon Society also sponsors books, field guides, and on-line nature activities, plus travel programs to exotic places like Antarctica, Africa, Baja California, and the Galápagos Islands.

For information about how you can become an Audubon member, subscribe to *Audubon Adventures,* or to learn more about our camps and workshops, please write or call:

NATIONAL AUDUBON SOCIETY
Membership Dept.
700 Broadway
New York, New York 10003
212-979-3000 or 800-274-4201
http://www.audubon.org/

Contents
Part One: Overview

Part Two: Flora and Fauna

Part Three: Parks and Preserves

Appendices

Natural Highlights

"Backbone of the World" was the name Native Americans gave to the sinuous uplift of stone reaching from Canada to South America, known today as the Continental Divide. The Rocky Mountains are part of this great span and the defining geographical feature of Colorado, Montana, Idaho, and Wyoming, a 431,708-square-mile region of soaring peaks, lush mountain meadows and forests, and high desert-like plains and grasslands. Meadows and forests shelter wolves, Bighorn Sheep, Elk, and Mountain Lions; where mountains meet plains, herds of Pronghorn graze while Golden Eagles soar overhead. High deserts are home to a fascinating variety of birds and small mammals.

Lochsa River, Idaho

Rivers

Born of snowmelt in high mountain meadows, the region's well-known rivers—the Snake, the Salmon, the Lochsa, the Colorado, the Yellowstone, the Missouri, and the Green—pound through glorious canyons and spread out in valleys to sculpt islands and sloughs and support rich deciduous forests of cottonwoods and willows.

Rock Formations

Scattered across arid plains, badlands are crumbling spires, ridges, and cliffs of soft, often beautifully colored sedimentary rock, shaped by the relentless action of wind and water. "Breaks" can be deep, labyrinthine worlds, with juniper, sagebrush, and Ponderosa Pine holding fast to drainages and bottoms. On volcanic plains, ancient lava flows and cinder cones are slowly being reclaimed by wildflowers, conifers, and wildlife.

Missouri Breaks, Montana

Mountains

San Juan Mountains, Colorado

The large ranges that make up the Rockies—among them the San Juans, the Sangre de Cristos, the Sawtooths, the Wind Rivers, the Bitterroots, and the Tetons—are evidence of the region's dramatic geologic history. Pushed skyward through faulting, carved by glaciers, covered with volcanic flows, and scoured by wind and water, they offer superb opportunities for the naturalist to experience life in one of the world's most dramatic environments.

Plains

The western edges of the Great Plains extend into Montana, eastern Wyoming, and Colorado, offering the definitive Western experience of great vistas and vast skies. Amid this seemingly endless expanse, it can be difficult to pinpoint wildlife. Listen for the Long-billed Curlew's namesake call, the rapid trill of a Vesper Sparrow, or the cry of a Red-tailed Hawk on the wing.

Pawnee National Grassland, Colorado

Forests

Coniferous forests sheath all of the region's major mountain ranges. From a distance, they appear monotonous, but closer inspection reveals a surprising array of species, each adapted to a unique combination of moisture, sunlight, elevation, and soil type. Ponderosa and Lodgepole Pines, Douglas Fir, and Engelmann Spruce are a few of the more widely distributed trees.

Wildflowers

Summer's brief visit to the high country begins an intense wildflower display of Glacier Lilies, Pasqueflowers, Balsam-roots, and other species, which bloom in a perfectly choreographed cycle with the first appearance of snow-free ground.

Pasqueflower

Topography

The spine of the Rocky Mountains marks a portion of the Continental Divide, a chain of mountains and plateaus stretching from Canada to South America from which water flows west toward the Pacific Ocean on one side and east toward the Atlantic Ocean and the Gulf of Mexico on the other. In some places, such as Colorado, the Divide is dramatic and unmistakable, while in others, such as Yellowstone National Park, it is almost undetectable. The spectacular peaks of the Rockies, formed during periods of uplift and volcanic action and further shaped by glaciers and erosion, are the dominant topographical feature of the Rocky Mountain states. Broad, horizontal expanses also characterize the region: the Great Plains stretch eastward from the Rockies at an average elevation of

Salmon River, Idaho

4,000 feet, while the tableland of the Colorado Plateau lies to the southwest. In places, the mountain ranges split, leaving isolated basins, such as the Great Divide Basin of south-central Wyoming. The Oregon Trail traverses this low spot. A topographical map of the region appears on the book's back endpaper.

Salmon River

Idaho's Salmon River, known for its deep, narrow canyons and wild rapids, was nicknamed "The River of No Return" by early explorers. It was here in 1805 that Lewis and Clark's first attempt to find a river route to the Pacific failed. The Salmon severs northern and southern Idaho; it is the longest undammed river system in any single state in the United States.

The Colorado Plateau

West of the Rocky Mountains, in the southwestern corner of Colorado, lies the arid desert of the Colorado Plateau, a high-elevation tableland deeply incised by steep canyons. The Colorado River and its tributaries cut through the plateau, forming a maze of cliffs, escarpments, canyons, and mesas. This is the site of the ancient Anasazi civilization, whose cliff dwellings at Mesa Verde date back to between A.D. 500 and 1300; the Black Canyon of the Gunnison, where the closely etched cliffs are as little as 40 feet across; and Colorado National Monument, the site of spectacular sandstone cliffs and canyons.

Colorado National Monument, Colorado

Flathead Lake

Flathead Lake, Montana

Montana's Flathead Lake is the largest—and one of the cleanest—natural freshwater lakes in the western United States. It was formed about 10,000 years ago from a large mass of stagnant ice that lingered after the retreat of the last great ice sheet in North America. Because of its huge volume—it measures 27 miles long, 14 miles wide, and 371 feet deep—as well as the high winter winds common in the area, the lake rarely freezes over, despite its northerly location.

The Great Plains

The western edges of the Great Plains extend into eastern Montana, Colorado, and Wyoming. These immense grasslands, which stretch for hundreds of miles through the central United States, were formed from gravel and sand eroded from the Rocky Mountains and trans-

Comanche National Grassland, Colorado

ported east by wind and rivers. The sediment was deposited as an extensive apron, which includes the gently sloping "gang plank" of easternmost Wyoming and Colorado.

Grand Teton

At 13,766 feet, the Grand Teton caps Wyoming's Teton Range, a jagged mountain range, 40 miles long and 15 miles wide, that rises 7,000 feet above the valley floor in a nearly sheer cliff. These are the youngest mountains in the Rockies, with a rugged topography sculpted mainly by extensive glaciation during the last ice age. Evidence of this remains in the dozen or so small glaciers than can still be seen in Grand Teton National Park.

Tectonic Origins

The Rocky Mountain region is characterized by a wealth of faults, lines along which the earth's crust separates and moves. Two major mountain-building periods contributed to the formation of the Rocky Mountains—the first beginning about 300 million years ago, when the ancestral Rockies were formed, and a more recent one that began about 60 million years ago. During these periods, the collision of plates (see box, below) caused the earth's crust to compress and the blocks along the faults to move, either up or down, a process known as vertical displacement. The youngest of the ranges, the Tetons in Wyoming, formed only 6 to 9 million years ago. Since then, earthquake activity has caused about 10 additional feet of movement every few thousand years. In the Tetons, there has been over 30,000 feet of vertical displacement overall, a result of normal faulting, which separated the peaks of the western Tetons from the floor of the Jackson Hole Valley.

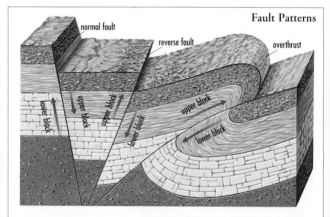

Fault Patterns

normal fault · reverse fault · overthrust · lower block · upper block · upper block · lower block · upper block · lower block

Faulting and Uplifting in the Rockies

According to the theory of plate tectonics, the earth's crust is broken into a dozen major plates that are kept in constant motion by convection currents, generated by earth's internal heat. This plate movement is responsible for the intense crustal deformation that results in mountain-building processes such as faulting, uplifting, and folding. Vertical movement along faults, or fractures in the crust, results in the uplifting and downdropping of adjacent blocks of rock. Faults are defined by the direction the blocks move. In normal faulting, the upper block is displaced downward while the lower block is uplifted; in a reverse fault, the upper block is forced upward. The upper block may be thrust over the lower block, called an overthrust.

Thrust Faults

A reverse fault is termed a thrust fault when the fault plane (the area over which the displacement occurs) is very shallow. About 170 million years ago, compressional forces in the earth's crust resulted in the thrusting of

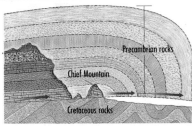

Lewis Overthrust: Most of the Precambrian rock that thrust over the younger Cretaceous rock has eroded away, leaving behind Chief Mountain and the ridge of the Continental Divide.

Precambrian rock, more than a billion years old, on top of much younger Cretaceous rock, more than 65 to 100 million years old. The nearly horizontal surface over which almost 50 miles of east-ward motion took place is called the Lewis Overthrust. Today, the rocks of Glacier National Park represent this ancient thrust slab.

Klippes

A klippe (German for "cliff") is a remnant of an overthrust slab that has been stranded after the rest of the slab has eroded away. Chief Mountain, an isolated peak located on the eastern margin of Glacier National Park, is a klippe that marks the easternmost point of the Lewis Overthrust. Here, Precambrian sedimentary rocks tower above rocks that are a billion years younger.

Chief Mountain, Glacier National Park, Montana

Intermountain Seismic Zone

Present-day earthquake activity in the Rocky Mountain region is concentrated in an area known as the intermountain seismic zone, which stretches through eastern Idaho and western portions of Montana and Wyoming. These northern Rockies are dissected by northwest–trending faults, formed over the past 50 million years. Blocks of the earth's crust aligned in this direction are still moving, a few feet at a time, raising the mountains and downdropping the valleys.

Volcanic Features

Volcanoes have shaped much of the Rocky Mountain region, and the effects of these relatively recent geologic events are easily observed. While Yellowstone National Park and Craters of the Moon National Monument are the best-known volcanic sites, other spectacular features exist. In Colorado, extensive outpourings of ash and lava occurred 10 to 40 million years ago, covering the area of the San Juan and West Elk Mountains and the White River Plateau; at Florissant Fossil Beds National Monument, gentle, rapid ashfalls 35 million years ago preserved delicate insect and plant fossils. Volcanic material dating back 50 million years is extensive, particularly in the Absaroka Range of Wyoming and Montana, Montana's Lowland Creek, and the vicinity of Challis, Idaho.

Yellowstone Geothermal Activity

A natural underground plumbing system that allows the circulation of hot water through fractured rocks results in the spectacular geothermal activity at Yellowstone National Park. Yellowstone's thousands of thermal features include hot springs, geysers, mudpots (hot springs with high concentrations of mud), and travertine terraces (raised layers of calcium carbonate deposited from hot springs). Its most famous geyser, Old Faithful, erupts on average every 79 minutes with a fountain of hot water that can reach 204° F and shoot to heights of 180 feet.

Old Faithful

Craters of the Moon

Craters of the Moon National Monument in southern Idaho represents the most recent volcanic action in the Rocky Mountain region, beginning about 15,000 years ago and continuing until as recently as 2,000 years ago. This 643-square-mile area on the Snake River Plain is covered with two types of basaltic lava flows: *pahoehoe* (thin, ropy flows) and *aa* (jagged, blocky flows). Many volcanic features dot the landscape: *Spatter cones* are steep-sided chimney-like structures, a few feet high, formed from globs of molten basalt that accumulated around steam vents; *cinder cones* are steep conical hills built up around volcanic vents from coarse rock fragments pushed out by escaping gases; *lava tube caves* are underground tunnels formed from the flow of molten lava through solidified crust.

Craters of the Moon National Monument

Devils Tower, Wyoming

Devils Tower

Wyoming's Devils Tower is the eroded core of an ancient volcano, famous for its central role in the movie *Close Encounters of the Third Kind*. The massive columns were formed from basaltic magma that cracked vertically as it cooled and contracted. The columns have a diameter of about 100 feet at their base; they rise 1,280 feet above the valley floor to an elevation of 5,117 feet.

Madison River and Madison Plateau, marking the edge of the Yellowstone Caldera

Yellowstone Volcano

The Yellowstone Volcano is one of the largest and most active resurgent volcanoes in the world. Resurgent volcanoes produce huge amounts of lava in eruptions spaced over hundreds of thousands of years. When the volcano last erupted 650,000 years ago, the magma chamber below was emptied and the overlying roof collapsed, leaving behind the remnant rim known as the Yellowstone Caldera.

HOT-SPOT VOLCANISM

A hot spot, or mantle plume, represents a region of localized melting within the earth that reaches the surface as a volcano. As the plates that form the surface of the earth pass over a hot spot, a linear chain of volcanoes is formed, with the oldest volcano farthest from the hot spot and the youngest lying just above the hot spot. The Yellowstone Hot Spot originated in Oregon about 17 million years ago, its origin possibly linked to the impact of a large meteorite. Its path can be traced across the Snake River Plain.

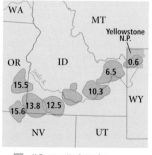

Yellowstone Hot Spot volcanoes
12.5 Ages of volcanoes (in millions of years)

Glacial Features

During the Pleistocene epoch, which began 2 million years ago, at least three major glacial advances left their mark on the Rocky Mountain states. In the most recent, powerful ice from the Cordilleran Ice Sheet, an extensive 1- to 2-mile-thick continental glacier, flowed through the area, scouring the underlying bedrock. This massive sheet, along with localized alpine glaciation, produced the magnificent jagged high peaks and the steep-walled valleys that characterize the Rocky Mountains. Most of the glaciers retreated about 15,000 to 20,000 years ago, marking the end of the last ice age. A few remain today, however, including three in Teton National Park, Wyoming: Skillet and Falling Ice Glaciers on Mount Moran and Teton Glacier on the Grand Teton. The Dinwoody Glaciers on the Wind River Range, Wyoming, form the largest existing ice field in the contiguous United States. There are tiny glaciers in the Front Range of Colorado, which some geologists speculate may have formed within the past few thousand years.

Lateral moraine (extending from lower left),
Rocky Mountain National Park

Moraines

Moraines are rubbly mixtures of rock and sand pushed ahead or along the side of advancing glaciers and left behind when the ice retreats. Terminal moraines form at the farthest point of glacial advancement; the more linear lateral moraines form along the sides of a glacier as it moves. Moraines are abundant throughout the Rocky Mountains. The ridge separating Hidden Valley from Horseshoe Park in Rocky Mountain National Park, Colorado, is an excellent example of a lateral moraine.

GLACIERS

Glaciers are masses of ice that move or spread over land. Ice sheets are continent-size glaciers that slowly advance outward from the center of ice accumulation; during ice ages, sheets of ice can extend across mountain ranges. Even outside of ice ages, smaller alpine glaciers form in cold, high mountains when accumulated snow compresses into ice and begins to move; like rivers of ice, alpine glaciers travel downhill. As they move, glaciers scour surfaces, erode bedrock, and deposit eroded debris in the form of erratics and moraines.

The Garden Wall, Glacier National Park

Aretes

Arete (French for "fish bone") refers to a long, narrow, serrated ridge, much like a knife-edge, that forms as glaciers carve away at either side of a mountain. The Garden Wall in Glacier National Park, Montana, is an arete separating Lake McDonald Valley from Many Glacier Valley. Aretes line the ridges of Idaho's Sawtooth Range and Wyoming's Wind River Range.

Giant Ripples

Ripples are long dunes of sediment formed at right angles to the overlying current. The giant ripples located on the Camas Prairie, between Perma and Hot Springs, Montana, range in height from 15 to 50 feet, and measure 100 to 250 feet from crest to crest. They formed about 15,000 years ago when a glacier that had blocked the Clark Fork river to create Glacial Lake Missoula broke free, causing a catastrophic flood. Similar events extended westward all the way to Washington.

Giant ripples on the Camas Prairie

Glacial erratics, Wind River Range, Wyoming

Erratics

Glacial erratics occur at high elevations throughout the Rocky Mountain states. Ice age glaciers moving across the landscape tens of thousands of years ago scoured the underlying bedrock, picking up boulders and transporting them far from their site of origin. These boulder-size rocks are found randomly scattered and are often recognized by their composition, which can be quite different from the surrounding rock.

Bird Woman Falls, Glacier National Park

Hanging Valleys

While large alpine glaciers formed deep U-shaped valleys, smaller tributary glaciers eroded through side canyons, cutting less deeply into the land. As the glaciers retreated, small valleys were left stranded on the mountainsides. These hanging valleys are common in previously glaciated areas of the Rocky Mountain states. Streams running through them precipitously plummet to the main trough of the larger valleys below, forming spectacular waterfalls. Bird Woman Falls cascades from a hanging valley on Oberlin Mountain in Montana's Glacier National Park.

Cirques

Cirques form at high elevations when bowls of rock are scooped out by ice at the heads of alpine glaciers. As the glacial ice melts, the bowl-shaped depressions often fill with water to form small lakes. Many such lakes dot the Rocky Mountain land-

Iceberg Lake, Glacier National Park

scape. Avalanche, Iceberg, and Gunsight Lakes in Glacier National Park, Montana, are all cirque lakes.

U-shaped Valleys

As glaciers traveled across the region they scoured the landscape, rounding and smoothing V-shaped valleys, previously cut by running water, into long U-shaped valleys with flat floors and steep

sides. When the ice receded, the U-shaped valleys remained, many of them filled with water. Colorado's Unaweep Canyon is an excellent example of a U-shaped valley. Lake McDonald in Glacier National Park, Montana, is another glacially gouged basin, with lateral moraines forming linear ridges on either side.

Unaweep Canyon, Colorado

Felsenmeers and Patterned Ground

Felsenmeers form when jagged rocks are thrust upward during repeated cycles of freezing and thawing. These "seas of rock" are common above the tree line in alpine areas. Patterned ground, similarly formed in regions with heavy frost activity, is characterized by cracks in the soil that form regular polygonal shapes. Patterned ground on Idaho's Snake River Plain dates back to the much colder conditions of the last glacial period.

Felsenmeers, Rocky Mountain National Park

Erosion by Wind and Water

Wind and water are powerful weathering agents, slowly wearing down mountains, deepening canyons and valleys, shaping unusual rock formations, and transporting sediment. Above the tree line in mountainous areas of the Rockies, the almost daily cycle of freezing and thawing significantly affects the appearance of the land, with water filling small cracks in the rocks during the day, then freezing and expanding at night to enlarge the cracks and break down the rock. Other areas show evidence of differential erosion, in which one type of rock erodes more easily or quickly than another; shale and volcanic ash, for example, erode more easily than hardened basaltic flows or well-cemented sandstones. Differential erosion is responsible for many unusual formations in the Rocky Mountain region, including hogbacks, badlands, and rock pinnacles.

Black Canyon of the Gunnison, Colorado

Canyons

Western Colorado's Black Canyon of the Gunnison is one of the narrowest and deepest canyons in the United States, in some places as little as 40 feet across at water level, with a maximum depth of 2,700 feet. The steep cliffs are maintained by the high resistance of the rocks to weathering. The nearly vertical walls of dark gray to purplish metamorphic rock are crisscrossed by lighter stripes of pink granite. Below, the waters of the Gunnison River appear bright green, the result of sunlight reflecting off sedimentary particles floating in the river.

Caverns

Underground cavities form when slightly acidic groundwater percolates through limestone and gradually dissolves it away. When the dripping water, rich in lime, evaporates, it leaves behind tiny crystals of calcium carbonate, which eventually grow into stalagmites,

Lewis and Clark Caverns, Montana

stalactites, and other cave formations. Montana's Lewis and Clark Caverns probably formed during the last ice age when the local climate was wetter, with more abundant groundwater and surface flow. Other notable caverns in the region are Minnetonka Cave in Idaho and Cave of the Winds in Colorado.

Great Sand Dunes, Colorado

Dunes

The 700-foot-tall Great Sand Dunes of the San Luis Valley, Colorado, are among the world's highest sand dunes. They formed from sand eroded by glaciers from the San Juan Mountains and carried by the meandering Rio Grande River; strong winds blew the sand northeast across the broad, flat San Luis Valley and piled it up to form dunes at the base of the Sangre de Cristo Mountains. The dune field covers an oval area about 6 miles wide and 6½ miles long. Because of prevailing southwest winds, the dunes are asymmetric, with much steeper eastern slopes. Their relatively dark color comes from a mixture of light-colored quartz and dark-colored volcanic grains.

Badlands

Badland-type weathering occurs in soft, easily eroded sedimentary rock that is cohesive enough to maintain steep faces. Rain splash and surface runoff over slopes devoid of vegetation carve a myriad of steep and narrow features, including columns, spires, and accordion-like folds. Beautiful reds, pinks, yellows, and greens are exposed in the weathered clay stones, shales, and sandstones of Hell's Half Acre, west of Casper, Wyoming. Other examples of badland weathering can be seen in Wyoming's Bighorn, Green River, Washakie, and Great Divide Basins, and in Montana at Terry Badlands and Makoshika State Park.

Hell's Half Acre, Wyoming

Dakota Hogback, Colorado Springs

Hogbacks

When uplifted and tilted rock layers of different composition and hardness weather at different rates (differential erosion), they can leave behind ridges of resistant composition, called hogbacks. The Dakota Hogback is a ridge of resistant sandstone that runs intermittently just east of Colorado's Front Range, from Wyoming to New Mexico, marking the edge of the Great Plains.

Garden of the Gods, Colorado

Garden of the Gods

The spectacular pinnacles, towers, and blades of Garden of the Gods in Colorado also resulted from differential erosion. These massive formations are composed of red sandstone "hardened" by a silica and iron cement and then tilted to a vertical position by tectonic uplift activity. Their imposing heights, shapes, and colors give them their name.

Honeycomb Weathering

This type of weathering is initiated when erosion by rain and moisture creates little depressions in the rock, which are then hollowed out by wind into deep, fist-size cavities. Collecting water and whirling eddies of sand continue to erode the holes. Honeycomb weathering is common in the sandstones of the Mesa Verde Formation in Colorado. The Mesa Verde is also the site of ancient cliff dwellings occupied by the Anasazi Indians.

Honeycomb weathering, Mesa Verde National Park

Minerals and Natural Resources

Minerals, the building blocks of rocks, are naturally occurring substances with characteristic chemical compositions and crystal structures that determine their external appearance. A mineral may be a single native element, such as copper or gold, or a compound of elements. Minerals are recognized by such physical properties as hardness, cleavage or fracture (the way they break), luster (the way the surface reflects light), and crystal structure. Minerals are *ductile* if they can be shaped into strings; they are *malleable* if they can be hammered into various shapes. Color may be an unreliable identifying feature, since it is often the result of impurities. The brief accounts below describe visible physical properties of common minerals found in the Rocky Mountain states, the rocks in which they occur, and areas where they are likely to be found.

COPPER
Cubic and 12-sided crystals; also scales, lumps, and branching forms. Copper-red turning black, blue, or green with tarnish; metallic luster. Can be scratched by a knife; ductile; malleable; lacks cleavage. Berkeley Pit copper mine, in Butte, Montana, often called the "richest hill on earth," contains high concentrations of copper, lead, silver, and manganese.

QUARTZ
Crystals commonly six-sided, with pyramidal ends. Many colors: white, gray, red, purple, pink, yellow, green, brown, black; transparent or milky; glassy luster. Abundant in the granites that are common throughout the peaks of the Rocky Mountain states.

GOLD
Grains, flakes, or nuggets. Rich, bright yellow; metallic luster. Ductile; malleable; lacks cleavage. Gold mines of the 1800s and 1900s in Idaho (Coeur d'Alene, Boise region, Clearwater River), Colorado (South Platte River, Central City, Idaho Springs, Cripple Creek, Leadville, Lake City, Creede), Montana (Gold Creek, Bull Mountains), and Wyoming (South Pass City).

SILVER

Scales, wires, or in massive form. Silvery white; exposed surfaces tarnished; metallic luster. Ductile; malleable; lacks cleavage. Silver mines in Idaho (Coeur d'Alene, Boise region, Silver City), Colorado (Aspen, Central City, Gilman, Leadville, Lake City, Silverton), and Montana (Berkeley Pit, Silver Star).

FELDSPAR

Flat crystals, square to rectangular in cross section. Color varies; depends on relative amounts of sodium, calcium, and potassium; most commonly white, pink, or gray. Orthoclase (a potassium-rich form; pictured) and andesine (a sodium and calcium form) very common in both igneous and metamorphic rocks.

MICA

Thin sheets or flakes. Dark brown to black (biotite), or colorless to white (muscovite); transparent to translucent; glassy luster. Common in igneous and metamorphic rocks.

GYPSUM

Thin flat crystals or in massive form. Whitish to gray; clear. Can be scratched with a fingernail. Common in Paradox, Sinbad, and Gypsum Valleys, Colorado, and in bluffs along the Eagle River, Colorado.

DIAMOND

Crystals 4-sided, 8-sided, and 12-sided. Generally colorless, but many colors possible. Hardest of all known minerals. Deep-seated cylindrical pipes, called "kimberlite diatremes," similar to those found in South Africa, carry diamonds upward from deep within the earth. So far, only small diamonds, less than 1 mm. across, have been found. First discovered in 1975 along the Wyoming–Colorado state line; this region has one of two diamond-bearing diatremes in the United States (the other is in Arkansas).

Rocks

A given rock may be composed of only one mineral or may be an aggregation of different kinds. A tangible record of the geologic processes that made them, rocks provide information about many such processes that are impossible to observe directly—for example, the melting of rocks in the earth's interior. Rock identification can be difficult, but clues are provided by the constituent minerals, color, grain size, and overall texture.

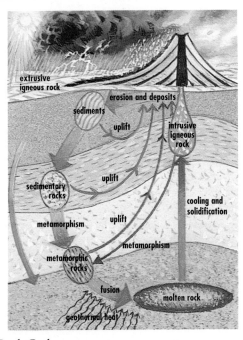

The Rock Cycle

The three basic classes of rocks undergo processes that convert them from one form to another. *Igneous* rocks form through solidification of molten material from the earth's interior: Extrusive igneous rock forms on the earth's surface from solidified molten material; intrusive igneous rock solidifies below the surface. *Sedimentary* rocks form from fragments of older, weathered rock ranging in size from submicroscopic particles to boulders, and from organic or chemical matter deposited at the earth's surface. *Metamorphic* rocks form when preexisting rocks are transformed, through heating, pressure, or both. Both igneous and metamorphic rocks are commonly associated with mountain building. As the small arrows on the drawing indicate, the cycle can be interrupted (and restarted) at any point. The Rocky Mountain states have an abundance of every rock type.

RHYOLITE

Extrusive igneous rock formed as lava erupts explosively at or near the earth's surface, or oozes out of the ground more slowly. *Constituent minerals:* quartz, feldspar, biotite mica. *Appearance:* light-colored, white, pink, or gray; very fine-grained or glassy; may contain vesicles. Common in the Snake River Plain, Idaho, and in Yellowstone National Park, Wyoming (beautiful exposures in the Grand Canyon of the Yellowstone).

BASALT

Extrusive igneous rock formed as lava erupts at or near the earth's surface. *Constituent minerals:* feldspar and pyroxene. *Appearance:* dark green to black; very fine-grained; shape depends on where rock came to surface. **Columnar basalt:** geometrically shaped pillars formed from cooling and contraction; common in Devils Tower, Wyoming. **Ropy and blocky-textured basalts:** twisted coils or jagged blocks; common in Craters of the Moon National Monument, Columbia Plateau, Idaho.

GRANITE

Intrusive igneous rock formed as magma cools beneath the surface of the earth. *Constituent minerals:* quartz (clear to white), feldspar (pink or white), and mica. *Appearance:* speckled pink, white, and gray-black; large coarse-grained crystals. Commonly found in the peaks of the Sawtooth Range of central Idaho (Idaho batholith); Colorado's Front Range (Pikes Peak); and Wyoming's Teton, Wind River, Bighorn, and Laramie Ranges.

SANDSTONE

Sedimentary rock; often contains fossils. *Constituent minerals:* predominantly quartz, with feldspar, mica, and other minerals. *Appearance:* fine- to medium-grained; often has cross-bedding (inclined layering due to grain movement by wind or water); dark-colored. Common throughout the Rocky Mountain states. The Dakota Hogback, or Devil's Backbone, is a ridge of sandstone tilted on its edge that runs along the eastern edge of the Rocky Mountains.

TRAVERTINE

Chemical sedimentary rock formed as deep, weakly acidic groundwater dissolves calcium carbonate in regions of circulating hydrothermal fluids; under lower pressures as the water reaches the surface, calcium carbonate precipitates out of the solution. *Constituent mineral:* calcium carbonate. *Appearance:* finely crystalline; light-colored, with porous, spongy texture. Associated with hot springs; common at Mammoth Hot Springs, Yellowstone National Park, Wyoming, and Soda Springs, Idaho.

LIMESTONE

Sedimentary rock; often contains fossils. *Constituent minerals:* predominantly calcium carbonate, with some quartz and clay. *Appearance:* fine- to medium-grained, with fossils of varying sizes; usually white or gray. Common throughout Glacier National Park and central Montana; on the cliffs of the Chinese Wall in the Bob Marshall Wilderness in Montana's Flathead National Forest; and in Idaho's Lost River Range.

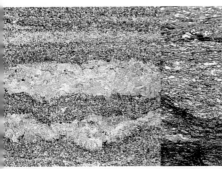

GNEISS

Metamorphic rock formed under conditions of high temperature and high pressure. *Constituent minerals:* quartz (clear to white), feldspar (pink to white), and mica (dark- and light-colored). *Appearance:* medium-grained; discontinuous alternating light and dark bands. Common in the Idaho panhandle, in Montana south of Butte and Bozeman, in Wyoming's Death Canyon of the Teton Range, and in Rocky Mountain National Park, Colorado.

SCHIST

Metamorphic rock formed under conditions of medium temperatures and pressures. *Constituent minerals:* quartz, feldspar, and mica; often segregated into layers with a foliated or wavy banding. *Appearance:* medium- to coarse-grained; minerals are oriented parallel to each other and often split into flat layers along these parallel planes. Common in Rocky Mountain National Park.

Fossils

A fossil is any indication of prehistoric life, including petrified wood, dinosaur bones, ancient seashells, footprints, and even "casts" in the shape of an animal left in rock after the organism has disintegrated. Almost all fossils are discovered in sedimentary rocks, usually in areas that were once underwater, which explains why most fossils are of aquatic species. Through uplift and erosion, these marine rocks are later exposed above sea level. An incredible diversity and abundance of fossils can be found in the Rocky Mountain states. Following is a list of some of the region's most notable fossil-rich areas.

DINOSAUR NATIONAL MONUMENT Colorado and Utah; dinosaurs, 145 mya (million years ago)

FOSSIL BUTTE NATIONAL MONUMENT Wyoming; Green River Formation fish, 50 mya

FLORISSANT FOSSIL BEDS NATIONAL MONUMENT Colorado; preservation of very delicate fossils, 35 mya

HAGERMAN FOSSIL BEDS NATIONAL MONUMENT Idaho; Hagerman Horse, 3.5 mya

SPECIMEN RIDGE, SPECIMEN CREEK, AND AMETHYST MOUNTAIN Yellowstone National Park, Wyoming; fossil forests, 50 mya

EGG MOUNTAIN Choteau, Montana; Duck-billed Dinosaurs and dinosaur eggs, 97 mya

RABBIT VALLEY PALEONTOLOGICAL SITE Grand Junction, Colorado; dinosaurs, 140 mya

DINOSAUR HILL Grand Junction, Colorado; dinosaurs, 140 mya

EOCENE FOSSIL FISH
About 50 million years ago, several large freshwater lakes existed in the region of Wyoming, Colorado, and Utah. The sediments formed in those lakes, known as the Green River Formation, are host to a wealth of fossils, including fossil fish. *Knightia eocaena,* a small herring, is one of the most common, occurring in massive groupings that indicate mass mortality.

STROMATOLITES
Stromatolites are reefs built out of colonies of blue-green algae that look similar to heads of cabbage with wavy laminations. These ancient creatures are estimated to have lived a billion years ago, probably in shallow water. Stromatolites are common in the gray to brown limestones of Glacier National Park, Montana.

DINOSAURS

Apatosaurus (better known as *Brontosaurus*) fossils are common at Dinosaur National Monument in Colorado and Utah. In the early 1900s, Earl Douglass, a paleontologist from the Carnegie Museum, discovered thousands of *Apatosaurus* bones here in a ridge of sandstone. The bones were probably originally deposited and concentrated on a river sandbar by floodwaters, mineralized by percolating groundwaters rich in dissolved silica, and preserved by overlying sedimentary deposits.

DINOSAUR EGGS

In 1978, fossilized dinosaur eggs were discovered west of Choteau, Montana. The nests of eggs, along with skeletons of adult duck-billed dinosaurs called *Maiasaura peeblesorum,* were probably killed by ash, debris, and poisonous gases from a volcanic eruption. From the site, dubbed "Egg Mountain," paleontologists have learned that these duck-billed dinosaurs probably parented their young much as modern-day birds do. *Maiasaura* means "good mother lizard."

HAGERMAN "HORSE"

Fossil remains indicate that *Equus simplicidens,* which lived between 3.5 and 1.7 million years ago, was about the same size as the modern Arabian horse. Despite the common name, details of its skull and the pattern of chewing surfaces on its teeth indicate that this species was more closely related to the zebra. The largest sample in the world of this extinct species is found in Idaho at Hagerman Fossil Beds National Monument, where more than 200 complete specimens have been collected.

INSECTS

A view of life 35 million years ago is preserved at Florissant Fossil Beds National Monument, Colorado. Although marine and terrestrial vertebrate remains are common, the area is particularly noted for abundant, well-preserved insects and plants. More than 1,100 insect species have been found here, including the Tsetse Fly, no longer living in North America.

Habitats

Beartooth Mountains, Montana

Habitats are discrete natural communities of plants and animals that have coexisted for thousands of years, and along the way formed dynamic interrelationships. Habitat types are influenced by many factors, including elevation, climate (temperature, precipitation, exposure, and wind), soil and geologic composition, and the availability of water. With its greatly varied topography, the Rocky Mountain region features a remarkable array of habitats, often in close proximity to one another. The seven general habitats covered here are mountains, forests, semiarid lands, plains and grasslands, wetlands and waterways, canyons, and disturbed habitats. Within these broad divisions important "sub-habitats" can exist. For example, mountain sub-habitats include alpine tundra and mountain meadows, and forest sub-habitats include montane and subalpine forests.

The habitats distribution map located on the back endpaper shows the distribution of important habitats and sub-habitats in the region: coniferous forests (most of the region's forests are coniferous), semi-arid lands, plains and grasslands, wetlands and waterways, disturbed areas (where natural habitats have been disrupted by human activities such as urban development or farming), and alpine tundra.

Because of the climatic influences of the region's mountains, the same habitat may occur at different elevations, depending on location. On the dry eastern slopes of the Rockies, for example, habitats begin at higher elevations than on the western slopes, where there is considerably more precipitation.

Food Chains and Webs

In any ecosystem there are three categories of organisms: producers, consumers, and decomposers. Green plants are food producers. Animals are consumers. Herbivores, which consume plant matter directly, are primary consumers. They may be leaf-eating grasshoppers, berry-eating Cedar Waxwings, or Moose browsing on all manner of vegetation. Secondary consumers, or primary carnivores,

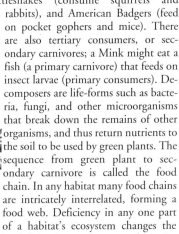

Food producer

are those that devour the primary consumers—examples are ladybugs (eat aphids), rattlesnakes (consume squirrels and rabbits), and American Badgers (feed on pocket gophers and mice). There are also tertiary consumers, or secondary carnivores; a Mink might eat a fish (a primary carnivore) that feeds on insect larvae (primary consumers). Decomposers are life-forms such as bacteria, fungi, and other microorganisms that break down the remains of other organisms, and thus return nutrients to the soil to be used by green plants. The sequence from green plant to secondary carnivore is called the food chain. In any habitat many food chains are intricately interrelated, forming a food web. Deficiency in any one part of a habitat's ecosystem changes the entire system somewhat. If the deficiencies are too great, the entire ecosystem can collapse; in such an event, many species would decline or disappear, and the ecosystem's diversity would be largely eliminated.

Primary consumer

Decomposers

Mountains

Mountains are responsible for much of the habitat diversity in the Rocky Mountain states, with elevation affecting temperature, precipitation, wind exposure, and soil depth and composition. Plant communities change with about every 1,000 feet of elevation gained, which on flat ground would be equivalent to traveling 600 miles northward. Plant life also varies within these elevational zones. North-facing slopes receive no direct sun and are cooler, wetter, and claimed by different species of conifers than warmer south-facing slopes. The Rockies cast a massive rain shadow on the plains to the east, where only compact or drought-tolerant species can survive. In spring and summer, the snowpack that accumulates in the peaks melts and recharges wet meadows, ephemeral streams, and entire watersheds in the lower valleys.

Tundra, Beartooth Plateau, Montana–Wyoming

Alpine Tundra

Wind-scoured and buried in snow for up to 10 months of the year, treeless alpine tundra occupies elevations typically above 10,000 feet. Tall plants here reach about 6 inches, a sound growing strategy when winds can exceed 150 miles per hour. Scattered shrubs grow in dense, ground-hugging domes; the occasional Subalpine Fir or Engelmann Spruce that dares encroach, usually in a low spot or on the leeward side of a boulder, grows in gnarled thickets of stunted limbs and roots called krummholz (German for "crooked wood"). Flowers sprout amid lichen-covered boulder fields and talus slopes (fields of shattered rock, cleaved from mountainsides and collected downslope); cinquefoils, phlox, buckwheats, and penstemons are common flowers. The few animals that inhabit the tundra year-round spend much of the year hibernating.

Mountain Meadows

Two distinct meadow habitats exist in the Rocky Mountains. Subalpine "wet" meadows are lush, spongy oases of sedges, wildflowers, and shrubs that occur at elevations above 6,000 feet where yearly precipitation is high. They occupy poorly drained areas, including the bowls and depressions of ancient glacier sites. Dry meadows of bunchgrasses and sagebrush occupy south-facing slopes. Elk, deer, pocket gophers, and rosy-finches are a few species that make use of both meadow habitats.

Uncompahgre National Forest, Colorado

Life in the High Peaks

Mountain Goat, Glacier National Park, Montana

The Mountain Goat moves easily over the cliff ledges, talus slopes, and razor-thin ridges of the Rocky Mountains. Its hooves are well-adapted to the terrain, with hard, sharp outer edges and soft, pliable soles providing excellent purchase on rock surfaces. Its shaggy, yellowish-white coat keeps it well camouflaged. But life remains perilous on the rocky peaks, with avalanches and rock slides accounting for many Mountain Goat deaths. Another popular denizen of the mountains, the irrepressible Yellow-bellied Marmot, makes its home in boulder-strewn meadows, rocky outcrops, and talus slopes up to 11,000 feet. Heard perhaps more often than seen, the marmot issues a distinctive chirp or whistle at the first hint of danger before retreating into its den.

Mountain Foothills

Foothills occur anywhere from 4,000 to 8,000 feet, forming a transition zone between grasslands below and montane forests above. The terrain is generally rocky and broken here, although occasionally there are more gentle, rolling areas. Depending on soil type, exposure to sun, and precipitation, foothill habitats of the Rocky Mountains can feature a variety of shrubs, including mountain mahogany, Serviceberry, and Bitterbrush, within a mosaic of bunchgrasses; the shrubs supply food and thermal protection for countless species of birds, as well as critical winter browse for Mule Deer and Elk when the higher elevations become buried in snow. Trees of the foothills include junipers, Gambel's Oaks (in Colorado), and a few Ponderosa Pines.

Mountain foothills, Yellowstone National Park

Forests

Coniferous forests are distributed throughout the region's major mountain ranges and cover at least one-third of each state's landscape. Conifers are well-suited to the thinner soils of mountainous areas, as they are highly efficient in their ability to use water and nutrients in arid conditions, including winter, when the ground freezes for extended periods. The region's most important deciduous trees are the aspens.

Montane Forests

Ponderosa Pines, Rocky Mountain National Park

Traveling upslope, this is the first forest type to appear on a mountain, beginning along the edges of grasslands or foothills and continuing up to about 7,000 feet. Ponderosa Pine and Douglas Fir are the dominant species, each with distinct growing preferences: Ponderosa Pines favor drier, warmer, often south-facing slopes, while Douglas Firs thrive in cooler, shaded areas and north-facing slopes. Given the region's endlessly varying topography, the two species are closely intermingled in some areas and grow as single-species stands in others. Where the Ponderosa dominates, mature trees are well spaced over an understory of bunchgrasses and shrubs, a landscape known as "pine savannah." Abert's and Red Squirrels, Elk, and Mule Deer are common mammals here; birds include Pine Siskins, Red Crossbills, and Northern Goshawks.

Subalpine Firs, Bitterroot Mountains, Idaho

Subalpine Forests

Dense and well-watered with snowmelt, moist subalpine forests occur on all slopes at elevations greater than about 6,500 feet and continue upward to the tree line. Typical subalpine trees include aspens, Engelmann Spruce, Subalpine Fir, and Lodgepole, Whitebark, and Limber Pines. Forest composition varies greatly throughout this habitat, though Lodgepole Pine is a dominant species almost everywhere. Tightly spaced and with a seemingly unbroken canopy, the forest provides wildlife with both protection from extreme temperatures and ideal hiding places. Grizzlies and Black Bears dig their winter dens here; American Martens, Elk, and rare Wolverines are other residents. Birds of the subalpine forest include the raucous Clark's Nutcracker, Cassin's Finch, and Blue Grouse.

Aspen Parks

Fall aspens, White River National Forest, Colorado

Aspens are a unique and important component of western forests. They grow in foothills, become more abundant in the montane forest, and may even extend into the lower reaches of the subalpine zone. These members of the wildflower family are fast-growing colonizers, the first trees to reclaim an area disturbed by wildfire, logging, or avalanche. Aspens grow as clones through a network of shallow roots; wildfire is a key regenerative agent, killing older trees and stimulating new sprouts, without which mature parks would eventually be replaced by conifers. Sunlight penetrates the aspen park canopy to nurture a lush understory of shrubs and grasses. Woodpeckers find easy drilling in the aspen's soft wood; many vireos and warblers seek aspen stands for nesting sites. Because they tend to grow in wet areas, aspen parks are important wildlife sites.

Inland Maritime Forests

Doused with wet Pacific air, the forests stretching from central Idaho to Montana's Glacier National Park, an area about 100 miles wide and 300 miles long, represent an ecological crossroads. These dense, prolific forests combine trees typical of northern and coastal rain forests (larch, cedar, hemlock, and Western White Pine) with species more common to the Rocky Mountain region (Grand

Cedar grove, Clearwater National Forest, Idaho

and Douglas Firs and Engelmann Spruce). Dry spells do occur here: In 1910, wildfires burned 3.5 million acres; around the same time, blister rust decimated the Western White Pine, reducing its presence from a historic level of 40 percent to 2–5 percent. Wildlife here includes Moose, Lynx, Snowshoe Hares, Western Tanagers, Pileated Woodpeckers, and Spruce Grouse.

Semiarid Lands

Stretched across southern Idaho, west-southwestern Colorado, portions of eastern Montana, and much of Wyoming are semiarid habitats—principally sagebrush grasslands and pinyon-juniper woodlands interspersed with shrub lands, at elevations of 4,000 to 8,000 feet. Often called "high desert" or "cold desert" regions, these plant communities have adapted to the extreme temperatures and sparse precipitation of lands situated in the rain shadows of the mountains. Sagebrush grasslands roll across broad, arid basins. Where the landscape is broken by canyons, rocky escarpments, or other irregularities, junipers and Colorado Pinyons grow in the dry, shallow soils. These trees seldom exceed 10 feet in height and are often referred to as "pygmy forests." In depressions or low basins, where the soil is too alkaline for sagebrush, a related community of salt desert shrubs thrives, including Greasewood, Saltbush, and horsebrush. These lands support unique communities of fauna, including kangaroo rats, Sage Grouse, Pronghorns, sparrows, finches, and numerous reptiles.

Sagebrush grasslands, Grand Teton National Park

Sagebrush Grasslands

Dominated by sagebrush with an understory of fescues, wheatgrasses, larkspurs, and other herbaceous plants, sagebrush grasslands are generally found at elevations above 4,000 feet, in areas where annual precipitation is less than 12 inches and where soils are deep enough to accommodate the sagebrush plant's massive taproot. The spreading boughs of this aromatic plant provide shade for an understory of grasses and wildflowers, the seeds and leaves of which are an important food source for many rodents, including mice and ground squirrels

Momma Sage

Few western plants serve as many critical functions for wildlife as the humble sagebrush. The porous soils of arid lands, extremely vulnerable to wind and erosion, are held in place by its aggressive root system, which for some species can spread to 90 feet in diameter. Healthy sage provides thermal relief, whether for a jackrabbit in a snowstorm, a newborn Pronghorn calf, or a nesting Brewer's Sparrow in blistering

Pronghorn calf

heat. Its leaves become a critical winter food source for Mule Deer, Elk, and Pronghorn. The Sage Grouse, Sage Thrasher, and Sagebrush Lizard all take their names from the plant they depend upon.

Pinyon-juniper woodland, Colorado

Pinyon-Juniper Woodlands

Pinyon-juniper woodlands occupy hills, escarpments, and broken terrain upslope from sagebrush-grassland communities. The Colorado Pinyon Pine and Rocky Mountain Juniper are principal species, although other juniper varieties also thrive here. To cope with powerful winds, extreme temperatures, and minimal moisture, trees average about 10 feet in height and seldom exceed 30 feet. Their nutritious fruits—pinyon nuts and juniper berries—are a favorite of many animals, from Clark's Nutcrackers and Desert Woodrats to Black Bears. The highly gregarious Pinyon Jay travels these woodlands in large, noisy flocks, searching for its staple food, the pinyon nut.

Wet Areas

Nestled in hidden canyons or breaks, on valley floors, and in other low-lying areas below 6,000 feet, shallow lakes, sinks, springs, seeps, and ephemeral streams form rich oases in the surrounding arid landscape. Willows, cottonwoods, and some deciduous shrubs thrive here, creating habitat for warblers, vireos, flycatchers, and other songbirds.

Wildlife inhabiting the drier sagebrush grasslands visit for water and relief from the extreme summer heat. The mudflats and open waters of ponds, marshes, and lakes may attract waterfowl, terns, and shorebirds such as American Avocets, White-faced Ibises, and Wilson's Phalaropes.

Sink pools, Sinks Canyon State Park, Wyoming

Plains and Grasslands

The Great Plains of North America reach their westernmost limit along the Rocky Mountain Front Range as it winds through Colorado, Wyoming, and Montana. These short- and midgrass prairies at elevations up to about 6,000 feet are well adapted to a rain-shadow climate of perpetual winds, searing heat, and scant rainfall. This was the habitat of the American Bison, perhaps 60 million of them prior to the arrival of Europeans. Agricultural practices have broken most of the original prairie sod, and cattle have replaced bison as primary grazers. Intact prairie lands still exist, however, spread across rolling hills with occasional ridges, buttes, and ravines. They feature a varied assortment of bunchgrasses, cacti, and scattered deciduous trees and shrubs. Wildlife on the plains is abundant, including many hawks, songbirds, small mammals such as prairie dogs and American Badgers, and fleet-footed herds of native Pronghorn.

Courtship on the Prairie

The region's prairies are home to four native upland birds renowned for their dramatic courtship displays. Sage Grouse, Sharp-tailed Grouse, and in eastern Colorado, Greater and Lesser Prairie-Chickens gather in early spring on their traditional leks—patches of open ground used for generations. Males spin, stomp, and bow, accompanying their danc-

Sage Grouse

ing with strange vocalizations, and rapidly popping or "booming" their colorful necks or chest sacs. Females appear at first unimpressed, but eventually they pair off to breed with the more dominant males. Dancing occurs at daybreak and in the evening; the morning displays are usually the most eventful.

Prairie Dogs and Other Wildlife

The Black-tailed Prairie Dog, a member of the squirrel family, is a keystone species in the prairie ecosystem. Its prolific burrowing loosens and aerates soils, dispersing nutrients and invigorating grasses. Burrows become nesting sites for Burrowing Owls, Bullsnakes, and rattlesnakes. Prairie dogs are a dietary staple of virtually all prairie carnivores, including American Badgers, Coyotes, and Ferruginous Hawks, the largest members of the buteo family. Extremely sensitive to the presence of people, these hawks quickly abandon their eggs if approached too closely; for reasons not entirely understood, they often line their nests with large intact "pies" of cow dung.

Yucca in bloom

How Plants Adapt on the Grasslands

The extensive root systems of prairie grasses spread horizontally near the surface, with the unraveled roots of a single plant sometimes measuring as long as 3 miles. This moisture-gathering adaptation is necessary in a region where annual precipitation averages just 10 inches and near-constant winds quickly evaporate the little rain that does fall. Blue Grama, Bluebunch Wheatgrass, and Little Bluestem are typical prairie grasses; their roots help block erosion by holding soil in place. The leaves of the yucca, another grassland plant, are pale green to reduce heat absorption, and have a smooth, waxy coating that helps the plant retain precious moisture; its branched taproot penetrates to depths of 20 feet.

Prairie Waters

Grassland waters include pothole lakes, sloughs, and marshes, as well as rivers and streams. Prior to the advent of management by agriculture or wildlife agencies, water supplies across prairie lands varied greatly from year to year, the key variables being snowmelt and spring rains. Today dikes and reservoirs make it possible to maintain higher water levels later into the year. Pothole lakes, depressions left by stranded blocks of glaciers, are scattered across the northern Plains and into Canada; they represent the single most important nesting habitat for North America's migratory waterfowl. Other birds that visit prairie waters include Black-crowned Night-Herons, Canada Geese, and Sandhill Cranes.

Pothole lakes, Montana

Wetlands and Waterways

Though accounting for a small fraction of the region's land mass, lakes, reservoirs, creeks, and rivers support a preponderance of wildlife in their bordering riparian communities. Along streams and rivers, verdant corridors of deciduous trees and shrubs provide nest sites and shelter for many birds, and habitat for Northern River Otters, American Beavers, and Mink. In the high country, alpine lakes are often bounded by lush meadow complexes; downslope, in the drier foothills and shrub lands, streamside habitats offer a striking contrast of lush growth. Prairie lakes, reservoirs, marshes, and wetlands serve as nesting and resting areas for waterfowl, shorebirds, and wading birds; during spring and fall migrations, hundreds of thousands of Snow Geese and Tundra Swans pass through the region.

Rivers

Yellowstone River

More than two dozen major rivers wind through the Rocky Mountain region, creating islands, sloughs, marshes, and oxbows. Undammed rivers are subject to seasonal flooding, which has numerous beneficial effects upon streamside forests. The Yellowstone, one of the nation's longest and last major undammed rivers, is recharged each spring with mountain snowmelt. Cottonwoods, willows, and shrubs dispense seeds during spring runoff, and pounding waters till the soils of islands and banks, leaving fresh deposits of silt that are ideal for the new seedlings. Dams on rivers reduce seasonal flooding and affect the regenerative capacity of streamside forests and riparian zones.

American White Pelican

American White Pelican

The majestic American White Pelican nests in large colonies on rocky islands, usually in waters of open, semiarid country. It is not unusual to see small groups of these birds soaring with 9-foot wingspans at heights more appropriate for a Golden Eagle. White Pelicans work in groups to herd their prey into shallow water, or they ease into a school of feeding fish, seizing unwary individuals close to the surface.

Lake Pend Oreille, Idaho

Lakes

The many thousands of alpine lakes that dot the region's mountainous areas are often nestled in cirques, small, glacially formed bowls or basins amid the high peaks. Fed by springs or snowmelt, a number of these pristine waters are a last stronghold for native Cutthroat Trout. Larger lakes also exist: Enormous blocks of stranded glacial ice melted to form Idaho's Lake Pend Oreille and Flathead Lake in Montana, the region's largest natural lake. Montana's Lake Koocanusa is home to native Kokanee Salmon, a land-locked cousin of the Pacific Sockeye. After spawning in autumn, the dead and dying Kokanee become a feast for migrating Bald Eagles that gather, often in very large numbers, along lake tributaries to feed and rest.

Mountain Creeks

Mountain creeks race and tumble down steep slopes flanked with riparian swaths of firs and aspens, and tangles of shrubs, ferns, and moss-covered boulders. Where gradients diminish, such as on meadows, they spread out and begin to cut deep meanders, creating ideal habitat for

Slough Creek, Yellowstone National Park

trout. The creeks nourish a diversity of grasses, forbs, and deciduous shrubs ideal for vireos, flycatchers, and Common Muskrats. Moose favor these wet meadows for browsing, especially with the shelter of a densely forested area close by.

Canyons

Some of the deepest, most inaccessible canyons in the United States are those carved by Rocky Mountain rivers, among them the colorful "Grand Canyon" of the Yellowstone, the Black Canyon of the Gunnison, and Hells Canyon on the Snake River. Over millions of years, these and other rivers have plowed through soft sedimentary plains, volcanic rocks, and harder, underlying crystalline or granitic formations. The spectacular layering of colors is today a text of each era's unique geologic history. The temperature on a canyon floor is often considerably higher than that of the surrounding area; this, combined with geographic isolation, makes some canyons ideal travel corridors as well as winter habitat for Bald Eagles, deer, and Elk.

Hells Canyon

At 5,000 feet the nation's deepest canyon, Hell's Canyon, features highly variable combinations of climate, geology, and topography that support rare or endemic plants and animals. The MacFarlane's Four-o'-clock, an endangered wildflower, is among the better-known of several plant species found only within Hells Canyon. The Townsend's Big-eared Bat, which feeds almost exclusively on moths, is another uncommon canyon resident. During summer, females form nursery colonies of as many as 200 bats.

Snake River, Hells Canyon, Idaho

Natural Protection

River canyons offer an increasingly precious commodity for wildlife: nesting sites and resting areas where human disturbance is minimal. The shaded cliff walls and outcrops are favored nesting sites for a host of raptors that hunt in the nearby arid lands. The Prairie Falcon is one of 14 raptor species that breed along the Snake River Birds of Prey Area, a preserve established in 1980. More than 700 pairs of birds nest along the basalt cliffs that tower 600 feet above the Snake

Bighorn Sheep

River. Canyon terrain provides Bighorn Sheep with high-elevation sites inaccessible to most predators and people. The ewes favor the secluded cliff ledges for bearing their lambs. By the end of its first day of life, a Bighorn lamb is walking and jumping with the prowess of an adult.

Disturbed Habitats

Humans have affected almost every corner of the Rocky Mountain states. Agricultural fields and ranches, cities, suburbs, river reservoirs, ski areas, and mines represent the more common disturbances to the natural landscape. Animals often continue to live close to or even within these disturbed areas. A few species have found them a boon, while others, such as bears, Mountain Lions, and various birds have suffered dramatic losses.

Ranch land, Little Bighorn River Valley, Montana

Agricultural and Range Lands

Agricultural and range lands make up the region's most widespread disturbed habitats. Both occur across historic sagebrush grasslands, prairie lands, and along rivers and streams. The vast fields of wheat, barley, and other grain crops have altered the population and distribution of many wild species. Traditional prairie wildlife such as prairie dogs, Greater and Lesser Prairie-Chickens, and Long-billed Curlews have suffered significant losses in habitat. More opportunistic and adaptable species, including pheasants, Gray Partridges, Canada Geese, and White-tailed Deer, have expanded. Many rodents feed upon waste grain and stubble, with predatory Coyotes and foxes multiplying accordingly. The economics of grain farming often lead landowners to plant every available acre, eliminating even brushy edges and shelterbelts.

Mule Deer on a grain stubble field

To increase forage for livestock, ranchers have introduced domestic annual grasses along streams and rivers. These lush "hay meadows" create a turnover of species: Native songbirds such as Baird's Sparrows, who prefer to nest amid sparse native grasses, disappear, while nonnative pheasants and ducks, like the Mallard, expand their territories. Sagebrush, long viewed by ranchers as a nuisance, is often replaced with more palatable exotic grass, which further reduces the diversity of forage and nesting cover for wildlife.

Impacts Old and New

The West's historic land-based industries—mining, agriculture, cattle grazing, and timber harvesting—continue to impose a wide range of deleterious effects on wildlife and natural systems. More recently, rapid population growth and increased recreational development have caused further irreversible impacts on water quality and habitat diversity. Even outdoor recreation, a concept often promoted as a nature-friendly economic alternative to extractive industries, has consequences for plant and animal communities.

Population

The intermountain West is growing faster than any other region of the United States. Montana's Gallatin County, which includes the city of Bozeman, experienced a 20 percent population boost between 1990 and 1996, and more than 100,000 acres have been developed over the past two decades. Valleys and mountain foothills, the historic winter range of Elk and deer, are typically the first areas to be developed.

Housing development, Bozeman, Montana

National Parks

Between 1984 and 1994, visitors to the country's national parks increased by 25 percent, and the major parks of the Rocky Mountain states are feeling the effects. To accommodate tourists, there has been rapid commercial and residential development along park borders, which eliminates critical "buffer zone" habitats and further isolates wildlife such as wolves, American Bison, and Elk.

Cheatgrass

In Idaho, millions of acres of historic sagebrush-grasslands habitat have been converted to monocultures of Cheatgrass, an exotic annual. Cheatgrass quickly establishes itself in spring, but then dries out and becomes potent fuel for wildfires. Hotter, larger wildfires result, killing off sagebrush. The loss of sagebrush reverberates throughout the ecosystem: jackrabbits, Sage Grouse, and ground squirrels lose food, shelter, and nesting cover; their decreased populations in turn diminish the prey base for raptors, snakes, and other carnivores.

Cheatgrass, Owyhee County, Idaho

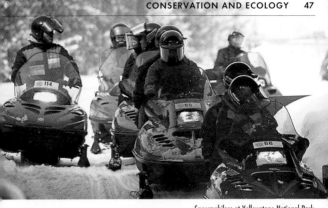

Snowmobilers at Yellowstone National Park

Off-road Recreation

Off-road recreation vehicles such as snowmobiles, ATVs (all-terrain vehicles), and motorcycles are problematic for public lands and natural areas. Greatly increased snowmobile use in Yellowstone has raised many concerns, particularly about air pollution and the effects of maintained roads on American Bison migration habits. Off-road vehicles are usually restricted to designated trails, but the region's sprawling, easily accessed mountains and grasslands make enforcement of these restrictions difficult. Thin soils are quickly disturbed, and reports of off-road vehicles damaging streams, trail switchbacks, and plant life are common.

Logging operation, Idaho

A Road Runs Through It

More than 380,000 miles of roads traverse national forest lands, more than eight times the total miles of the United States interstate highway system. Built to facilitate timber harvesting, forest roads also enable greater numbers of outdoor enthusiasts to penetrate deeper into undisturbed backcountry. As many as eight Grizzly Bears are killed each year in self-defense by big-game hunters during surprise encounters on public lands.

Cattle Grazing

More than 250 million acres of federal lands, the vast majority of which are located in the West, are leased for livestock grazing. When cattle grazing is properly managed, the negative effects can be minimized; grazing can even assist in keeping native grasslands vigorous. Without adequate fencing and rotation methods, however, cattle quickly wreak havoc on fragile riparian habitats, trampling or overgrazing shrubs and grasses and depleting nesting cover and food sources for wildlife. Overgrazing may compact soils and weaken native grasses, enabling exotic weeds and nonnative grasses to take over.

Impacts on Water

Human activity has adversely affected water quality throughout the region in many ways. Livestock waste and overgrazing along stream and river banks, chemical and nutrient runoff from agricultural operations, and erosion from timber harvesting and road building increase sedimentation and introduce pesticides and other chemicals into watersheds. Mining represents an especially serious threat to water supplies, for both people and wildlife. Rapid urban and residential growth is raising new concerns about the increased demands for water and the potential for depletion or degradation of underground aquifers.

Mountain creek, Glacier National Park

Mining

From historic "mom and pop" works to today's massive industrial-scale operations, mining is inextricably linked with both the region's cultural history and some of its deadliest environmental woes. Most mining occurs in mountainous areas, within or adjacent to nascent watersheds. When waste rock and tailings, byproducts of mining operations, are exposed to air and water, potent chemical reactions take place, creating sulfuric acid that in turn leaches out toxic materials like lead and arsenic. Many idle or abandoned mining operations are today listed by the Federal Environmental Protection Agency as "superfund sites," which means they pose a serious threat to drinking water and human health. The Berkeley Pit, a vast body of heavy metal–laced water in Butte, Montana, is one such site. Modern open-pit mining occurs on a staggering scale; one such operation near the Salmon River, in Idaho, features a pit more than a mile long, with a 500-acre waste pond.

Open-pit silver mine, Idaho

Irrigation Returns

To irrigate hay meadows and croplands, ranchers and farmers divert water from streams and onto fields through a system of ditches or pipes. Depending on the type of crop and irrigation method, water not taken up by plants either seeps into the aquifer or returns to the

Irrigation returns

stream via return ditches. These "irrigation returns" to streams or lakes may contain toxic agents, pesticides, herbicides, fertilizers, salts, or animal waste. Irrigation return flows are today among the most serious unregulated forms of water pollution in the region. A federal report on water issues in the West notes that western irrigated cropland accounts for 89 percent of quality-impaired river mileage.

Irrigating an alfalfa field

A Drop in the Bucket

The management and allocation of water is one of the most contentious issues in the West. Water, in the form of mountain snowmelt, is a finite commodity, and a host of interests compete for it: urban areas, agricultural and hydroelectric industries, recreationists, and wildlife. To store water and generate electricity, almost all the region's major rivers are dammed. This manipulation of stream flows has degraded river ecosystems, affecting everything from wetlands and bottomland forests to native fish species. An estimated 78 percent of western water currently goes to the region's agricultural operations; in drought years, taking away water from streams for irrigation damages aquatic and riparian communities.

Conservation

Compared with the Rocky Mountain states, there are few other regions of the United States where wildlife and natural resource issues garner as much day-to-day attention in the media and in the minds of citizens. Local and state chapters of national conservation groups like National Audubon Society, the Nature Conservancy, and Sierra Club, along with regional organizations and citizen coalitions, carry on the work of conserving wildlife and habitats, often in partnership with state and federal agencies. Much of the work of conservation is sociological—bringing together conflicting interests and managing an often complex array of values and beliefs to reach consensus.

Forest ranger conducting a controlled burn

Forests and Forest Fire

Nature has long "managed" forest ecosystems through wildfire, periodic disease and insect infestations, and long-term climatic fluctuations. Today's forests also bear the influence of human activities, foremost among them wildfire suppression and timber harvesting. Though the nation grieved when massive fires swept through Yellowstone's forests and meadows in 1988, ten years later the park was bursting with new life, its soils, grasses, and forests reinvigorated. Building upon the lessons of nature, forest managers today conduct limited prescribed burning on public lands in an effort to duplicate the natural effects of wildfire. Low-intensity fires in Ponderosa Pine forests clear out small trees and needle mats, and release nutrients to stimulate a fresh undergrowth of grasses and forbs. Burns in Lodgepole Pine forests create new openings in the dense forest canopy, as well as snag trees, which are beneficial to wildlife. Aspen stands are also managed with fire, which serves to trigger new sprouts around the bases of mature parent trees, adding age diversity to the forest.

Clearcut, northern Idaho

Timber Harvesting

Excessive timber harvesting can reduce the number and distribution of slower-growing species, as well as the natural accumulation of decaying trees on the forest floor. The result is less complex habitat for such species as Pine Martens, Fishers, Wolverines, and a variety of birds, particularly cavity-nesters like woodpeckers. Timber harvesting on national forest lands is slowing in the region, but the damage—sometimes severely altered habitats, endangered species, siltation in rivers and streams—has been significant. With fire suppression a reality in most areas, timber harvesting is one substitute for managing forest ecosystems. Well-regulated timber harvests can help maintain age diversity in some forests, and can serve to thin the forest canopy and create openings for grasses, shrubs, and other plants beneficial to wildlife.

Oil and Gas Drilling

Oil and natural gas reserves scattered throughout the Rocky Mountain region draw the interest of corporate concerns. Drilling for oil and gas requires road building, pipelines, and other major disruptions to natural areas. Montana residents and others in the country cheered in 1997 when Lewis and Clark National Forest Supervisor Gloria Fiora declared forest lands along the Rocky Mountain Front off-limits to oil and gas drilling. The Rocky Mountain Front is the dramatic western limit of the Great Plains, where grasslands abruptly yield to high mountain peaks. Grizzly Bears, wolves, and large herds of Elk, deer, and Pronghorn inhabit the region, along with numerous rare plants.

New World Mine press conference

Buyouts and Leases

Land swaps, buyouts, and lease agreements are some of the more frequently employed strategies for safeguarding lands or securing public access. In 1997 the Clinton Administration brokered a $65 million buyout of the New World Mine, a proposed gold mining operation at the edge of Yellowstone National Park.

Gray Wolf and Grizzly Bear

Reestablishing Wildlife

While political wrangling continues, in the minds of most the reintroduction of Gray Wolves to Yellowstone National Park and central Idaho has been a success. As this book goes to press, the 67 wolves transplanted from Canada in 1995 and 1996 have established many thriving packs. In Yellowstone, visitors with spotting scopes have witnessed wolf pups frolicking near their den and adult pack members delivering fresh kills. Hoping to build upon the lessons learned through wolf reintroduction, a coalition of nonprofit conservation groups, federal agencies, and timber industry representatives have collaborated on a proposal for reintroducing the threatened Grizzly Bear into the Selway–Bitterroot and Frank Church River of No Return Wildernesses of western Montana and central Idaho. The plan calls for reintroducing a minimum of 25 bears, with a tentative long-term population goal of about 280 animals.

Endangered or Threatened Water Life

The problems of the charismatic Gray Wolf and Grizzly Bear are fairly well documented, but species declines in the region's waterways receive less notoriety. More than 100 native fish species across the West are now listed as threatened, endangered, or of special concern; 22 species already have gone extinct in this century. The Bull Trout, which survives in Idaho, Montana, and portions of three

other western states, is the most recent casualty, listed as a threatened species in June 1998. Voracious feeders that prey primarily on smaller fish, Bull Trout thrive in only the coldest, cleanest waters, and need sediment-free gravel for their spawning beds.

Bull Trout

Monitoring Elusive Mammals

Forest carnivores, including Lynx, Wolverines, Fishers, and American Martens, inhabit the more remote coniferous forests of the northern Rockies. Interest in the status of these mammals is growing throughout the conservation community, but collecting accurate information about them is extremely difficult, given their historically sparse populations and secretive habits. Most state and federal wildlife agencies lack the resources for such intensive work even as they recognize the need. Smaller, local groups are stepping in. In western Montana, for example, a group of Seeley Lake residents have developed a program to monitor long-term population trends by conducting snow-track surveys throughout the winter.

Slaughtering Bison

When the bitter winter of 1996 subsided, more than 1,100 of Yellowstone's wild American Bison—nearly half the park population—had been shot and killed as they crossed over the park border in Montana. Since Yellowstone has existed, its Elk, bison, and other

American Bison, Yellowstone National Park

hoofed mammals have coped with harsh winters by migrating to low-elevation ranges, a sizable portion of which lies outside park boundaries in private hands. Roughly half the bison herd is thought to carry brucellosis, a bacterium that causes spontaneous miscarriage in domestic cows and undulant fever in people. There has not yet been a documented case of bison transmitting the disease to livestock, but the potential risks prompted a threat from the USDA Animal and Plant Health Inspection Service: It would revoke the "brucellosis-free" status on the livestock of any state in which bison intermingled with cattle. Ranchers would be unable to ship their cows across state lines until costly testing and quarantine requirements were met. Park officials and the state of Montana have yet to develop a nonlethal alternative to shooting and shipping to slaughter any bison leaving the park. The situation has spurred protests, petitions, and finger-pointing between park leaders and elected officials. For everyone in the region, forced to bear witness to the annual spectacle of bison collapsing under rifle fire, winter in Yellowstone has lost its innocence.

Weather

The highly irregular topography of the Rocky Mountain states causes a wide range of weather conditions and phenomena, as well as unique local climates. Generally, peaks and western slopes receive copious amounts

Wildflowers, Uncompahgre National Forest, Colorado

of rain and snow, while eastern slopes and regions east and west of the mountains are relatively dry. In winter, periodic easterly winds blowing against the foothills rise, form clouds, and produce heavy snows, while westerly winds channeled through mountain valleys create dry downslope "chinook" windstorms that rapidly melt snow cover on the eastern slopes. In spring, severe thunderstorms and tornadoes rumble across the semiarid grasslands of the eastern plains, while blizzards and avalanches swirl about the high peaks. Summer is usually pleasant and warm at higher elevations and notably hot on the plains below. In fall, the region experiences crisp, cool weather and a stunning display of golden aspen forests.

Rocky Mountain Weather Patterns

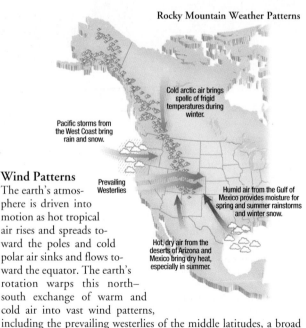

Cold arctic air brings spells of frigid temperatures during winter.

Pacific storms from the West Coast bring rain and snow.

Prevailing Westerlies

Humid air from the Gulf of Mexico provides moisture for spring and summer rainstorms and winter snow.

Hot, dry air from the deserts of Arizona and Mexico bring dry heat, especially in summer.

Wind Patterns

The earth's atmosphere is driven into motion as hot tropical air rises and spreads toward the poles and cold polar air sinks and flows toward the equator. The earth's rotation warps this north–south exchange of warm and cold air into vast wind patterns, including the prevailing westerlies of the middle latitudes, a broad west-to-east current of air that flows over most of the United States and southern Canada. Most of the weather systems affecting the Rocky Mountains approach from the west.

Highs and Lows

Embedded in the prevailing westerlies is a succession of whirls and eddies: systems of high pressure (fair weather) and low pressure (high humidity, cloudiness, and storms) that form and dissipate along fronts, the boundaries between warm and cold air masses. Winds blow in a circular pattern around the centers of these weather systems; in the Northern Hemisphere they blow counterclockwise around low pressure and clockwise around high pressure. The large-scale weather patterns in the Rocky Mountain states are dominated by alternating influences of high and low pressure, with each system usually lasting three to five days before being replaced by a new one.

Mountain Weather

The Rocky Mountains provide a formidable barrier to the flow of air across the region and profoundly influence local climates. They disrupt the flow of the prevailing westerlies, directing the air sharply upward and causing heavy precipitation on the western slopes and rain shadows to the east. Strangely shaped lenticular clouds form from this disruption of air flow and can extend eastward for hundreds of miles. Wind is rarely steady or predictable in mountainous terrain. Chinooks (see page 57) are warm, dry winds channeled down eastern slopes. Mountain and valley breezes are localized wind systems caused by temperature differentials between mountains and adjacent valleys; they cause winds to blow up mountain slopes during the day and downward toward the valleys at night. Valley breezes are caused by the daytime heating and rising of valley air. Mountain breezes occur at night when the air at high elevations cools and descends toward the valleys.

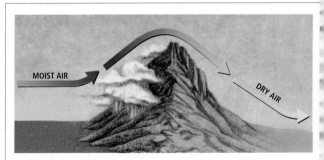

MOIST AIR

DRY AIR

THE RAIN SHADOW EFFECT
When moist westerly winds are forced to ascend a ridge to get to the other side, the air cools to the condensation temperature (dew point), and clouds and precipitation develop. Because of this upslope effect, the western slopes of the Rockies are among the snowiest places in the United States. As the air descends the eastern slopes, however, there is little moisture left; the dry areas created by this phenomenon are called rain shadows.

Rain

Annual rainfall averages anywhere from 7 inches (in south-central Colorado) to 43 inches (in northern Idaho). Much of the region's rainfall is produced by terrain-induced vertical air motions, when tall mountain ranges cause air to rise, cool, and condense into clouds. Low-pressure systems traversing the region produce still more rain. Spring and summer rainfall, particularly in the eastern Rockies, is most often associated with afternoon or evening thunderstorms, caused by rising warm air.

Thunder and Lightning

Lightning is an electrical discharge between one part of a cloud and another, between two clouds, or between a cloud and the earth. In a typical year, lightning strikes in the Rocky Mountain states nearly 500,000 times, and perhaps ten times as many flashes arc across the sky without reaching the ground. Thunder, the sound of air expanding explosively away from the intense heat of lightning bolts, is a common sound in late spring, summer, and early fall.

Flash Floods

Mountainous areas are particularly susceptible to flooding, as narrow valleys channel water that originates over large tracts of upstream areas. Slow-moving thunderstorms can dump enormous amounts of rain over these valleys, causing raging torrents of water that can destroy everything in their path. Springtime melting of deep winter snowpacks can also cause serious flooding.

Record-setting Rockies Weather

LOWEST TEMPERATURE –70° F at Rogers Pass, Montana, January 20, 1954.

HIGHEST TEMPERATURE 118° F at Bennett, Colorado, July 11, 1888, and at Orofino, Idaho, July 28, 1934.

GREATEST 24-HOUR RAINFALL June 20, 1921. 11.5 inches fell in Circle, Montana.

GREATEST SNOWFALL March 23–30, 1899. 141 inches buried Ruby, Colorado.

CLOUDIEST CITY Kalispell, Montana, is the sixth-cloudiest city in the United States, with an average of 213 cloudy days per year.

WORST FLASH FLOOD July 31, 1976. More than 10 inches of rain fell in four hours in Big Thompson Canyon, Colorado, causing 135 deaths and $35.5 million in property damage.

GREATEST RAPID TEMPERATURE CHANGE January 19, 1893. Chinook winds in Fort Assiniboine, Montana, caused temperatures to rise 42° F, from –5° F to 37° F, over a 15-minute period.

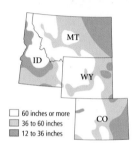

Snow

As with rain, much of the region's snow is produced by rising air motions over the mountains, although significant amounts also fall when cold, dry, southward-moving Canadian air masses collide with warm, moist subtropical air from the south. Annual snowfall exceeds 60 inches throughout much of the Rocky Mountains, which helps to support a healthy ski industry. However, in some areas, such as the Great Plains and sections west of the mountains, only 12 to 36 inches of snow fall annually.

- 60 inches or more
- 36 to 60 inches
- 12 to 36 inches

Teton Range, Grand Teton National Park

Avalanches

In high mountains, powdery snow atop a base of older hard, icy snow occasionally lets loose and cascades down a mountainside. During an avalanche, up to 100,000 tons of snow can fall at speeds of more than 60 miles per hour. Incredibly destructive and dangerous, avalanches are especially common on very steep mountain slopes.

Chinook Winds

The chinook (which means "snow eater") is a warm, dry wind that descends the eastern slopes of the Rocky Mountains. Because dry air is more dense than humid air, air descending the eastern slopes accelerates as it sinks. Additional speed and warmth are gained as the air is compressed by the higher air pressures close to the ground. Chinook winds cause temperatures to rise sharply, sometimes as much as 30° F in a single hour, which can rapidly melt snow for about 20 miles eastward. These high winds often reach hurricane force (sustained winds of 74 mph or greater) and loft dust and debris into the air.

Seasons

Because of its location in the interior of the North American continent, the Rocky Mountain region experiences dramatic seasonal changes in the weather. In Denver, Colorado, for example, high temperatures approach 90° F in July but only 40° F in January. Situated approximately halfway between the equator and the North Pole, this area is particularly sensitive to the changing angles of sunlight striking the ground over the course of a year.

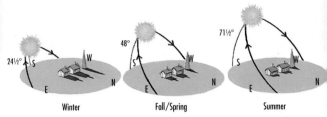

Winter	Fall/Spring	Summer

At 42 degrees north latitude (the latitude of the Utah–Idaho border), the noontime sun at the summer solstice has an altitude above the horizon of 71½ degrees; at the spring and fall equinoxes, its altitude is 48 degrees; and at the winter solstice, the noontime sun rises only 24½ degrees above the horizon.

As the earth moves around its orbit, its 23½-degree tilt on its axis means that for half the year the Northern Hemisphere is inclined toward the sun and the sun's rays shine on it more directly; for half the year it is tilted away from the sun and the sun's rays are more oblique. The latitude that receives the greatest heat from the sun is farther north during the summer months (though the earth's surface—land and sea—takes a while to warm up, so that early August is actually hotter than late June). As a result, large-scale wind patterns, like the prevailing westerlies, shift toward the north. Higher sun angles and longer days in the Arctic during summer warm up the polar air masses, and this, together with the northern position of the westerlies, keeps the coldest air north of the Rocky Mountain states during summer.

Wildflowers, Glacier National Park

Spring

Spring officially begins on March 21 or 22, called the spring (or vernal) equinox, when the sun, heading north, appears directly overhead at noon at the equator. In spring, the first incursions of mild air from the tropical Pacific Ocean arrive in the region, but the Arctic can still send south bitter-cold air masses, and the clash provides some of the most violent weather of the year. March is often snowy and cold, with frequent blizzards in the high altitudes. Sunshine begins to increase in April and May, as do showers, thunderstorms, and occasional tornadoes over the eastern plains.

Summer

The sun reaches its peak over the Northern Hemisphere on June 21 or 22, the longest day (that is, daylight period) of the year, known as the summer solstice. As the sun's more direct rays heat the high Arctic, tempering the Rocky

Storm clouds and rainbow, Idaho

Mountain states' source of cold air, the region begins to warm up. Temperatures above 90° F are common along the eastern plains and the high plateaus of southern Idaho, but frequent showers and thunderstorms bring temporary relief. Beautiful rainbows following a late afternoon thunderstorm are a common sight.

Fall aspens, Grand Teton National Park

Fall

As it does at the spring equinox, the sun "crosses" the equator again at the fall (or autumnal) equinox, on September 21 or 22, this time heading south. At high elevations the first frost occurs in August, but throughout the eastern plains and in southern Idaho it occurs typically in September or October. Cold polar air masses dropping down from the north clash with warm tropical air, creating the cold season's first organized snowstorms.

Winter

The sun reaches its lowest point over the Northern Hemisphere at the winter solstice, on December 21 or 22. Winter is a time of heavy snows, high winds, and bitter cold in the higher elevations of the Rocky Mountain states. Along the eastern plains and foothills, three- to five-day periods of cold, snowy weather alternate with three- to five-day periods of milder conditions as large-scale high and low pressure systems traverse the region. Warm, dry chinook winds regularly howl down the eastern slopes and melt away the snow cover.

American Bison, Yellowstone National Park

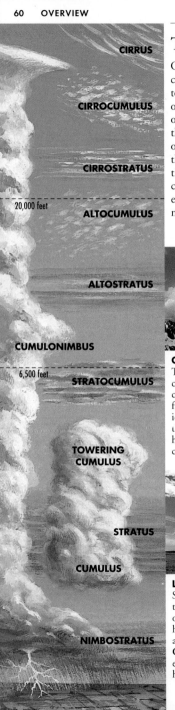

CIRRUS

CIRROCUMULUS

CIRROSTRATUS

20,000 feet

ALTOCUMULUS

ALTOSTRATUS

CUMULONIMBUS

6,500 feet

STRATOCUMULUS

TOWERING
CUMULUS

STRATUS

CUMULUS

NIMBOSTRATUS

Typical Clouds

Clouds form when moist air is cooled, causing water molecules to condense into water droplets or ice crystals. While most types of clouds can be spotted over the Rocky Mountain states, the ones described here are among the most common. The illustration at left shows the relative common altitudes of the different cloud types; distances are not shown to scale.

CUMULONIMBUS

Tallest of all cloud types; commonly called thunderheads. Lower part composed of water droplets; fuzzy, fibrous top—the "anvil"—made of ice crystals. Produce lightning, thunder, heavy rain, and sometimes hail, high winds, or tornadoes. Most common from May to September.

LENTICULAR CLOUDS

Stationary, smooth-edged clouds that form at crests of air currents over mountainous terrain. Indicate high winds at mountaintop level and turbulence above mountains. **Cap clouds,** with more ragged edges, form directly on summits of higher mountains.

CUMULUS

Water-droplet clouds formed at tops of rising air currents set in motion by uneven heating of ground by sun. Domed tops, like bright white cotton balls. Typical clouds of fine summer days, but can occur any time of year. Very common throughout the Rocky Mountain states.

TOWERING CUMULUS

Cumulus clouds grow into towering, or swelling, cumuli (also called cumuli congesti) if atmospheric moisture is sufficient and it is much warmer at ground level than in the air aloft. Can grow taller and develop into thunderstorms—watch for rapid billowing in tops.

CIRRUS

High (5 miles or more), thin, wispy cloud made of ice crystals; may be seen in any season, anywhere in the Rocky Mountain states. Cirrus thickening from west or south may signal approaching rain or snow; however, cirrus often come and go without bringing any lower clouds or rain.

ALTOSTRATUS

Middle-level clouds, mainly of water droplets; usually appear as featureless gray sheet covering sky. Thickening, low altostratus from west or south often bring steady widespread rain or snow within hours. May be seen in the Rocky Mountains at any time of year; most common in winter.

FOG

Clouds formed at ground level; occur up to 40 days per year throughout the mountainous portions of the Rocky Mountain states. **Radiation fog:** caused by overnight cooling of still air; burns off as sun rises; common in mountain valleys.

STRATUS AND NIMBOSTRATUS

Stratus: low, indistinct gray water-droplet clouds, usually covering sky in calm conditions; may become fog if close to ground. **Nimbostratus:** stratus clouds from which precipitation falls; almost always present during steady rain or snow.

Our Solar System

The sun, the nine planets that revolve around it, and their moons make up our solar system. Venus, Mars, Jupiter, and Saturn are easily visible to the naked eye; Mercury, Uranus, Neptune, and Pluto are more difficult to see. Other objects in our solar system are transient: the large orbits of comets make them rare visitors near earth, and meteors flash brightly for only seconds before disappearing.

Sky-observing in the Rockies

The Rocky Mountain region, with its high elevations and generally low humidity, provides fair to good conditions for viewing the night sky, particularly away from the urbanized Boulder–Denver area, which produces considerable light pollution. About one out of three nights are clear (one out of four in Montana, which is cloudier and colder due to winter Arctic blasts from Canada).

FULL MOON

The full moon rises at sunset and sets at sunrise. It is highest in the sky in December, culminating at up to 78 degrees above the horizon in Boulder, Colorado (in summer, it culminates as low as 22 degrees). Some lunar features show up best when the moon is full: the dark "seas" (hardened lava flows) and the "rays" of bright material splattered from craters. Craters and mountain ranges are best seen before and after full moon, when the angle of sunlight throws them into relief; look especially near the terminator, the dividing line between the moon's day and night sides. Because the moon is locked in earth's gravitational grip, the same side of the moon always faces us.

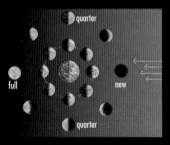

PHASES OF THE MOON

As the moon makes its monthly orbit around the earth, the illuminated lunar surface area appears to grow (wax), shrink (wane), and even disappear (at new moon). The center of the illustration shows the phases, with sunlight coming from the right. The outer drawings show how the moon looks from our perspective on earth.

VENUS

Cloud-shrouded Venus alternates between being our "morning star" and "evening star," depending on where it is in its orbit in relation to the earth and sun. This brilliant planet usually outshines everything in the sky except for the sun and moon. As it circles the sun, Venus displays phases, which can be viewed through a small telescope or high-power binoculars.

Venus (left) and the moon

MARS

Every 25½ months, when earth is aligned between Mars and the sun, Mars is closest to us and at its brightest and most colorful, appearing orange-red to the naked eye. At this time, called opposition (opposite in the sky from the sun), Mars rises at sunset and remains in the sky all night. Bright, white polar caps and dusky surface markings may be glimpsed through a small telescope at opposition. Mars rivals Jupiter in brightness at opposition, but fades at other times.

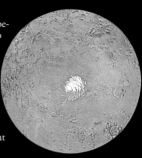

JUPITER

Visible in our morning sky for about five months at a stretch and in our evening sky for five months, Jupiter appears brighter than any star in the night sky at all times. The largest planet in our solar system, it has a diameter of 88,850 miles, 11.2 times that of the earth. Jupiter's four largest moons—Io, Europa, Ganymede, and Callisto—can often be spotted with binoculars.

Jupiter (top) and moons

SATURN

Visible most of the year, Saturn appears to the naked eye as a slightly yellowish, moderately bright star. A small telescope reveals its rings, composed mainly of rocky chunks of ice, and the two largest (Titan and Rhea) of its more than 20 known moons.

METEORS

These "shooting stars" are typically chips ranging from sand-grain to marble size that are knocked off asteroids (tiny planets) or blown off comets and burn up as they strike our atmosphere. The strongest annual meteor showers are the Perseids, which peak around August 12, and the Geminids, which peak around December 13.

COMETS

Comets are irregular lumps of ice and rock left over from the formation of the solar system. Occasionally a notable comet approaches the sun as it travels in its far-ranging elliptical orbit. The sun's energy vaporizes the comet's surface, generating a tail of gas and dust that may be millions of miles long.

Comet Hale-Bopp, 1997

Stars and Deep-sky Objects

As earth orbits the sun in its annual cycle, our planet's night side faces in steadily changing directions, revealing different stars, constellations, and views of our own Milky Way. People in ancient times named constellations after mythological figures and familiar creatures whose shapes they saw outlined by the stars. The best known of these constellations lie along the ecliptic, the imaginary line that traces the apparent annual path of the sun through the sky. Earth, our moon, and other planets orbit in nearly the same plane, all traveling along a band roughly 16 degrees wide centered on the ecliptic and called the zodiac. The zodiac is traditionally divided into 12 segments, but 13 constellations are actually intersected by the ecliptic.

Modern constellations are simply designated regions of the celestial sphere, like countries on a map. Most constellations bear little resemblance to their namesakes. Beyond the approximately 6,000 stars visible to the naked eye lie other fascinating deep-sky objects—star clusters, galaxies, nebulas (gas clouds)—that can be seen, a few with the naked eye but most requiring binoculars or a small telescope.

The Zodiac

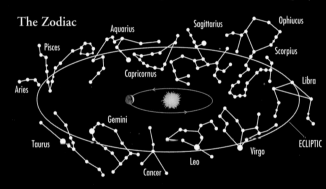

Ophiucus • Sagittarius • Aquarius • Pisces • Scorpius • Capricornus • Aries • Libra • Gemini • Taurus • Virgo • ECLIPTIC • Leo • Cancer

Seasonal Sky Maps

The following pages show star maps for each of the four seasons, drawn at a latitude of 45 degrees north for the specific times and dates given. (If you wish to observe at a different time or date, note that the same stars appear two hours earlier each month, or one hour earlier every two weeks.) The map for each season divides the sky into four quadrants: northeast, northwest, southeast, and southwest. Start by facing the direction in which you have the clearest view; if your best view is southeastward, use the southeast map. The maps plot the constellations and major stars; the wavy, pale blue areas represent the band of the Milky Way; the zenith, the point directly overhead, is indicated. The key to finding your way around the sky is to locate distinctive constellations or star groups, and then use them to find others. The maps do not chart the planets of our solar system, whose positions change continually; their locations are often listed in the weather section of newspapers.

WINTER: ORION

On winter evenings, we look outward through a spiral arm of our disk-shaped galaxy. Many hot, young blue or white stars (such as Sirius, Rigel, and Procyon), along with some older, cooler yellow and reddish stars (Betelgeuse, Capella, and Aldebaran), dominate the sky. New stars are being born in the Orion Nebula, a mixture of young stars, gases, and dust visible to the naked eye or with binoculars as a fuzzy area in Orion's sword, which hangs from his bright, three-starred belt.

SPRING: THE DIPPERS

The spring sky features the well-known Big Dipper, part of the constellation Ursa Major, the Great Bear. The two stars at the end of the Big Dipper's bowl point almost directly at Polaris, the North Star, a moderately bright star (part of the Little Dipper, or Ursa Minor) that lies slightly less than one degree from the true north celestial pole. Polaris sits above the horizon at an altitude equal to the observer's latitude (for example, its altitude is about 40 degrees in Denver and 46 degrees in Helena).

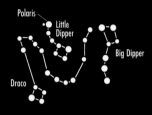

SUMMER: MILKY WAY

During the summer months, earth's night side faces toward the bright center of the Milky Way, making that hazy band of light a dominant feature in the sky. A scan with binoculars through the Milky Way from Cygnus to Sagittarius and Scorpius reveals a dozen or more star clusters and nebulas. High to the northeast, the hot, white stars of the Summer Triangle—Vega, Deneb, and Altair—are usually the first stars visible in the evening.

FALL: ANDROMEDA GALAXY

On autumn evenings, earth's night side faces away from the plane of our galaxy, allowing us to see other, more distant ones. The Andromeda Galaxy can be found northeast of the Great Square of Pegasus, just above the central star on the dimmer northern "leg" of Andromeda. (On the Fall Sky: Southeast map the galaxy is near the first D in Andromeda.) Appearing as an elongated patch of fuzzy light, it is 2.5 million light-years away.

The Winter Sky

The chart is drawn for these times and dates, but can be used at other times during the season.

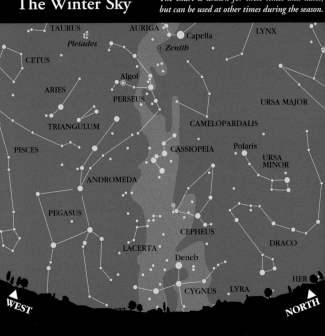

TAURUS
Pleiades
AURIGA
Capella
+ *Zenith*
LYNX
CETUS
Algol
ARIES
PERSEUS
URSA MAJOR
TRIANGULUM
CAMELOPARDALIS
PISCES
CASSIOPEIA
Polaris
URSA MINOR
ANDROMEDA
PEGASUS
CEPHEUS
DRACO
LACERTA
Deneb
CYGNUS
LYRA
HER
WEST
NORTH

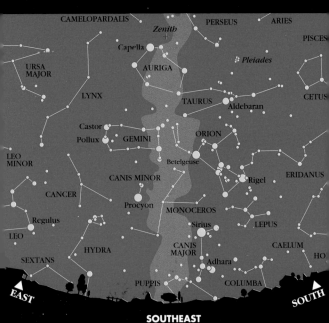

CAMELOPARDALIS
Zenith +
PERSEUS
ARIES
Capella
PISCES
URSA MAJOR
AURIGA
Pleiades
LYNX
TAURUS
Aldebaran
CETUS
Castor
Pollux
GEMINI
ORION
LEO MINOR
Betelgeuse
CANIS MINOR
Rigel
ERIDANUS
CANCER
Procyon
MONOCEROS
LEPUS
Regulus
Sirius
CAELUM
LEO
HYDRA
CANIS MAJOR
Adhara
HO
SEXTANS
PUPPIS
COLUMBA
EAST
SOUTH
SOUTHEAST

December 1, midnight; January 1, 10 P.M.; February 1, 8 P.M.; March 1, 6 P.M.

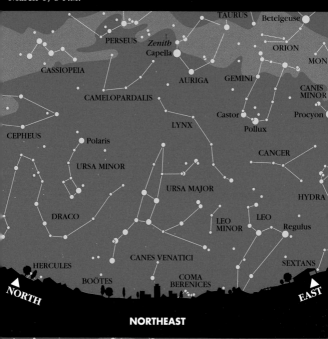

NORTHEAST

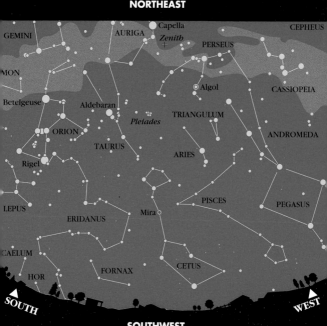

SOUTHWEST

The Spring Sky

The chart is drawn for these times and dates, but can be used at other times during the season.

LEO

LEO MINOR

Zenith

URSA MAJOR

DRACO

CANCER

Pollux

Castor

LYNX

URSA MINOR

CANIS MINOR

GEMINI

Polaris

CEPHEUS

MON

Capella

CAMELOPARDALIS

CASSIOPEIA

Betelgeuse

AURIGA

ORION

Aldebaran

Algol

PERSEUS

LACERTA

TAURUS

Pleiades

TRIANGULUM

ANDROMEDA

WEST

NORTH

NORTHWEST

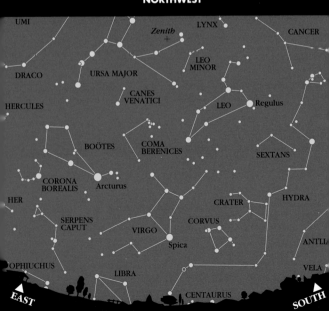

UMI

LYNX

Zenith

CANCER

DRACO

URSA MAJOR

LEO MINOR

HERCULES

CANES VENATICI

LEO

Regulus

BOÖTES

COMA BERENICES

SEXTANS

CORONA BOREALIS

Arcturus

HER

CRATER

HYDRA

SERPENS CAPUT

CORVUS

VIRGO

ANTLI

Spica

OPHIUCHUS

LIBRA

VELA

EAST

CENTAURUS

SOUTH

SOUTHEAST

March 1, midnight; April 1, 10 P.M. (11 P.M. DST); May 1, 8 P.M. (9 P.M. DST)

NORTHEAST

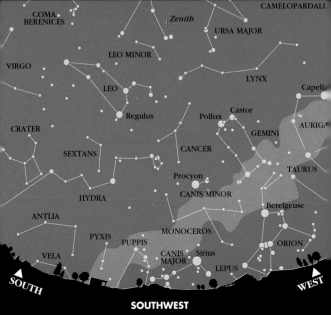

SOUTHWEST

The Summer Sky

The chart is drawn for these times and dates.

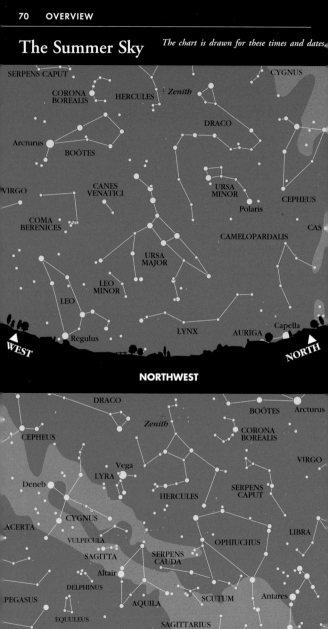

June 1, midnight (1 A.M. DST); July 1, 10 P.M. (11 P.M. DST);
August 1, 8 P.M. (9 P.M. DST).

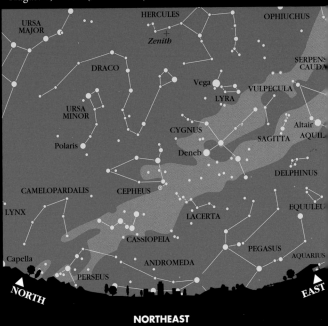

NORTHEAST

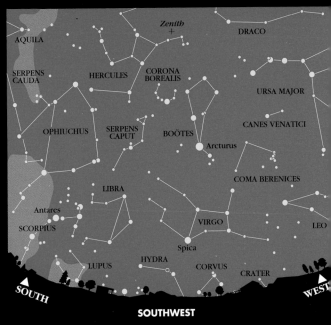

SOUTHWEST

The Fall Sky

The chart is drawn for these times and dates, but can be used at other times during the season.

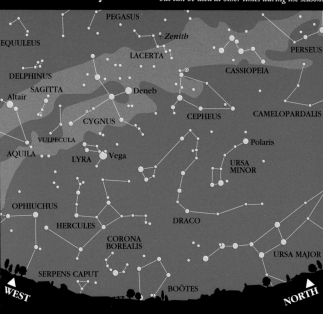

EQUULEUS

PEGASUS

LACERTA

+*Zenith*

PERSEUS

CASSIOPEIA

DELPHINUS

SAGITTA

Deneb

CEPHEUS

CAMELOPARDALIS

Altair

CYGNUS

AQUILA

VULPECULA

Polaris

LYRA   Vega

URSA MINOR

OPHIUCHUS

HERCULES

DRACO

CORONA BOREALIS

URSA MAJOR

SERPENS CAPUT

BOÖTES

◁ **WEST**

NORTH ▷

NORTHWEST

CAMELOPARDALIS

LACERTA

CYGNUS

Zenith +

CASSIOPEIA

DELPHINUS

ANDROMEDA

PEGASUS

EQUULEUS

Algol

AQUARIUS

PERSEUS

TRIANGULUM

Pleiades

ARIES

PISCES

CAPRICORNUS

TAURUS

PISCIS AUSTRINUS

Aldebaran

Mira

Fomalhaut

ORION

CETUS

GRUS

ERIDANUS

SCULPTOR

◁ **EAST**

SOUTH ▷

SOUTHEAST

September 1, midnight (1 A.M. DST); October 1, 10 P.M. (11 P.M.

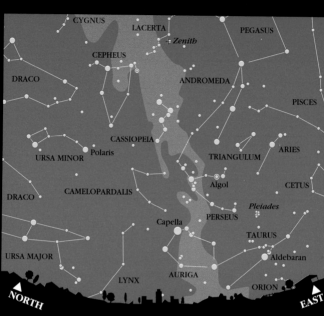

NORTHEAST

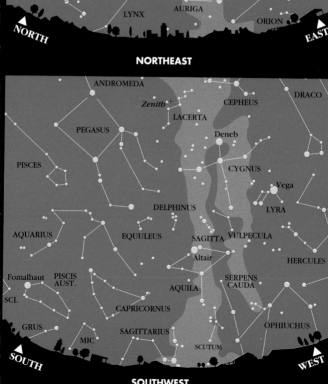

SOUTHWEST

Flora and Fauna

How to Use the Flora and Fauna Section

Part Two of this book presents nearly 1,000 of the most common species found in the Rocky Mountain States, beginning with mushrooms, lichens, ferns, and other spore plants, and continuing with large and small trees, wildflowers, invertebrates (mostly insects), fishes, amphibians, reptiles, birds, and mammals. Flora species are presented alphabetically by family name. Fauna species are sequenced according to their taxonomy, or scientific classification. The classification and the names of species in this guide are based on authoritative sources when these exist for a given group.

Introductions and Other Essays

Most major sections of Part Two—for example, trees, wildflowers, marine invertebrates, birds—have an introduction, and some groups within the larger sections are also described in brief essays. The introductions should be read along with the species accounts that follow, as they present information that is fundamental for understanding the plants or animals in question. For groups without introductory essays, shared features are sometimes given in the opening sentence of the first species in the sequence.

Names

Each account begins with the common name of the species. Common names can change and may differ in other sources; if a species has a widely used alternate name, that is given within quotation marks, directly below the common name. The scientific species name, shown below the common name, is italicized (alternate scientific names are also sometimes listed). In a few cases (some flowers and invertebrates), organisms are best known on the genus level and are presented as such here. For example, the Mosquitoes are presented as a group: the *Aedes* species. Below the scientific name is the name of the group (class, order, family) with which the species is most commonly associated.

Description

The species accounts are designed to permit identification of species in the field. An account begins with the organism's typical mature or adult size: length (L), height (H), width (W), diameter (D), tail length (T), and/or wingspan (WS). The size is followed by physical characteristics, including color and distinctive markings. We use the abbreviations "imm." (immature) and "juv." (juvenile). The term "morph" describes a distinctive coloration that occurs in some individuals.

Other Information

For every species, the typical habitat is described. Other information may also be given, such as seasonality (bloom times of flowers or periods of activity for mammals) or the need for caution (species that can cause irritation, illness, or injury). Similar species are some-

adult (left), immature (right)

Names

AMERICAN ROBIN
Turdus migratorius
THRUSH FAMILY

Description

10″. Male breast and sides rufous-orange; back and wings gray-brown; head blackish; partial white eye ring; throat striped; bill yellow; tail black, with tiny white corners. Female head, back duller brown. Tail fairly long. Imm. buffy white below, with heavy blackish spots; pale buffy scaling on back. In spring and summer, eats earthworms; in fall and winter, roams in berry-searching flocks and roosts communally. **VOICE** Song: prolonged, rising and

Other
Information

falling *cheery-up cheery-me*. Calls: *tut tut tut* and *tseep*. **HABITAT** Woods, shrubs, lawns. **RANGE** Resident in entire region. In winter, withdraws from high mtns. and n MT.

times described at the end of an account. The range (the area in which the species lives) is not stated if the species occurs throughout the Rocky Mountain region; the one exception to this rule is the birds, for which the range is always given. The term "local" means that a species occurs in spotty fashion over a large area, but not throughout the entire area. In describing the geographic range of species, we use the abbreviations e (east), w (west), n (north), s (south), c (central), and combinations of these (sc for south-central). For state names, we use the two-letter postal codes.

Readers should note that color, shape, and size may vary within plant and animal species, depending on environmental conditions and other factors. Bloom, migration, and other times can vary with the weather, latitude, and geography.

Classification of Living Things

Biologists divide living organisms into major groups called kingdoms, the largest of which are the plant and animal kingdoms. Kingdoms are divided into phyla (or divisions, in plants), phyla are divided into classes, classes into orders, orders into families, families into genera (singular: genus), and genera into species. The species, the basic unit of classification, is generally what we have in mind when we talk about a "kind" of plant or animal. The scientific name of a species consists of two words. The first is the genus name; the second is the species name. The scientific name of the Western Jumping Mouse is *Zapus princeps*. *Zapus* is the genus name, and *princeps* is the species name.

Species are populations or groups of populations that are able to interbreed and produce fertile offspring themselves; they usually are not able to breed successfully or produce fertile offspring with members of other species. Many widespread species have numerous races (subspecies)—populations that are separated from one another geographically; races within a species may differ in appearance and behavior from other populations of that species.

Flora

The flora section of this guide includes flowering and nonflowering plants, as well as mushrooms, which are no longer considered part of the plant kingdom. Mushrooms are covered here because they are somewhat plant-like in appearance and are often found on plants or plant matter.

The first part of the Rocky Mountain flora section begins with mushrooms, followed by lichens. The next group is the nonflowering spore plants such as liverworts, mosses, clubmosses, horsetails, and ferns. Trees follow, beginning with conifers, then large broadleaf trees, and finally small broadleaf trees and shrubs. Wildflowers, including flowering vines, grasses, and water plants in addition to terrestrial herbaceous plants, end the flora section.

In most of the flora subsections, species are grouped by family and sequenced alphabetically by the English family name. The measurements in the species accounts are typical mature sizes in the Rocky Mountain region. Colors, shapes, and sizes may vary within a species depending on environmental conditions. Bloom times vary throughout the region—they are later northward and at higher elevations—and can be affected by weather conditions in a given year. The geographic range is given only for species that are not found in all parts of the region where the described habitat occurs. The abbreviation "Cont. Div." refers to the Continental Divide.

Users of this guide are warned against eating or otherwise consuming any plants or parts of a plant (including fiddleheads or fruits) or any mushrooms based on the information in this guide.

Mushrooms

The organisms known as fungi—including molds, yeasts, mildews, and mushrooms—range from microscopic forms to mammoth puffballs. Unlike plants, they do not carry out photosynthesis and thus must obtain food from organic matter, living or dead. The fungi in this book are of the type commonly known as mushrooms.

Most mushrooms that grow on the ground have a stalk and a cap. The stalks of different species vary in shape, thickness, and density. There is often a skirt-like ring midway up or near the top of the stalk, and the stalk base is often bulbous or enclosed by a cup at or just below the surface of the ground. Bracket (or shelf) mushrooms, which grow on trunks or logs, are often unstalked or short-stalked. A mushroom's cap may be smooth, scaly, warty, or shaggy, and its shape may be round, flat, convex (bell- or umbrella-shaped), or concave (cup- or trumpet-shaped). The caps of many species change as they mature, from closed and egg-shaped to open and umbrella-like; the cap color may also change with age.

Fungi reproduce through the release of single-celled bodies called spores. Many mushrooms bear their microscopic, spore-producing structures on the underside of the cap, either on radiating blade-like gills or within tiny tubes that terminate in pores. In others, the spore-producing structures line the inside of a cup-shaped cap or are located in broad wrinkles or open pits on the sides or top of the cap. Puffball mushrooms produce their spores within a ball-shaped body; the spores are released when the mature ball breaks open at the top or disintegrates.

Mushroom seasons often begin earlier in wet areas than in dry ones. In the accounts that follow, sizes given are typical heights (for stalked species) and cap widths of mature specimens.

CAUTION

Of the many hundreds of mushroom species occurring in the Rocky Mountain region, at least six are deadly poisonous to eat, even in small amounts, and many others cause mild to severe reactions. The brief descriptions and few illustrations in this guide are not to be used for determining the edibility of mushrooms. Inexperienced mushroom-hunters should not eat any species they find in the wild.

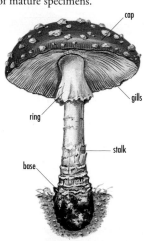

Parts of a Mushroom

FLY AMANITA
"Fly Agaric"
Amanita muscaria
AMANITA FAMILY
H 5″; W 5″. Cap umbrella-shaped, faded orange (occ. bright red) with white warts. Stalk white, cylindrical or tapered upward, has fragile skirt, bulbous base. Gills white. **CAUTION** Poisonous. **SEASON** July–Oct. **HABITAT** Under aspens or conifers.

KING BOLETUS
Boletus edulis
BOLETUS FAMILY
H 6″; W 6″. Cap round, muffin-like, spongy, tan to reddish or dark brown, sticky when wet. Stalk stout, often pear-shaped, pale brown, partly covered with fine white netting. Cap underside white to green or yellow, with pores. **SEASON** June–Sept. **HABITAT** Under aspens or conifers.

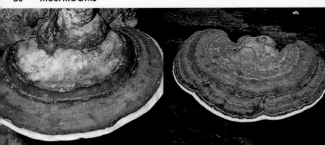

PINE DESTROYER
"Red-belted Conk"
Fomitopsis (Fomes) pinicola
BRACKET FAMILY

W 10″. Cap hoof-shaped to shelf-shaped, glossy, very hard; bright rust red (the youngest, outermost belt) darkening in belts to reddish black. Underside white or yellowish, does not discolor where bruised; pores too tiny to see. Causes brown rot, mainly in already-dead trees. **SEASON** Year-round. **HABITAT** Trunks of dead or dying trees.

ARTIST'S BRACKET
"Artist's Conk"
Ganoderma applanatum
BRACKET FAMILY

W 16″. Cap flat to convex, semicircular; shiny dark brown or gray, lighter and brighter at edge; wrinkled, hard, attached directly to wood. Underside white, bruises brown; with pores. **SEASON** Year-round. **HABITAT** Low on trunks of dead or dying trees.

PURPLE-TIPPED CORAL
"Clustered Coral"
Ramaria botrytis
CORAL FUNGUS FAMILY

H 5″; W 5″. Cauliflower-like; massive white stem (usu. buried) branches into many crowded, blunt, dull pink to lilac tips; fragrant. Firm, opaque throughout. **SEASON** Aug.–Oct. **HABITAT** Thick needle humus under conifers. **Orange Coral** (*R. largentii*) is rich orange throughout and has erect tubular tips.

BLACK HELVELLA
Helvella lacunosa
FALSE MOREL FAMILY

H 3″; W 1½″. Cap dark gray, saddle-shaped, resembling crumpled piece of leather. Stalk pale gray, with vertical ridges outside, several hollow chambers inside. **SEASON** July–Sept. **HABITAT** Soil containing rotten wood, esp. in burned areas.

SADDLE-SHAPED FALSE MOREL
Gyromitra infula
FALSE MOREL FAMILY

H 3″; W 2½″. Cap tan to brown, resembling crumpled piece of leather, usu. low-centered like a saddle. Stalk pale tan to brown, hollow, convoluted; brittle. **CAUTION** Poisonous. **SEASON** July–Oct. **HABITAT** Soil containing rotten wood.

TREE EARS
Auricularia auricula (auricula-judae)
TREE EAR FAMILY

W 4″. Dark brown, rubbery, wavy, ear-shaped disks or cups; hard when dry. Upper surface smooth, wavy; attachment-side ribbed, minutely silky-hairy. Attached at center. **SEASON** May–June, Sept.–Oct. **HABITAT** Dead, usu. coniferous, wood.

WITCH'S BUTTER
Tremella mesenterica
JELLY FUNGUS FAMILY

W 2″. Gelatinous, bright yellow, earlike lobes; in dry conditions shrivels and turns dark, hard, and brittle, but revives in moist conditions. **SEASON** Year-round, ex. when dry or frozen. **HABITAT** On deciduous trees. **Orange Jelly** *(Dacrymyces palmatus)* grows on conifers, is deeper yellow to orange, and has a whitish attachment layer.

GREEN-GILL
Chlorophyllum molybdites
LEPIOTA FAMILY

H 7″; W 7″. Cap umbrella-shaped or broadly conical, white, with coarse cinnamon scales at maturity. Stalk slender, slightly tapers upward; broad, often movable skirt. Gills white in youth, aging gray-green. Often grows in rings. **CAUTION** Poisonous. **SEASON** Aug.–Sept. **HABITAT** Lawns, pastures, disturbed ground. **RANGE** Mainly CO.

HORSE MUSHROOM
Agaricus arvensis
MEADOW MUSHROOM FAMILY

H 5″; W 5″. Cap umbrella-shaped, white, bruises yellowish; smooth or slightly fibrous; sweet anise or almond fragrance. Stalk usu. cylindrical, with felty white skirt. Gills fine, crowded, white in youth, maturing pinkish gray to blackish brown. Often grows in rings. **SEASON** June–Oct. **HABITAT** Among grasses.

SCULPTURED PUFFBALL
Calvatia sculpta
PUFFBALL FAMILY

H 4″; W 4″. White "baseball" covered with pyramidal bumps that are often tall, bent. Pear-shaped (with narrowed base); no stem or gills. Splits open on top, releasing spores. Interior pure white, turning yellow to greenish brown as spores mature. **SEASON** June–Aug. **HABITAT** Subalpine forests and clearings. **Warted Giant Puffball** (*Calbovista subsculpta*) has low pyramidal bumps that eventually flake off.

BLACK MOREL
Morchella elata (angusticeps)
MOREL FAMILY

H 5″; W 1½″. Cap conical to egg-shaped, blackish brown, often pale between ridges or in hollows; varying from ridged to honeycombed, with patterns vertically aligned; hollow. Stalk hollow, whitish; maturing very thick. Spores produced in pits on cap. **SEASON** Apr.–June. **HABITAT** Conifer or aspen stands, esp. after fires; dirt roads.

YELLOW MOREL
Morchella esculenta
MOREL FAMILY

H 4″; W 1½″. Cap conical to egg-shaped, yellow-brown to grayish, honeycombed with deep pits rarely vertically aligned; hollow. Stalk hollow, enlarged at base, whitish. Spores produced in pits on cap. **SEASON** Apr.–June. **HABITAT** Usu. under deciduous trees, esp. cottonwoods, and in old orchards.

SCALY PHOLIOTA
Pholiota squarrosa
STROPHARIA FAMILY

H 5"; W 4". Clustered. Cap umbrella-shaped, buff, covered with raised brown scales; veil shreds hang from edges; may smell garlicky. Stalk cylindrical; similarly scaly, but smooth white above high, thick ring. **CAUTION** Poisonous. **SEASON** June–Aug. **HABITAT** Logs, stumps, bases of trees, esp. aspens.

WHITE MATSUTAKE
"Pine Mushroom"
*Tricholoma magnivelare
(Armillaria ponderosa)*
TRICHOLOMA FAMILY

H 5"; W 6". Cap convex to flat; white to pale tan, becoming brown-scaly in center; firm. Stalk white above thick ring, scaly and dirty below; tapers downward. Gills broad; white to creamy, bruises pinkish brown. Strange sharp fragrance. **SEASON** Sept.–Oct. **HABITAT** Under Lodgepole or Limber Pines.

Lichens

A lichen is a remarkable dual organism made up of a fungus and a colony of microscopic green algae or cyanobacteria ("blue-green algae"). Such a relationship—dissimilar organisms living in close association—is known as *symbiosis* and may be harmful to one of the participants (parasitism) or beneficial to both (mutualism). In a lichen, the fungus surrounds the algae and takes up water and minerals that come its way from rainwater, fog, and dust; the algae supply carbohydrates produced by photosynthesis. It is not definitely known whether symbiosis in lichens is mutually beneficial or mildly to wholly parasitic—the balance is probably different in each species.

Lichens occur in a range of habitats, including forests, along roadsides, on buildings, and on mountaintops; and in some of the harshest environments on earth, such as deserts and the Arctic. Lichens vary in color, occurring in white, black, gray, and various shades of green, orange, brown, yellow, or red. Their color often varies dramatically with moisture content.

Most lichens grow very slowly, about $1/25$ inch to $1/2$ inch per year, and can have extremely long lifetimes; specimens estimated to be at least 4,000 years old have been found. Many lichens have special structures for vegetative reproduction—tiny fragments that break off easily or powdery spots that release tiny balls of algae wrapped in microscopic fungal threads. In others, the fungal component produces spores carried on conspicuous fruiting bodies, which may be disk-like, cup-like, or globular.

HORSEHAIR LICHEN
Bryoria fremontii

L 15". Dense clumps of hanging, branched, somewhat twisted brown strands, sometimes with yellow powdery spots. Fruiting bodies inconspicuous, rare. Grows intermingled with several very similar species of *Bryoria*. **HABITAT** Branches, twigs of conifers, esp. pines, larches, and Douglas Firs, in mtn. forests. **RANGE** c CO and north.

TRUMPET CLADONIA
"Trumpet Pixie Cup"
Cladonia fimbriata

H 1". Pale greenish, powdery, flaring cups arising from cluster of small, pale green lobes. Fruiting bodies rare; reproduces via powder on surface. **HABITAT** Soil, moss, rotting wood, or tree bases in low- to mid-elev. wooded areas. **RANGE** Scattered throughout. Several other "pixie cup" *Cladonia* species are similar, esp. **Mealy Pixie Cup** *(Cladonia chlorophaea)*.

NEW MEXICO RIM-DISK LICHEN
Lecanora novomexicana

W 1". Rounded, pale yellowish-green patches with narrow lobes at edges; flat and tightly attached to rock. Fruiting bodies disk-like; pale yellowish green rims with darker centers; crowded. **HABITAT** Exposed rocks at all elevs. Can be confused with **Green Rock-Posy** *(Rhizoplaca melanophthalma)*, which is attached to rock only at a central point.

FIELD DOG-LICHEN
Peltigera rufescens

W 5". Gray-brown rosette of wide lobes, often whitish at edges. Fruiting bodies brown to black, somewhat round; on lobe extensions that curl upward, exposing white underside. Underside darker in center, with raised veins and tufts of root-like hairs. **HABITAT** Widespread on soil or moss in low-elev. to alpine open areas.

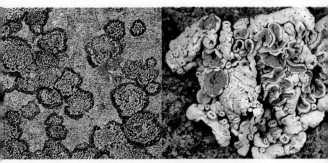

MAP LICHEN
Rhizocarpon geographicum

W 2″. Thin, yellow to yellow-green crust, with black outline; black cracks contain black, disk-like fruiting bodies. **HABITAT** Exposed rocks at high elevs., esp. mountaintops. There are several species of *Rhizocarpon* that are similar. Some can be found on rocks near creeks, or even submerged at times.

ROCK-POSY LICHEN
Rhizoplaca chrysoleuca

W 1″. Whitish to pale yellow-green lumpy rosettes attached to rock at central point. Fruiting bodies flat to folded disks, pale orange to salmon or tan, with pale rims. Underside tan to brown. **HABITAT** Exposed rocks at all elevs. **RANGE** Scattered throughout. **Green Rock-Posy** *(Rhizoplaca melanophthalma)* is similar in form, but is yellowish green with dark greenish fruiting bodies.

WHITEWORM LICHEN
Thamnolia vermicularis

W 2″. Stark white, slender, pointed, worm-like strands; occ. branching, usu. prostrate. No fruiting bodies; reproduces by simple fragmentation. **HABITAT** On exposed soil, rock, or moss above tree line; tundra.

PEBBLED ROCKTRIPE
Umbilicaria hyperborea

W 1″. Mainly circular, dark brown lobes, often with lacerated edges, attached only in center. Upper surface lumpy. Fruiting bodies disk-like, raised, dark gray with minute ridges forming complex patterns. **HABITAT** Exposed rocks at high elevs.

BRISTLY BEARD LICHEN
Usnea hirta
H 2″. Pale greenish-yellow, stringy, pendent, branching tufts, with short, dense, perpendicular bristles. May have small powdery spots for reproduction; no fruiting bodies. **HABITAT** Branches and trunks of conifers and deciduous trees in low-elev. open areas.

ALPINE GOLD-TWIST
Vulpicida tilesii
W 1″. Bright yellow, twisted, narrow straps with curly, irreg. edges. Fruiting bodies rare. **HABITAT** On soil or tundra sod at high elevs. **Pine Gold-twist** *(Vulpicida pinastri),* with powdery lobe edges for reproduction, grows on tree bases and dead wood. **Channeled Snow Lichen** *(Flavocetraria cucullata)* and **Crinkled Snow Lichen** *(F. nivalis)* are pale yellow.

CUMBERLAND ROCKSHIELD
Xanthoparmelia cumberlandia
W 4″. Round, yellowish to greenish patches of crowded lobes, with scattered, tiny black dots. Fruiting bodies large, brown, cup-like to nearly flat; in center of patches. Underside tan to brown. **HABITAT** Low- to mid-elev. rocks.

ELEGANT SUNBURST LICHEN
Xanthoria elegans
W 1″. Bright orange patches of radiating narrow lobes. Fruiting bodies orange, disk-like. Underside white, coarse-hairy. Easily separated from rock. **HABITAT** Exposed rocks at all elevs. **Flame Lichens** *(Caloplaca* species) cannot be separated from rock.

Spore Plants

Spore plants are green land plants such as liverworts, mosses, club-mosses, horsetails, and ferns (ferns are introduced separately on page 89) that do not reproduce from seeds. Among the earliest evolved land plants still present on earth, these plants do not produce flowers or fruits. The most conspicuous part of their reproduction is the spore, a reproductive cell that divides and eventually develops the structures producing the sperm and egg, which fuse to form a new adult plant.

Liverworts and mosses are mat-forming plants typically found in shady, damp to wet habitats; they typically absorb water and nutrients directly from the environment, as they lack a sophisticated vascular system for conducting water and nutrients internally. When "fruiting," their spores are released from a lidded capsule often elevated on a fertile stalk. Some liverworts consist of flat green lobes, while others are feathery-looking and thus easily mistaken for mosses.

Like ferns, clubmosses and horsetails have well-developed vascular systems. Clubmosses often look like upright green pipe cleaners or tiny conifers rising from the ground in shady woodlands. When fruiting, their spores are produced in tiny but visible sacs, called *sporangia,* between the leaves. In some species the leaves and sporangia are densely clustered into a long, narrow, cone-like structure. Horsetails have conspicuously jointed stems with whorls of tiny, scale-like leaves and branches at most joints. Sporangia are produced along the edges of umbrella-like structures clustered into a cone-like configuration atop a brownish, whitish, or green stem.

In the accounts that follow, the size given is the typical height of a mature specimen unless otherwise noted; sizes are not given for very low, mat-forming species.

PEAT MOSSES
Sphagnum species
MOSS CLASS
6". Yellow-green to red mats of long spongy stalks with thick, whorled branches covered with tiny, scale-like leaves. **HABITAT** Swamps, bogs, ponds, streams; sometimes floating.

HAIRCAP MOSS
"Narrowleaf Moss"
Polytrichum juniperinum
MOSS CLASS
3". Green carpet of erect, wiry stems; narrow leaves taper to reddish point. Fertile stalks reddish, each topped by golden-brown capsule covered with hairy, pointed cap until mature. **HABITAT** Forests or open areas; disturbed or burned ground. **RANGE** West of Cont. Div.

LUNG LIVERWORT
Marchantia polymorpha
LIVERWORT CLASS
Bright green, flat, leathery, ½″ lobes with close rows of pale, bubble-like bumps, often with tiny cups. Fertile stalks each topped with flat disk (male) or star-shaped female organ. **HABITAT** Streamsides; wet, disturbed, or burned ground.

STIFF CLUBMOSS
Lycopodium annotinum
CLUBMOSS FAMILY
6″. Cylindrical, pale green to tan, spore-bearing spikes rise from tops of dark green leafy stems that rise from network of runners. Leaves ¼″, needle-like, usu. spreading. **HABITAT** Moist ground under willows or Engelmann Spruce; subalpine bogs. **RANGE** Esp. n part of region.

ROCKY MOUNTAIN SPIKEMOSS
Selaginella densa
SPIKEMOSS FAMILY
1½″. Erect, 4-sided, spore-bearing spikes rise from small mats of prostrate branches covered with closely pressed, tiny, needle-like leaves, each tipped with a white hair. Spikes and leaves grayish when dry, greener when moist. **HABITAT** Dry gravels, foothills to alpine.

COMMON HORSETAIL
"Field Horsetail"
Equisetum arvense
HORSETAIL FAMILY
24″. Dense clusters of green, jointed, hollow (sterile) stalks with many whorls of narrow jointed branches. Fertile stalks pale brown, unbranched, each topped by 1″ spore cone. **HABITAT** Ditches, floodplains; at all elevs.

SCOURING RUSH
Equisetum (Hippochaete) hyemale
HORSETAIL FAMILY
4′. Clusters of green, jointed, hollow, usu. unbranched stalks, each topped by sharp ¾″ spore cone; evergreen. **HABITAT** Streamsides, ditches, seeps, old wet pastures; to mid-elevs.

Ferns

Ferns, the largest group of seedless vascular plants still found on earth, are diverse in habitat and form. In the Rocky Mountain states they occur both in shady forests and on cliffs, rockpiles, and other sunny areas. Most ferns grow in soil, often in clumps or clusters; some grow on rocks or trees, and a few float on water.

Ferns have a stem called a *rhizome* that is typically thin and long and grows along the surface or below the ground. The rhizome bears the roots and leaves and lives for many years. Fern leaves, called *fronds,* are commonly compound and may be *pinnate* (divided into leaflets), *bipinnate* (subdivided into subleaflets), or *tripinnate* (divided again into segments); they are often lacy or feathery in appearance.

Frond types

| simple | pinnate | bipinnate | tripinnate |

Ferns reproduce through the release of spores from tiny sacs called *sporangia,* which commonly occur in clusters *(sori)* on the underside of the frond. The sori may cover the entire frond underside, may form dots or lines, may occur only beneath the frond's curled-under edges, or may be covered by specialized outgrowths of the frond. Fronds that bear sporangia are called fertile fronds; those that do not are called sterile fronds. In some species the sterile and fertile fronds differ in size and shape.

Some ferns are evergreen, but the foliage of most Rocky Mountain ferns dies back each year with the autumn frosts. Each spring the rhizome gives rise to coiled tender young fronds called *fiddleheads.* Fiddleheads of some ferns are popular delicacies, but identification is difficult: the shoots of some deadly poisonous flowering plants (including various poison hemlocks) can be mistaken for fern fiddleheads, and many fiddleheads are edible at certain stages and poisonous at others. Only local experts should collect fiddleheads for consumption.

In the accounts that follow, sizes given are typical mature heights. For illustrations of leaf shapes, see page 122.

segment

sori

Parts of a Fern

leaflet

subleaflet

stalk

fiddlehead

rhizome

BRACKEN
Pteridium aquilinum
BRACKEN FAMILY

5′. Stalks robust, longer than fronds. Fronds divided into 3 broadly triangular, stalked, bi- or tripinnate leaflets, each with many pinnate subleaflets. Sori dot curled-under leaflet edges. Colonizes aggressively, impedes reforestation in mid-elev. burns and clearcuts. **HABITAT** Mtn. ravines, forest clearings.

WESTERN MAIDENHAIR FERN
Adiantum aleuticum (pedatum)
MAIDENHAIR FERN FAMILY

18″. Stalks black to dark red, shiny, wiry. Fronds bipinnate, fan-shaped; leaflets lobed along one side. Sori under rolled lobe tips. **HABITAT** Seeps, streamsides, wet cliffs. **RANGE** n ID, nw MT; elsewhere local at high elevs.

WESTERN POLYPODY
"Western Licorice Fern"
Polypodium hesperium
POLYPODY FERN FAMILY

8″. Fronds oblong overall, pinnately divided into broad, round-tipped leaflets, connected at bases; from scaly licorice-scented rhizomes. Sori round; in 2 rows. **HABITAT** Cool, shaded rock surfaces at forested elevs. **RANGE** ID, w MT; local in sw CO.

LADY FERN
Athyrium filix-femina
WOOD FERN FAMILY

3′. Stalks blackish, scaly. Fronds arch outward, bi- or tripinnate, tapered at both ends, with lobed, fine-toothed leaflets. Sori kidney-shaped. **HABITAT** Wet ground, forests; to tree line in Tetons. **Alpine Lady Fern** *(A. alpestre),* which grows on wet alpine or subalpine talus, is smaller, lacier.

FRAGILE FERN
"Brittle Fern"
Cystopteris fragilis
WOOD FERN FAMILY

8". Stalks smooth, fragile, straw-colored. Fronds usu. bipinnate, tapered at both ends, with fine-toothed, hairless leaflets. Sori partly covered by translucent pouch that soon withers. Abundant. HABITAT Cliff crevices, usu. where wet at least in spring; plains to tree line.

OAK FERN
Gymnocarpium dryopteris
WOOD FERN FAMILY

10". Stalks slender, scaly at base; usu. scattered in patches. Fronds divided into 3 broadly triangular leaflets, lower 2 tripinnate; upper 1 bipinnate. Subleaflets deeply cut into blunt segments. Few sori on each side of leaflet midrib. HABITAT Moist sites in conifer shade.

WESTERN SWORD FERN
Polystichum munitum
WOOD FERN FAMILY

4'. Stalks light brown, scaly, robust. Fronds pinnate, tapered at both ends, coarsely cut into finely toothed leaflets; evergreen. Sori covered by round shields, in 2 rows. HABITAT Low- to mid-elev. forests. RANGE n ID, nw MT. Holly Fern (*P. lonchitis*), with broad, spiny-toothed leaflets, grows at high elevs., s to nw CO.

ROCKY MOUNTAIN WOODSIA
Woodsia scopulina
WOOD FERN FAMILY

8". Stalks reddish brown, scaly; in clumps with last year's broken leaf bases. Fronds bipinnate; undersides white-hairy. HABITAT Dry rocky slopes, foothills to tree line. Similar Oregon Woodsia (*W. oregana*) lacks hairs.

Trees and Shrubs

Trees and shrubs are woody perennial plants. Trees typically have a single trunk and a well-developed crown of foliage and grow to at least 16 feet tall; some attain heights of more than 300 feet. Shrubs are usually less than 20 feet tall and often have several woody stems rather than a single trunk. This book covers two major categories of trees and shrubs. Conifers begin on page 93. Broadleaf trees and shrubs begin on page 101.

Individual tree sizes vary according to age and environmental factors. The heights given in the following sections are for average mature individual trees on favorable sites in the Rocky Mountain states. Younger trees and those exposed to harsh conditions are smaller; older specimens may attain greater heights in optimal conditions. Trunk diameter, which also varies greatly within a species, is cited only for very large species.

Identifying a Tree

Trees can be identified by three key visual characteristics: crown shape, bark color and texture, and leaf shape and arrangement (illustrated on page 122). Below are common crown shapes for mature conifers and broadleaf trees. These shapes are idealized and simplified for illustrative purposes.

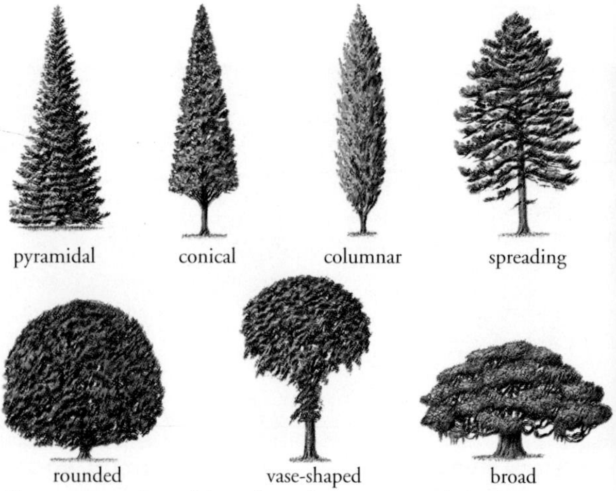

The roots, trunk, and branches of most trees and shrubs are covered in bark, a protective layer consisting mainly of dead cells. The bark of young trees often differs in color and texture from mature bark. As a tree grows, the bark splits, cracks, and peels. In some trees, such as birches, the bark peels horizontally. In cedars the bark shreds in vertical strips. In many trees the bark may develop furrows, ridges, or fissures, may break up into plates, or may flake off. The species accounts describe mature bark unless otherwise noted.

Beneath the bark is the wood, most of which is dense, dark, dead tissue (heartwood) that provides structural support for the plant.

Between the heartwood and the bark are many pale, thin layers of living tissue (including sapwood) that transport water and minerals, and produce new wood and bark. Concentric rings, each representing a period (often a year) of growth, are visible in cut trunks and branches.

Conifers

Gymnosperms ("naked seeds") are trees and shrubs that produce exposed seeds, usually in cones, rather than seeds enclosed in an ovary, as in the angiosperms (flowering plants). Conifers and the odd shrub Ephedra (which are Rocky Mountain natives) and ginkgos and cycads (which are not) are all gymnosperms.

Conifers (also known as "softwoods") have needle-like (long and slender) or scale-like (small and overlapping) leaves, are typically evergreen, and are well adapted for drought and freezing temperatures, thanks to a thick waxy coating and other protective features.

The distinctive cone is a reproductive structure comprised of a central axis with spirally arranged scales bearing pollen or seeds. A single tree usually has both pollen-bearing (male) and seed-bearing (female) cones; males are usually carried on lower branches or lower down on the same branches as females. Male cones appear in spring, shed pollen, and soon fall from the tree. Female cones are larger, more woody, and have scales that protect the seeds until the cones expand to release them. Cones described in this guide are female.

Most conifer species in the Rocky Mountain region belong to the pine family. In our area, those commonly known as pines (genus *Pinus*) bear long needles in bundles of two to five. Other pine family members have much shorter needles. Larches (genus *Larix*) bear needles in brush-like clusters that are deciduous (shed seasonally) and that turn yellow in autumn; cones are stalked and round to egg-shaped. Hemlocks (genus *Tsuga*) bear needles on woody cushions and have small cones at the branch tips. Spruces (genus *Picea*) have rough twigs, hanging cones, and sharp, four-sided needles borne on tiny, raised, woody pegs. Douglas Firs (genus *Pseudotsuga*) also have hanging cones and flat needles, but the needles grow directly from the branches. True firs (genus *Abies*) have upright cones that shed their scales and seeds while still on the tree and needles arising from tiny depressions on the branches.

Other conifers in the Rocky Mountains include those of the cypress family (cedars and junipers) and the yew family. Most members of the cypress family have narrow, scale-like leaves covering their branches; their small cones are round and bell-shaped or (in the junipers) fleshy and berry-like. Yews have needles in two opposite rows and bear seeds not in cones but individually and surrounded by a fleshy, cup-shaped, berry-like structure called an *aril*.

Most conifers are pyramidal in shape when young, especially if they grow in an open area; they mature to a ragged columnar shape with a conical (commonly broken) top and a limbless lower half. The following species accounts give overall shape only if it differs from this description. Leaf shapes, including the needles and scale-like leaves of conifers, are shown on page 122. Unless otherwise noted in the individual species account, needle or scale color is green, fading to yellowish or brown when shedding, and cone color is brown.

COMMON JUNIPER
Juniperus communis
CYPRESS FAMILY

2′. Usu. sprawling, mat-forming shrub. Needles ½″, whitish above, sharp, crowded. Cones ¼″, berry-like, green, ripening in second year to blue-black, resinous. Bark reddish, shreddy. **HABITAT** Rocky sites, esp. high ridges.

UTAH JUNIPER
Juniperus (Sabina) osteosperma
CYPRESS FAMILY

H 20′. Rounded, often many-stemmed shrub or tree. Scales mostly tiny, gray-green, in pairs; stem 4-sided; some leaves (esp. on young plants) ¼″, needle-like. Cones ⅜″, berry-like, tan to red-brown under variable bluish coating, resinous. Bark gray-brown, aging whitish, shreddy. **HABITAT** Steppes. **RANGE** w CO, s ID, local in WY and s MT.

ROCKY MOUNTAIN JUNIPER
Juniperus (Sabina) scopulorum
CYPRESS FAMILY

30′. Dense, pyramidal to rounded small tree; occ. a shrub. Scales mostly tiny, gray-green, in pairs; stem 4-sided; some leaves (esp. on young plants) ¼″, needle-like. Cones ¼″, berry-like, blackish under variable bluish coating, resinous. Bark red-brown, shreddy. May live more than 2,000 years, become massive. **HABITAT** Steppes; invasive where fire has been excluded.

WESTERN RED CEDAR
Thuja plicata
CYPRESS FAMILY

H 180′; D 5′. Trunk base flared, buttressed; branchlets droop. Scales tiny, in opposite pairs; cover flat twigs. Cones ½″, elliptical; in upright clusters. Bark gray to reddish, fibrous. **HABITAT** Forests with water table near surface. **RANGE** n ID, nw MT.

EPHEDRA
"Mormon Tea"
Ephedra species
EPHEDRA FAMILY

3′. Almost leafless, many-branched shrub. Leaves minute, short-lived, non-functional. Cones ¼″, few-scaled, whorled at stem nodes; male and female on separate plants. Stems green to gray-green, photosynthetic. **HABITAT** Sagebrush steppes. **RANGE** w CO, sw WY.

WHITE FIR
Abies concolor
PINE FAMILY

H 140'; D 3'. Crown pointed. Needles 1¾", white-striped, flat, blunt-tipped. Cones 3", cylindrical, yellow, brown, or purple; upright. Bark gray-brown, strongly furrowed. **HABITAT** Low-elev. mtns. **RANGE** CO, se ID.

GRAND FIR
Abies grandis
PINE FAMILY

H 130'; D 3'. Crown pointed. Needles 1½", white-striped below, glossy green above; flat, notch-tipped; fragrant when crushed. Cones 3½", cylindrical; upright. Bark gray-brown, smooth and blistered or shallowly furrowed. **HABITAT** Low- to mid-elev. mtns. **RANGE** n and c ID, nw MT.

SUBALPINE FIR
Abies lasiocarpa (bifolia)
PINE FAMILY

H 90'; D 18". Tree with spire-shaped crown; matted shrub above tree line. Needles 1", white-striped, flat, usu. up-curved; camphor-like aroma when crushed. Cones 4", cylindrical, purplish; upright. Bark gray, smooth to fissured. **HABITAT** Subalpine forests or parkland clumps.

WESTERN LARCH
Larix occidentalis
PINE FAMILY

H 180′; D 4′6″. Needles 1½″, yellow-green, soft; in bundles of 15–30, or single near branch tips; deciduous; turn yellow. Cones 1½″, elliptical; scales with long-pointed bracts; upright. Bark red-brown, scaly, furrowed. Largest larch. **HABITAT** Mid-elev. mtns. **RANGE** n ID, nw MT.

ENGELMANN SPRUCE
Picea engelmannii
PINE FAMILY

H 150′; D 3′. Tree with drooping branchlets; dense low shrub above tree line. Needles 1¼″, blue-green, white-striped, sharp, 4-sided. Cones 2¼″, cylindrical, with papery thin scales; hang down. Bark grayish, thin, scaly; young twigs minutely fuzzy. **HABITAT** Subalpine forest.

COLORADO BLUE SPRUCE
Picea pungens
PINE FAMILY

H 100′; D 2′. Pyramidal; branches stiff. Needles 1¼″, bluish or green, white-striped, sharp, stiff, 4-sided. Cones 3″, cylindrical; hang down. Bark gray or brown, thick, furrowed. **HABITAT** Foothill canyons, to 9,500′. **RANGE** CO, se ID, sw WY.

WHITEBARK PINE
Pinus albicaulis
PINE FAMILY

H 50′; D 3′. Tree with spreading to irreg. crown and many-stemmed trunk; dense shrub above tree line. Needles 2½″, yellow-green; in bundles of 5, concentrated near branch tips. Cones 2½″, egg-shaped, purplish; disintegrate at maturity. Bark whitish gray, smooth to scaly. Decimation of this species by fungal disease is changing alpine ecology in MT. **HABITAT** High-elev. forests or near tree line. **RANGE** ID, w MT and south to Wind River Range, WY.

ROCKY MOUNTAIN BRISTLECONE PINE
Pinus aristata
PINE FAMILY

H 40′. Crown irreg., twisted. Needles 1¼″, deep blue-green with sticky resin droplets; usu. curved; in bundles of 5. Cones 3½″, purplish; scales end in slender, in-curved ¼″ prickle. **HABITAT** Rocky ridges near tree line. **RANGE** CO.

LODGEPOLE PINE
Pinus contorta
PINE FAMILY

H 80′. Tree with narrow, dense crown; or shrub. Needles 2½″, yellow-green, flat; in bundles of 2. Cones 2″, egg-shaped, asymmetrical at base. Bark red-brown to gray, thin, scaly. **HABITAT** Mtn. forests, esp. where dry or disturbed.

COLORADO PINYON
Pinus edulis
PINE FAMILY

H 30'. Crown conical to rounded; trunk contorted. Needles 1¼", usu. in bundles of 2, fragrant. Cones 1½", egg-shaped; seeds edible, in hard ½" shells. Bark yellowish to reddish brown, scaly. Source of American pine nuts; choice firewood. **HABITAT** Dry rocky places, 4,500–8,000'. **RANGE** CO, s WY.

LIMBER PINE
Pinus flexilis
PINE FAMILY

H 45'; D 4'. Contorted tree with spreading crown, many-stemmed trunk; dense shrub above tree line. Branchlets flexible. Needles 2½", yellow-green; in bundles of 5, concentrated near branch tips. Cones 5", egg-shaped, purplish; fall from tree whole. Bark gray, smooth, becoming checked. **HABITAT** High-elev. forests; at tree line in CO.

WESTERN WHITE PINE
Pinus monticola
PINE FAMILY

H 200'; D 5'. Needles 4", blunt, blue-green with white-striped inner surfaces; in bundles of 5. Cones 9", cylindrical, usu. curved, reddish to silvery; hang down. Bark gray, square-plated. **HABITAT** Mtn. forests, 1,600–6,000'. **RANGE** n ID, nw MT.

DOUGLAS FIR
Pseudotsuga menziesii
PINE FAMILY

H 140'; D 3'6". Needles 1¼", blue-green, flat. Cones 2½", egg-shaped; scales have protruding, paper-thin, 3-pointed bracts. Bark reddish brown, furrowed. **HABITAT** Moist forests, 2,000–10,000'; in WY and esp. CO grow mainly on northern slopes.

PONDEROSA PINE
"Yellow Pine"
Pinus ponderosa
PINE FAMILY

H 130'; D 4'. Needles 5", yellow-green; usu. in bundles of 3, concentrated near branch tips. Cones 4", broad, egg-shaped, reddish. Bark yellow-brown, thick, scaly. **HABITAT** Steppe; plains; southern slopes in low-elev. mtns.

WESTERN HEMLOCK
Tsuga heterophylla
PINE FAMILY

H 150'; D 4'. Treetop and branch tips droop. Needles ½", white-striped below, flat with rounded tip. Cones 1", elliptical; hang down. Bark reddish, scaly, finely furrowed. **HABITAT** Mid-elev. forests. **RANGE** n ID, nw MT.

PACIFIC YEW
Taxus brevifolia
PINE FAMILY

H 35'; D 18". Tree with few branches; dense, thicket-forming shrub at higher elevs. Needles ¾", soft, flat, in 2 rows. Seed covering (aril) ¼", red, cup-shaped, berry-like, juicy. Bark brown, purple, and red; smooth, flaky. **CAUTION** Seeds and arils are deadly poisonous. **HABITAT** Various; esp. shady forests. **RANGE** n ID, nw MT.

Broadleaf Trees and Shrubs

Trees belonging to the angiosperm (flowering plant) group are called broadleaf trees because their leaves are generally broad and flat, in contrast to the needle-like leaves of most conifers. Whereas the seeds of conifers and other gymnosperms are exposed, those of angiosperms are enclosed in an ovary that ripens into a fruit. The fruit may take the form of an edible drupe or berry, such as a cherry or mulberry, a hard-cased nut, the paired winged key of a maple, or a dried-out seedpod, such as that of a locust tree.

In warmer regions of North America, many broadleaf species (known in the timber industry as "hardwoods") maintain active green leaves year-round, but in the Rocky Mountain region most flowering trees and shrubs are deciduous, shedding their leaves for the winter because the leaves cannot survive freezing weather.

The individual species descriptions in this guide note leaf color only if it is not green. The term "turn" indicates the fall color of the leaves. The various types of leaf arrangements and shapes mentioned in the species descriptions are illustrated on page 122. As most broadleaf trees bear their leaves in an alternate arrangement, only exceptions are noted in the species descriptions. Leaf measurements indicate length unless otherwise stated. Leaflet measurements are given for compound leaves.

Illustrations of flower types and parts, and a discussion of flower structure and function, are given on pages 123–125. Because the flowers of many trees are inconspicuous, only prominent ones are emphasized in the species accounts that follow. In the Rocky Mountain states, trees generally flower in the spring, from April through May (later at higher elevations); fruits of broadleaf trees mature mainly from July to October. Months of maturation are given only for edible fruit.

To facilitate identification, descriptions of large broadleaf trees (which begin on page 102) are grouped separately from small broadleaf trees and shrubs (which begin on page 105).

Fall Foliage of the Rocky Mountain Region

The Rocky Mountain region has a preponderance of evergreen trees, which add little to the fall color display. One well-known deciduous tree more than compensates for the lack of diversity—the Quaking Aspen, whose glowing yellow leaves (sometimes ranging to orange or red) stand out against its distinctive white trunks. Because aspens most often reproduce by root suckers rather than seeds, whole stands covering tens of acres are clones, in which every stem is a genetic copy of every other stem and turns color at exactly the same time. By looking for large patches of bright color on a mountainside in autumn, you can see the extent of aspen clones graphically laid out.

In some parts of Montana and Idaho, larch trees (which are deciduous conifers) exhibit a golden display that rivals that of the aspens. Cottonwoods and birches also turn yellow, but are less dramatic. Shrubs, including the nearly tree-sized Rocky Mountain Maple, also provide fall color. Cliffbush, Red Osier Dogwood, and sumacs turn various shades of scarlet, purple, russet, and crimson, and the tiny leaves of some blueberries can turn subalpine parklands in the northern Rockies into exquisite heathery patchworks.

Each blaze of color represents a change in leaf chemistry. In late summer, leaves begin forming layers of cells at the leafstalk base that help the leaf detach and heal the resulting scar on the branch. As these layers grow, the veins of the leaves become clogged. The dominant pigment of the green leaf, chlorophyll, is no longer renewed and disintegrates quickly, revealing the yellow and orange pigments that had been masked by the chlorophyll. Under the right conditions, some species convert colorless compounds in their leaves into new red, scarlet, and purple pigments. Because these red pigments require high light intensity and elevated sugar content for their formation, the colors appear after a period of bright autumn days and cool nights, which prevent accumulated sugar from leaving the dying leaf.

GAMBEL'S OAK
Quercus gambelii
BEECH FAMILY

10′. Thicket-forming shrub; occ. tree to 40′ or more. Leaves 4″, elliptical, bluntly 6- to 10-lobed; turn brown, stay on tree. Bark light gray or brown, scaly. Acorns ¾″, solitary or paired. **HABITAT** Pinyon-juniper forests, chaparral. **RANGE** CO, local in WY.

PAPER BIRCH
Betula papyrifera
BIRCH FAMILY

70′. Crown narrow, open. Leaves 3″, ovate, long-pointed, toothed; turn light yellow. Bark when young chalky to creamy white, with thin, horizontal stripes; peels in papery strips to reveal orange inner bark; later brown, furrowed. Cones 1¾″, cylindrical, brown, scaly; hang down. **HABITAT** Moist lowland forests; floodplains. **RANGE** n ID, ne MT; local (usu. hybridized) east of Cont. Div.

BOX ELDER
"Ashleaf Maple"
Acer negundo var. *interius (Negundo aceroides)*
MAPLE FAMILY

65′. Crown broad, irreg.; trunk often crooked; branches wide-spreading. Leaves 5″, opposite, pinnately compound, with 3–5 elliptical, coarse-toothed, 3″ leaflets. Bark light brown to gray, furrowed. Fruit 1½″, red-brown keys. **HABITAT** Low-elev. ravines. **RANGE** Mainly east of Cont. Div. in MT, WY; mtns. in CO.

SIBERIAN ELM
Ulmus pumila
ELM FAMILY

60′. Crown rounded, open. Leaves 2″, elliptical, toothed; turn yellow. Bark gray-brown, rough, furrowed. Introduced from Asia as blight-resistant replacement for American Elm; tolerates poor soil, drought, pollution. **HABITAT** Disturbed ground; naturalizes on floodplains. **RANGE** s MT and south.

GREEN ASH
Fraxinus pennsylvanica
OLIVE FAMILY

50′. Crown rounded or irreg., dense. Leaves 8″, opposite, pinnately compound, with usu. 7 lanceolate, short-stalked, shiny, 4″ leaflets; turn yellow. Bark gray, furrowed. Fruit 2″, very narrow, 1-winged keys; in dense, hanging clusters. **HABITAT** Escaping from cultivation and persisting, esp. in ravines. **RANGE** Great Plains.

BLACK COTTONWOOD
"Balsam Poplar"
Populus balsamifera (trichocarpa)
WILLOW FAMILY

90". Crown vase-shaped. Leaves 6",
usu. ovate; toothed, shiny, sticky
above, dull gray below; sweet-
smelling; turn yellow. Bark gray,
deeply furrowed. Flowers in 1½"
(male) or 3" (female) catkins; bloom
Mar.–May. Fruit tiny brown capsules; contain cottony seeds. **HABITAT**
Streamsides at all elevs. **RANGE** ID, w
MT; local elsewhere.

NARROWLEAF COTTONWOOD
Populus angustifolia
WILLOW FAMILY

50'. Crown columnar. Leaves 3",
gray, lanceolate, fine-toothed; sweet-
smelling leafstalks finely grooved;
turn yellow. Bark gray, rough. Flowers in 1" (male) or 3" (female), reddish catkins; bloom Apr.–May.
HABITAT Streamsides; floodplains in
mtns., foothills, high plains.

PLAINS COTTONWOOD
Populus deltoides ssp. *monilifera*
(P. sargentii)
WILLOW FAMILY

H 60'; D 3'. Crown spreading.
Leaves 3", flat-based, heart-shaped,
long-pointed, coarse-toothed; turn
yellow. Bark dark gray, rough; twigs
yellowish. Flowers in 2½" catkins,
growing to 5" in seed; bloom
Apr.–May. **HABITAT** Low-elev. streamsides. **RANGE** Mainly east of Cont.
Div.

QUAKING ASPEN
Populus tremuloides
WILLOW FAMILY

50". Crown narrow, rounded. Leaves 2½", heart-shaped to rounded, fine-
toothed; turn yellow. Bark greenish white, smooth. Flowers in 2" brownish
catkins; bloom Apr.–May, before leaves. Fruit tiny green capsules in 4"
catkins; contain cottony seeds. Reproduces mainly in clones from root suckers. **HABITAT** Foothills to mtns., often following burns.

Small Broadleaf Trees and Shrubs

To facilitate identification, we have separated most small broadleaf trees and shrubs from the large broadleaf trees. The species in this section generally reach an average mature height of 40 feet or less. Cacti, with their often shrub-like shapes, are included here as well.

Trees typically have a single woody trunk and a well-developed crown of foliage, whereas shrubs usually have several woody stems growing in a clump. Many of the Rocky Mountain region's small trees and shrubs have beautiful and conspicuous spring flowers

Curl-leaf Mountain Mahagony

and/or colorful late-summer or autumn fruits. Flower and leaf arrangements and shapes are illustrated on pages 122–123. The majority of species covered here are deciduous.

SILVER SAGEBRUSH
Artemisia (Seriphidium) cana
ASTER FAMILY
30″. Rounded shrub. Leaves 1½″, narrowly oblanceolate, occ. 3-lobed at tip, fuzzy gray-green, spicy-aromatic. Flowers tiny, yellow, in slender, leafy, 8″ spikes; bloom Aug.–Sept. **HABITAT** Meadows, plains, streamsides. **RANGE** West of Cont. Div. **Sand Sagebrush** (*A. filifolia*) is a 3′ erect shrub with linear (occ. lobed) leaves and 2″ flower spikes; grows on sandy plains, mainly east of Cont. Div.

BIG SAGEBRUSH
Artemisia (Seriphidium) tridentata
ASTER FAMILY
5′. Rounded gnarled shrub, or low, spreading shrub at high elevs. Leaves 1½″, narrowly oblanceolate, usu. with 3-lobed tip, fuzzy gray-green; spicy-aromatic. Stems brown, shreddy. Flowers tiny, drab yellow, in slender spikes; bloom Sept.–Oct. **HABITAT** Steppes; dry mtn. slopes at all elevs.

GRAY RABBITBRUSH
"Rubber Rabbitbrush"
Ericameria (Chrysothamnus) nauseosa
ASTER FAMILY

3'. Dense, broom-like shrub. Leaves 3", linear, soft, gray-hairy. Stems shreddy; twigs fuzzy. Flowers tiny, bright yellow, profuse, in rounded clusters; bloom Aug.–Oct. Increases with overgrazing. HABITAT Steppes, plains, roadsides.

SPINELESS HORSEBRUSH
Tetradymia canescens
ASTER FAMILY

2'. Rounded shrub. Leaves 1", linear to oblanceolate, white-wooly. Stems finely wooly. Flower heads ½", vase-shaped, with several cream to yellow petal lobes sticking out at odd angles; heads clustered at branch tips; bloom June–Sept. HABITAT Sagebrush steppes, pinyon-juniper woodlands, dry forests.

CREEPING OREGON GRAPE
Berberis (Mahonia) repens (aquifolium)
BARBERRY FAMILY

8". Prostrate shrub. Leaves 9", pinnately compound, with 3–9 ovate, spiny-edged, 3" leaflets; evergreen. Flowers ⅜", yellow, with 15 petal-like parts in concentric whorls; bloom Apr.–June. Berries ⅜", blue, edible (tart); ripe Aug. Spreads by runners. HABITAT Low- to mid-elev. dry forests.

MOUNTAIN ALDER
Alnus incana (tenuifolia)
BIRCH FAMILY

15'. Thicket-forming, low to almost tree-like shrub. Leaves 3", ovate, doubly toothed, wavy-edged; finely white-wooly below. Male flowers in 3" green catkins, females in ½" brown cones; bloom Mar.–Apr. HABITAT Foothill to subalpine streamsides.

WATER BIRCH
Betula occidentalis (fontinalis)
BIRCH FAMILY

25′. Tall shrub, or tree with rounded crown. Leaves 2″, ovate, toothed singly or doubly; shiny above; turn yellow-brown. Bark shiny red-brown, smooth, with horizontal chalky slits; young twigs pebbly. Flowers in 1½″ catkins; males drooping and yellowish, females upright and greenish; bloom Mar.–June. **HABITAT** Foothill to subalpine streamsides. **Bog Birch** *(B. nana* or *glandulosa)* is a 4′ shrub with 1″ leaves; grows in sunny, wet places in mtns.

BEAKED HAZEL
Corylus cornuta
BIRCH FAMILY

15′. Many-stemmed shrub. Leaves 4″, ovate, doubly toothed, usu. asymmetrical at base. Bark tawny brown, smooth, with horizontal slits. Flowers 2¾″ yellowish catkins; bloom Feb.–Mar. Fruit paired, bristly, green, ½″ husks; each contain tiny, edible nut in heavy shell. **HABITAT** Foothill valleys. **RANGE** ID; local in e CO.

MOUNTAIN LOVER
"Oregon Boxwood"
Paxistima myrsinites
BITTERSWEET FAMILY

30″. Low shrub. Leaves ¾″, opposite, elliptical, shallowly toothed, dark, glossy, evergreen. Twigs reddish, 4-sided. Flowers minute, red and white, in leaf axils; bloom May–June. **HABITAT** Mid- to high-elev. forests.

WESTERN WHITE VIRGIN'S BOWER
Clematis ligusticifolia
BUTTERCUP FAMILY

L variable. Prolific climbing, woody vine. Leaves 6″, pinnately compound, with 5–7 coarse-toothed, 2″ leaflets. Flowers ¾″, creamy, with usu. 4 petal-like sepals; in open 2″ clusters; bloom June–July. Seeds with 1″ white plumes, in copious fluffballs. **HABITAT** Streamsides, ditches, low-elev. forests, thickets.

PURPLE VIRGIN'S BOWER
Clematis (Atragene) occidentalis
BUTTERCUP FAMILY

L variable. Climbing, half-woody vine. Leaves compound, with 3 ovate, smooth or few-toothed, 2″ leaflets. Flowers 1¾″, blue to purple, with 4 petal-like sepals, many white-and-yellow stamens; bloom June–July. Seeds with 2″ white plumes, in ball-like clusters. Called *C. columbiana* before 1980, but differs from small alpine *C. columbiana* of recent books. **HABITAT** On trees or in thickets, low- to mid-elevs. in mtns.

Cacti

The cactus family consists of about 2,000 species of fleshy, spiny plants native to the Western Hemisphere. Although cacti are especially well suited to hot climates, a few Rocky Mountain species cross the Canadian border on both sides of the Continental Divide; 17 cactus species can be found in the four Rocky Mountain states.

Cactus plants have spiny stems and roots. Their most distinctive feature is the *areoles*—small spots on the stems from which the spines arise. Although most areoles have one or more spines, some areoles instead have many *glochids*—microscopic hairs or barbed structures. Prickly pears and chollas have, in addition to spines, a small, fleshy, pointed leaf beneath each areole on new joints; these leaves drop within a few months.

The succulent, swollen stems of cacti are well adapted for water storage: the extensive root system lies close to the surface of the soil in order to take advantage of even the lightest rains. Leaves are usually absent or reduced, with nearly all photosynthesis carried out by the stems. Cactus flowers are generally large and showy, and the fruits are fleshy and brightly colored.

CLARET-CUP CACTUS
"King's Crown Cactus"
Echinocereus triglochidiatus
CACTUS FAMILY

10". Ribbed barrel cactus in dense mounds. Spines 1", usu. gray, clustered on ribs. Flowers 3", red to orange, funnel-shaped; bloom Apr.–May. Fruit 1", egg-shaped, pink to red, initially spiny. **HABITAT** Deserts, pinyon-juniper forests. **RANGE** s CO.

FRAGILE PRICKLY PEAR
Opuntia fragilis
CACTUS FAMILY

8". Spiny clump. Stems form flattish joints; upper ones break off easily. Spines 1", yellowish, in star-like clusters with white wool at base. Flowers 1½", usu. yellow, with many petals and red-stalked stamens; bloom May–June. Fruit ½", tan, egg-shaped. **CAUTION** Barbed spines. **HABITAT** Ponderosa Pine forests; dry plains.

TREE CHOLLA
"Walking-stick Cholla"
"Candelabra Cactus"
Opuntia (Cylindropuntia) imbricata
CACTUS FAMILY

5'. Branched, shrub-like. Stem segments 8", cylindrical, with spiny knobs. Spines hook-tipped, clustered. Flowers 2½" with many purple-pink petals; bloom May–July. Fruit 1½", yellow, egg-shaped. **HABITAT** Plains, deserts, pinyon-juniper forests. **RANGE** sw CO.

SMOOTH SUMAC
Rhus glabra
CASHEW FAMILY

5′. Few-branched, scrawny shrub. Leaves 12″, pinnately compound, with 11–13 lanceolate, toothed leaflets, each 2½″; turn red or orange. Bark smooth, brown; twigs gray or red. Flowers tiny, yellowish, in open, 7″ clusters; bloom June–July. Berries tiny, red, sticky-hairy; in upright, dense, conical 8″ clusters. **HABITAT** Dry, low-elev. mtn. slopes.

SKUNKBUSH
Rhus aromatica var. *trilobata*
CASHEW FAMILY

5′. Rounded shrub. Leaves 2″, usu. compound with 3 round-lobed, 1″ leaflets; bad-smelling; turn orange-red. Flowers tiny, yellow, in clusters at branch tips; bloom Apr.–May, before leaves. Berries ¼″, red-orange, flattish, sticky-hairy; used for ersatz lemonade. **HABITAT** Dry foothills, plains, mtns. to 8,000′.

Poisonous Plants

Poisonous plants are those that contain potentially harmful substances in high enough concentrations to cause injury if touched or swallowed. Determining whether a plant species is "poison" or "food" requires expertise. The information in this guide is not to be used to identify plants for edible or medicinal purposes.

Sensitivity to a toxin varies with a person's age, weight, physical condition, and individual susceptibility. Children are most vulnerable because of their curiosity and small size. Toxicity can vary in a plant according to season, the plant's different parts, and its stage of growth. Plants can also absorb toxic substances, such as herbicides, pesticides, and pollutants from the water, air, and soil. Among the potentially deadly plants in the Rocky Mountain states are Death Camas and Water Hemlock. The berry-like fruits of the Pacific Yew are deadly poisonous; those of the Pacific Red Elderberry are mildly toxic.

Physical contact with plants that contain irritating resinous compounds causes rashes in many individuals. The main offender in the region is that notorious member of the cashew family, Western Poison Ivy. All parts of the plant contain the irritating compounds. Stinging Nettle and Devil's Club have needle-like hairs or spines that release stinging substances when touched.

WESTERN POISON IVY
Toxicodendron rydbergii (radicans)
CASHEW FAMILY

5′. Lanky shrub. Leaves 4″, compound, with 3 ovate, usu. coarse-toothed, shiny 3″ leaflets; turn red in fall, and often some red much earlier. Flowers tiny, in yellowish-white 3″ clusters; bloom May–June. Berries ¼″, greenish white. **CAUTION** Causes severe skin inflammation. Berries poisonous. **HABITAT** Low-elev. hills, canyons, disturbed ground.

GOLDEN CURRANT
Ribes aureum
CURRANT FAMILY

6′. Thicket-forming shrub. Leaves 2″, with 3 rounded lobes, usu. toothed, on 2″ stalks. Bark gray, smooth. Flowers ½″, yellow, tubular, in loose clusters; bloom Feb.–Apr., before fully leaved. Berries tiny, orange to yellow to blue-black; edible, ripe Apr.–June. **HABITAT** Low-elev. forests, sagebrush steppes, roadsides, streamsides.

WAX CURRANT
"Squaw Currant"
Ribes cereum
CURRANT FAMILY

5′. Bushy, weak-stemmed shrub. Leaves 1″, nearly round to shallowly 3- or 5-lobed, toothed, grayish; musky when crushed. Flowers ¾″, white to pink, tubular, 5-lobed; bloom Apr.–June. Berries ¼″, red. **HABITAT** Low-elev. forests, clearings, plains.

PRICKLY CURRANT
"Swamp Gooseberry"
Ribes lacustre
CURRANT FAMILY

5′. Thorny, straggly shrub. Leaves 1¾″, palmately 5-lobed. Small fine thorns cover stems; larger ½″ spines in whorls at leaf nodes. Flowers tiny, dull pink, saucer-shaped, in drooping clusters; bloom May–July. Berries ¼″, dark purple; edible but bitter. **HABITAT** Mtn. streamsides, wet meadows.

RED OSIER DOGWOOD
Cornus (Swida) sericea (stolonifera)
DOGWOOD FAMILY

10'. Many-stemmed, spreading shrub. Leaves 5", opposite, elliptical, with curved veins; turn purple to russet. Young stems red to purple, smooth. Flowers tiny, white, in dense flat clusters; bloom May–July. Berries tiny, pale blue-green, in broad clusters. HABITAT Riparian, at lower mtn. elevs. Low-elev. mtn. streamsides.

DEVIL'S CLUB
Oplopanax horridus
GINSENG FAMILY

5'. Shrub with gnarly, sparsely branched, cane-like stems. Leaves 12", toothed, palmately lobed; stalks and veins spiny. Stems light brown, very spiny. Flowers ¼", whitish, in 10" clusters; bloom June–July. Berries ¼", red, in conical 10" clusters. CAUTION Spines irritate skin. HABITAT Streamsides and seeps in mtns. RANGE ID, MT.

FOUR-WINGED SALTBUSH
"Shadscale"
Atriplex canescens
GOOSEFOOT FAMILY

5'. Rounded shrub; sprawling low shrub east of Cont. Div. Leaves 1¼", oblanceolate, scaly, gray-green. Young bark whitish scaly; later peeling. Flowers minute, greenish; males may be reddish; bloom June–Aug. Fruit ⅜", reddish 4-winged capsule. HABITAT Dry, often salty soils.

SPINY HOPSAGE
Grayia (Atriplex) spinosa
GOOSEFOOT FAMILY

2'. Rounded shrub. Leaves 1", oblanceolate, rough-hairy, gray-green. Bark gray, shreddy; twig tips spine-like. Flowers tiny, females green to red-tinged, in tight axillary clusters; bloom May–June. Fruit tiny, reddish, 2-winged disks. HABITAT Foothills, deserts, lake pans. RANGE West of Cont. Div.

GREASEWOOD
Sarcobatus vermiculatus
GOOSEFOOT FAMILY

5'. Dense shrub. Leaves 1½", linear, bright green, fleshy. Bark pale gray, smooth. Flowers tiny, greenish, in catkin-like 1¼" spikes; bloom June–Aug. Poisonous to stock; invasive and hard to get rid of. HABITAT Alkaline flats.

KINNIKINNICK
"Bearberry"
Arctostaphylos uva-ursi
HEATH FAMILY

6". Sprawling shrub. Leaves 1", obovate, glossy, leathery; evergreen. Flowers tiny, white or pink, jug-shaped, in drooping clusters at branch tips; bloom May–June. Berries ¼", red. **HABITAT** Rocky sites, low-elev. forests to tree line.

WHITE MOUNTAIN HEATHER
Cassiope mentensiana
HEATH FAMILY

8". Thick, mat-forming shrub. Leaves minute, scale-like, densely packed along stem in 4 rows; evergreen. Flowers ¼", white with small reddish sepals, bell-shaped, 5-lobed, mostly nodding in clusters; bloom July–Aug. Fruit tiny, round, brown capsule. **HABITAT** Alpine. **RANGE** ID, MT.

FOOL'S HUCKLEBERRY
"Rustyleaf"
Menziesia ferruginea
HEATH FAMILY

5'. Straggly shrub. Leaves 2", elliptical, bumpy, finely brown-hairy; concentrated at branch tips; turn red-orange. Flowers ¼", pale orange, jug-shaped, 4-lobed with 8 stamens; bloom June–Aug. Fruit ¼" dry, brown, 4-celled capsule. **HABITAT** Mtn. forests, esp. streamsides. **RANGE** ID, MT, WY.

PINK MOUNTAIN HEATHER
Phyllodoce empetriformis
HEATH FAMILY

12". Thick mat-forming shrub. Leaves ½", needle-like, evergreen. Flowers ¼", pink, bell-shaped, 5-lobed, mostly in nodding clusters; bloom July–Aug. Fruit tiny, round, brown capsule. **HABITAT** Alpine and subalpine streamsides and snowbed sites. **RANGE** ID, MT and south to Wind River Range.

GROUSEBERRY
Vaccinium scoparium
HEATH FAMILY

10". Small broom-like shrub. Leaves ½", lanceolate, fine-toothed. Flowers tiny, pink, jug-shaped, minutely 5-lobed; bloom May–Aug. Stems green, crowded, sharply angled. Berries tiny, red; edible, ripe July–Sept. Widespread; dominant under spruce or Whitebark Pine. **HABITAT** Subalpine forests and clearings.

WESTERN BOG LAUREL
Kalmia microphylla (polifolia)
HEATH FAMILY

20″. Mat-forming shrub. Leaves 1½″, opposite, elliptical, grayish below, edges roll under; evergreen. Flowers ¾″, pink, bowl-shaped, 5-lobed; 10 stamens spring free when pollinated; bloom June–Aug. **HABITAT** Subalpine bogs and lakesides.

ORANGE HONEYSUCKLE
Lonicera ciliosa
HONEYSUCKLE FAMILY

L variable. Climbing woody vine. Leaves 2″, opposite, ovate. Flowers 1¼″, red-orange, tubular, 5-lobed; in clusters of 8–12 above round leaf surrounding stem; bloom June–July. Stems hollow. Berries ⅜″, in 1″ clusters. **CAUTION** Berries may be poisonous. **HABITAT** Low-elev. thickets, open woods. **RANGE** ID, w MT.

TWINBERRY
"Bush Honeysuckle"
Lonicera involucrata
HONEYSUCKLE FAMILY

6′. Erect shrub. Leaves 5″, opposite, elliptical. Bark shreddy, light brown. Flowers ¾″, pale yellow, tubular, 5-lobed; in pairs, with 4 green bracts that turn magenta; bloom May–Aug. Berries ⅜″, black, paired. **HABITAT** Mtn. streamsides; low- to mid-elevs.

BLUE ELDERBERRY
Sambucus mexicana (cerulea)
HONEYSUCKLE FAMILY

14′. Tall shrub. Leaves 12″, opposite, pinnately compound, with 5–9 lanceolate, fine-toothed, 5″ leaflets. Bark gray, furrowed. Flowers tiny, white, in flattish, branched, 8″ clusters; bloom June–July. Berries tiny, blue or white, in flattish 8″ clusters; edible, ripe Aug.–Sept. **HABITAT** Valley bottoms, low-elev. forest slopes. **RANGE** ID, w MT.

PACIFIC RED ELDERBERRY
"Black Elderberry"
Sambucus racemosa
HONEYSUCKLE FAMILY

6′. Weak-stemmed shrub. Leaves 10″, opposite, pinnately compound, with 5–7 lanceolate, fine-toothed, 5″ leaflets. Flowers tiny, white, in 4″ conical clusters; bloom May–July. Berries tiny, red to black; edible, used for jam and wine, ripe July–Sept. **CAUTION** Raw berries mildly toxic. **HABITAT** Streamsides, moist forests.

CLIFF FENDLERBUSH
Fendlera rupicola
HYDRANGEA FAMILY

5′. Bushy shrub. Leaves 1″, opposite, elliptical, usu. hairy, edges usu. rolled under. Twigs tan to red, age gray. Flowers 1¼″, white, pink in bud, with 4 spoon-shaped petals; single to clusters of 3; profuse; bloom May–June, sometimes repeating later. **HABITAT** Canyons, mesa rims. **RANGE** sw and c CO.

CLIFFBUSH
Jamesia americana
HYDRANGEA FAMILY

6′. Rounded to straggly shrub. Leaves 2″, opposite, ovate, toothed, gray-wooly below; turn bright red. Bark reddish, peeling. Flowers ¾″, waxy white to pink, with 5 narrow lobes, in clusters; bloom June–Sept. **HABITAT** Cliffs, foothills to occ. subalpine. **RANGE** CO, s WY.

MOCK ORANGE
"Syringa"
Philadelphus lewisii
HYDRANGEA FAMILY

6′. Erect shrub. Leaves 3″, opposite, ovate. Flowers 1¼″, white, with 4 petals, many yellow stamens; fragrant; in terminal clusters of 3–11; bloom May–July. Fruit ¼″ woody capsules. ID state flower. **HABITAT** Rocky slopes. **RANGE** ID, w MT.

ROCKY MOUNTAIN MAPLE
Acer glabrum
MAPLE FAMILY

12′. Shrub or small tree. Leaves 2½″, opposite, toothed, palmately 3- or 5-lobed or occ. compound with 3 lanceolate leaflets; turn red-orange. Bark gray to reddish, smooth. Flowers tiny, greenish, saucer-shaped, in branched clusters; bloom May–June. Fruits reddish 1″ keys. **HABITAT** Canyons, foothills to low-elev. mtns.

PURPLE SAGE
"Grayball Sage"
Salvia dorrii
MINT FAMILY

20″. Broad round shrub; branches rigid, spine-tipped. Leaves 1¼″, opposite to whorled, oblanceolate, silvery; aromatic; some persist through winter. Flowers ½″, blue-violet, tubular, with 6 odd lobes; in whorled clusters; bloom May–June. **HABITAT** Sagebrush steppes. **RANGE** sw ID.

RUSSIAN OLIVE
Elaeagnus angustifolia
OLEASTER FAMILY

30′. Small tree with dense, rounded crown. Leaves 4″, lanceolate, sage-green above, silvery below. Bark gray-brown, shreds in strips. Flowers ½″, yellow, bell-shaped, 4-lobed; single or paired in leaf axils; bloom May–June. Berries ½″, yellow to brown; pulp edible, ripe Aug.–Oct. Planted as windbreak. **HABITAT** Steppe areas where water table has been raised by irrigation.

SILVER BUFFALOBERRY
"Silverberry"
Shepherdia argentea
OLEASTER FAMILY

18′. Shrub or small tree with silvery, scaly leaves, young twigs, berries; branches opposite; twigs often spine-tipped. Leaves 1½″, opposite, oblong. Flowers tiny, yellowish, 4-lobed, in clusters; bloom Apr.–May. Berries tiny, red or yellow, egg-shaped, often crowded and showy; edible, sour, best after frost in Nov. **HABITAT** River bottoms, ditches, meadows. **RANGE** Plains of MT and ne WY; local elsewhere.

BITTER BUFFALOBERRY
"Soapberry" "Soopolallie"
Shepherdia canadensis
OLEASTER FAMILY

3'. Usu. small rounded shrub. Branches opposite; young twigs brownish, scaly. Leaves 2", opposite, elliptical; scaly, brownish below. Flowers tiny, yellowish, 4-lobed; bloom Apr.–May. Berries ¼", red or yellow, egg-shaped. **HABITAT** Open forests at all elevs.; rocky n slopes.

WESTERN SERVICEBERRY
"Saskatoon" "Shadbush"
Amelanchier alnifolia
ROSE FAMILY

10'. Rounded shrub. Leaves 1¾", rounded to ovate, outer part toothed. Flowers 1¼", white, with 5 narrow petals, in clusters; bloom Apr.–July. Berries ⅜", purple; edible, ripe June–Aug. **HABITAT** Low-elev. to subalpine sunny slopes.

CURL-LEAF MOUNTAIN MAHOGANY
Cercocarpus ledifolius
ROSE FAMILY

6'. Gnarled shrub, or tree with rounded crown. Leaves 1¼", lanceolate, with rolled edges; dark green above, white-wooly below; evergreen. Bark reddish, furrowed. Flowers ⅜", funnel-shaped, yellowish, hairy; bloom Apr.–June. Seeds tiny, with white, hairy, twisted, 3" tail. **HABITAT** Desert foothills, dry forests, tree line. **RANGE** s ID, s MT, w WY, w CO.

BIRCHLEAF MOUNTAIN MAHOGANY
Cercocarpus montanus (betuloides)
ROSE FAMILY

6'. Gnarled shrub or occ. tree. Leaves 1", elliptical, outer part coarse-toothed; white, hairy below; persist in winter. Bark gray-brown, smooth. Flowers tiny, yellowish, funnel-shaped, usu. hairy; bloom Apr.–June. Seeds tiny, with white, hairy, twisted, 2½" tail. Sprouts from roots after fire. **HABITAT** Desert foothills, dry forests; to 10,000'. **RANGE** ID, WY, CO.

BLACKBRUSH
Coleogyne ramosissima
ROSE FAMILY

3'. Bristly, rounded shrub. Leaves ¼", linear, gray. Stems opposite; young stems pale gray, aging black and rough. Flowers ⅜", with 4 yellowish sepals; bloom May–July. **HABITAT** Dry steppes. **RANGE** sw CO.

BLACK HAWTHORN
Crataegus douglasii (rivularis)
ROSE FAMILY

15'. Thicket-forming shrub; small tree with rounded crown. Leaves 2½", ovate, toothed. Bark reddish, ages gray; twigs red; dark red 1" spines on trunk and twigs. Flowers ½", white, 5-petaled, stamens pink; in clusters; bloom May–June. Berries ½", reddish black, in drooping clusters. **HABITAT:** Streamsides to 10,000'. **RANGE** ID, MT, w WY, w CO.

OCEAN SPRAY
Holodiscus discolor
ROSE FAMILY

10'. Many-branched shrub. Leaves 3", ovate, toothed, slightly lobed. Bark reddish, flaking. Flowers tiny, creamy; in conical, 7" clusters; bloom June–Aug. **HABITAT** Dry open forests. **RANGE** n ID, nw MT. **Mountain Spray** (*H. discolor* var. *dumosus*) has elliptical ⅝" leaves, grows in CO and WY canyons.

SHRUBBY CINQUEFOIL
Pentaphylloides floribunda (Potentilla fruticosa)
ROSE FAMILY

24". Rounded to mat-forming shrub. Leaves 1½", pinnately compound, with usu. 5 linear, hairy, ¾" leaflets. Stems red, smooth to shreddy. Flowers 1", yellow, 5-petaled; bloom July–Aug. Seedpods tiny, white, hairy. **HABITAT** Plains buttes to wet subalpine meadows and alpine slopes.

MALLOW NINEBARK
Physocarpus malvaceus
ROSE FAMILY

5'. Lanky shrub. Leaves 2", usu. 3-lobed, toothed. Bark peeling in papery layers. Flowers tiny, white, 5-petaled; in round, 1½" clusters; bloom June–July. Fruits usu. paired, hairy, tiny reddish seedpods. **HABITAT** Rocky slopes, pine–Douglas Fir forests. **RANGE** ID, MT, n WY. **Rocky Mountain Ninebark** (*P. monogynus*) has 1", nearly round, toothed leaves with a few deep incisions, grows in CO and s WY.

AMERICAN PLUM
"Wild Plum"
Prunus americanus
ROSE FAMILY

8′. Thicket-forming shrub; small tree with short trunk, spreading crown. Leaves 3″, elliptical, toothed; turn red. Some twigs spine-like. Bark dark brown. Flowers 1″, white, 5-petaled, in clusters; bloom Apr.–May. Plums 1″, yellow to purplish; edible, ripe June–Aug. **HABITAT** Streamsides, valley forests. **RANGE** Mainly e of Cont. Div.

CHOKECHERRY
Prunus virginiana var. *melanocarpa*
ROSE FAMILY

12′. Thicket-forming tall shrub. Leaves 4″, elliptical, fine-toothed; turn red or yellow. Bark reddish brown, smooth. Flowers ½″, white, 5-petaled, in drooping, 4″ clusters; bloom May–June. Cherries ½″, red to black; astringent, edible, used for jam; ripe July–Sept. **CAUTION** Pits poisonous. **HABITAT** Streamsides, valley slopes.

CLIFFROSE
Purshia (Cowania) stansburiana (mexicana)
ROSE FAMILY

8′. Straggly shrub; tree with crooked trunk, open crown. Leaves ⅜″, with narrow lobes, leathery; crowded at branch tips. Bark reddish; ages shreddy. Flowers ¾″ with 5 yellowish petals; bloom May–June. Seeds ¼″, with 2″ curling plumes. **HABITAT** Canyons, to 8,000′. **RANGE** sw CO.

BITTERBRUSH
"Antelope Brush"
Purshia tridentata
ROSE FAMILY

6′. Stiff bushy shrub. Leaves ¾″, oblanceolate, with 3-lobed tip, edges rolled under; white-hairy below. Flowers ¾″, yellow, funnel-shaped, with 5 flat petals; bloom May–June. Fruit ¾″ green seedpods. **HABITAT** Grasslands, pinyon-juniper forests. **RANGE** Mainly west of Cont. Div.

WOODS'S ROSE
Rosa woodsii
ROSE FAMILY

6′. Thicket-forming weak-stemmed shrub. Leaves 4″, pinnately compound; with 5–9 ovate, toothed, 1½″ leaflets. Stems thorned sparsely or near base only. Flowers 2″, pink, 5-petaled, in small clusters; fragrant; bloom May–July. Fruit ½″ red rose hips. **HABITAT** Open forests, grasslands. Great Plains variety (*R. woodsii* var. *woodsii*) is 3′ with ¾″ leaflets.

WILD RED RASPBERRY
Rubus idaeus
ROSE FAMILY

6'. Many-stemmed shrub. Leaves compound, with 3 or 5 ovate, toothed, 3" leaflets. Stems cinnamon-brown, peeling; usu. prickly; live 2 years, flowering the 2nd. Flowers ½", white, 5-petaled, usu. in small clusters; bloom May–Aug. Berries ⅜", red; edible, ripe July–Sept. **HABITAT** Clearings, rockslides, burns, streamsides, alpine slopes.

ROCKY MOUNTAIN RASPBERRY
"Boulder Raspberry"
Rubus (Oreobatus) deliciosus
ROSE FAMILY

4'. Many-stemmed shrub. Leaves 2", rounded. Stems cinnamon-brown, peeling, usu. thornless; young shoots pink. Flowers 2", white, 5-petaled, usu. in clusters; bloom May–July. Berries ¾", red, tasteless. **HABITAT** Rocky foothills to mid-elevs. **RANGE** CO, WY; mainly east of Cont. Div.

THIMBLEBERRY
Rubus parviflorus
ROSE FAMILY

4'. Weak-stemmed shrub. Leaves 5", 5-lobed, toothed, hairy. Stems green to light brown, thornless. Flowers 2", white, with 5 rounded, crinkly petals; bloom May–July. Berries ¾", crimson, broadly cup-shaped; edible, ripe June–Aug. **HABITAT** Cool ravines at all forested elevs.

WESTERN MOUNTAIN ASH
Sorbus scopulina
ROSE FAMILY

10'. Dense-clumping shrub or small tree. Leaves 7", pinnately compound, with 11–13 lanceolate, toothed, 3" leaflets. Bark gray or reddish, smooth. Flowers ½", white, 5-petaled, in 4" broad clusters; bloom June–July. Fruit ⅜", bright orange-red; resemble . tiny apples. **HABITAT** Moist ravines in mtns.

SUBALPINE SPIRAEA
Spiraea splendens (densiflora)
ROSE FAMILY

3'. Small to prostrate shrub. Leaves 1¼", rounded-ovate, toothed on outer part. Flowers tiny, pink to red, with many stamens; in fuzzy, flat to rounded, 2" clusters; bloom July–Aug. **HABITAT** Streamsides and moist slopes to near tree line. **RANGE** n ID, w MT, nw WY. **Birchleaf Spiraea** (*S. betulifolia*) has white to slightly pinkish flowers; grows in aspen forests, moist forests, meadows to 9,000'.

TAMARISKS
"Saltcedars"
Tamarix species
TAMARISK FAMILY

16′. Lacy shrub or small tree. Leaves minute, scale-like; deciduous in cold climates; exude salt. Bark red-brown, furrowing in age. Flowers tiny, pink to white, 5-petaled, in several spikes; bloom May–July. **HABITAT** Along canals, reservoirs, streams, saline flats.

PEACHLEAF WILLOW
Salix amygdaloides
WILLOW FAMILY

40′. Tree with spreading crown, several trunks. Leaves 4″, lanceolate, thin, toothed; glossy green above, whitish below; turn yellow. Bark dark brown, furrowed. Flowers tiny, in 2″ yellowish catkins; bloom Apr.–May, same time as leaves. **HABITAT** Riversides, floodplains; to 7,000′.

BEBB WILLOW
Salix bebbiana
WILLOW FAMILY

15′. Thicket-forming shrub; small tree with rounded crown. Leaves 3″, oblong, fine-toothed, wavy-edged; turn yellow. Older bark gray, rough, furrowed; often has diamond-shaped patterns caused by fungi. Flowers tiny, in ¾″ (male) or 1½″ (female) catkins; bloom Apr.–May. **HABITAT** Streamsides, mtn. slopes, to 10,000′.

COYOTE WILLOW
"Sandbar Willow"
Salix exigua (interior)
WILLOW FAMILY

4′. Thicket-forming shrub; small tree. Leaves 3″, linear, usu. gray-wooly; turn yellow. Twigs reddish or yellowish. Flowers tiny, in 2″ yellowish catkins; bloom Apr.–May, some with leaves, some later. **HABITAT** Ditches, sandbars, riversides, floodplains; up to 7,500′.

SCOULER WILLOW
Salix scouleriana
WILLOW FAMILY

20′. Thicket-forming shrub; many-stemmed tree. Leaves 3″, obovate, dark green above, white- or rusty-hairy below. Bark gray to brown, fissured, aromatic. Flowers tiny, in 2″ yellow-tipped male or blackish female catkins ("pussy willows"); bloom Mar.–May, before leaves. **HABITAT** Open forests, clearings, burns, streamsides in mtns.; to 9,500′.

Leaf Shapes

scales

needles in bundle

needles in cluster

linear

oblong

lanceolate

oblanceolate

obovate

ovate

rounded

heart-shaped

arrowhead-shaped

elliptical

toothed

lobed

palmately lobed

pinnately lobed

palmately compound

pinnately compound

bipinnately compound

Leaf Arrangements

axil
alternate

opposite

whorled

basal

clasping

sheathing

Flower Types

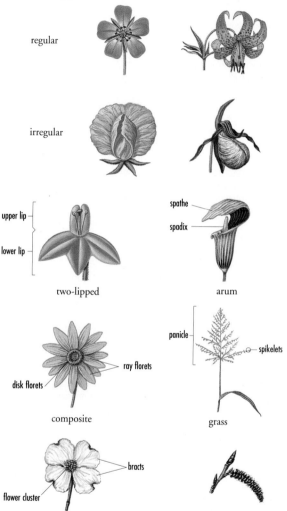

regular

irregular

upper lip
lower lip
two-lipped

spathe
spadix
arum

disk florets
ray florets
composite

panicle
spikelets
grass

bracts
flower cluster
bracts and flower cluster

catkin

Flower Cluster Types

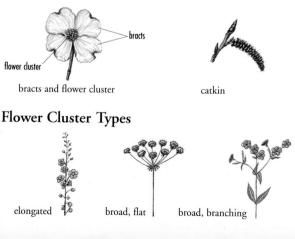

elongated

broad, flat

broad, branching

Wildflowers

The Rocky Mountain states have more than 3,000 species of flowering plants in more than 110 families. This section covers a broad selection of common and interesting wildflowers, including vines, grasses, and a few water plants. In this guide, wildflowers are defined as relatively small, noncultivated flowering plants that die back after each growing season.

The wildflowers included here are mainly herbaceous (nonwoody); some are woody but too small to be placed with the shrubs; a few have a woody base with herbaceous stems. These plants come in many forms. Many have a single delicate, unbranched, erect stem terminated by a single flower or a flower cluster. Some have very robust stems; others are many-branched and bushy. In some, the stems trail along the ground, sometimes spreading by runners. Those known as "vines" have long, slender, often flexible stems that either trail on the ground or climb, sometimes with tendrils to hold them in place. Plants of the grass family have erect, jointed stems and blade-like leaves; some other plants, such as rushes and sedges, are described as grass-like because they have narrow leaves and slender stems. Aquatic plants are adapted to life in or along water.

Wildflowers are most often identified by their flowers. The flowers or flower clusters may be borne in the leaf axils along the main stem or on branches off the stem. Modified leaves called *bracts* are often situated at the base of the flower or cluster. Flowers are typically composed of four sets of parts. The outermost set in a "complete" flower is the leaf-like *sepals* (known collectively as the *calyx*) that protect the often colorful second set—the *petals*. The next set is the *stamens*, the "male" part of the flower, each consisting of pollen sacs *(anthers)* typically on a stalk *(filament)*. The innermost set is the "female" part of the flower, with one or more *pistils*, each of which typically has a swollen base, the *ovary* (containing the ovules that after fertilization become the seeds), and a stalk *(style)* topped by the pollen-collecting *stigma*. The fruit develops from the ovary, forming a covering for the seed or seeds. The form of the fruit varies from species to species.

Some plants have unisexual flowers that may occur on the same or separate plants. Many wind-pollinated species, such as grasses and sedges, have reduced flowers that lack petals and/or sepals. These flow-

Parts of a Flower

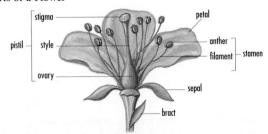

ers tend to be inconspicuous, unlike flowers that need to attract insects for pollination. Seed dispersal is often aided by animals that eat fruit or seeds and disperse seeds in their droppings; fruits that are bur-like or covered with sticky hairs attach to animals on contact and later fall off or are shed along with fur. Plants such as dandelions bear tiny fruits that have parachute-like tops and are carried by the wind far from the parent plant.

Flowers of a few representative types are illustrated on page 123. The buttercup and the lily are *regular* flowers; their parts radiate in a wheel-like (radially symmetrical) fashion. In this guide, pea and orchid flowers are considered *irregular:* they can be divided evenly only along one plane (bilateral symmetry). Many plants in the mint and snapdragon families have tubular, *two-lipped* flowers. The tiny flowers of the arum family are clustered on a club-like *spadix,* which is usually enfolded by a leaf-like *spathe.* The *composite* "flower" of the daisy or aster is actually a head of many flowers; tiny tubular *disk florets* form a disk in the center, encircled by petal-like *ray florets.* (Dandelions have flower heads made up of all ray florets; true thistles have all disk florets.) Grasses have tiny, reduced florets enclosed in scale-like bracts; these are organized in overlapping arrangements called *spikelets,* which typically form a larger spike, if each spikelet attaches directly to the main stem, or a *panicle,* spikelets share tiny branched stalks from the main stem. Dogwood "flowers" in fact consist of a dense head of tiny flowers encircled by several large, petal-like bracts. The tiny unisexual flowers of oaks and many other species of trees and shrubs are clustered into slender spikes called *catkins.* Many plants bear flowers in clusters along or atop the stems or branches. Flower clusters take many forms, such as small round bunches, elongated spikes, feathery plumes, and broad, flat-topped, or branching arrangements.

Unless otherwise noted, in the accounts that follow, sizes given are typical heights of mature specimens. Rather broad time spans are given for bloom times in order to account for normal variations due to elevation, latitude, and timing of snowmelt, but not for every errant blossom.

SOAPWEED YUCCA
Yucca glauca
AGAVE FAMILY

4'. Thick, round clump of leaves. Flowers 2", greenish white, cup-shaped, leathery, mostly drooping, abundant; on annual stalk. Leaves 2', linear, stiff, sharp; edges white, fibrous, shreddy. **BLOOMS** June–July. **HABITAT** Dry plains, foothills, mesas. **RANGE** Mainly east of Cont. Div.

NARROWLEAF ARROWHEAD
"Wapato"
Sagittaria cuneata
ARROWHEAD FAMILY

16" (from roots). Emergent from water. Male flowers 1¼", white, with 3 round petals, in whorls of 3 along stem; females green, ball-like, whorled lower on stem. Leaves 2½" wide, with 2 pointed side lobes shorter than main lobe; on long stalks from base. **BLOOMS** June–Sept. **HABITAT** Ponds, swamps, quiet streams, shores. **Broadleaf Arrowhead** (*S. latifolia*) has 2 side lobes as long as main lobe.

YELLOW SKUNK CABBAGE
Lysichiton americanum
ARUM FAMILY

12". Flowers minute, yellow, on thick 4" spadix hooded by 8", yellow, parallel-veined spathe; skunky-smelling. Leaves huge, ovate, net-veined, to 3'. **BLOOMS** May–June. **HABITAT** Wet ground, bogs, swamps. **RANGE** ID, w MT.

YARROW
Achillea millefolium (lanulosa)
ASTER FAMILY

24". Flowers ¼", with 3–5 white to pink rays around yellow disk; in dense, flat, or slightly rounded 3" clusters. Single stem. Leaves fern-like, finely cut, narrow; sharply fragrant when crushed. **BLOOMS** May–Sept. **HABITAT** Sunny sites at all elevs.

PALE MOUNTAIN DANDELION
Agoseris glauca
ASTER FAMILY

17"; less than 6" in alpine zone. Flowers ¾", with pale, waxy, yellow rays that dry pinkish; 1 per stem. Stems unbranched, with milky juice. Leaves lanceolate, sometimes wavy-edged. Seed heads dandelion-like. **BLOOMS** May–Sept. **HABITAT** Mid-elev. to alpine meadows.

ROMAN RAGWEED
Ambrosia artemisiifolia
ASTER FAMILY

3'. Coarse, hairy, branched stems bear tiny, inconspicuous greenish flowers in open clusters of 3" spikes. Leaves light green, deeply bipinnately dissected into many lobes, each 4". Wind-borne pollen among primary causes of hay fever. **BLOOMS** July–Oct. **HABITAT** Roadsides, disturbed ground.

ROSY PUSSYTOES
Antennaria rosea (microphylla)
ASTER FAMILY

10″. Slender stalk above leafy mat. Flowers tiny tufts of minute white bristles surrounded by pink- or white-tipped, greenish-based papery bracts; in rounded 1″ clusters. Leaves oblanceolate, whitish-wooly, mostly basal. **BLOOMS** June–Aug. **HABITAT** Open forests, plains, alpine meadows.

NUTTALL'S PUSSYTOES
Antennaria parvifolia (aprica)
ASTER FAMILY

6″. Short, stout stalk above leafy mat. Flowers tiny tufts of minute white bristles surrounded by pink-to-white-tipped papery bracts; in rounded 1″ clusters. Leaves oblanceolate, whitish-wooly, mostly basal. **BLOOMS** May–July. **HABITAT** Plains, dry meadows to tree line.

HEARTLEAF ARNICA
Arnica cordifolia
ASTER FAMILY

12″. Flowers 2½″, yellow, with 8–15 rays around disk. Leaves heart-shaped, toothed; 2–4 opposite pairs per stem, lowest pair long-stalked. Leaves often ovate and untoothed on 6″ alpine variety. **BLOOMS** May–Aug. **HABITAT** Mtn. forests, alpine to subalpine gravels.

ALPINE ASTER
"Hayden's Aster"
Aster alpigenus var. haydenii
ASTER FAMILY

5″. Flowers 1″, with 10–30 lavender to deep purple rays around yellow disk; cupped by purple-and-green bracts; 1 per stem. Leaves linear, smooth, mostly basal. **BLOOMS** July–Aug. **HABITAT** Alpine meadows, rocky tundra. **RANGE** MT, c ID, n WY.

WESTERN SHOWY ASTER
Aster conspicuus
ASTER FAMILY

30″. Flowers 1¼″, with 15–35 violet to blue rays around yellow disk; cupped by sticky bracts; in broad clusters. Leaves broadly elliptical, toothed, thick, rough; clasping. **BLOOMS** July–Sept. **HABITAT** Open forests, foothills to mid-elevs. **RANGE** ID, MT, n WY.

ENGELMANN'S ASTER
Aster engelmannii
ASTER FAMILY

3′. Flowers 2″, with about 8–20 white to pinkish rays around yellow disk; cupped by purple-tinged papery bracts; several per stem. Leaves elliptical, smooth, all on stem. BLOOMS July–Sept. HABITAT Mtn. meadows and open forests.

ARROWLEAF BALSAMROOT
Balsamorhiza sagittata
ASTER FAMILY

20″. Robust clumps. Flowers 3″, yellow, with 8–25 rays around disk; 1 per stem. Leaves arrowhead-shaped, silvery, with felt-like wool when young. BLOOMS Apr.–July. HABITAT Valleys to mid-elev. slopes, often with sagebrush.

SPOTTED KNAPWEED
Centaurea (Acosta) maculosa (biebersteinii)
ASTER FAMILY

24″. Flowers 1½″, pink to purple, thistle-like, with large, 5-lobed outer "rays"; cupped by black-tufted, bulbous, green, ½″ base. Stems stiff, many-branched. Leaves narrowly pinnately lobed. Invasive; introduced from Eurasia. BLOOMS June–Oct. HABITAT Disturbed ground.

DUSTY MAIDEN
Chaenactis douglasii
ASTER FAMILY

18″; 5″ at high elevs. Flower heads ¾″, white to pinkish, with 50–70 5-lobed disk flowers; in flat clusters. Leaves fern-like, white-wooly, thick. Resembles Yarrow but lacks fragrance. BLOOMS May–Sept. HABITAT Dry forests, gravelly subalpine meadows.

HAIRY GOLDEN ASTER
Heterotheca (Chrysopsis) villosa
ASTER FAMILY

14″. Many-stemmed, erect to spreading. Flowers 1″, golden yellow, with about 16 rays around disk; numerous. Stems and leaves usu. coarsely hairy. Leaves oblanceolate, mainly on stem. BLOOMS May–Oct. HABITAT Sandy or rocky areas; to subalpine elevs.

CHICORY
"Blue Sailors"
Cichorium intybus
ASTER FAMILY

3'. Flowers 1½", bright blue (rarely white), with rays toothed at tips. Stem juice milky. Leaves 10", deeply pinnately lobed; midrib often red. Introduced from Europe. **BLOOMS** July–Sept. **HABITAT** Disturbed areas.

CANADA THISTLE
Cirsium (Breea) arvense
ASTER FAMILY

3'. Colony-forming; prickly, white-hairy. Flowers ½" pink to purple disk on ¾" spiny green base. Leaves irregularly shaped, with curling, very spiny lobes. Introduced from Europe; invasive. **BLOOMS** July–Aug. **HABITAT** Disturbed areas.

ELK THISTLE
"Leafy Thistle"
Cirsium scariosum (foliosum or *tioganum)*
ASTER FAMILY

8" to 5'. Prickly, white-hairy. Flowers 1¼" pink to white disk borne close to stem, surrounded by long leaves. Stem thick or absent, with flowers close to ground. Leaves pinnately lobed, spiny pale green, often with cobwebby white hairs. **BLOOMS** June–Aug. **HABITAT** Wet meadows and pastures; mid- to high elevs.

WAVYLEAF THISTLE
Cirsium undulatum
ASTER FAMILY

3'. Prickly, white-wooly. Flowers 1½" pink-purple to white disk on 1½" spiny, bulbous, usu. green-and-white-striped base. Leaves with spine-tipped pinnate lobes. **BLOOMS** June–Sept. **HABITAT** Dry prairies, foothills, disturbed areas.

SUBALPINE DAISY
Erigeron peregrinus
ASTER FAMILY

16". Flowers 1½", with 30–60 pink or lavender to pale blue rays around yellow disk. Stem finely sticky-wooly just below flowers. Leaves lanceolate, mainly basal. **BLOOMS** June–Aug. **HABITAT** Open rocky slopes; mid-elevs. to alpine elevs.

SHOWY FLEABANE
"Showy Daisy"
Erigeron speciosus
ASTER FAMILY

2'. In clumps or thick patches. Flowers 1¾", with 80 or more narrow blue to pink to white rays around yellow disk; 1 to several per stem. Stems smooth. Leaves ovate to lanceolate, 3-veined; mainly on stem; slightly clasping. **BLOOMS** June–Aug. **HABITAT** Mtn. forest clearings, subalpine meadows.

WOOLY SUNFLOWER
Eriophyllum lanatum
ASTER FAMILY

14". White-wooly. Flowers 1¼", daisy-like, yellow, with 9–15 rays around disk. Leaves linear or divided into finger-like lobes. **BLOOMS** May–Aug. **HABITAT** Steppes, rocky areas, subalpine meadows. **RANGE** ID, w MT, nw WY.

BLANKETFLOWER
"Brown-eyed Susan"
Gaillardia aristata
ASTER FAMILY

20". Flowers 3", with 8–16 golden yellow, 3-pointed rays around broad brown disk; 1–4 per stem. Stems hairy. Leaves 4", lanceolate or pinnately lobed. **BLOOMS** June–Sept. **HABITAT** Grasslands, roadsides, low-elev. forests.

CURLYCUP GUMWEED
Grindelia squarrosa
ASTER FAMILY

2'. Flowers 1½", yellow, with about 30 rays around disk; on gummy, bulbous base with long down-curved bract tips. Leaves dark green, linear to oblong to elliptical, fine-toothed to smooth; clasping or basal. **CAUTION** Mildly toxic; used medicinally. **BLOOMS** July–Sept. **HABITAT** Overgrazed rangeland, roadsides.

PRAIRIE SUNFLOWER
Helianthus petiolaris
ASTER FAMILY

30". Bristly hairy. Flowers 3", with about 13 golden yellow rays around ¾", initially white-centered brown disk. Leaves broadly lanceolate, usu. untoothed. **BLOOMS** June–Sept. **HABITAT** Sandy plains, roadsides. **Common Sunflower** (*H. annuus*) (4') has 5" flowers lacking white center.

ORANGE HAWKWEED
Hieracium aurantiacum
ASTER FAMILY

12″. Coarse-hairy. Flowers ¾″, brilliant red-orange, dandelion-like, with strap-like, 5-toothed rays; in tight, 2″, single cluster atop stem. Stems milky-juiced. Leaves basal, oblanceolate. **BLOOMS** June–Aug. **HABITAT** Trailsides, roadsides. **Slender Hawkweed** *(Hieracium gracile or triste)* has yellow flowers and little or no hair; grows in meadows throughout region.

ALPINE GOLD
Hulsea algida
ASTER FAMILY

10″. Tufted. Flowers 2″, yellow, with 25–40 rays around disk; 1 per stem. Leaves oblong, with blunt, shallow teeth rolled upward; finely hairy, somewhat succulent; aromatic. **BLOOMS** July–Aug. **HABITAT** Alpine rocks. **RANGE** c ID, sw MT, Absarokas of WY.

ALPINE SUNFLOWER
"Old Man of the Mountain"
Hymenoxys (Rydbergia) grandiflora
ASTER FAMILY

6″. Showy dwarf. Flowers 3″, yellow, with 20–30 3-toothed rays around broad disk; 1 per stem. Stems and leaves sparsely wooly. Leaves pinnately divided into several linear lobes. **BLOOMS** July–Aug. **HABITAT** Alpine meadows. **RANGE** c ID, sw MT, WY, CO.

PRICKLY LETTUCE
Lactuca serriola
ASTER FAMILY

4′. Lanky, many-branched. Flowers tiny, yellow, with rays only. Stems milky-juiced. Leaves pinnately lobed; spiny below midvein and along edges; clasping with 2 "ears"; twisted at base to vertical plane. Introduced from Europe. **BLOOMS** July–Sept. **HABITAT** Croplands, yards, roadsides.

OXEYE DAISY
Leucanthemum vulgare
(Chrysanthemum leucanthemum)
ASTER FAMILY

16″. Blooms profusely. Flowers 1½″, daisy-like, with white rays around yellow disk. Basal leaves obovate, deeply lobed; stem leaves oblanceolate, toothed. Introduced; takes over meadows. **BLOOMS** June–Sept. **HABITAT** Moist, disturbed ground.

DOTTED GAYFEATHER
Liatris punctata
ASTER FAMILY

14″. Spire-like, clump-forming. Flower heads ¾″ long, pink-purple, with 4–6 disk flowers only, each with 2 curling pistil branches; in dense 8″ spike. Leaves linear, resin-speckled, rough. **BLOOMS** Aug.–Sept. **HABITAT** Dry, grassy areas. **RANGE** East of Cont. Div.

PINEAPPLE-WEED
Matricaria discoidea (matricarioides)
ASTER FAMILY

10″. Soft, sprawling, many-branched. Flowers tiny, yellow, conical, rayless disks. Leaves lacy, bipinnately compound, with tiny, thread-like leaflets; fruity-fragrant when crushed. Native, but invasive. **BLOOMS** May–Sept. **HABITAT** Roadsides, parking areas, croplands.

PRAIRIE CONEFLOWER
"Mexican Hat"
Ratibida columnifera
ASTER FAMILY

3′. Leggy, in clumps. Flowers 2″, with 3–7 drooping yellow rays around 1½″-long columnar, red-brown disk. Leaves pinnately narrowlobed; all on stem. **BLOOMS** June–Sept. **HABITAT** Prairies, roadsides. **RANGE** Native on Great Plains; local elsewhere.

CUTLEAF CONEFLOWER
Rudbeckia laciniata (ampla)
ASTER FAMILY

6′. Leggy, single-stemmed. Flowers 4″, yellow, with 6–16 somewhat droopy rays around domed yellowish disk. Leaves 8″, palmately narrowlobed and/or compound. **BLOOMS** July–Oct. **HABITAT** Streamsides, ditches, wet meadows. **RANGE** Entire region, ex. n ID.

ARROWLEAF GROUNDSEL
Senecio triangularis
ASTER FAMILY

3′. Flowers ¾″, yellow, with 5–9 raggedy rays around small disk; in 3″ flat cluster. Leaves triangular, narrow, toothed. **BLOOMS** July–Sept. **HABITAT** Moist mtn. meadows, avalanche tracks, streamsides.

CANADA GOLDENROD
Solidago canadensis
ASTER FAMILY

3'. Patch-forming. Pyramidal clusters of many tiny golden flowers form dense branching 5" plume atop each minutely hairy stem. Leaves lanceolate, 3-veined, crowded. **BLOOMS** Aug.–Oct. **HABITAT** Moist mtn. meadows, open forests, roadsides. **Smooth Goldenrod** *(S. gigantea)* lacks fine hairs on most of stem.

MISSOURI GOLDENROD
Solidago missouriensis
ASTER FAMILY

14". Patch-forming. Many tiny golden flowers form open, branching 3" plume atop each smooth stem. Leaves lanceolate, becoming linear and smaller upward; thick, somewhat 3-veined. **BLOOMS** June–Oct. **HABITAT** Sandy plains and basins.

FIELD SOW-THISTLE
Sonchus arvensis
ASTER FAMILY

4'. Lanky, patch-forming. Flowers 1½", yellow, many strap-shaped rays, no disk; in a sparse spray. Stems succulent, milky-juiced. Leaves to 16", prickly-edged, pinnately lobed; become smaller and less lobed up stem; clasping. Introduced from Europe. **BLOOMS** July–Oct. **HABITAT** Ditches, croplands.

TANSY
Tanacetum vulgare
ASTER FAMILY

4'. Many tiny, button-like, yellow flowers in dense clusters; rays minute, barely visible around large disk. Leaves dark green, fern-like, tripinnately compound; aromatic when crushed. **CAUTION** Poisonous. **BLOOMS** Aug.–Sept. **HABITAT** Roadsides, ditches, pastures.

DANDELION
Taraxacum officinale
ASTER FAMILY

11". Flowers 1", yellow, from rosette of leaves at stem base. Stems unbranched, hollow, with milky juice. Leaves lanceolate, lobed, toothed; flattened near ground. Seed heads globular; seeds wind-borne on umbrella-shaped bristles. **BLOOMS** Apr.–Dec. **HABITAT** Lawns, fields, roadsides.

YELLOW SALSIFY
Tragopogon dubius
ASTER FAMILY

30". Flowers 2", yellow, dandelion-like, with narrow, long-pointed bracts; fold up in midday heat. Seed heads huge, dandelion-like. Stems milky-juiced, branched. Leaves grass-like, clasping. **BLOOMS** May–July (some to Sept.). **HABITAT** Roadsides, dry fields; to near tree line.

SHOWY GOLDENEYE
Heliomeris (Viguiera) multiflora
ASTER FAMILY

3'. Many-stemmed. Flowers 1¼", yellow, with 10–16 rays around domed disk. Leaves linear (in CO lowlands) to elliptical; finely hairy, rough; lower ones opposite. **BLOOMS** June–Sept. **HABITAT** Dry slopes, steppes; to just above tree line. **RANGE** e ID, sw MT, WY, CO.

NORTHERN MULE'S EARS
Wyethia amplexicaulis
ASTER FAMILY

24". Patch-forming. Flowers 4", bright yellow, with 8–21 rays around disk; usu. 2–5 per stem. Leaves elliptical, with varnish-like sheen and thick yellow midrib. **BLOOMS** May–July. **HABITAT** Open slopes, dry meadows; foothills to mid-elevs. **RANGE** Mainly west of Cont. Div.

WHITE MULE'S EARS
Wyethia helianthoides
ASTER FAMILY

20". Flowers 4", white to cream, with 13–21 rays around yellow disk; usu. 1 per stem. Leaves elliptical, heavy, felty. **BLOOMS** Apr.–June. **HABITAT** Moist meadows; foothills to mid elevs. **RANGE** ID, w MT, extreme nw WY.

HAREBELL
Campanula rotundifolia
BELLFLOWER FAMILY

16". Bell-shaped, pale blue, 1" flowers nod on slender stalks. Stem leaves linear; basal leaves stalked, oblanceolate to heart-shaped, often wither before flowers open. Seed pods nodding. Alpine form 4". **BLOOMS** June–Aug. **HABITAT** Diverse open habitats to alpine elevs.

SULPHUR BUCKWHEAT
Eriogonum umbellatum
BUCKWHEAT FAMILY

8". Tiny cream, bright yellow, or red-tinged flowers in tight balls that form domed clusters. Stems unbranched. Leaves obovate, in whorls, mainly basal. **BLOOMS** June–Aug. **HABITAT** Rocky foothills to alpine slopes; sagebrush steppes in mtn. basins.

MOUNTAIN SORREL
Oxyria digyna
BUCKWHEAT FAMILY

11". Flowers minute, greenish, in dense spikes from leaf rosette at stem base; swell and become reddish in seed. Leaves reddish, kidney- to heart-shaped; edible, sour. Round, reddish, papery husks enclose seeds. **BLOOMS** July–Aug. **HABITAT** Moist rocky areas at alpine and subalpine elevs.

WATER SMARTWEED
Polygonum (Persicaria) amphibium
BUCKWHEAT FAMILY

4" (flower cluster stalks). Sprawling; afloat or on watersides; forms pink "fields" in water. Flowers tiny, deep pink, in 1 or 2 dense, egg-shaped, 1" clusters. Leaves elliptical to oblong, with whitish midvein. **BLOOMS** June–Sept. **HABITAT** Fresh water.

AMERICAN BISTORT
Polygonum (Bistorta) bistortoides
BUCKWHEAT FAMILY

20". Tiny, white to pinkish flowers in fuzzy 1" balls atop slender, unbranched, reddish stems; usu. fetid. Leaves lanceolate, mostly at stem base. Abundant. **BLOOMS** June–Aug. **HABITAT** Moist alpine to subalpine meadows.

CURLY DOCK
Rumex crispus
BUCKWHEAT FAMILY

30". Flowers tiny, greenish, in dense branching clusters. Stem single, erect. Leaves 8", oblong or lanceolate, wavy-edged. Bears thousands of red-brown winged seedpods. Introduced from Eurasia; invasive. **BLOOMS** June–July. **HABITAT** Low-elev. ditches, gardens. **Sheep Sorrel** *(R. acetosella)* has reddish flowers and tenderer arrow-head-shaped leaves; reaches tree line; invasive.

WESTERN MONKSHOOD
Aconitum columbianum
BUTTERCUP FAMILY

4'. Tall spike of 1" blue-purple flowers with 5 petal-like sepals; uppermost sepal forming a large, helmet-shaped hood. Leaves deeply palmately 5-lobed, long-toothed. **CAUTION** Poisonous, esp. roots. **BLOOMS** June–Aug. **HABITAT** Mtn. streamsides, moist forests, subalpine meadows.

RED BANEBERRY
Actaea rubra
BUTTERCUP FAMILY

3'. Flowers tiny white pom-poms of stamens and smaller stamen-like petals; in 4" conical cluster. Leaves compound with ovate, lobed, fine-toothed leaflets. Berries ⅜", shiny red or pure white; in 4" conical cluster. **CAUTION** Berries poisonous. **BLOOMS** June–July. **HABITAT** Shady moist forests.

PASQUEFLOWER
"Prairie Cactus"
Anemone (Pulsatilla) patens
BUTTERCUP FAMILY

6". Clump-forming. Flower 1¾", dull red to purple or blue (rarely white); cup-shaped, with 5–7 crinkled, wooly, petal-like sepals, many yellow stamens; 1 per stem. Stems hairy. Leaves fern-like, bi- or tripinnately compound. Seeds have 1", straight, silky, reddish plumes. **BLOOMS** June–Aug., as snow melts. **HABITAT** Foothills to rocky tundra, subalpine meadows.

WESTERN PASQUEFLOWER
Anemone (Pulsatilla) occidentalis
BUTTERCUP FAMILY

6". Clump-forming. Flower 1¼", white, cup-shaped, with 5–8 crinkled, petal-like sepals, many yellow stamens; 1 per stem. Stems hairy. Leaves fern-like, bi- or tripinnately compound. Seeds have 1¼", drooping, silky, light green plumes. **BLOOMS** June–Aug., as snow melts. **HABITAT** Subalpine meadows. **RANGE** ID, w MT.

COLORADO BLUE COLUMBINE
Aquilegia coerulea
BUTTERCUP FAMILY

20". Bushy. Flowers 2½", with 5 white to blue, spreading, petal-like sepals; 5 tubular white petals with rearward spurs; many yellow stamens. (Rich blue form mainly in CO at lower elevs.) Leaves repeatedly divided into round-lobed leaflets. CO state flower. **BLOOMS** June–Aug. **HABITAT** Open forests, aspen groves, high meadows. **RANGE** c and s ID, sw MT, WY, CO.

YELLOW COLUMBINE
Aquilegia flavescens
BUTTERCUP FAMILY

20". Bushy. Flowers 2"; all pale yellow, with 5 spreading, petal-like sepals; 5 tubular petals with inward-hooked rearward spurs. Leaves repeatedly divided into round-lobed leaflets. **BLOOMS** June–Aug. **HABITAT** Alpine and subalpine meadows, rockpiles. **RANGE** ID, w MT, w WY.

RED COLUMBINE
Aquilegia formosa
BUTTERCUP FAMILY

24". Bushy. Flowers 2", with 5 red to orange, spreading, petal-like sepals; 5 tubular yellow petals with red rearward spurs; many yellow stamens. Leaves repeatedly divided into round-lobed leaflets. BLOOMS June–July. HABITAT Mid-elev. forest clearings. RANGE ID, extreme w MT.

WHITE MARSH MARIGOLD
Caltha (Psychrophila) leptosepala
BUTTERCUP FAMILY

5". Succulent, patch-forming. Flowers 1", white or rarely bluish, bowl-shaped, with 6–11 petal-like sepals, many yellow stamens; usu. 1 per stem. Stems smooth. Leaves oblong, notched at base. CAUTION Poisonous. BLOOMS June–July, as snow melts. HABITAT Alpine to subalpine streams, seeps, marshes.

SUGARBOWL
"Leatherflower"
Clematis (Coriflora) hirsutissima
BUTTERCUP FAMILY

16". Wooly clumps. Flowers 1¼", lavender to brown, jar-shaped, hang down; 4 petal-like sepals hairy, leathery, curved outward. Leaves opposite, finely divided, fern-like. Seeds with 1½" plumes. BLOOMS Apr.–July. HABITAT Grasslands, Ponderosa Pine forests.

SHOWY LARKSPUR
Delphinium bicolor
BUTTERCUP FAMILY

12". Flowers 1¼", with 5 indigo sepals (upper 1 spurred) around 4 smaller indigo petals; lower 2 petals scarcely notched; in 1 short spike. Stems usu. single. Leaves rounded, deeply divided into narrow lobes; basal, long-stalked. BLOOMS May–July. HABITAT Dry gravels; from foothills to alpine elevs., plains in MT. RANGE ID, MT, nw WY.

NUTTALL'S LARKSPUR
Delphinium nuttallianum (nelsonii)
BUTTERCUP FAMILY

12". Flowers 1¼", with 5 indigo sepals (upper 1 spurred) around 4 smaller, white to brownish-purple petals; lower 2 petals deeply notched; in 1 loose spike per delicate stem. Leaves deeply divided into narrow lobes; mostly basal. CAUTION Poisonous. BLOOMS Mar.–July. HABITAT Gravelly slopes with Ponderosa Pine or sagebrush.

DUNCECAP LARKSPUR
"Tall Larkspur"
Delphinium occidentale
BUTTERCUP FAMILY

5'. Flowers 1¼", indigo to pale blue or spotted, with 5 sepals (upper 1 spurred) around 4 smaller petals; in tall spike. Leaves deeply, palmately divided into many narrow lobes. BLOOMS July–Aug. HABITAT Aspen flats, mtn. streamsides.

SAGEBRUSH BUTTERCUP
Ranunculus glaberrimus
BUTTERCUP FAMILY

5". Flowers 1", saucer-shaped, with 5 or more glossy yellow petals, 5 sepals, many stamens. Leaves elliptical, round, or shallowly 3-lobed. Plant withers away in midsummer. BLOOMS Mar.–June. HABITAT Ponderosa Pine forests, sagebrush grasslands.

SUBALPINE BUTTERCUP
Ranunculus eschscholtzii
BUTTERCUP FAMILY

5". Flowers 1", saucer-shaped, with 5 glossy yellow petals, 5 sepals, many stamens. Leaves vary from deeply 3-lobed to compound with 3 several-lobed leaflets. BLOOMS June–Aug., as snow melts. HABITAT Wet alpine to subalpine meadows; moist subalpine forests.

AMERICAN GLOBEFLOWER
Trollius albiflorus (laxus)
BUTTERCUP FAMILY

12". Flowers 1¼", creamy white or greenish, bowl-shaped, with 5–9 petal-like sepals, many yellow stamens; 1 per stem. Stems smooth. Leaves deeply palmately 5-lobed, each lobe doubly toothed. BLOOMS June–Aug., as snow melts. HABITAT Wet ground; mainly subalpine elevs.

YELLOW BEE PLANT
"Yellow Spiderflower"
Cleome lutea
CAPER FAMILY

30". Rounded clusters of ½" yellow flowers with 4 petals and very long, protruding stamens; atop bluish, waxy stems. Leaves palmately compound, with several lanceolate leaflets. Rich nectar source. BLOOMS May–July. HABITAT Sandy lowlands. RANGE w CO and north and west.

ROCKY MOUNTAIN BEE PLANT
Cleome serrulata
CAPER FAMILY

30". Rounded clusters of ½" pink to purple flowers (occ. white), with 4 petals and usu. long protruding stamens. Leaves compound, with 3 linear leaflets; sharply fetid. Rich nectar source. BLOOMS June–Aug. HABITAT Low-elev. rangelands and roadsides.

CLAMMYWEED
Polanisia dodecandra (trachysperma)
CAPER FAMILY

24″. Sticky-hairy, bushy, fetid. Rounded clusters of ½″, purple-tinged, white flowers with 4 petals and 6–20 protruding purple stamens of unequal length. Leaves compound, with 3 oblanceolate to obovate leaflets. Seed pods 2½″, erect. **BLOOMS** June–Sept. **HABITAT** Dry, sandy lowlands.

WATER HEMLOCK
Cicuta maculata (douglasii)
CARROT FAMILY

5′. Domed, loose, 4″ clusters of many tiny white flowers. Stems smooth, sturdy, branched, magenta-streaked. Leaves doubly or triply divided into toothed, lanceolate leaflets. **CAUTION** All parts deadly poisonous. **BLOOMS** July–Aug. **HABITAT** Marshes, ditches, streamsides.

QUEEN ANNE'S LACE
"Wild Carrot"
Daucus carota
CARROT FAMILY

3′. Flat, lacy, 3″ clusters of tiny white flowers. Branches of old clusters curl inward, resemble bird's nests. Leaves bipinnately compound, lacy, fern-like. Introduced from Europe. **BLOOMS** July–Aug. **HABITAT** Disturbed ground.

COW PARSNIP
Heracleum lanatum (sphondylium)
CARROT FAMILY

6′. Domed 7″ clusters of tiny white flowers atop thick, succulent, strong-smelling stems. Leaves 16″ long and wide, compound with 3 palmately lobed leaflets, hairy, not fern-like. **BLOOMS** June–Aug. **HABITAT** Mtn. streamsides, moist thickets.

NARROWLEAF DESERT PARSLEY
Lomatium triternatum
CARROT FAMILY

20″. Minute yellow flowers in flat-topped, 3″ clusters. Leaves hairy, at least twice-compound in 3s and 5s; leaflets linear; leaf base a broad sheath. **BLOOMS** May–July. **HABITAT** Roadsides, dry slopes; foothills to tree line. **RANGE** ID, MT, c WY, w CO.

YAMPAH
Perideridia montana (gairdneri)
CARROT FAMILY

32″. Slender, dill-like, fragrant. Minute white flowers in flat to concave clusters. Stems single. Leaves compound with extremely narrow, soft, linear, 5″ leaflets; all along stem, withering early. Tubers (usu. 2) edible. **BLOOMS** July–Aug. **HABITAT** Open forests, grassy slopes, mid-elev. meadows.

BROADLEAF CATTAIL
Typha latifolia
CATTAIL FAMILY

6'. Minute flowers in dense, 2-part spike: tapering, light brown male part (fluffy, then withered) above dense, dark brown, cylindrical female part (releases fluffy seeds); each to 6". Leaves sheathing, as tall as stem. Cause sediment to collect; make water shallower; turn lakes into marshes. **BLOOMS** June–July. **HABITAT** Marshes, ditches. **Narrowleaf Cattail** *(T. angustifolia)* has short length of stem between male and female parts of spike, leaves ¼" wide.

SPREADING DOGBANE
Apocynum androsaemifolium
DOGBANE FAMILY

16". Shrub-like. Fragrant, pinkish, bell-shaped ¼" flowers in loose clusters. Stem has milky juice. Leaves ovate, opposite, drooping. Fruit 4", very narrow, paired seedpods. **CAUTION** Foliage poisonous. **BLOOMS** June–Sept. **HABITAT** Dry low-elev. forests.

BUNCHBERRY
"Ground Dogwood"
Cornus canadensis
DOGWOOD FAMILY

5". Flowers 2", each made up of 4 white, petal-like bracts around dense greenish flower cluster. Stems erect, from creeping rootstock. Leaves ovate, whorled. Berries bright red-orange, densely clustered. **BLOOMS** June–July. **HABITAT** Forests. **RANGE** More common northward.

FIREWEED
Chamerion (Epilobium) angustifolium
EVENING-PRIMROSE FAMILY

5'. Flowers 1¼", with 4 round petals, 4 linear sepals, all pink to purple; in conical spikes. Leaves linear, 5", grayish-green, turn red. Seedpods 2½", reddish, slender; release fluffy white seeds. **BLOOMS** June–Aug. **HABITAT** Clear-cuts, burned areas, avalanche tracks, river bars, subalpine meadows.

RIVER BEAUTY
"Dwarf Fireweed"
Chamerion (Epilobium) latifolium
EVENING-PRIMROSE FAMILY

8". Flowers 1¾", with 4 deep pink, round petals, 4 crimson, linear sepals; clustered atop stem. Leaves lanceolate, 2½", grayish green. Seedpods 3", reddish, slender; release fluffy white seeds. **BLOOMS** July–Aug. **HABITAT** Alpine to subalpine wet gravels.

DEERHORN CLARKIA
"Ragged Robin" "Pink Fairies"
Clarkia pulchella
EVENING-PRIMROSE FAMILY

12". Flowers 1½", brilliant pink, with 4 petals, each divided into 3 long lobes, side petals often twisted. Leaves linear. **BLOOMS** June–July. **HABITAT** Steppes, pine forests. **RANGE** ID, w MT, nw WY.

SCARLET GAURA
Gaura coccinea
EVENING-PRIMROSE FAMILY

10". Slender, in clumps. Flowers ½"; 4 petals turn from white in evening to pink, red, or maroon by midmorning; 8 stamens; bloom in sequence upward; fragrant. Stems sprawl, bend upward. Leaves lanceolate. **BLOOMS** May–July. **HABITAT** Grasslands, steppes, roadsides. **RANGE** Mainly east of Cont. Div.

TUFTED EVENING-PRIMROSE
Oenothera caespitosa
EVENING-PRIMROSE FAMILY

6". Stemless clumps. Flowers 3", with 4 wide, white petals that turn pink or purple; bloom around sunset, wither by end of next day; fragrant; stem-like flower base to 6". Leaves 7", oblanceolate, jaggedly toothed, all basal. **BLOOMS** Apr.–Aug. **HABITAT** Dry sand or clay sites; all elevs.

WESTERN BLUE FLAX
Linum (Adenolinum) lewisii (perenne)
FLAX FAMILY

18". Flowers 2", sky blue, with 5 flat petals around yellow center. Leaves linear. **BLOOMS** Apr.–Aug. **HABITAT** Steppes to alpine slopes. **Yellow Flax** (*L. rigidum*) is a straggly annual of the Great Plains and foothills.

MINER'S CANDLE
Cryptantha (Oreocarya) virgata
FORGET-ME-NOT FAMILY

18". Painfully sharp, hairy. Flowers ⅜", white with yellow eye, trumpet-shaped, 5-lobed; in small groups in leaf axils along unbranched stem. Leaves linear. Biennial; stemless rosette first year. **BLOOMS** May–July. **HABITAT** Gravelly foothills, plains. **RANGE** CO, WY. **Butte Candle** (*C. celosioides*) has rounded oblanceolate leaves; found in entire region.

ALPINE FORGET-ME-NOT
Eritrichum nanum (aretioides)
FORGET-ME-NOT FAMILY

1–4″. Alpine cushion plant. Flowers ¼″, blue with yellow "eye," trumpet-shaped, 5-lobed. Stems sometimes so short that flowers sit on leaf mat. Densely matted leaves, oblong, hairy-tufted. BLOOMS July–Aug. HABITAT Dry alpine to subalpine meadows, rocky tundra. **Mountain Forget-me-not** *(Myosotis alpestris)* is 8″ subalpine version (not a cushion).

MANY-FLOWERED STICKSEED
Hackelia floribunda
FORGET-ME-NOT FAMILY

30″. Slender, hairy. Flowers ¼″, blue with yellow "eye," trumpet-shaped, 5-lobed; in open clusters that uncoil as they bloom. Leaves lanceolate. Seeds stick to clothes with barbed prickles. BLOOMS June–Aug. HABITAT Thickets, meadows, streamsides, mtn. roadsides.

FRINGED PUCCOON
"Stoneseed" "Gromwell"
Lithospermum incisum
FORGET-ME-NOT FAMILY

14″. Clump-forming, hairy. Trumpet-shaped, fragrant, bright yellow 1¼″ flowers with 5 fine-toothed lobes; crowded together with leaves at stem ends. Leaves linear, stalkless. Fruit stony nutlets borne mainly in lower leaf axils. BLOOMS Apr.–July. HABITAT Open plains, foothills. RANGE MT, WY, CO.

WESTERN PUCCOON
"Stoneseed" "Gromwell"
Lithospermum ruderale
FORGET-ME-NOT FAMILY

16″. Clump-forming, hairy. Trumpet-shaped, 5-lobed, fragrant, ⅜″ pale yellow flowers crowded together with leaves at stem ends. Leaves linear, stalkless. BLOOMS Apr.–June. HABITAT Dry areas; foothills to mid-elevs. RANGE West of Cont. Div.

MOUNTAIN BLUEBELLS
Mertensia ciliata
FORGET-ME-NOT FAMILY

3′. Forms lush clumps. Flowers ½″, light blue (initially pink-tinged), narrowly bell-shaped, 5-lobed; in hanging clusters. Stems smooth, often bluish. Leaves elliptical, veiny, smooth, stalked. BLOOMS June–Aug. HABITAT Streamsides, wet cliffs, meadows; alpine to mid-elevs. RANGE c ID, sw MT, WY, CO.

NARROWLEAF BLUEBELLS
Mertensia lanceolata (viridis)
FORGET-ME-NOT FAMILY

12″. Clump-forming. Flowers ½″, light blue (initially pink-tinged), narrowly bell-shaped, 5-lobed; in hanging clusters. Leaves variable, usu. lanceolate, hairy or smooth. **BLOOMS** June–Aug. **HABITAT** Sunny dry slopes; foothills to alpine elevs.

BROADLEAF BLUEBELLS
"Tall Bluebells"
Mertensia paniculata
FORGET-ME-NOT FAMILY

3′. Forms lush clumps. Flowers ½″, light blue (initially pink-tinged), narrowly bell-shaped, 5-lobed, in hanging clusters. Leaves veiny; hairy or smooth; ovate or heart-shaped; stalked. **BLOOMS** June–Aug. **HABITAT** Mtn. streamsides, wet cliffs, meadows. **RANGE** n ID, extreme w MT.

SNOWBALL SAND VERBENA
Abronia elliptica
FOUR-O'CLOCK FAMILY

16″. Clumps with fragrant pom-poms of ¾″, white to pink, long-necked, trumpet-shaped, 5-lobed flowers. Stems sticky, wooly, whitish, sometimes red. Leaves obovate to oblong; opposite. Pod has 2–5 pliable papery wings, 1 seed. **BLOOMS** June–Aug. **HABITAT** Sandy grasslands, juniper woods. **RANGE** w CO, w WY.

MONUMENT PLANT
"Elkweed" "Green Gentian"
Frasera speciosa
GENTIAN FAMILY

4′. Robust, conical. Flowers 1¼″, pale green with purple spots; saucer-shaped with 4 petals, 4 linear sepals; clustered in upper leaf axils. Leaves lanceolate, in whorls; basal ones longest, to 20″. Blooms once after several years of growth. **BLOOMS** June–Aug. **HABITAT** Mtn. slopes with pine or sagebrush; to 10,000′.

ARCTIC GENTIAN
Gentiana (Gentianodes) algida
GENTIAN FAMILY

5″. Flowers 1¾″, white or pale yellow (often purple-streaked), vase-shaped, 5-lobed, with pleats in notches. Leaves opposite, linear, clasping. **BLOOMS** Aug.–Sept. **HABITAT** Alpine bogs and wet meadows.

MOUNTAIN BOG GENTIAN
"Explorer's Gentian"
Gentiana calycosa
GENTIAN FAMILY

8". Flowers 1½", deep blue, vase-shaped, 5-lobed, with 2- to 4-pointed fringes in notches. Leaves opposite, ovate, clasping. **BLOOMS** Aug.–Sept. **HABITAT** Wet subalpine to alpine areas. **Parry's Gentian** *(G. parryi)* has fringes of tiny hairs on sepals and stems; replaces this species in CO.

WESTERN FRINGED GENTIAN
Gentianopsis thermalis (detonsa)
GENTIAN FAMILY

15". Flowers 1¾", indigo (occ. white or pink), vase-shaped, with 4 finely fringed, flat-spreading rounded lobes, 4 sepals; single atop stems. Leaves oblanceolate; basal or opposite. **BLOOMS** July–Sept. **HABITAT** Mid-elev. to lower alpine wet meadows.

STAR GENTIAN
"Felwort"
Swertia perennis
GENTIAN FAMILY

16". Delicate. Flowers ¾", pale blue-purple, star-like; 5 petals, 5 linear sepals; in loose spike. Leaves lanceolate, mostly basal, long-stalked; 1 or 2 smaller pairs on stem. **BLOOMS** July–Sept. **HABITAT** Wet subalpine to alpine areas.

REDSTEM FILAREE
"Storksbill"
Erodium cicutarium
GERANIUM FAMILY

6". Flowers ½", deep pink, 5-petaled; 2–10 per cluster. Stems red, usu. prostrate. Leaves pinnately compound, mostly prostrate at stem base. Fruits have 1½" protruding "bills." **BLOOMS** Apr.–July. **HABITAT** Disturbed ground.

STICKY GERANIUM
"Sticky Cranesbill"
Geranium viscosissimum
GERANIUM FAMILY

24". Flowers 1", bright pink to purple, 5-petaled, in loose clusters. Leaves deeply 5- to 7-lobed, toothed. Fruits have 5-tipped, 1½" "bills." **BLOOMS** June–Aug. **HABITAT** Aspen forests, mtn. sagebrush grasslands, open forests, ditches. Very similar **Richardson's Geranium** *(G. richardsonii)* has whiter, purple-veined petals and shorter "bills."

HALOGETON
Halogeton glomeratus
GOOSEFOOT FAMILY

16″. Succulent clumps. Pale blue-green in spring, turning red (esp. stems) or yellow by late summer. Flowers minute, green, along stems. Leaves pointed-tubular, fleshy. Seriously invasive. Palatable to livestock but deadly. **BLOOMS** July–Sept. **HABITAT** Roadsides, waste sites, overgrazed rangelands. **RANGE** Mainly west of Cont. Div. but spreading.

BURNING BUSH
"Summer Cypress"
Kochia scoparia (sieversiana)
GOOSEFOOT FAMILY

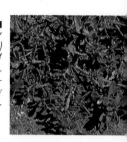

4″. Bushy. Often turns entirely rust red by fall. Flowers minute, greenish, along stems. Leaves linear; usu. with silky hairs below. Introduced; partly descended from garden escapes. **BLOOMS** July–Sept. **HABITAT** Neglected yards, roadsides, waste sites.

RED GLASSWORT
"Pickleweed" "Swampfire"
Salicornia europaea (rubra)
GOOSEFOOT FAMILY

7″. Jointed, reddish, succulent stems with minute flowers in club-like spikes at branch tips. Leaves scale-like, minute. Intense red by fall. **BLOOMS** June–Sept. **HABITAT** Saline or alkaline ground, esp. lakeshores, river bars.

RUSSIAN THISTLE
"Tumbleweed"
Salsola tragus (kali, iberica, or australis)
GOOSEFOOT FAMILY

3′. Bushy, ferociously spiny. Flowers tiny, magenta or green. Stems purple-striped. Leaves linear, soft; become thorn-like. Dies, turns rigid in fall; tumbles over open areas, scattering seeds. **BLOOMS** July–Sept. **HABITAT** Open, disturbed areas; esp. along fences.

BUFFALO GOURD
Cucurbita foetidissima
GOURD FAMILY

L variable. Coarse sprawling vine. Flowers 2½″, yellow-orange, funnel-shaped with 5 lobes; hidden under leaves. Stems succulent, rough; fetid when crushed. Leaves 8″, narrowly heart-shaped, rough. Fruit 3″ hard, spherical gourd, striped pale and dark green, ripening yellow. **CAUTION** Poisonous. **BLOOMS** Apr.–July. **HABITAT** Steppes. **RANGE** CO.

INDIAN RICEGRASS
Achnatherum (Oryzopsis) hymenoides
GRASS FAMILY

18″. Forms thick clumps. Flowers in delicate, open, 4½″ panicles of tiny white plumes. Leaves tightly in-rolled. **BLOOMS** May–June. **HABITAT** Grassland steppes, pinyon-juniper woods.

SIDEOATS GRAMA
Bouteloua curtipendula
GRASS FAMILY

28″. Forms open patches, scarcely clumping. Purplish spikelets hang flag-like from one side of uppermost 7″ of stem. Valuable graze species. **BLOOMS** July–Sept. **HABITAT** Low-elev. dry areas. **RANGE** Mostly east of Cont. Div.

BLUE GRAMA
Bouteloua (Chondrosum) gracilis
GRASS FAMILY

12″. Sod-forming. Bristly, often purplish spikelets form 1–3 distinctive flag- or sickle-like, 1-sided, tight, 1½″ spikes. Leaves mostly basal, from rhizome. Short-grass prairie dominant; valuable graze and soil-building species. **BLOOMS** July–Sept. **HABITAT** Dry areas below tree line. **RANGE** Mainly east of Cont. Div.

MOUNTAIN BROME
Bromus marginatus (carinatus)
GRASS FAMILY

40″. Forms small tufts. Flattened 1″ spikelets of 5–10 bristle-tipped flowers; in tall panicles with branches spreading to erect. Leaves rather broad, finely hairy. **BLOOMS** May–Aug. **HABITAT** Mtn. and tree line meadows, open forests.

CHEATGRASS
"Downy Brome" "Downy Chess"
Bromus (Anisantha) tectorum
GRASS FAMILY

14″. Forms small tufts. Flowers in loose, arching, reddish panicles of stiff-hairy, ¾″ spikelets. Leaves flat, finely hairy. Introduced; stubbornly invasive. Dies in midsummer, becoming fire hazard. **BLOOMS** May–June. **HABITAT** Locally abundant on disturbed ground.

BLUEJOINT REEDGRASS
Calamagrostis canadensis
GRASS FAMILY
40″. Sod-forming. Flowers in 6″, purplish or straw-colored, open, usu. conical panicles. Leaves flat, rough, soft. **BLOOMS** July–Aug. **HABITAT** Mtn. streamsides, bogs, wet meadows; to tree line.

IDAHO FESCUE
Festuca idahoensis
GRASS FAMILY

24″. Forms clumps; usu. bluish. Flowers in narrow 4″ panicles. Leaves 5″, extremely narrow, inrolled, mostly basal. **BLOOMS** May–Aug. **HABITAT** Mtn. grass-steppes, open forests; to tree line.

NEEDLE-AND-THREAD
Hesperostipa (Stipa) comata
GRASS FAMILY
28″. Clumps with windblown horsetail tops. Flowers in 10″ spikes; each floret (or, later, each seed) ends in 5″ crooked "thread"; base needle-sharp, barbed, can injure mouths of livestock. Leaves inrolled, rough. **BLOOMS** May–July. **HABITAT** Dry, sandy grasslands; to lower forests.

SWITCHGRASS
Panicum virgatum
GRASS FAMILY

5′. Sod-forming. Flowers tiny, in loose, open panicles. Stems tough, smooth, often bluish-coated. Leaves mainly smooth, ¼″ wide. Native tall-grass prairie species; good forage species. **BLOOMS** June–Sept. **HABITAT** Moist prairies, open forests. **RANGE** Mainly east of Cont. Div.

TIMOTHY
Phleum pratense
GRASS FAMILY
30″. Thickly clumped grass. Flowering spikes dense, slender, yellowish, 4″ cylinders. Stems bulbous just above root crown. Leaves flat. Introduced; top U.S. crop hay; hay fever allergen. **BLOOMS** June–Aug. **HABITAT** Roadsides, pastures.

KENTUCKY BLUEGRASS
Poa pratensis
GRASS FAMILY

24″. Sod-forming. Flowers purple, 2–4 per flattened spikelet; in open, delicate, conical or arching panicles. Leaves slender, soft, abundant, sometimes bluish. Introduced; popular for lawns but invasive. **BLOOMS** May–Oct. **HABITAT** Lawns, gardens, roadsides, moist areas; to alpine tundra.

BLUEBUNCH WHEATGRASS
Pseudoroegneria (Agropyron) spicata
GRASS FAMILY

32″. Forms thick clumps; often bluish-coated. Hairy spikelets spaced along stem tips form 4½″ spikes. Originally a steppe dominant; now decimated where grazed but still common. **BLOOMS** June–Aug. **HABITAT** Dry mtn. slopes with sagebrush, oak. **RANGE** w CO, WY, MT, ID.

LITTLE BLUESTEM
Schizachyrium (Andropogon) scoparius
GRASS FAMILY

40″. Robust clumped grass. Flowers few and large, bristly, each with bent ½″ tip; in several 1½″ spikes on stem branches. Stems purplish to bluish-white-coated. Native tall-grass prairie species. **BLOOMS** July–Sept. **HABITAT** Dry lowlands. **RANGE** Mainly east of Cont. Div.

INDIAN GRASS
Sorghastrum nutans (avenaceum)
GRASS FAMILY

4′. Sod-forming. Flowers each with crooked ½″ tip; in red-gold narrow 10″ panicles that usu. nod at tip. Leaves 8″, rough, flat, ¼″ wide; leaf nodes wooly. Native tall-grass prairie species; good forage species. **BLOOMS** Aug.–Sept. **HABITAT** Prairies. **RANGE** Great Plains.

PRAIRIE CORDGRASS
Spartina pectinata
GRASS FAMILY

6′. Colony-forming giant grass. Several dense 3″ flower spikes alternate in 10″ panicle. Leaves 16″, dangerously rough-edged, ⅜″ wide. **BLOOMS** June–Sept. **HABITAT** Ditches, floodplains, marshes, lakeshores. **RANGE** Mainly Great Plains.

SPIKE TRISETUM
Trisetum spicatum
GRASS FAMILY

15″. Dense tufts. Flowers in dense, often purplish, spike-like 3″ panicles; shaggy with bent ¼″ bristles. Leaves narrow; smooth to finely hairy. **BLOOMS** July–Sept. **HABITAT** Moist alpine to subalpine (occ. mid-elev.) meadows.

PIPSISSEWA
Chimaphila umbellata
HEATH FAMILY

8″. Flowers ½″, pink to white, nodding, with 4–5 petals spread flat around fat, knob-like pistil. Stems slender, woody. Leaves elliptical, fine-toothed, leathery, dark green, evergreen, mostly whorled. **BLOOMS** June–Aug. **HABITAT** Shady conifer forests.

PINEDROPS
Pterospora andromedea
HEATH FAMILY

28″. Fleshy stalk with no green parts. Flowers ¼″, amber, jar-shaped, 5-lobed; nodding in tall spike. Stem red-brown, sticky. Obtains all nutrients from soil fungi, which draw nutrients from trees. **BLOOMS** June–Aug. **HABITAT** Shady conifer forests; to mid-elevs.

PINK PYROLA
"Heartleaf Pyrola"
Pyrola asarifolia (rotundifolia)
HEATH FAMILY

11″. Narrow spike of bowl-shaped, pink to red, ½″ flowers with 5 petals and curved, off-center style. Leaves elliptical to heart-shaped, leathery, dark green, evergreen; in rosette at stem base. **BLOOMS** June–Aug. **HABITAT** Moist conifer forests.

TWINFLOWER
Linnaea borealis
HONEYSUCKLE FAMILY

5″ (flower stalks). Evergreen creeper. Flowers ½″, pink to white, 5-lobed, bell-shaped, fragrant, paired. Stems woody, reddish. Leaves 1″, obovate, fine-toothed, glossy dark green. **BLOOMS** June–Aug. **HABITAT** Moist conifer forests.

ROCKY MOUNTAIN IRIS
"Western Blue Flag"
Iris missouriensis
IRIS FAMILY

18″. Forms dense clumps. 1–4 pale blue or blue-violet, 3½″ flowers with petal-like parts in 3s (down-curved sepals, erect petals, style branches). Leaves sword-like. **BLOOMS** May–July. **HABITAT** Mtn. streamsides, marshes, wet meadows; to subalpine elevs.

IDAHO BLUE-EYED GRASS
Sisyrinchium idahoense (angustifolium or occidentale)
IRIS FAMILY

11″. Grass-like. Flowers ¾″, blue with yellow center, saucer-shaped, with 6 petal-like parts tipped with slender points. Stems flat. Leaves very narrow. **BLOOMS** May–July. **HABITAT** Grassy mtn. areas that are wet in spring; to near tree line. **Mountain Blue-eyed Grass** (*S. montanum*), more common in CO, has a notch on either side of the slender point at each petal's tip.

HOOKER'S ONION
Allium acuminatum
LILY FAMILY

9″. Grass-like; onion-scented. Flowers ½″, rose-purple to white, vase-shaped, in rounded branched cluster atop bare, slender, single stem. Leaves linear, rolled, basal. **BLOOMS** May–July. **HABITAT** Dry, rocky sites; to mid-elevs. **RANGE** ID, sw WY, w CO.

SIBERIAN CHIVES
Allium schoenoprasum
LILY FAMILY

18″. Grass-like. Onion-scented. Flowers ⅜″, rose, vase-shaped, in ball-like cluster atop bare, slender, single stem. Leaves tubular, hollow, basal. **BLOOMS** Apr.–Aug. **HABITAT** Mtn. streamsides, marshes, wet meadows; to mid-elevs.

CAT'S EARS
"Elegant Mariposa Lily"
Calochortus elegans
LILY FAMILY

5". Usu. 1 or 2 grayish-white, ¾" flowers; 3 elliptical sepals; 3 broad petals with inner surface hairy and usu. purple-blotched. Single leaf taller than stem. **BLOOMS** May–June. **HABITAT** Grassy slopes. **RANGE** c ID, extreme w MT.

SEGO LILY
Calochortus nuttallii
LILY FAMILY

14". Showy 2", lilac-tinged white flowers, 1–4 per stem; 3 very broad, small-pointed petals with maroon crescent and yellow blush at base; 3 shorter, lanceolate white sepals. Leaves grass-like, few. **BLOOMS** June–July. **HABITAT** Dry foothills and plains. **RANGE** WY, s MT, e ID, w CO. **Gunnison's Sego Lily** *(C. gunnisonii)* replaces this species in c CO and at high elevs., WY and s MT.

SAGEBRUSH MARIPOSA LILY
Calochortus macrocarpus
LILY FAMILY

14". Flowers 3", lavender or rose-purple; 3 broad, sharp-tipped petals, each with dark purple band and yellowish hairy base; 3 longer, linear, petal-like sepals. Leaves linear, curled at tips. Palatable to livestock, disappearing where cattle graze. **BLOOMS** May–July. **HABITAT** Dry lowlands. **RANGE** ID, w MT.

COMMON CAMAS
Camassia quamash
LILY FAMILY

18". Grass-like. Tall conical clusters of many 1½", bright blue-violet flowers with nearly flat-spreading petals. Leaves linear, sheathing. **BLOOMS** Apr.–June. **HABITAT** Meadows moist in spring; to mid-elevs. **RANGE** ID, w MT, nw WY.

GLACIER LILY
Erythronium grandiflorum
LILY FAMILY

9". Flowers 2½", yellow, with 6 curved-back petals, 6 long stamens. Leaves and stalk tulip-like. Leaves elliptical, basal. **BLOOMS** May–July. **HABITAT** High-elev. meadows, aspen groves, sagebrush slopes; often near melting snow. **RANGE** Entire region, ex. sc CO.

LEOPARD LILY
"Checker Lily" "Spotted Mountain Bells"
Fritillaria atropurpurea
LILY FAMILY

14". Flowers 1", purplish or greenish brown speckled with light green; bowl-shaped, with 6 petals; 1–4 nodding atop stem. Leaves linear, grass-like, on stem. Seedpod a hexagonal box. **BLOOMS** Apr.–July. **HABITAT** Open forests or shrublands; to mid-elevs. **RANGE** ID, sw MT to nc CO.

YELLOW BELL
Fritillaria pudica
LILY FAMILY

6". Flowers ¾", yellow to orange, narrowly bell-shaped, with 6 petals; usu. 1, nodding, atop stem. Leaves linear, grass-like, few. **BLOOMS** Mar.–June. **HABITAT** Grasslands, sagebrush, open forests; foothills to mid-elevs. **RANGE** nw CO and north and west.

STAR LILY
"Sand Lily"
Leucocrinum montanum
LILY FAMILY

5". Stemless rosette. Flowers 1¼", white, trumpet-shaped, with 6 protruding stamens; 6 lanceolate lobes on tubular base emerging from below ground. Leaves 6" linear, grass-like, bluish, basal. **BLOOMS** Apr.–June. **HABITAT** Grasslands, vacant lots; to low-elev. forests. **RANGE** s MT and south.

ALP LILY
Lloydia serotina
LILY FAMILY

4". Flowers ¾", white with fine purple veins, 6 flaring petals; 1 or 2 atop stem. Leaves grass-like; 2 basal, a few smaller ones on stem. **BLOOMS** June–Aug. **HABITAT** Alpine gravels, meadows, rock crevices.

FALSE SOLOMON'S-SEAL
Smilacina (Maianthemum) racemosa (amplexicaule)
LILY FAMILY

24″. Minute, white, fragrant flowers form many-branched 4″ clusters. Stems arch out from rootstock. Leaves elliptical, parallel-veined. Berries speckled green; ripen red. **BLOOMS** Apr.–July. **HABITAT** Shady forests.

STARRY FALSE SOLOMON'S-SEAL
Smilacina (Maianthemum) stellata
LILY FAMILY

16″. Fragrant, white, ⅜″ flowers form open clusters of 3–15. Stems arch out from rootstock. Leaves elliptical, parallel-veined. Berries green; ripen dark red. **BLOOMS** Apr.–June. **HABITAT** Moist sites, plains, arroyos; to mid-elev. forests.

FALSE ASPHODEL
"Sticky Tofieldia"
Tofieldia glutinosa
LILY FAMILY

14″. Grass-like. Flowers ¼″, white, bowl-shaped, 6-petaled, atop stems; in 1″ egg-shaped clusters Stems sticky-hairy. Leaves 6″, linear, mostly basal. **BLOOMS** June–Aug. **HABITAT** High-elev. streamsides, meadows, lakeshores. **RANGE** MT, nw WY, n and c ID.

DOUGLAS'S TRITELEIA
Triteleia grandiflora (Brodiaea douglasii)
LILY FAMILY

18″. Grass-like. Round clusters of ¾″, bell-shaped, blue flowers; 6-lobed, with inner 3 lobes ruffled. 1 or 2 narrow 20″ leaves. **BLOOMS** May–July. **HABITAT** Dry foothills. **RANGE** ID, w MT, w WY.

CALIFORNIA CORN LILY
"False Hellebore"
Veratrum californicum
LILY FAMILY

5′. Many 1″ flowers with 6 petals, each white with a green V at base; in dense 12″ cluster with erect branches. Leaves 12″, elliptical, strongly pleated. **CAUTION** Poisonous. **BLOOMS** June–Aug. **HABITAT** Mtn. meadows and streamsides. **Rocky Mountain Corn Lily** *(V. tenuipetalum)* replaces this species in CO.

GREEN CORN LILY
Veratrum viride
LILY FAMILY

5'. Many ½", green flowers with 6 finely ragged-edged petals; in loose 18" cluster with long, drooping branches. Leaves 12", elliptical, strongly pleated. **CAUTION** Poisonous. **BLOOMS** June–Sept. **HABITAT** Mtn. meadows and streamsides. **RANGE** ID, MT.

BEARGRASS
"Indian Basket Grass"
Xerophyllum tenax
LILY FAMILY

5'. Flowers ½", saucer-shaped, white to cream, 6-petaled, fragrant; in elongating cluster atop stout stalk. Leaves tough, sharp-edged, grass-like; in massive basal bunch. **BLOOMS** June–Aug. **HABITAT** Open subalpine forests and ridges. **RANGE** Tetons and north and west.

ELEGANT DEATH CAMAS
"Alkali Grass"
Zigadenus (Anticlea) elegans
LILY FAMILY

20". Open 8" spike of ¾", saucer-shaped, greenish-white flowers; 6 petals all same length, with heart-shaped green spot near base. Leaves 10", grass-like. **CAUTION** Possibly poisonous. **BLOOMS** June–Aug. **HABITAT** Open forests, moist meadows, alpine tundra (where dwarfed).

DEATH CAMAS
Zigadenus (Toxicoscordion) venenosus
LILY FAMILY

19". Pointed 4" cluster of ½", cup-shaped, white to cream flowers with 6 petals (3 long, 3 short); with round, green spot near base of each petal. Leaves 10", grass-like. **CAUTION** Deadly poisonous. **BLOOMS** May–July. **HABITAT** Grasslands, open low-elev. forests.

NORTHERN BEDSTRAW
Galium boreale (septentrionale)
MADDER FAMILY

18". Many flat ¼", 4-lobed, white flowers form lacy clusters. Stems 4-sided. Leaves linear, blunt-tipped, in whorls usu. of 4. **BLOOMS** June–Aug. **HABITAT** Mid-elev. forests and moist meadows; plains.

STREAMBANK GLOBE MALLOW
"Mountain Hollyhock"
Iliamna rivularis
MALLOW FAMILY

5′. Hollyhock-like. Flowers 1½″, pink to lavender, with 5 petals, 5 sepals, many stamens; in tall spikes. Leaves palmately 3- to 7-lobed. **BLOOMS** June–Aug. **HABITAT** Mtn. streamsides, ditches.

SCARLET GLOBE MALLOW
"Copper Mallow"
Sphaeralcea coccinea
MALLOW FAMILY

8″. Velvety, patch-forming. Flowers 1″, brick red to red-orange; 5 petals, many stamens; in numerous small, elongated clusters. Stems often weak, leaning; in clumps. Leaves grayish, compound with 3 narrow-lobed leaflets. **BLOOMS** May–July. **HABITAT** Dry plains, foothills. **RANGE** Mainly east of Cont. Div.

SHOWY MILKWEED
Asclepias speciosa
MILKWEED FAMILY

3′6″. Coarse, gray-wooly. Broad clusters of ¾″, pink to maroon flowers, with 5 sharply bent-back petals and 5 curved-in, horn-like structures. Stem and leaf juice milky. Leaves 6″, opposite, lanceolate. Seed-pods velvety, spiny; release silky white fluff. **CAUTION** Poisonous. **BLOOMS** June–July. **HABITAT** Streamsides, roadsides, fields, waste sites.

FIELD MINT
Mentha arvensis
MINT FAMILY

15″. Tiny pale pink flowers nearly hidden in leaf axils encircle weak, hairy, 4-sided stems. Leaves opposite, elliptical, sharp-toothed. **BLOOMS** July–Sept. **HABITAT** Wet areas; plains and low valleys.

WILD BERGAMOT
"Bee Balm"
Monarda fistulosa
MINT FAMILY

2′. Flowers 1¼″, lavender, tubular, 2-lipped; in rounded clusters atop square stems. Leaves opposite, ovate to lanceolate, toothed, grayish. **BLOOMS** July–Aug. **HABITAT** Ravines, meadows, roadsides; plains to lower mtns.

SELF-HEAL
"Heal-all"
Prunella vulgaris
MINT FAMILY
7". Flowers ½", violet or pink, tubular, 2-lipped, with hood-like upper lip and fringed lower lip; in oblong heads atop 4-sided stems. Leaves opposite, ovate. **BLOOMS** June–Sept. **HABITAT** Moist areas, foothills; to mid-elevs.

DWARF MISTLETOES
Arceuthobium species
MISTLETOE FAMILY
1". Tiny, branching, olive to dull blue-green or orange-green growths with bud-like tips; on tree limbs. Parasitic; grows long thread-like roots inside tree branches, inflicts slow death; conspicuous only in causing host trees to branch into dense vertical "witches brooms." Most common on upper branches, but occ. visible near eye level. **HABITAT** Conifer limbs.

FIELD BINDWEED
Convolvulus arvensis
MORNING GLORY FAMILY
H/L variable. Aggressive twining vine. Flowers 1", white to purplish, funnel-shaped, shallowly 5-lobed. Leaves triangular to arrowhead-shaped. Introduced; crop-smothering pest; regrows from deep roots when pulled out. **BLOOMS** May–Oct. **HABITAT** Fields, gardens, disturbed areas.

WESTERN WALLFLOWER
Erysimum capitatum (asperum)
MUSTARD FAMILY
22". Foliage grayish. Flowers ¾", with 4 petals; orange, occ. yellow or purplish. Leaves narrowly lanceolate, finely toothed. Seedpods slender, 4-sided. **BLOOMS** Apr.–June. **HABITAT** Dry sites; plains to tundra (where dwarfed).

DOUBLE BLADDERPOD
"Rydberg's Twinpod"
Physaria acutifolia (australis)
MUSTARD FAMILY
3". Rosette. Flowers ⅜", yellow, bell-shaped with 4 flaring petals; in small clusters. Stems flop. Leaves mostly basal, obovate to oblanceolate. Fruit a puffy 2-lobed pod. **HABITAT** Dry open forests to alpine gravels. **BLOOMS** June–Aug. **RANGE** West of Cont. Div.; Beartooth R. and south.

PRINCE'S PLUME
"Desert Plume"
Stanleya pinnata
MUSTARD FAMILY

4′. Stout columnar plant. Flowers 1″, yellow, spidery, with 4 linear, hairy petals and 4 sepals; elongated 12″ clusters mature bottom-to-top into slender 2½″ pods. Leaves lanceolate; pinnately lobed, smaller and shallowly or not lobed upward. **BLOOMS** May–July. **HABITAT** Arid lowlands. **RANGE** s MT and south.

WILD CANDYTUFT
"Alpine Pennycress"
Thlaspi (Noccaea) montanum
MUSTARD FAMILY

12″. Slender. Flowers ¼″, white, narrow, 4-petaled bells; in dense cluster atop stem. Basal rosette of stalked ovate leaves; smaller stem leaves clasping. **BLOOMS** Apr.–Aug. **HABITAT** Widespread; foothills to alpine tundra (where dwarfed).

STINGING NETTLE
Urtica dioica (gracilis)
NETTLE FAMILY

5′. Stems and leaf edges covered with stinging hairs. Loose clusters of minute green flowers dangle from leaf axils. Stems spindly, 4-sided. Leaves opposite, ovate, toothed. **CAUTION** Painful skin irritant; do not touch. **BLOOMS** May–Sept. **HABITAT** Ditches, streamsides; foothills to lower mtns.

BUFFALO BUR
Solanum rostratum
NIGHTSHADE FAMILY

2′. Prickly herb. Flowers 1″, yellow, trumpet-shaped, with 5 flat-spreading, shallow lobes. Stems very spiny. Leaves 5″, deeply pinnately lobed. Burs covered with long straight spines. **BLOOMS** June–Sept. **HABITAT** Waste sites, fields. **RANGE** Great Plains; widely scattered elsewhere.

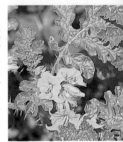

FAIRY SLIPPER
Calypso bulbosa
ORCHID FAMILY

5″. Purple scaly stem topped with single 1″ pink flower with 5 narrow, ascending petals and sepals above large, slipper-shaped lip mottled with orange, yellow, and white. 1 ovate leaf; grows in fall, withers in summer. **BLOOMS** May–July. **HABITAT** Moist forests, bogs; to near tree line.

SPOTTED CORALROOT
Corallorhiza maculata
ORCHID FAMILY

12″. Fleshy. Seemingly leafless, dull reddish stem bears tall spike of 1″, brownish-purple flowers with magenta-spotted white lip petal; pale-yellow albinos also common. Obtains all nutrients from soil fungi, which draw nutrients from trees. **BLOOMS** June–July. **HABITAT** Under aspens or pines; to mid-elevs.

GIANT HELLEBORINE
Epipactis gigantea
ORCHID FAMILY

28″. Flowers 1¼″; lip petal like a pink tongue, other 2 petals like floppy brownish-purple ears; backed by 3 lanceolate bronzy-greenish sepals; 3–10 flowers facing one way along upper stem. Leaves pleated, lower ones ovate; becoming smaller, lanceolate up stem; clasping. **BLOOMS** Apr.–Aug. **HABITAT** Low-elev. wet mtn. meadows, desert seeps.

WHITE BOG ORCHID
"White Rein Orchid"
Platanthera (Habenaria or *Limnorchis) dilatata*
ORCHID FAMILY

18″. Single, straight, hollow stem bears dense 8″ spike of ¾″, white, spicy-scented orchids; "rein" refers to long, strap-shaped lowest petal. Leaves lanceolate, sheathing. **BLOOMS** June–Aug. **HABITAT** Wet areas; lower forests to above tree line.

HOODED LADIES' TRESSES
Spiranthes romanzoffiana
ORCHID FAMILY

8″. Single straight stem bears dense, twisted, 4-sided, 2″ spike of ½″, white to creamy, rather closed-up, hood-like orchids. Leaves lanceolate, sheathing; mostly on lower ¼ of stem. **BLOOMS** July–Sept. **HABITAT** Wet areas; foothills to subalpine elevs.

FRINGED PARNASSIA
Parnassia fimbriata
PARNASSIA FAMILY

10″. Flowers 1″, white; with 5 petals fringed near base and 5 stamens; 1 per stem. 1 to several stems. Basal leaves heart- to kidney-shaped, long-stalked; 1 small clasping leaf halfway up stem. **BLOOMS** July–Sept. **HABITAT** Mtn. streamsides, seeps, lakeshores, wet meadows.

PURPLE PRAIRIE CLOVER
Dalea (Petalostemum) purpurea
PEA FAMILY

16″. Tiny, slightly irregular, 5-petaled, purple flowers in numerous dense, rounded, 1½″ spikes. Grayish hair on sepals and usu. all over. Leaves compound, with 3 or 5 linear, folded leaflets; speckled underneath. **BLOOMS** July–Aug. **HABITAT** Dry plains and foothills. **RANGE** East of Cont. Div.

NORTHERN SWEETVETCH
"Northern Chainpod"
Hedysarum boreale
PEA FAMILY

18″. Unbranched or few-branched stems bear open spikes of ½″, pink to maroon pea-flowers. Leaves pinnately compound with 7–15 ovate leaflets. Seedpod narrows sharply between each of the 2–4 beans. **BLOOMS** May–Aug. **HABITAT** Diverse open dry areas; plains to tree line.

STEPPE SWEETPEA
"Few-flowered Pea"
Lathyrus pauciflorus
PEA FAMILY

18″. Climber. Angled stems bear clusters of pink to purple or blue, ¾″ pea-flowers. Leaves with tendrils at tips, pinnately compound, with 8 or 10 linear to ovate, fleshy leaflets, plus 1 pair clasping stem. **BLOOMS** Apr.–July. **HABITAT** Open forests or brush steppes, usu. where moist in spring. **RANGE** s ID, sw CO.

SILVERY LUPINE
Lupinus argenteus
PEA FAMILY

18″. Blue or bicolored (pink or white), ¾″ pea-flowers, whorled in conical clusters. Silver-hairy leaves (usu. only below), stems, seedpods, sepals. Stems often purple. Leaves palmately compound. **BLOOMS** Apr.–July. **HABITAT** Partial shade at mid-elevs., alpine gravels (where dwarfed).

DWARF LUPINE
Lupinus caespitosus (lepidus)
PEA FAMILY

3″. Hairy. Blue, ⅜″ pea-flowers whorled in columnar cluster close to ground. Silver-hairy leaves (both sides), seedpods, sepals, back of upper petal. Leaves palmately compound, basal, long-stalked. **BLOOMS** June–Aug. **HABITAT** Mid-elev. to alpine gravels and dry meadows.

SILKY LUPINE
Lupinus sericeus
PEA FAMILY

24". Blue or white, ½" pea-flowers whorled in conical clusters. Brown-silky leaves, stems, seedpods, sepals, back of upper petal. Leaves palmately compound; mainly on stem. **BLOOMS** June–Aug. **HABITAT** Steppes, grasslands, forest openings; to mid-elevs. **RANGE** MT, ID; mainly west of Cont. Div. in CO and WY.

YELLOW SWEET CLOVER
Melilotus officinalis
PEA FAMILY

4'. Pale yellow ¼" pea-flowers in 3½" spikes on most branches. Leaves divided into 3 obovate, fine-toothed leaflets. Introduced from Europe. Sweet scent attracts bees. **BLOOMS** June–Aug. **HABITAT** Roadsides, fields, river bars, seeps; low- to mid-elevs. **White Sweet Clover** *(M. alba)* has white flowers.

SILKY LOCOWEED
"Silky Crazyweed"
Oxytropis sericea
PEA FAMILY

12". Unbranched stalks bear columnar spikes of ¾" white or pale yellow pea-flowers, usu. purple-tipped. Silver-silky leaves, stalks, seedpods, sepals. Leaves pinnately compound, with 9–19 lanceolate leaflets; basal. Pods ¾", grooved on 1 side; hardening and long-persistent. **BLOOMS** May–July. **HABITAT** Rocky grassy sites; plains to (occ.) tree line.

SHOWY LOCOWEED
Oxytropis splendens
PEA FAMILY

12". Unbranched stalks bear dense spikes of ½", reddish-purple to blue pea-flowers. Silver-silky leaves, stalks, seedpods, sepals. Leaves compound, with 30 or more leaflets whorled around leafstalk; basal. Pods ¾", grooved on 1 side, tapered. **BLOOMS** June–Aug. **HABITAT** River bars, aspen groves, rocky subalpine meadows. **RANGE** Great Plains in MT; near and east of Cont. Div. in MT, WY, CO.

MOUNTAIN GOLDEN PEA
"Golden Banner" "False Lupine"
Thermopsis montana
PEA FAMILY

20". Yellow ¾" pea-flowers whorled in columnar clusters. Leaves compound, with 3 oblanceolate, 3", true leaflets, and 2 smaller bracts clasping stem. Pods fine-wooly, slender, straight, erect. **BLOOMS** May–Aug. **HABITAT** Moist mtn. meadows near tree line.

PARRY'S CLOVER
Trifolium parryi
PEA FAMILY

5". Tuft-forming. Reddish purple ⅝" flowers in round heads. All green parts hairless. Leaves divided into 3 elliptical leaflets. **BLOOMS** June–Sept. **HABITAT** Subalpine clearings, alpine tundra. **RANGE** CO, WY, sw MT. **Alpine Clover** *(T. dasyphyllum),* has fine hair below leaves, varying amounts of white in flowers; on tundra in CO and s WY.

WHITE CLOVER
"Dutch Clover"
Trifolium repens
PEA FAMILY

5". Tiny white or pinkish flowers in ¾" round heads. Leaves divided into 3 round, fine-toothed leaflets with slightly notched tips. Roots freely from runners. Cultivated for hay and honey; escapes and naturalizes. **BLOOMS** Apr.–Sept. **HABITAT** Croplands, lawns, trailsides, mtn. meadows.

SKYROCKET
"Scarlet Gilia"
Ipomopsis (Gilia) aggregata
PHLOX FAMILY

21". Flowers 1", trumpet-shaped, with 5 pointed lobes; scarlet, pink, or cream with or without red speckles. Leaves finely pinnately lobed, skunky-smelling. Hummingbird favorite. **BLOOMS** May–Aug. **HABITAT** Rocky slopes; foothills to tree line.

ROCKY MOUNTAIN PHLOX
Phlox multiflora
PHLOX FAMILY

5". Mat-forming. Flowers ¾", white (occ. pink or bluish), with 5 lobes spreading flat from tubular base. Prostrate stems woody. Leaves ¾", linear. **BLOOMS** June–Aug. **HABITAT** Dry rocky areas; foothills to alpine elevs. **RANGE** sw MT, e ID, WY, CO.

LONGLEAF PHLOX
Phlox longifolia
PHLOX FAMILY

10". Flowers 1", pink with white center, lilac, or pure white; 5 lobes spread flat from tubular base. Stems erect, semiwoody. Leaves at least 1", linear. **BLOOMS** Apr.–July. **HABITAT** Dry rocky areas in lower mtns. and basins.

SHOWY JACOB'S LADDER
Polemonium pulcherrimum
PHLOX FAMILY

9″. Flowers ½″, blue to lavender with yellow center, broadly bell-shaped, 5-lobed, densely clustered. Leaves pinnately compound, with 11–25 elliptical leaflets; often skunky-scented. **BLOOMS** June–Aug. **HABITAT** Dry subalpine forests, rock crevices, tundra; mid-elevs. to highest peaks.

SKY PILOT
Polemonium viscosum
PHLOX FAMILY

7″. Skunky-smelling, sticky herb. Flowers ¾″, purple (rarely white) with orange stamens, narrowly funnel-shaped, 5-lobed, densely clustered. Leaves compound, with many tiny leaflets whorled around stalk. **BLOOMS** June–Aug. **HABITAT** Moist, rocky alpine to subalpine areas.

FIELD CHICKWEED
"Field Mouse-ear"
Cerastium arvense (strictum)
PINK FAMILY

9″. Several slender weak stems. Flowers white, ½″, with 5 deeply notched rounded petals, 5 separate sepals; 2–4 atop stem. Leaves opposite, lanceolate, few; lower leaf axils bear tiny leaflets or shoots. **BLOOMS** Apr.–Aug. **HABITAT** Sandy or gravelly areas; foothills to alpine elevs.

WHITE CAMPION
"Evening Lychnis"
Silene (Lychnis) latifolia (alba)
PINK FAMILY

30″. Sticky-hairy, much branched. Flowers ¾″, white or pinkish, sweet-scented, with 5 deeply notched petals. Females: 5 protruding pistils; 20-veined calyx swells as it matures. Males: on separate plants: slender, 10-veined calyx, 10 stamens. Leaves opposite, lanceolate. Blooms at night; pollinated by moths. Spreading into region from East. **BLOOMS** June–Aug. **HABITAT** Disturbed areas.

MOSS CAMPION
Silene acaulis
PINK FAMILY

2″. Moss-like cushion. Flowers ½″, pink (rarely white), with tubular calyx, 5 usu. notched petals, 3 protruding styles; nearly cover surface of leaf mat. Leaves linear, sharp, crowded. Cushion shape protects alpine plants from drying winds. **BLOOMS** June–Aug. **HABITAT** Alpine tundra.

BROADLEAF PLANTAIN
"Common Plantain"
Plantago major
PLANTAIN FAMILY

16". Dense, narrow, 4" spikes of minute, drab white flowers rise on wiry stems above basal rosette of ovate 5" leaves. Introduced from Europe; invasive. **BLOOMS** May–Aug. **HABITAT** Lawns, ditches, river flats.

PRICKLY POPPY
Argemone polyanthemos
POPPY FAMILY

2'. White, 3" flowers with 4–6 wide, crinkly petals, many golden stamens. Stems have yellow sap, sparse yellow spines. Leaves 7", pinnately lobed, bluish; main veins spiny. **CAUTION** Spines contain substance irritating to skin. **BLOOMS** Apr.–July. **HABITAT** Sandy or gravelly areas. **RANGE** Great Plains and foothills of WY; local in MT and CO.

GOLDEN SMOKE
"Scrambled Eggs"
Corydalis aurea
POPPY FAMILY

12". Sprawling, soft, with watery juice. Yellow, ⅝", irreg. flowers; tube-like with open mouth and swollen tongue; attached at midlength; in elongated clusters. Leaves bluish, fern-like. Bean-pod small, curved. **BLOOMS** May–Aug. **HABITAT** Roadsides, ravines, creek flats.

STEER'S HEAD
Dicentra uniflora
POPPY FAMILY

3". Pinkish, ⅝" flower resembles steer's head; 2 back-curved petals, 2 fused petals; 1 flower per stalk. Leaves much divided, rather lacy, round-tipped, long-stalked; basal. Leaf and flower stalks joined below ground. **BLOOMS** Mar.–June. **HABITAT** Sandy or gravelly areas; foothills to tree line. **RANGE** Extreme w WY, sw MT, c ID.

FEW-FLOWERED SHOOTING STAR
Dodecatheon pulchellum (pauciflorum)
PRIMROSE FAMILY

9". Single stem bears deep pink, dart-like, 1" flowers; 5 petals upswept from dark purple stamens; yellow "neck," white "collar." Leaves lanceolate, basal, somewhat succulent. **BLOOMS** May–Aug. **HABITAT** Wet mtn. meadows and streamsides; to near tree line.

ROCKY MOUNTAIN DOUGLASIA
Douglasia montana
PRIMROSE FAMILY

1½". Moss-like cushion. Flowers ⅜", pink, with tubular base, 5 slightly notched lobes; styles unbranched, hidden; nearly cover surface of leaf mat. Leaves ¼", linear, crowded. Cushion shape protects this and other alpine plants from drying winds. **BLOOMS** May–July. **HABITAT** Dry gravels; foothills to (mainly) alpine elevs. **RANGE** WY, MT, e ID.

FAIRY PRIMROSE
Primula angustifolia
PRIMROSE FAMILY

3." Short stems bear 1–3 deep pink, yellow-throated, ⅜" flowers with tubular base, 5 notched lobes. Leaves 3", oblanceolate, somewhat fleshy, with heavy midvein; basal. **BLOOMS** June–Aug. **HABITAT** Alpine to subalpine meadows near melting snow. **RANGE** CO.

PARRY'S PRIMROSE
Primula parryi
PRIMROSE FAMILY

12". Single stem bears several fetid, ¾" flowers; deep pink with yellow throat; tubular base, 5 slightly notched lobes. Leaves 10", oblanceolate, somewhat fleshy with heavy midvein; basal. **BLOOMS** June–Aug. **HABITAT** Wind-sheltered alpine to subalpine streamsides, rock crevices. **RANGE** CO, WY, c ID, c MT.

PUSSY PAWS
Calyptridium (Cistanthe, Spraguea) umbellatum
PURSLANE FAMILY

3". Alpine rosette plant. Ball-like, 1" clusters of rusty-pink-edged cream flowers on several reddish, often prostrate stems. Leaves rounded-oblanceolate, fleshy, prostrate. **BLOOMS** June–Aug. **HABITAT** Dry gravelly mtn. areas; esp. subalpine elevs. **RANGE** Wind R. Range and north and west.

WESTERN SPRING BEAUTY
Claytonia lanceolata
PURSLANE FAMILY

8". Flowers ½", 5-petaled, white to pinkish with fine red veins; several atop succulent stem. 1 pair of rather fleshy oval or lanceolate leaves. **BLOOMS** Apr.–Aug. **HABITAT** Meadows, esp. subalpine, usu. near snowbanks.

MINER'S LETTUCE
Claytonia (Montia) perfoliata
PURSLANE FAMILY

8″. Small cluster of white, 5-petaled, ½″ flowers emerges from center of round stem leaf. Other leaves basal, spoon-shaped. **BLOOMS** Apr.–Aug. **HABITAT** Moist shady forests. **RANGE** WY, MT, ID; local in CO.

PYGMY BITTERROOT
Lewisia (Oreobroma) pygmaea
PURSLANE FAMILY

2″. Alpine dwarf plant. Several short stems each bear 1 rose-pink (occ. white), ½″ flower with 6–9 petals and 2 green to red sepals. Leaves fleshy, basal, linear, taller than stems; 1 pair of tiny papery leaflets midway up stem. **BLOOMS** June–Aug. **HABITAT** Dry alpine to subalpine meadows.

BITTERROOT
Lewisia rediviva
PURSLANE FAMILY

5″. Deep pink (occ. to white), 2″ flowers with 10–18 petals, many stamens; atop inconspicuous stems with linear fleshy leaves that wither at flowering. MT state flower. **BLOOMS** Apr.–June. **HABITAT** Arid lowlands to Ponderosa Pine forests.

WHITE MOUNTAIN AVENS
"Mountain Dryad"
Dryas octopetala
ROSE FAMILY

6″. Mat-forming. Flower 1″, white, usu. 8-petaled; single on naked stem. Leaves evergreen, oblong with scalloped, rolled-under edges. Seeds have silky yellowish-white plumes, initially twisted together. **BLOOMS** July–Aug. **HABITAT** Alpine rock fields, mid-elev. gravel bars. **Yellow Mountain Avens** *(D. drummondii)* has yellow flowers; common in n MT.

WOODLAND STRAWBERRY
Fragaria vesca
ROSE FAMILY

5″. Groundcover. Flowers ¾″, white to pinkish, with 5 rounded petals. Leaves divided into 3 elliptical, toothed leaflets; on hairy stalks. Strawberries red, ½″; edible, delicious, ripe July–Aug. **BLOOMS** June–July. **HABITAT** Open forests or streamsides in mtns; talus at tree line.

PRAIRIE SMOKE
"Old Man's Whiskers"
Geum (Erythrocoma) trifolium
ROSE FAMILY

12″. Thick clumps or scattered. Small clusters of nodding, ¾″, hairy, dusty-rose flowers with 5 narrow and 5 wide lobes. Leaves 4″, mostly basal, fern-like, hairy. Seeds have long (2″ in Great Plains, 1¼″ in mtns.), showy, purplish plumes. BLOOMS May–Aug. HABITAT Plains; moist mtn. meadows to alpine elevs.

PARTRIDGEFOOT
Luetkea pectinata
ROSE FAMILY

4″. Carpet-forming. Dense, round, ¾″ clusters of tiny cream-white flowers with many long stamens. Stems red, unbranched, somewhat woody, from runners. Leaves crowded, divided into 9 narrow lobes. BLOOMS July–Aug. HABITAT Subalpine and lower alpine meadows. RANGE Bitterroot Mtns. and west.

ROCKMAT
"Rock-spiraea"
Petrophyton caespitosum
ROSE FAMILY

3″. Sprawling shrubby mat. Dense, round, 1½″ spikes of minute cream-white flowers with many long pink stamens. Stems unbranched, somewhat woody. Basal leaves oblanceolate, crowded, grayish-silky; stem leaves tiny, few. BLOOMS Aug–Sept. HABITAT Mtn. rock crevices, usu. limestone. RANGE sw MT, s ID, WY, w CO.

SLENDER CINQUEFOIL
Potentilla gracilis
ROSE FAMILY

18″. Spindly. Flowers ½″, yellow, with 5 petals, 10 apparent sepals, many stamens; in loose clusters. Leaves palmately compound, with 5–9 deeply toothed, elliptical, hairy leaflets; long-stalked. BLOOMS June–Aug. HABITAT Moist meadows, rocky tundra, open forests, grasslands, disturbed ground.

MARSH CINQUEFOIL
Potentilla (Comarum) palustris
ROSE FAMILY

24″. Erect to prostrate or floating. Flowers 1″, wine-red, flattish, with 5 sepals, 5 shorter petals, 20–25 stamens. Stems usu. reddish; thick; rooting at nodes. Leaves pinnately compound with 5–7 oblong, sharp-toothed leaflets. BLOOMS June–Aug. HABITAT Bogs, lakeshores. RANGE MT, n and c ID, w WY; local in CO.

MERTENS' RUSH
Juncus mertensianus
RUSH FAMILY

10". Dark green grass-like clumps of tubular stems with round, ½" clusters of blackish-brown flowers; usu. 1 cluster per stem. Leaves tubular, uppermost 1 alongside flower head. **BLOOMS** July–Sept. **HABITAT** Mid-elev. to alpine meadows, often where wet.

WESTERN ST.-JOHN'S-WORT
Hypericum formosum (scouleri)
ST.-JOHN'S-WORT FAMILY

16". Many showy, 1", star-shaped, yellow flowers from red buds; 5 flat-spreading petals with black-speckled edges, long stamens, 4 ovate sepals. Leaves ovate, black-speckled. **BLOOMS** July–Sept. **HABITAT** Moist, rocky slopes; mid-elevs. to lower alpine elevs.

COMMON ST.-JOHN'S-WORT
"Klamath Weed"
Hypericum perforatum
ST.-JOHN'S-WORT FAMILY

24". Many showy, ¾", yellow flowers; 5 flat-spreading petals with black-speckled edges, long stamens, 5 linear sepals. Leaves linear to oblong, black-speckled. Introduced; invasive; used medicinally. **BLOOMS** June–Sept. **HABITAT** Lowland roadsides, dry fields.

BASTARD TOADFLAX
Comandra umbellata
SANDALWOOD FAMILY

9". Pale gray-green, patch-forming. Flowers tiny, white, 5-lobed, cobwebby on inner faces; in rounded clusters atop stems. Leaves linear, thick, gray-coated. Roots blue where cut. Root parasite. **BLOOMS** May–Aug. **HABITAT** Plains, sagebrush steppes.

LITTLELEAF ALUMROOT
Heuchera parvifolia
SAXIFRAGE FAMILY

16". Leafless sticky-hairy stalks above matted leaf clump. Flowers tiny, greenish-white, funnel-shaped, 5-lobed, stamens not protruding; in 3" spike-like panicle. Leaves heart-shaped, shallowly lobed, round-toothed; basal on long stalks. **BLOOMS** May–Sept. **HABITAT** Rocky slopes and crevices; valleys to alpine elevs.

PRAIRIE STAR
Lithophragma parviflorum
SAXIFRAGE FAMILY

12". Slender. Flowers ¾", white, with 5 narrowly 3-lobed petals; several atop stem. Stems grayish-hairy, often purplish. Leaves deeply palmately 9-lobed, long-stalked; mostly basal. **BLOOMS** Apr.–July **HABITAT** Grassy open forests, sagebrush steppes.

FIVE-POINT BISHOP'S CAP
Mitella pentandra
SAXIFRAGE FAMILY

12". Slender. Flowers tiny, whitish, with 5 petals like branched threads; several, along upper third of stem. Leaves heart-shaped, doubly toothed, long-stalked; all basal. **BLOOMS** June–Aug. **HABITAT** Moist forests, mtn. meadows and stream-sides.

SPOTTED SAXIFRAGE
Saxifraga bronchialis (Ciliaria austromontana)
SAXIFRAGE FAMILY

4". Juniper-like mat of leaves. Flowers ⅜", white with tiny red and yellow dots; 5 petals, 10 stamens; in a sparse spray. Leaves linear, stiff, bristle-edged; densely packed around sprawling stem bases; plus a few on erect, flowering upper stems. **BLOOMS** June–Sept. **HABITAT** Rocky areas; foothills to (esp.) alpine elevs.

PURPLE MOUNTAIN SAXIFRAGE
Saxifraga oppositifolia
SAXIFRAGE FAMILY

1". Showy alpine miniature. Flowers ⅜", purple (occ. white), bell-shaped; scattered over mound of leaves. Leaves opposite, minute, obovate, bristly-edged, crowded; persisting after withering. **BLOOMS** June–July, as snow melts. **HABITAT** Alpine rock crevices. **RANGE** Wind R. Range and west and north.

WESTERN FOAMFLOWER
Tiarella trifoliata (unifoliata)
SAXIFRAGE FAMILY

14". Delicate. Flowers tiny, white; 5 thread-like petals, 5 calyx lobes, 10 protruding stamens; in panicle. Leaves 3-lobed (somewhat maple-like) to compound with 3 leaflets; long-stalked. **BLOOMS** June–Aug. **HABITAT** Moist forests, stream-sides. **RANGE** w MT, n ID.

TALL COTTONGRASS
Eriophorum angustifolium (polystachion)
SEDGE FAMILY
20″. Grass-like marsh plant bearing 1¼″ white, flower heads like cotton balls; 2 to several per stem. Leaves bright green; uppermost 1 or 2 alongside flowers. **BLOOMS** July–Aug. **HABITAT** Alpine to subalpine bogs.

HARDSTEM BULRUSH
"Tule"
Scirpus (Schoenoplectus) acutus (lacustris)
SEDGE FAMILY
7′. Colony-forming. Thick, grass-like stems with many brownish spikelets in loose sprays. Leaves form long sheaths around stem base. **BLOOMS** June–Aug. **HABITAT** Marshes, lakes, streamsides; lower elevs.

BLACK ALPINE SEDGE
Carex nigricans
SEDGE FAMILY
6″. Turf-forming. Blackish flower spike atop 3-sided, sharp-angled stem; upper flowers (males) dangle conspicuous straw-colored stamens; females have 3 stigmas. Leaves flat, narrow. **BLOOMS** June–Aug. **HABITAT** Alpine or subalpine elevs., usu. by water or where late snowbeds melt.

DESERT PAINTBRUSH
"Early Paintbrush"
Castilleja chromosa
SNAPDRAGON FAMILY

12″. Flowers and brightly colored bracts form ragged red to orange (rarely yellow) "paintbrush" spikes. Outer floral bracts and upper leaves have several long narrow lobes; lowest leaves linear. This and other paintbrush species are partly parasitic; their roots connect with and draw from those of other plants. **BLOOMS** May–June. **HABITAT** Brush steppes, Pinyon-juniper woods. **RANGE** w CO, c and s WY, s ID.

WYOMING PAINTBRUSH
"Longleaf Paintbrush"
Castilleja linariifolia
SNAPDRAGON FAMILY
20″. Flowers and brightly colored bracts form ragged scarlet (occ. yellow) "paintbrush" spikes. Outer floral bracts and upper leaves have 3 long narrow lobes; other leaves linear. WY state flower. Usu. parasitic on sagebrush. **BLOOMS** July–Aug. **HABITAT** Brush steppes, pine forests. **RANGE** s MT and s.

GIANT RED PAINTBRUSH
Castilleja miniata
SNAPDRAGON FAMILY
20″. Flowers and brightly colored bracts form ragged scarlet "paintbrush" spikes. Outer floral bracts usu. lobed near tip. Leaves linear. Can hybridize with Alpine Paintbrush, producing intermediate characteristics. **BLOOMS** July–Aug. **HABITAT** Moist clearings; mid-elevs. to tree line.

ALPINE PAINTBRUSH
Castilleja rhexifolia
SNAPDRAGON FAMILY
16″. Flowers and brightly colored bracts form ragged rose-purple "paintbrush" spikes. Outer floral bracts typically with 2 or 4 side lobes near midlength. Leaves linear. **BLOOMS** July–Aug. **HABITAT** Low subalpine open forests to alpine meadows.

SULPHUR PAINTBRUSH
Castilleja sulphurea
SNAPDRAGON FAMILY
18″. Flowers and brightly colored bracts form ragged pale yellow "paintbrush" spikes. Outer floral bracts unlobed or with 2 tiny side lobes near tip. Leaves linear. **BLOOMS** June–Aug. **HABITAT** Alpine to subalpine meadows.

DALMATIAN TOADFLAX
Linaria dalmatica (genistifolia)
SNAPDRAGON FAMILY
28″. Dense spikes of 1½″, yellow, 2-lipped flowers with deeper yellow center and long, straight, rearward spur. Leaves ovate, clasping. Introduced from Europe; invasive. **BLOOMS** June–Sept. **HABITAT** Rangelands, roadsides. **Butter-and-eggs** (*L. vulgaris*) has 1″ flowers and linear leaves.

COMMON MONKEYFLOWER
Mimulus guttatus
SNAPDRAGON FAMILY
14″. Flowers 1″, snapdragon-like, brilliant yellow, with red-spotted and usu. hairy throat. Leaves opposite, ovate, toothed. Variable in size, hairiness, branching. **BLOOMS** June–Aug. **HABITAT** Seeps and streams; foothills to tree line.

PINK MONKEYFLOWER
Mimulus lewisii
SNAPDRAGON FAMILY

20". Lush, sticky-hairy, clumping. Flowers 1½", magenta, with yellow throat; upper lip 2-lobed, lower lip 3-lobed. Leaves opposite, ovate to lanceolate. BLOOMS July–Aug. HABITAT Seeps and streams; mid-elevs. to tree line. RANGE n CO and north.

YELLOW OWL'S-CLOVER
Orthocarpus luteus
SNAPDRAGON FAMILY

12". Sticky-hairy, usu. unbranched stem bears flowers and partly colored bracts in ragged, pale yellow "paintbrush" spike. Flowers ½", tubular; tips divided into upper and lower lips equal in length, extending past yellow-tipped bracts. Floral bracts 3-lobed. Leaves linear. BLOOMS July–Aug. HABITAT Mtn. meadows, often with sagebrush or aspens.

BRACTED LOUSEWORT
"Wood Betony"
Pedicularis bracteosa
SNAPDRAGON FAMILY

20". Dense tall spike of many yellow (or red in n ID and MT) 1" flowers resembling hooked beaks. Leaves mostly on stem, fern-like, pinnately compound, with lanceolate toothed leaflets. BLOOMS June–Aug. HABITAT Moist forest openings; mid-elevs. to tree line.

ELEPHANT'S HEAD
Pedicularis groenlandica
SNAPDRAGON FAMILY

16". Dense spike of many ¾" pink flowers, each unmistakably shaped like an elephant's head with up-curved trunk. Leaves fern-like, pinnately lobed, toothed. BLOOMS July–Aug. HABITAT Wet, high-elev. meadows, bogs, shallow streams.

PARRY'S LOUSEWORT
Pedicularis parryi
SNAPDRAGON FAMILY

8". Dense spike of many ¾" flowers resembling hooked beaks; from Wind R. Range north, pink-purple; to south, pale yellow. Leaves fern-like, pinnately lobed; mostly basal, a few small ones on stem. BLOOMS July–Aug. HABITAT Alpine to subalpine slopes.

WASATCH PENSTEMON
Penstemon cyananthus (glaber)
SNAPDRAGON FAMILY
20″. Tall sparse spike of whorled, bright blue, tubular, 1″ flowers; upper lip 2-lobed, lower lip 3-lobed; hairless ex. on anthers. Leaves lanceolate; opposite and clasping, or basal. **BLOOMS** May–July. **HABITAT** Various: roadsides, open forests, alpine scree; foothill canyons to tree line. **RANGE** e ID, w WY, sw MT.

HOT ROCK PENSTEMON
Penstemon deustus
SNAPDRAGON FAMILY
14″. Clustered erect stems from a woody base bear several whorls of 2-lipped flowers, ½″ long, dingy white with fine purple lines; minutely sticky-hairy. Leaves opposite, elliptical, sharp-toothed. **BLOOMS** May–July. **HABITAT** Dry rocky (often volcanic) areas. **RANGE** s and c ID, sw MT, w WY.

FIRECRACKER PENSTEMON
Penstemon eatoni
SNAPDRAGON FAMILY
18″. Flowers 1″, scarlet, narrow, tubular, with 5 lobes almost alike and not curled back; in tall, usu. 1-sided cluster. Leaves opposite, obovate, basal, clasping stem. Like other tubular scarlet flowers, it attracts hummingbirds. **BLOOMS** June–July. **HABITAT** Brush steppes, juniper woods. **RANGE** sw CO; common in Mesa Verde N.P.

ROCKY LEDGE PENSTEMON
"Northern Shrubby Beardtongue"
Penstemon ellipticus
SNAPDRAGON FAMILY
4″. Clustered woody stems bear several 2-lipped, 1½″, violet flowers; yellow- or white-hairy throat. Leaves elliptical, fine-toothed or smooth; mat-forming, basal, and opposite on stem. **BLOOMS** June–Sept. **HABITAT** Subalpine to alpine cliffs or talus. **RANGE** n ID, nw MT; common in Glacier N.P.

WHIPPLE'S PENSTEMON
Penstemon whippleanus
SNAPDRAGON FAMILY

18". Clustered erect stems from a woody base bear several whorls of 2-lipped, wooly-throated, 1¼" flowers, either dark purple or cream with purple tinge; minutely sticky-hairy. Leaves variable, basal and opposite on stem. **BLOOMS** July–Aug. **HABITAT** Subalpine forests to alpine tundra. **RANGE** sw MT and south.

WOOLY MULLEIN
Verbascum thapsus
SNAPDRAGON FAMILY

5'. Robust stalk of yellow, 5-lobed, ¾" flowers. Leaves lanceolate, thick, gray-wooly; large (12") at plant base, smaller up stem. Biennial; produces only large rosette of leaves in first year. **BLOOMS** June–Aug. **HABITAT** Dry roadsides, burns, overgrazed ranges.

AMERICAN BROOKLIME
Veronica americana
SNAPDRAGON FAMILY

10". Flowers ⅜", blue, with 4 unequal lobes, 2 stamens; in paired elongate clusters from upper leaf axils. Stems often branch, may lean and root from nodes. Leaves opposite, ovate to lanceolate, usu. toothed or scalloped. **BLOOMS** July–Aug. **HABITAT** In mud or shallow water of mtn. springs, seeps, slow creeks.

SHOWY PENSTEMON
Penstemon speciosus
SNAPDRAGON FAMILY

20". Tall sparse spike of whorled, bright blue, tubular, wooly-throated, 1" flowers; upper lip 2-lobed, lower lip 3-lobed. Leaves opposite, oblanceolate. **BLOOMS** June–July. **HABITAT** Open juniper or pine forests, sagebrush steppes. **RANGE** sw ID.

ALPINE SPEEDWELL
Veronica wormskjoldii (nutans)
SNAPDRAGON FAMILY

5". Clumps of unbranched stems. Flowers ⅜",
deep blue, with 4 unequal lobes, 2 stamens; 1
short cluster atop stem. Leaves opposite, elliptical, clasping. **BLOOMS** July–Aug. **HABITAT** Wet
alpine to subalpine meadows.

WESTERN SPIDERWORT
Tradescantia occidentalis
SPIDERWORT FAMILY

14". Flowers 1", blue (occ. lavender in south),
between 2 green bracts; 3 wide petals, 6 hairy
stamens all alike; blooming 1 at a time in
morning, wilting midday. Leaves linear;
sheathing stem at knobby nodes. **BLOOMS**
May–July. **HABITAT** Sandy or rocky areas.
RANGE Great Plains.

LEAFY SPURGE
Euphorbia esula (Tithymalus uralensis)
SPURGE FAMILY

30". Dense patches. Flowers minute, between
1" pair of showy, heart-shaped, greenish-yellow bracts; in broad, domed clusters. Stems
have milky juice. Leaves linear, numerous.
Seed pods explode open. Introduced from
Eurasia; invasive, esp. in MT. **CAUTION** Poisonous; irritates skin; kills cattle if eaten in quan-
tity. **BLOOMS** May–Aug. **HABITAT** Rangelands,
mtn. meadows.

NORTHERN BLAZING STAR
Mentzelia (Nuttallia) laevicaulis
STICKLEAF FAMILY

30". Many 3½" yellow flowers at
branchtips; 5 petals, many showy 1"
stamens. Leaves 8", pinnately lobed,
very rough, cling to clothes. **BLOOMS**
June–Aug. **HABITAT** Dry gravels in
inter-mtn. lowlands. **RANGE** MT,
WY, ID. **Giant Blazing Star** (*M. de-
capetala*) blooms evenings; has 5 petal-
like stamens alternating with 5 broader
petals; mainly east of Cont. Div.

LANCELEAF STONECROP
Sedum (Amerosedum) lanceolatum
STONECROP FAMILY

6″. Flowers ½″, yellow, often red-tinged; bell-shaped with 5 flaring petals; in rounded clusters. Leaves ⅜″, almost round in cross-section, succulent, pale green to reddish; numerous on flower stalks, crowded on short basal branches. **BLOOMS** June–Aug. **HABITAT** Sunny rocky areas; all elevs.

SITKA VALERIAN
Valeriana sitchensis
VALERIAN FAMILY

30″. Flowers ½″, white, tubular, with 5 unequal lobes, 3 protruding stamens; in rounded clusters. Leaves pinnately compound, with 3–7 leaflets. Seeds have umbrella-shaped plumes. **BLOOMS** June–Aug. **HABITAT** Moist subalpine meadows, mtn. forests. **RANGE** n and c ID, nw MT. **Western Valerian** *(V. occidentalis)* has tiny flowers in rounded 1″ clusters; stem leaves pinnately compound, basal leaves simple or with 3 leaflets; throughout region.

DAKOTA VERBENA
Verbena (Glandularia) bipinnatifida (ambrosifolia)
VERBENA FAMILY

16″. Hairy. Many short, broad spikes of ⅜″ pink-purple flowers; slightly irreg.; stamens and pistil hidden. Stems sprawl in spreading mat; turn erect. Leaves opposite, lanceolate, deeply pinnately lobed, toothed. **BLOOMS** June–Aug. **HABITAT** Plains and foothills. **RANGE** Great Plains of WY, CO.

NEW MEXICO VERBENA
Verbena macdougalii
VERBENA FAMILY

30″. Hairy, slender. Several dense spikes of ¼″, slightly irregular, blue-violet, 5-lobed flowers bloom upward, 1 ring at a time; stamens and pistil hidden. Stems 4-sided. Leaves opposite, lanceolate, coarse-toothed; all on stem. **BLOOMS** June–Sept. **HABITAT** Ponderosa Pine forests. **RANGE** sw and sc CO, occ. s WY.

WESTERN BLUE VIOLET
Viola adunca (labradorica)
VIOLET FAMILY

5″. Flowers ½″, with 5 blue to violet petals, often white at base; lowest petal longest, with long, hooked, rearward spur. Leaves ovate to heart-shaped, scalloped. **BLOOMS** May–July. **HABITAT** Moist areas; foothill ravines to alpine meadows (where dwarfed, 1½″).

CANADA VIOLET
Viola canadensis (scopulorum or rydbergii)
VIOLET FAMILY

9″. Flowers ¾″, with 5 white petals with yellow bases, purple veins and backs; fragrant; from leaf axils. Leaves heart-shaped, toothed. **BLOOMS** May–July. **HABITAT** Moist ravines; lower mtns. to tree line.

YELLOW PRAIRIE VIOLET
Viola nuttallii (vallicola, praemorsa)
VIOLET FAMILY

6″. Flowers ½″; with 5 yellow, veined petals, some brownish-purple backs; 1 per stem. Leaves ovate to linear, smooth-edged, long-stalked; all basal. Tolerates drier sites by going dormant in summer heat. **BLOOMS** Apr.–Aug. **HABITAT** Various: plains to subalpine snowbeds, in full or partial sun.

BALLHEAD WATERLEAF
Hydrophyllum capitatum
WATERLEAF FAMILY

7″. Flowers ¼″, pale lavender or blue (occ. white), bell-shaped, 5-lobed; in 1½″ ball-like clusters usu. lower than leaves. Leaves few, with 5–11 deep pinnate lobes, each shallowly lobed. A dwarf variety grows in sw ID mtns. **BLOOMS** May–July. **HABITAT** Mid-elev. open forests, brushy slopes. **RANGE** w CO and north and west.

WHITELEAF PHACELIA
"Scorpionweed"
Phacelia hastata (leucophylla)
WATERLEAF FAMILY

14". Silvery with stiff flat hairs. Flowers ¼", bright purple to lavender, or dirty white; 5 bristly sepals; 5 hairy, protruding stamens; in short (sometimes uncoiling) clusters. Several unbranched stems, prostrate or leaning. Leaves narrowly elliptical, mostly unlobed. **BLOOMS** May–Aug. **HABITAT** Sunny, often sandy areas; all elevs.

THREADLEAF PHACELIA
Phacelia linearis
WATERLEAF FAMILY

10". Flowers lavender, ½", saucer-shaped, 5-lobed; in small clusters in upper leaf axils and atop stem. Sepals, stems, and leaves have fine hairs. Leaves linear or with a few linear lobes near base; all on stem. **BLOOMS** Apr.–June. **HABITAT** Sagebrush plains, foothills. **RANGE** ID, n WY, MT.

SILKY PHACELIA
"Purple Fringe"
Phacelia sericea
WATERLEAF FAMILY

10". Silvery-silky. Flowers deep blue-purple, ¼", with ½" yellow-tipped stamens; in dense, cylindrical clusters. Stems silky-hairy (less so at mid-elevs.). Leaves deeply pinnately lobed. **BLOOMS** June–Aug. **HABITAT** Rocky sites; to high peaks.

YELLOW POND LILY
"Spatterdock"
Nuphar polysepala (lutea)
WATER-LILY FAMILY

Flowers and leaves float on or emerge from water. Flowers 3½", cup-shaped, yellow, with 5 thick, waxy, petal-like sepals around broad pistil and purplish stamens. Leaves massive (12"), heart-shaped. **BLOOMS** June–Aug. **HABITAT** Shallow lakes, ponds; subalpine elevs. in CO; all elevs. in north.

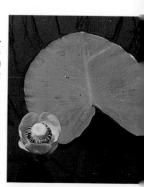

Invertebrates

Biologists divide the animal kingdom into two broad groupings—vertebrates, animals with backbones, and invertebrates, those without. While this distinction seems apt, perhaps because we are vertebrates ourselves, it is really one of mere convenience. Vertebrates are but a small subphylum in the animal kingdom, while invertebrates comprise the vast majority of animal life forms that inhabit water, air, and land. Invertebrates have thrived on earth for more than a billion years, with species evolving and disappearing through the eons; they include a fascinating spectrum of phyla with extraordinarily diverse lifestyles and evolutionary developments. This guide describes selected species of invertebrates from two phyla found in terrestrial and freshwater environments:

Phylum Annelida	Earthworms
Phylum Arthropoda	Crustaceans, centipedes, millipedes, arachnids, and insects

There are two basic invertebrate body structures. *Radially symmetrical* invertebrates, like many marine invertebrates, have a circular body plan with a central mouth cavity and a nervous system encircling the mouth. *Bilateral* invertebrates have virtually identical left and right sides like vertebrates, with paired nerve cords that run along the belly, not the back, and a brain (in species with a head). All invertebrates are cold-blooded, and most become dormant or die in extreme temperatures.

Tens of thousands of invertebrate species thrive in the freshwater and terrestrial environments of the Rocky Mountain states. Ponds and meadows are home to billions of invertebrates per acre; even sheer rock faces and acidic bogs support a varied assortment.

The phylum Annelida includes the earthworms, which can occur at an average of 1,000 pounds per acre; they help fertilize and oxygenate soil by pulling vegetation underground. The phylum Arthropoda comprises the largest number of freshwater and land invertebrates, with five classes covered here: crustaceans, millipedes, centipedes, arachnids, and insects. Crustaceans include the terrestrial pillbugs, commonly found under rocks and rotting logs. Terrestrial millipedes and centipedes look like worms with legs—two pairs per segment for vegetarian millipedes and one pair per segment for predatory centipedes. Arachnids include spiders, scorpions, daddy-long-legs (harvestmen), and ticks. Insects comprise many well-known invertebrate orders, including dragonflies, grasshoppers, beetles, flies, butterflies, and ants, wasps, and bees (see their separate introductions within the section).

Our coverage of invertebrates begins with non-insect classes: millipedes, centipedes, pillbugs, and earthworms (all on page 179), followed by spiders and their kin (starting on page 180). Insects begin on page 182.

MILLIPEDES
Spirobolus and other genera
MILLIPEDE CLASS

L 2½″. Body often cylindrical, rounded at both ends. 2 short antennae; 2 pairs short legs per segment. Slow-moving; rolls into ball if threatened, releasing foul-smelling secretion to repel predators. **HABITAT** Meadows, woods.

CENTIPEDES
Scolopendra and other genera
CENTIPEDE CLASS

L 3″. Body flattened; black or reddish brown, some with pale red, yellow, or orange sides. 12–20 large segments. 1 pair legs per segment; 2 rear-facing legs at rear. Antennae long. Fast moving; venom paralyzes insects, spiders. **HABITAT** Woods; under bark, logs, trash.

COMMON PILLBUG
"Sowbug"
Armadillidium vulgare
CRUSTACEAN CLASS

L ⅓″. Body convex, with gray, shrimp-like plates, 7 pairs short legs; can roll into ball. Head has 2 short antennae. Feeds on decaying plant matter. **HABITAT** Common under rocks, leaves, and logs.

EARTHWORMS
"Night Crawlers"
Lumbricus and other genera
EARTHWORM CLASS

L to 8″. Body soft, cylindrical, legless, with dozens of segments; purplish orange or pink. Aerates moist soil; common on surface after heavy rains. Feeds on decaying plant matter. **HABITAT** Moist soils in woodlands, meadows, yards.

Spiders and Kin

The class Arachnida includes spiders, ticks, daddy-long-legs (harvestmen), and windscorpions. These generally dreaded invertebrates are much maligned; in fact, most species are harmless to humans, many are beneficial to the environment, and all have habits worthy of the naturalist's attention.

Spiders have two body parts and eight legs. Most also have eight simple eyes, the arrangement of which differs from family to family. On jumping spiders, which hunt without benefit of a web, two eyes are tremendously enlarged, a trait that enables them to accurately judge distances to their prey. All spiders extrude up to three or four types of silk from spinnerets on their undersides: one to make cocoons for their eggs; another, much finer, for lowering themselves; sturdy strands to construct radial web lines; and finally, the sticky silk they use to entrap prey.

8 eyes

Head of spider

Spiders hunt by stalking, ambushing, or ensnaring their victims, then subduing or killing them with a poisonous bite. Their venom acts as a powerful digestive fluid, which liquefies their prey so they can suck it up. Almost all spiders are venomous, but most are entirely harmless to humans, and indeed retreat quickly when we arrive on the scene. Spiders are not parasitic on humans or domesticated animals, nor do they transmit any diseases to humans. They can be incredibly abundant, especially in meadows, where hundreds of thousands can inhabit a single acre. Their hearty appetites help to control the insect population.

In addition to spiders, there are many other arachnids among us. Daddy-long-legs, also called harvestmen, are nonvenomous and have one body part and very long, fragile legs. They are normally solitary, but in winter they may be seen huddling together in masses. Windscorpions look like long, slender spiders with forward-projecting jaws. Ticks are parasites with little foreclaws that grasp on to passing animals; to feed, they bury their heads under the skin and draw blood.

Arachnids in buildings may be active all year; at high elevations they are active chiefly from April to October. The accounts below give typical lengths of females, not including legs; the rarely seen males are often much smaller.

WESTERN BLACK WIDOW
Latrodectus hesperus
ARACHNID CLASS
¾". Female black, glossy; abdomen bulbous, with red hourglass pattern below. Male and imm. appear paler, due to fine white, yellow, or red lines. Web irregular, with funnel-like exit. Nocturnal. **CAUTION** Poisonous (mainly female). **HABITAT** Woodpiles, debris, crawl spaces. **SEASON** Year-round.

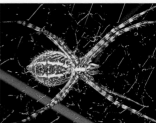

AMERICAN HOUSE SPIDER
Achaearanea tepidariorum
ARACHNID CLASS

¼". Body pale brown; abdomen large, mottled black and gray on sides. Male's legs orange; female's banded black and yellow. Builds irregular web in corners of ceilings and windows. **HABITAT** Buildings. **SEASON** Year-round.

BANDED GARDEN SPIDER
Argiope trifasciata
ARACHNID CLASS

¾". Head/thorax has silvery hair; abdomen yellow, with reddish markings. Legs spotted. Female waits for prey in center of large web; male builds small web in corner of female's. **HABITAT** Dry grasslands, meadows. **SEASON** Apr.–Sept.

BLACK-AND-YELLOW GARDEN SPIDER
Argiope aurantia
ARACHNID CLASS

1". Head/thorax has short silvery hair. Abdomen large, egg-shaped; black with bold yellow or orange markings. Legs long, hairy; banded yellow or reddish and black. Web large, with central thick vertical zigzag pattern; placed among plants in sunny, sheltered area. **HABITAT** Gardens, shrubby meadows. **SEASON** May–Sept.

GOLDENROD CRAB SPIDER
Misumena vatia
ARACHNID CLASS

⅜". Female yellow or white, with red streaks on abdomen. Male head/thorax and legs dark reddish brown; abdomen creamy white with red bands. Legs thick. Hides in flowers, snatching insects. Changes color over 5–7 days between yellow and white. **HABITAT** Gardens, meadows. **SEASON** Late Apr.–Sept.

STRIPED LYNX SPIDER
Oxyopes salticus
ARACHNID CLASS

⅓". Body light gray, with lengthwise dark stripes. Legs armed with conspicuous dark spines. Very active runner and jumper; does not spin web. **HABITAT** Sagebrush grasslands. **SEASON** Apr.–Sept.

WINDSCORPIONS
Eremobates species
ARACHNID CLASS
1¼". Head pointed; abdomen large, oval. Large appendages on head. Very fast runners; named for speed and resemblance to true scorpions. Nonvenomous. **HABITAT** Arid, non-urban areas. **SEASON** Apr.–Sept.

DADDY-LONG-LEGS
Phalangium and other genera
ARACHNID CLASS
¼". Body oval. Legs extremely long, thin; second pair longest, used as antennae. Most often seen singly, but sometimes massed together with legs intertwined. Nonvenomous. **HABITAT** Varied, from deserts to woodlands. **SEASON** Mar.–Oct.

ROCKY MOUNTAIN WOOD TICK
Dermacentor andersoni
ARACHNID CLASS
⅛". Female reddish brown with small white shield on back; male shield mottled gray, covers entire back. Waits on grasses for passing mammals. 3 meals in lifetime: first 2 on small mammals, last on large mammal (often a human). **CAUTION** Can transmit serious diseases: Rocky Mountain spotted fever, Colorado tick fever, tularemia, and tick paralysis. **HABITAT** Open, rocky and grassy areas. **SEASON** June–Sept.

Insects

Insects (class Insecta) bring out special feelings in people: They fascinate children with their forms and colors; they bewilder naturalists with their ecological intricacies; they cause rational adults to cringe at their mere presence. Their vast repertory of environmental adaptations is overwhelming, as are their sheer numbers and staying power. Try as we might (and we have tried mightily), we have not succeeded in exterminating any insect pests from the Rocky Mountain region. Perhaps instead we should spend more time observing their beauty and variety.

All insects have three main body parts—head, thorax, and abdomen—to which various other organs are attached. The head has a pair of antennae, which may be narrow, feathery, pointed, short, or long (sometimes much longer than the body). The eyes are compound and the mouthparts are adapted to chewing, biting, piercing, sucking, and/or licking. Insect wings (usually four) and legs (six) attach at the thorax. The abdomen, usually the largest section, houses the reproductive and other internal organs.

A remarkable aspect of insect life is the transformation from egg to adult, known as metamorphosis. In complete metamorphosis, which includes a pupal stage and is unique to insects, the adult females lay eggs from which the larvae are hatched. The larva feeds and grows, molting its skin several times, until it prepares for its immobile pupal state by hiding or camouflaging itself. Within the pupa, larval organs dissolve and adult organs develop. In incomplete metamorphosis, there is no pupal stage, and insects such as dragonflies, grasshoppers, and true bugs gradually develop from hatched nymphs into adults. The metamorphic timetable varies widely; some insects complete the transformation in a matter of days while others, such as cicadas, can take up to 17 years.

The importance of insects to the ecological health of the planet cannot be overstated. In the Rocky Mountains and other temperate regions, insects pollinate approximately 80 percent of the flowering plants. They are a vital link in every ecosystem.

This book introduces representative species or genera of insects from many orders in a sequence from primitive to more advanced. We have placed the large butterfly and moth section last, although traditionally these insects precede the ants, bees, and wasps. For many insects, there is no commonly accepted English name at the species level. We give orders for all members of the class Insecta, except for the familiar group of butterflies and moths, in which we give families. Descriptions and seasonal information refer to typical adult forms unless otherwise noted. Measurements indicate typical adult body lengths, except in the butterfly accounts, in which wingspan measurements are given.

WESTERN GREEN DRAKE
Drunella grandis
MAYFLY ORDER

nymph (left), adult (right)

¾″. Body dark green with fine yellow bands; 3 long tails; 4 transparent wings. Nymph aquatic; adult hatches during day. Most important western mayfly hatch for trout. **HABITAT** Fast mtn. streams. **SEASON** Early June–early July. **RANGE** ID and east to eastern slopes of Rockies.

Dragonflies

Dragonflies are large predatory insects, many of which specialize in killing mosquitoes. The order is 300 million years old and comprises two major groups—dragonflies and damselflies. Both have movable heads and large compound eyes that in dragonflies nearly cover the head and in damselflies bulge out from the sides. Their legs are attached to the thorax just behind their heads, a feature that makes walking all but impossible but greatly facilitates their ability to grasp and hold prey while tearing into it with sharp mouthparts. They have four powerful wings that move independently, allowing for both forward and backward flight. At rest, the wings are held horizontally by dragonflies and together over the top of the abdomen by damselflies. The wings have a noticeable, usually dark, stigma patch near the front outer edge. Nymphs, called naiads, live among the vegetation and muck in ponds and streams and feed on mosquito larvae, other insects, tadpoles, and small fish. Many of the Rocky Mountain region's colorful species have captured the interest of bird and butterfly enthusiasts. A few species are migratory, gathering in the fall for southbound flights. In the accounts that follow, all species not noted as damselflies are dragonflies. The size given for dragonflies is the typical adult body length (not the wingspan).

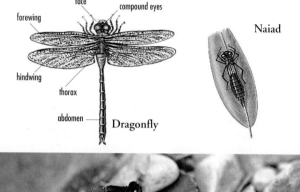

Dragonfly (labeled): face, compound eyes, forewing, hindwing, thorax, abdomen

Naiad

WESTERN RED DAMSEL
Amphiagrion abbreviatum
DRAGONFLY ORDER

1″. Damselfly. Male thorax black with reddish sides; abdomen shortish, stout, mostly red with black tip. Female dull reddish brown. Wings clear; extend almost to tip of abdomen. Perches low amid vegetation. **HABITAT** Marshy ponds, sloughs. **SEASON** May–Aug.

BOREAL BLUET
Enallagma boreale
DRAGONFLY ORDER

1¼″. Damselfly. Male brilliant blue, with black markings on head and abdomen. Female lighter, with more black on abdomen. Wings clear. **HABITAT** Ponds, lakes. **SEASON** May–Sept. **Northern Bluet** (*E. cyathigerum*) virtually identical.

EMERALD SPREADWING
Lestes dryas
DRAGONFLY ORDER

1½″. Damselfly. Body broad for a damselfly. Above bright metallic green; below and sides of thorax yellow to yellowish brown. Eyes blue. Wings clear. **HABITAT** Ponds, incl. temporary ponds. **SEASON** June–Aug.

WESTERN FORKTAIL
Ischnura perparva
DRAGONFLY ORDER

1″. Damselfly. Male head and thorax black with blue to blue-green markings; abdomen greenish with black markings above, blue tip. Female blue-violet above; thorax sides green; abdomen sides red-violet. Wings clear. **HABITAT** Ponds, lakes, slow streams. **SEASON** May–Oct.

PADDLE-TAILED DARNER
Aeshna palmata
DRAGONFLY ORDER

3″. Body large, dark. Male thorax with several greenish stripes; abdomen with many paired blue spots above. Female head and back of thorax green; abdomen with paired light green spots. Wings clear. **HABITAT** Ponds, lakes. **SEASON** July–Oct.

PALE SNAKETAIL
Ophiogomphus severus
DRAGONFLY ORDER

2″. Thorax green; head and abdomen greenish yellow, abdomen with extensive black markings, more on female. Abdomen tip swollen in characteristic "clubtail." Wings clear. **HABITAT** Sand and gravel banks of streams, rivers. **SEASON** May–Oct.

AMERICAN EMERALD
Cordulia shurtleffi
DRAGONFLY ORDER

2″. Head and thorax bright green. Abdomen unpatterned, dark bronze-green; swells significantly near tip. Wings clear. **HABITAT** Ponds, lakes. **SEASON** May–Aug.

MOUNTAIN EMERALD
Somatochlora semicircularis
DRAGONFLY ORDER

2″. Body blackish; thorax metallic green with 2 yellowish spots on sides; abdomen has yellowish markings at base. Wings clear. Hovers above sedges. **HABITAT** Marshy bogs, shallow mtn. ponds. **SEASON** June–Sept.

HUDSONIAN WHITEFACE
Leucorrhinia hudsonica
DRAGONFLY ORDER

1⅜". Male thorax mottled red and black; abdomen black with red spots above. Face white. Hindwings have small black area at base. **HABITAT** Marshy ponds. **SEASON** June–Sept.

FOUR-SPOTTED SKIMMER
Libellula quadrimaculata
DRAGONFLY ORDER

1¾". Body olive-brown with narrow yellow stripe along sides; base of head and thorax yellow. Wings clear with yellowish leading edge; 2 black spots on each. **HABITAT** Ponds, lakes. **SEASON** May–Sept.

BLACK MEADOWHAWK
Sympetrum danae
DRAGONFLY ORDER

1". Male thorax blackish with yellow lines on sides; abdomen black with several yellowish side spots; face greenish yellow. Female similar, but with more yellow on abdomen sides. Wings golden at base. **HABITAT** Marshy ponds. **SEASON** June–Oct.

WHITE-FACED MEADOWHAWK
Sympetrum obtrusum
DRAGONFLY ORDER

1⅜". Body red, with black triangular markings along abdomen sides. Face white. Wings clear, tinged orange at base. **HABITAT** Ponds, wet meadows. **SEASON** June–Oct.

ARID LAND SUBTERRANEAN TERMITE
Reticulitermes tibialis
TERMITE ORDER

¼". Worker yellowish white with darker abdomen; soldier has large yellow head, blackish mandibles. Builds tube-like underground nest of dirt and saliva. Common and very destructive; eats wood from inside out. **HABITAT** Humid areas, incl. buildings. **SEASON** Year-round.

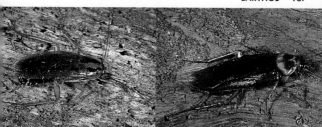

GERMAN COCKROACH
Blattella germanica
COCKROACH ORDER

¾". Body brown; 2 blackish stripes on pale yellow-brown shield behind head. With adhesive pads on pale legs, can climb vertical smooth glass. Introduced from Eurasia; common pest in cities; secreted liquid leaves unpleasant odor. HABITAT Buildings. SEASON Year-round.

AMERICAN COCKROACH
Periplaneta americana
COCKROACH ORDER

2". Body reddish brown; large, pale yellow head shield; antennae longer than body. Yellow stripe on front margin of forewings. A nonnative species, now living throughout N. Amer. HABITAT Municipal sewer systems, warm buildings. SEASON Year-round.

COMMON STONEFLIES
Acroneuria species
STONEFLY ORDER

1". Body long, slender; yellowish to brownish. Forewings with many cross veins, hindwings wide; wings held flat over abdomen at rest. Aquatic nymph (1") robust, with 2 tail-like appendages, long antennae. Adult does not feed. HABITAT Streams and nearby areas. SEASON Apr.–Sept.

CALIFORNIA GIANT STONEFLY
Pteronarcys californica
STONEFLY ORDER

1½". Body long, cylindrical; brownish gray, with red line across thorax; head blackish. Wings black-veined. Mostly nocturnal; crawls over rocks in streams; sometimes attracted to lights. Adult does not feed. HABITAT Fast-flowing mtn. streams. SEASON July–Aug.

EUROPEAN EARWIG
Forficula auricularia
EARWIG ORDER

½". Body slender, brownish to black; legs yellowish. Antennae bead-like. Pincers at abdomen tip curved (male) or straight (female). Female guards eggs, feeds young nymphs. HABITAT Decaying logs, leaf litter, trees, sheds. SEASON Apr.–Oct.

Grasshoppers and Kin

Members of the order Orthoptera are beloved for their musical abilities and despised for their voracious appetites. All species have mouthparts designed to bite and chew, and straight, membranous wings. Grasshoppers, locusts, and crickets have greatly developed hindlegs for jumping. Female grasshoppers and locusts have short ovipositors for digging, while crickets and katydids have long ovipositors, straight in crickets and sickle-shaped in katydids; they lay eggs in soil or tree vegetation. While no insects have true voices, orthopterans manage to make themselves heard in a variety of distinctive ways; most melodies are produced by males trying to attract mates. Crickets and katydids raise their wings and rub together specialized parts to produce their well-known calls. Most crickets are "right-winged," rubbing their right wings over their left, while katydids are "left-winged." Grasshoppers rub their hindlegs and wings together, and also make rattling, in-flight sounds by vibrating their forewings against their hindwings.

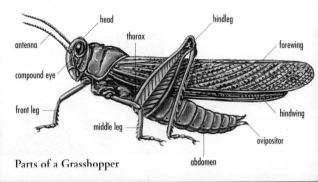

Parts of a Grasshopper

MORMON CRICKET
Anabrus simplex
GRASSHOPPER ORDER

1¾". A katydid. Body yellow-brown to blackish; large head shield, swordlike ovipositor. Antennae as long as body. Wings small, obscured by shield. Serious pest to crops; California Gull monument in Utah commemorates when cricket-hungry gulls saved the Mormons' crops in 1848. **HABITAT** Fields. **SEASON** Mainly June–Oct.

PALLID-WINGED GRASSHOPPER
Trimerotropis pallidipennis
GRASSHOPPER ORDER

1½". Body gray to brown, with dark camouflaging bands. Hindwings translucent pale yellow with dark edge; visible in flight. Several related "band-winged" grasshoppers have blue, red, yellow, or orange hindwings. **HABITAT** Varied, below 9,500'. **SEASON** June–Sept.

SPECKLED RANGELAND GRASSHOPPER
Arphia conspersa
GRASSHOPPER ORDER

1¼″. Forewings brownish gray. Body and most of hindwings variably colored; hindwings visible in flight. HABITAT Prairies, fields, croplands. SEASON Apr.–Oct.

TWO-STRIPED GRASSHOPPER
Melanoplus bivittatus
GRASSHOPPER ORDER

1¼″. Body olive to dark brown. Front of thorax and forewings with prominent light stripe on each side. Hindlegs with dark longitudinal stripes. Very destructive to crops. HABITAT Fields, croplands. SEASON June–Oct.

MIGRATORY GRASSHOPPER
Melanoplus sanguinipes
GRASSHOPPER ORDER

1¼″. Body mottled light brown to yellowish. Lower hindlegs red. Among the most destructive crop insects in U.S., although swarms not reported in recent decades; migratory swarm in 1870s thought to have included over 120 billion. HABITAT Fields, croplands. SEASON June–Oct.

AGILE GROUND MANTID
Litaneutria minor
MANTID ORDER

1⅛″. Body elongated; head mobile, triangular. Reddish or yellowish brown. Males have brown spot above. Forelegs spined, folded, used to grasp insects. Wings long. HABITAT Open areas. SEASON July–Oct.

COMMON WATER STRIDER
Gerris remigis
TRUE BUG ORDER

½″. Body slender, blackish with pale sides. Middle and hindlegs very long, slender, spider-like. Skates over water using surface tension; eats mosquito larvae and small insects. HABITAT Lakes, ponds. SEASON Mar.–Nov.

WATER BOATMEN
Corixa and other genera
TRUE BUG ORDER

⅜″. Body oval; dark brown to gray; often patterned above with fine lines. Middle and hindlegs elongated, used as paddles to swim on water's surface. Feeds on algae. Many similar species in several related genera. **HABITAT** Ponds, pools. **SEASON** Apr.–Nov.

ASSASSIN BUGS
Apiomerus species
TRUE BUG ORDER

¾″. Body hourglass-shaped; variably colored: red with dark markings or brown with yellowish markings. Head, thorax, and legs with short hairs. **HABITAT** Meadows, fields, gardens. **SEASON** May–Nov.

JAGGED AMBUSH BUG
Phymata erosa
TRUE BUG ORDER

½″. Body broad, angular; yellowish with black mottling above. Front legs short, wide, powerful; used to capture insects. Sits motionless on flowers; ambushes insects as large as bumble bees. **HABITAT** Meadows, gardens; common on goldenrods, thistles. **SEASON** July–Nov.

SMALL MILKWEED BUG
Lygaeus kalmii
TRUE BUG ORDER

½″. Body oval, black; red band behind head. Forewings have large bright red X. Toxic to predators. Lays eggs on milkweeds; adult and nymph incorporate plant's toxins and become unpalatable. **HABITAT** Meadows with milkweeds. **SEASON** Apr.–Oct.

SQUASH BUG
Anasa tristis
TRUE BUG ORDER

⅝″. Body hourglass-shaped; grayish brown, with orange edging on abdomen sides. Hindlegs cylindrical (flattened, leaf-like on related bugs). Serious pest of gourds, squashes, pumpkins, cucumbers. **HABITAT** Cultivated croplands. **SEASON** May–Oct.

HARLEQUIN BUG
Murgantia histrionica
TRUE BUG ORDER

¾″. Body shield-shaped, shiny; black with red-orange (and occ. whitish) markings. Nymph with orange or yellow markings at rear. Eggs resemble tiny barrels. Nymph and adult feed on mustards; damage crops. **HABITAT** Low-elev. weedy fields, open hillsides. **SEASON** Year-round. **RANGE** CO.

SAY'S STINK BUG
Chlorochroa sayi
TRUE BUG ORDER

¾″. Body shield-shaped, bright green; raised white dots on back, 3 white or orange spots on mid-back. Feeds on many plants, incl. alfalfa seeds; can be pest of cotton plants. **HABITAT** Fields, croplands. **SEASON** Mar.–Sept.

PUTNAM'S CICADA
Platypedia putnami
CICADA ORDER

1″. Body triangular, black. 2 orange lines: 1 behind head, 1 across body in front of wing base. 2 orange spots at abdomen base. Feeds on plant juices; imm. lives several years underground. Adult male produces loud whirring sound. **HABITAT** Woods. **SEASON** Mar.–July.

BUFFALO TREEHOPPERS
Stictocephala species
CICADA ORDER

⅜″. Body triangular-shaped, green to yellow-green. Well camouflaged; resembles thorn. Feeds on plant juices. Female lays eggs in tree slits, often killing twigs. Pest of many crops, incl. apple, cherry, alfalfa. **HABITAT** Meadows, fields, woods. **SEASON** June–Sept.

MEADOW SPITTLEBUG
Philaenus spumarius
CICADA ORDER

⅜″. Adult (froghopper) body long, pear-shaped; gray, green, yellow, or brown; spotted. Antennae and wings short. Hops about on leaves like a tiny frog. Nymph (spittlebug) oval, pale yellow; emits conspicuous bubbly protective froth. **HABITAT** Brushy meadows, roadsides. **SEASON** May–Sept. **RANGE** Great Plains.

SNOW SCORPIONFLIES
Boreus species
SCORPIONFLY ORDER

⅛". Body spindle-shaped, with greatly elongated face; dark. Female's ovipositor long. Wings tiny. Hops about on snow on warm winter days. A dozen western species. **HABITAT** On mosses in woodlands. **SEASON** Year-round (usu. noticed on snow).

SNAKEFLIES
Raphidia species
NERVEWING ORDER

½". Body elongated, dark brown. Long head and thorax give serpent-like appearance. Female ovipositor long, thin. Wings transparent with many dark veins. Voracious; eats destructive aphids, bark beetles, caterpillars. **HABITAT** Forests, orchards; larva lives under bark; occ. at high elevs. **SEASON** June–Aug.

ANTLION
Bracynemurus ferox
NERVEWING ORDER

1½". Adult body like a damselfly's, but softer; brownish gray to gray. Antennae long, clubbed. Wings heavily veined. Weak flier; sometimes attracted to lights. Larva, called doodlebug or antlion, lives in sandy areas, on or just below surface; preys on insects. **HABITAT** Woodland edges. **SEASON** June–Sept.

GREEN LACEWINGS
Chrysopa species
NERVEWING ORDER

½". Body elongated, pale green; head narrow; eyes large; antennae long. Wings clear, heavily veined, longer than body; fold together over back. Adult and larva eat aphids, mealybugs. Often attracted to lights. **HABITAT** Gardens, woodland edges. **SEASON** Apr.–Oct.

GREAT SILVER-STRIPED SEDGE
Hesperophylax designatus
CADDISFLY ORDER

¾". Body bright olive. Antennae and legs ginger. Wings light ginger, veined. Caddisfly larvae, called caseworms, live in underwater cases built from sand and vegetation, held together with silk. Trout feed on larvae and emerging adults. **HABITAT** Rivers, streams. **SEASON** July.

Beetles

There are more species of beetles (order Coleoptera) than any other group of animals on earth. Beetles' forewings are hardened dense sheaths known as elytra, which meet in a straight line down the back. Their hindwings underneath function as the organs of flight. Beetle legs and antennae vary from long and straight to stout and angled. Both adults and larvae, known as grubs, have mouthparts adapted for biting and chewing. They are vegetarians, predators, scavengers, and in a few instances parasites. Some, like lady beetles, are highly prized by gardeners because they eat aphids and other garden pests, while others are nuisances at best. They range in size from microscopic organisms to some of the largest insects in the world.

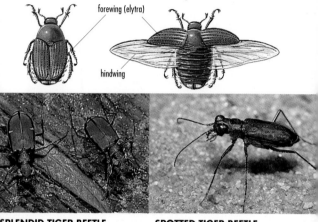

forewing (elytra)

hindwing

SPLENDID TIGER BEETLE
Cicindela splendida
BEETLE ORDER
½″. Body an elongated oval, with large head, large, sharp jaws; coppery red or bright green. Forewings have metallic blue-green markings along margins. **HABITAT** Sandy areas, esp. in coniferous forests. **CAUTION** Bites if handled. **SEASON** May–Sept. **RANGE** WY, CO.

SPOTTED TIGER BEETLE
Cicindela punctulata
BEETLE ORDER
½″. Head large, forewings widen toward rear; bronzy. Forewings pitted, lighter along edges, with a few light spots, small green or copper-colored dots. Fast, wary predator; runs or flies after prey, then tears it to pieces. **CAUTION** Bites if handled. **HABITAT** Sandy areas. **SEASON** June–Sept.

**BOAT-BACKED
GROUND BEETLES**
Scaphinotus species
BEETLE ORDER
⅝″. Body long, narrow; black to deep violet. Head elongated, with slender mandibles, long antennae. Feeds on snails. **HABITAT** Moist woods. **SEASON** May–Sept.

LARGE DIVING BEETLES
Dytiscus species
BEETLE ORDER

1¼". Body oval, smooth, hard; blackish with yellow along margins; hindlegs flattened, fringed; used as paddles to pursue tadpoles, insects, small fishes. Antennae long, slender. Sometimes comes to lights. HABITAT Quiet streams, ponds. SEASON Adult: May–Nov.; larva: summer.

WHIRLIGIG BEETLES
Gyrinus and *Dineutus* species
BEETLE ORDER

⅛–⅝". Body oval, flattened; shiny black. Hindlegs paddle-shaped. Swims in circles on water's surface. Feeds on aquatic insects and insects that fall into water. HABITAT Ponds, slow-moving streams. SEASON Apr.–Oct.

GIANT BLACK WATER BEETLE
Hydrophilus species
BEETLE ORDER

1½". Body oval, convex above, keeled below; shiny black. Hindlegs flattened, hairy. Antennae short, clubbed. Adult and larva feed on dead and living animals. Adult may leave water at night; attracted to lights. HABITAT Stream pools, lake shallows. SEASON May–Oct.

HAIRY ROVE BEETLE
Creophilus maxillosus
BEETLE ORDER

⅝". Body elongated, shiny black. Forewings short, extend to middle of body. Wings and several abdominal segments have yellow bands. Feeds on dead animals; appears at first sign of decay. HABITAT On dead animals. SEASON Apr.–Oct.

MARGINED BURYING BEETLE
Nicrophorus marginatus
BEETLE ORDER

1". Body cylindrical; shiny black, with several prominent orange patches on forewings. Antennae clubbed. Lives and lays eggs on carrion, burying it for larvae to hatch and feed on. Often found on dead snakes. HABITAT On dead animals. SEASON Mar.–Oct.

MAY BEETLES
"June Bugs"
Phyllophaga species
BEETLE ORDER

1″. Body tan to chestnut brown. Forewings smooth; hindwings well developed. Antennae with finger-like, angled club. Attracted to lights; slow, noisy, buzzing flight. May defoliate trees. Larva (white grub) lives in soil. **HABITAT** Broadleaf woods, fields. **SEASON** Apr.–Aug.

TEN-LINED JUNE BEETLE
Polyphylla decemlineata
BEETLE ORDER

1¼″. Body oval; brownish with white stripes on head, thorax, and forewings; each wing has 1 short and 4 long stripes. Eats conifer needles. Larva white, eats shrub and tree roots; serious pest in nurseries. Adults attracted to lights. **HABITAT** Woodlands. **SEASON** May–Sept.

CLICK BEETLES
Ctenicera species
BEETLE ORDER

2″. Body dark brown to black; often with dark thorax shield. Forewings often orange-brown, banded, with 2 dark spots. If overturned, uses lobe on underside of thorax to snap itself upright with audible click. Larva (wireworm) feeds on roots. **HABITAT** Decaying trees. Sometimes in high elevs. **SEASON** May–July.

CONVERGENT LADY BEETLE
Hippodamia convergens
BEETLE ORDER

¼″. Body oval. Thorax has converging white stripes. Forewings reddish orange with many black spots. Adult and larva eat aphids, soft-bodied insects. In fall, large masses migrate to overwinter under leaves in mtn. canyons. **HABITAT** Gardens, meadows, woodlands. **SEASON** Mar.–Oct.

DARKLING GROUND BEETLES
"Circus Beetles"
Eleodes species
BEETLE ORDER

¾″. Body oval, shiny; black, sometimes with reddish above. Forewings fused; flightless. Runs with body raised 45 degrees, as if standing on its head; sprays foul-smelling secretion if disturbed. Mainly nocturnal. **HABITAT** High plains, deserts. **SEASON** Apr.–Sept.

CALIFORNIA PRIONUS
Prionus californicus
BEETLE ORDER

2″. Body elongated; dark brownish black. Thorax has 3 large spines on each side. Antennae long, segmented; legs long. Nocturnal; crashes against lighted windows. Larva in burrow whitish; eats dead wood. **HABITAT** Coniferous forests. **SEASON** July–Aug.

WESTERN MILKWEED LONGHORN BEETLE
Tetraopes femoratus
BEETLE ORDER

½″. Body cylindrical; above red with black dots, below black. 4 eyes. Antennae long, blackish with thin gray bands. Adult and larva eat milkweeds (and are tolerant of its poison); poisonous to birds. **HABITAT** On or near milkweeds. **SEASON** Summer.

SPOTTED BLISTER BEETLES
Epicauta species
BEETLE ORDER

⅜″. Body elongated, oval, with wide head. Forewings gray with black spots. Abundant at a given site for a day or two, then disappears. Adult eats many vegetables and flowers; larva eats grasshopper eggs. **CAUTION** When disturbed, secretes blood that causes blisters. **HABITAT** Agricultural fields, gardens. **SEASON** June–Sept.

LONG-HORNED PINE SAWYERS
Monochamus species
BEETLE ORDER

¾″. Body cylindrical; black or dark gray, often with glossy sheen above. Male's antennae very long, twice body length; female's shorter. Adult feeds on needles and bark of burned or recently felled conifers. **HABITAT** Coniferous woodlands. **SEASON** July–Sept.

COLORADO POTATO BEETLE
Leptinotarsa decemlineata
BEETLE ORDER

⅜″. Body oval. Head and thorax orange, with numerous black spots. Forewings striped black and yellowish white. Larva red to orange, with black head and spotted sides. Formerly confined to CO, but spread throughout N. Amer. with introduction of potato. **HABITAT** Potato fields, meadows. **SEASON** Apr.–Sept.

ROSE WEEVIL
Rhynchites bicolor
BEETLE ORDER

¼". Body stout, curved, with elongated snout. Thorax and forewings red; rest of body black. Eats rose hips, buds, and pith of canes (stems). **HABITAT** Fields, gardens. **SEASON** May–Sept.

Flies and Mosquitoes

Flies and mosquitoes, some of humankind's least favorite insects, nonetheless belong to an important and interesting order, worthy of a second glance. All species in the order have two wings, and their mouthparts are formed for sucking, or piercing and sucking combined. The larvae, which are legless and wingless, undergo complete metamorphosis. Some species have terrestrial larvae, called maggots, which are almost always whitish or grayish in color. Other species lay eggs in water and have aquatic larvae, which have various names; those of mosquitoes are called wrigglers. Adults of this order beat their wings extremely rapidly in flight. Their wingbeat frequency is usually in the range of 100 to 300 beats per second, but in tiny species can be even higher. It is this incredible speed that produces the familiar (and often annoying) in-flight buzzing sound. Flies feed on decomposing matter, nectar, other insects, and in the case of biting flies, blood. Male mosquitoes feed on plant juices, while females drink the blood of animals, including humans. Their lower lips form an organ called a proboscis with six knife-sharp parts, some smooth and some saw-toothed, that cut into skin.

CRANE FLIES
Tipula species
FLY ORDER

½–2½". Body narrow, delicate, gray to gold; legs long, slender, fragile. Antennae long. Wings clear to spotted, often veined; held at 60-degree angle from body. Often mistaken for giant mosquito, but does not bite. **HABITAT** Damp areas; may enter houses. **SEASON** May–Sept.

MOSQUITOES
Aedes and other genera
FLY ORDER

½". Body black, brown, or striped. Male's antennae feathery, female's thread-like. Wings narrow, scaly; banded, black, or clear. Sharp proboscis; female sucks blood; male and female drink nectar. **CAUTION** Bites. **HABITAT** Woodlands, towns, watersides. **SEASON** Apr.–Sept.

BLACK FLIES
Simulium species
FLY ORDER

⅛". Body humpbacked, with head pointed down; black. Wings clear. Larvae pupate in cocoons that coat rocks in streams. **CAUTION** Bites; female sucks blood; not known to transmit diseases to humans in N. Amer. **HABITAT** Woodlands, watersides. **SEASON** Apr.–July.

DEER FLIES
Chrysops species
FLY ORDER

½". Body somewhat flattened; yellow and black to dull gray-brown or black. Wings have brownish-black patches. **CAUTION** Often buzzes around head, giving nasty bite upon landing. **HABITAT** Woodlands, roadsides near water. **SEASON** May–Sept.

BIG BLACK HORSE FLY
Tabanus punctifer
FLY ORDER

⅞". Body large, black; thorax, above, edged with pale hairs. Wings dark at base, paler at tip. Male's eyes large, contiguous. Male drinks nectar; female sucks blood, esp. of livestock. **CAUTION** Gives painful bite. **HABITAT** Marshy ponds, streamsides; occ. at high elevs. **SEASON** June–Aug.

GIANT ROBBER FLIES
Proctacanthus species
FLY ORDER

1". Thorax bulging; abdomen long, tapering. Brownish gray, with many bristly spines on body and legs. Distinct, bristly "mustache." Effective predator; snatches insects from ground and vegetation. **HABITAT** Meadows, fields. **SEASON** July–Aug.

AMERICAN HOVER FLY
Eupeodes americanus
FLY ORDER

⅜". Body stout; black to metallic green; abdomen has 3 yellow crossbands. Wings clear. Coloring mimics a bee's, but hover flies do not sting or bite. Hovers above flowers; drinks nectar. Larva eats aphids. **HABITAT** Fields, open woods. **SEASON** June–Aug.

HOUSE FLY
Musca domestica
FLY ORDER
¼". Body gray with dark stripes. Wings clear. Eyes large, red-brown; legs hairy. Egg hatches in 10–24 hours; matures to adult in 10 days; male lives 15 days, female 26. Sucks liquid sugars from garbage; spreads disease. **HABITAT** Buildings, farms. **SEASON** Mainly May–Oct.

Ants, Wasps, and Bees

The insects of the order Hymenoptera include narrow-waisted bees, wasps, and ants. Hymenopterans have two pairs of membranous, transparent wings, mouthparts modified to chew and lick, and in adult females, an ovipositor. All species of ants, bees, and wasps undergo complete metamorphosis.

The narrow-waists are divided into two broad groupings. The first, parasitic wasps, includes the large and varied assemblage of nonstinging ichneumon wasps, which live as parasites during their larval stage. Some ichneumons are greatly feared by humans for their astonishingly long ovipositors, which in fact are used not for stinging but to probe about in woody vegetation for suitable insects on which to lay eggs. The second group of narrow-waists are stinging insects, with ovipositors that have been modified into stinging organs. These include vespid wasps (such as hornets and yellow jackets), bees, and many ants.

Paper Wasp nest

Ants and some wasps and bees are highly social creatures, while other species in this order live solitary lives. Their nests vary in complexity from a single-celled hole in the ground to the Honey Bee's elaborate comb structure. Many ant species excavate in soil or wood, building multichambered homes mostly hidden from sight. Yellow jackets and some hornets build similar homes. Unlike ants, though, they build a separate six-sided chamber for each of their young, made of a papery material that consists of wood or bark and adult saliva. Bald-faced Hornets often construct their nests in open situations, while Honey Bees utilize man-made hives or hollow trees or logs. The Honey Bees' two-sided, vertically hanging beeswax combs can contain more than 50,000 cells.

Bees and flowering plants have developed a great many interdependencies over the eons as they have evolved together. We would lose many of our flowers and fruits were we to let our bees be poisoned out of existence. We would also lose some of the greatest known examples of animal industry.

The following species accounts give typical body lengths of the commonly seen workers; queens are generally larger.

CARPENTER ANTS
Camponotus species
ANT, WASP, AND BEE ORDER

⅜″. Body large; reddish to black. Antennae elbowed. Tunnels into soft wood to make nest, but does not eat it; causes structural damage to buildings. **CAUTION** Bites. **HABITAT** Forests, in trees, logs; wooden structures. **SEASON** Apr.–Nov.

WESTERN THATCHING ANT
Formica obscuripes
ANT, WASP, AND BEE ORDER

⅛–½″. Head and thorax rusty red; abdomen and legs blackish brown. Builds dome-like nest mound, decorating entrance with grass and twigs. Eats larvae, flower nectar, aphid honeydew (a sugar-rich secretion). Tends herds of aphids; enslaves larvae of other *Formica* species. **CAUTION** Bites. **HABITAT** Open woodlands. **SEASON** Spring–fall.

HARVESTER ANTS
Pogonomyrmex species
ANT, WASP, AND BEE ORDER

⅜″. Body reddish brown. Head and thorax hairy; abdomen shiny. Builds underground nests with gravel mound near entrance. Clears vegetation around burrow; multiple colonies can cause extensive defoliation. **CAUTION** Bites and stings. **HABITAT** Plains, grasslands. **SEASON** Apr.–Sept.

PAPER WASPS
Polistes species
ANT, WASP, AND BEE ORDER

¾″. Body slender, with narrow waist; reddish brown to black, with narrow yellow bands; face pointed. Wings translucent smoky brown. Builds gray, papery nest under eaves and overhangs. Adult feeds on nectar and fruit juices; chews insects for larva. **CAUTION** Stings, but usu. not aggressive. **HABITAT** Gardens, meadows. **SEASON** Apr.–Sept.

WESTERN YELLOW JACKET
Vespula pensylvanica
ANT, WASP, AND BEE ORDER

⅝″. Body stout, yellow, with heavy black bands and spots. Antennae long, curving. Wings clear. Aggressively defends nests in burrows, logs. Raids picnic food, trash cans. **CAUTION** Stings. **HABITAT** Open areas. **SEASON** Apr.–Oct.; large colonies in late summer.

BALD-FACED HORNET
Vespula maculata
ANT, WASP, AND BEE ORDER

¾″. Body stout, black. Yellowish-white spots on head, thorax, and abdomen tip. Builds football-size paper nest under branch or overhang. CAUTION Stings nest visitors. HABITAT Woodland edges, meadows, gardens. SEASON May–Sept.

BLACK-AND-YELLOW MUD DAUBER
Sceliphron caementarium
ANT, WASP, AND BEE ORDER

1″. Body slim, with long waist; black with yellow markings; legs mostly yellow. Wings dark. Feeds on flower nectar. Constructs tubular mud nests on cliffs, overhangs, walls; puts paralyzed spider into each cell to feed young. HABITAT Buildings, cliffs, rock faces. SEASON May–Aug.

HONEY BEE
Apis mellifera
ANT, WASP, AND BEE ORDER

½″. Body rounded. Thorax hairy, brown; abdomen banded black and golden. Wings dusky. Makes honey; pollinates crops; nests in tree holes. Introduced from Eurasia. CAUTION Stings, but is not aggressive; if stung, remove stinger immediately. HABITAT Fields, orchards. SEASON Apr.–Oct.

BUMBLE BEE
Bombus appositus
ANT, WASP, AND BEE ORDER

⅝″. Body stout, hairy, black. Hair dense, mostly yellow on head and thorax, with rusty tinge and dark bands on abdomen. CAUTION Stings, but is not aggressive. HABITAT Meadows, woodland clearings. SEASON May–Sept.

Butterflies and Moths

The order Lepidoptera comprises the familiar groups of moths and butterflies. *Lepidoptera* means "scale-winged" and refers to the minute scales that cover the four wings of all butterfly and moth species. All lepidopterans share the same generalized life cycle—egg to larva to pupa to adult. Eggs are laid singly, or in rows, stacks, or masses, depending on the species. The emergent larva, usually referred to as a caterpillar, feeds on plant life and grows through several stages, or instars, shedding its skin each time. When fully grown, the caterpillar prepares to pupate by spinning a silken co-

coon (moth) or finding a secure hiding place (butterfly). Then the caterpillar sheds its last larval skin, revealing the pupa, an outer shell with no head or feet within which the wings and other adult features fully develop. Finally, the pupal skin breaks open and the winged moth or butterfly emerges. The time required for this process is different for each species. Many have only one emergence of adults per year; others have two or three. Because of the significant variations in elevation and latitude within the region, a species' emergence is frequently staggered—earlier at southern and lowland locales and later in more northern and mountainous areas. Most Rocky Mountain lepidopterans live out their entire lives within the region, although a few species, such as the world-famous Monarch, migrate to

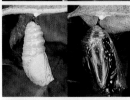

Metamorphosis of a Monarch

warmer regions in the fall. The thousands that stay behind survive the winter as eggs, larvae, or pupae, although a few overwinter as adults.

Several key differences distinguish moths and butterflies. Moths' antennae are either feather-like or wiry and lack the clubbed tips of butterflies' antennae. Moths rest with their wings outstretched or at an angle above the body; butterflies rest with their wings outstretched or held together vertically, like a sail. Moths can fly day and night, while butterflies fly only by day. Color and size are poor general distinguishing features between the two groups.

When trying to identify a species, pay special attention to the wing colors, shape, and pattern. Most of the characteristic wing markings on moths are found on the uppersides. In butterflies, look at the uppersides of those species that rest with outstretched wings and on the undersides of those that rest with their wings folded up.

Butterflies drink nectar from many species of wildflowers and shrubs. Among the best wild nectar plants in the Rocky Mountain states are locoweeds, daisies, groundsels, penstemons, lupines, eriogonums, Gayfeather, Golden Banner, and Orange Sneezeweed. Excellent garden flowers that attract butterflies and moths include milkweeds, asters, coneflowers, zinnias, geraniums, lavenders, mints, and Butterfly Bush. Nocturnal moths are also drawn to lights.

Each caterpillar species has its own select food plants, and the accounts that follow list many of these. Measurements are of typical wingspans for adult forms, from tip to tip.

PHOEBUS PARNASSIAN
Parnassius phoebus
SWALLOWTAIL FAMILY

2¾". Translucent chalky white above and below; forewings have 1 red, 2 black short bars in front, dark wing margins; hindwings have red spots. Caterpillar black with rows of yellow spots. **HABITAT** Meadows, tundra, forest edges. **FOOD PLANTS** Sedums. **SEASON** Late May–Sept. **RANGE** Entire region, ex. e WY, e CO.

ANISE SWALLOWTAIL
Papilio zelicaon
SWALLOWTAIL FAMILY

2¾". Black above and below, with broad yellow band on each wing; hindwings have small blue spots, orange eyespot, tail. Caterpillar green with yellow-spotted black bands. **HABITAT** Mtn. meadows and valleys. **FOOD PLANTS** Carrot family. **SEASON** Apr.–July.

INDRA SWALLOWTAIL
Papilio indra
SWALLOWTAIL FAMILY

2¾". Mostly black above and below, with 2 narrow bands of creamy spots; hindwings have row of blue spots, orange eyespot, very short tail. Caterpillar banded yellow and black, with orange spots. **HABITAT** Canyons, arid mtn. slopes. **FOOD PLANTS** Carrot family. **SEASON** May–early July. **RANGE** Entire region, ex. e CO, ne MT.

WESTERN TIGER SWALLOWTAIL
Papilio rutulus
SWALLOWTAIL FAMILY

3½". Bright yellow above, with black "tiger" stripes and black, yellow-spotted margins; hindwings have several blue and 2 orange spots near long tail. Paler yellow below; hindwings have blue line near outer margin. Caterpillar green with 2 large yellow eyespots. **HABITAT** Meadows, moist canyons, parks. **FOOD PLANTS** Willows, poplars, cherries, ashes, aspens. **SEASON** June–July.

TWO-TAILED SWALLOWTAIL
Papilio multicaudata
SWALLOWTAIL FAMILY

4¼". Very large. Yellow above, with black borders; forewings have 4 narrow black stripes; hindwings have 1 narrow black stripe, blue spots near rear edge; 2 distinct tails. Below, bright yellow with narrow black stripes. **HABITAT** Canyons, gardens. **FOOD PLANTS** Cherries, plums, ashes. **SEASON** May–July, Aug. (2 broods).

PALE SWALLOWTAIL
Papilio eurymedon
SWALLOWTAIL FAMILY

3½". Creamy white above, with black stripes, broad black borders, long tail. Below paler, with distinct black veins. Frequents hilltops to mate. Caterpillar pale green with yellow and black eyespots. **HABITAT** Moist canyons, hilltops. **FOOD PLANTS** Rose and buckthorn families. **SEASON** May–July. **RANGE** Entire region, ex. e CO, ne MT.

PINE WHITE
Neophasia menapia
WHITE AND SULPHUR FAMILY

2". White above, with black markings at tip and leading edge of forewings; female hindwings have black lines near outer margin. Below, hindwings veined with narrow (male) or broad (female) dark lines; female's outlined with orange. **HABITAT** Pine forests. **FOOD PLANTS** Pines. **SEASON** July–Sept. **RANGE** Entire region, ex. e CO, ne MT.

WESTERN WHITE
Pontia occidentalis
WHITE AND SULPHUR FAMILY

1⅜". Male white above, with scattered grayish checkering, more obvious near forewing tip; female spots extend onto hindwings. Below, hindwings veined with greenish lines. Caterpillar light green with fine bands. **HABITAT** Meadows, mountaintops. **FOOD PLANTS** Mustard family. **SEASON** Apr.–Oct.

MUSTARD WHITE
Pieris napi
WHITE AND SULPHUR FAMILY

1⅝". Nearly pure white above; forewing tips with some dark dusting; with or without black spots (male 1, female 2). Below, creamy to yellowish white, veined. **HABITAT** Moist forest clearings. **FOOD PLANTS** Mustard family. **SEASON** June–Aug. **RANGE** Entire region, ex. e CO, ne MT.

CABBAGE WHITE
Pieris rapae
WHITE AND SULPHUR FAMILY

1⅝". White above; forewings have slaty tip, 1 black spot (male) or 2 (female). Yellowish white below. Introduced from Europe; common. Caterpillar green with yellow stripes; feeds heavily on commercial crops. **HABITAT** Fields, gardens. **FOOD PLANTS** Mustard family. **SEASON** Mar.–Oct.

LARGE MARBLE
Euchloe ausonides
WHITE AND SULPHUR FAMILY

1¾". Creamy white above; forewings have black markings near tip, black patch along leading edge. Below, hindwings white with golden veins and extensive green marbling. **HABITAT** Open woodlands, meadows, forest trails. **FOOD PLANTS** Mustard family. **SEASON** May–Sept.; most common early in season. **RANGE** Entire region, ex. e CO.

SARA ORANGETIP
Anthocharis sara
WHITE AND SULPHUR FAMILY

1¼". White above (female sometimes yellow); forewings have bright orange tip. Below, hindwings have dark gray marbling; forewing tip paler orange. Flies very low among vegetation; unmistakable. **HABITAT** Open slopes, streamsides, meadows. **FOOD PLANTS** Mustard family. **SEASON** Mar.–Aug. **RANGE** Rockies and west.

CLOUDED SULPHUR
Colias philodice
WHITE AND SULPHUR FAMILY

1⅝". Lemon yellow above, with prominent blackish borders (solid in males, yellow-spotted in females), brownish spots near margins; female sometimes white. Below, yellow to greenish yellow; silvery spot in center of hindwings. **HABITAT** Open areas, mud puddles. **FOOD PLANTS** Pea family, esp. White Clover. **SEASON** Apr.–Oct.

RUDDY COPPER
Lycaena rubidus
GOSSAMER-WING FAMILY

1¼". Male bright red-orange above, with narrow white fringe; female dull yellow with small black spots, brownish shading. Below, both sexes pale yellow or white; forewings have black spots. **HABITAT** Open dry meadows, shrub lands, esp. with Shrubby Cinquefoil. **FOOD PLANTS** Docks, Wild Rhubarb. **SEASON** May–Aug.

BLUE COPPER
Lycaena heteronea
GOSSAMER-WING FAMILY

1¼". Above, male blue with black veins and borders; female gray-blue to gray with dark spots. Below, both sexes silvery white; forewings spotted; hindwings clear or spotted. **HABITAT** Sagebrush grasslands, canyons. **FOOD PLANTS** Wild Buckwheat. **SEASON** July–Aug. **RANGE** Entire region, ex. e CO, ne MT.

PURPLISH COPPER
Lycaena helloides
GOSSAMER-WING FAMILY

1¼". Coppery above (male has purplish wash), with black spots, brown outer margins; hindwings have wavy orange line (aurora) at rear. Below, forewings ocher, black-spotted; hindwings with scalloped red submarginal band. **HABITAT** Roadsides, meadows in prairies and foothills. **FOOD PLANTS** Knotweeds, docks, Sheep Sorrel. **SEASON** Apr.–Oct.

COLORADO HAIRSTREAK
Hypaurotis crysalus
GOSSAMER-WING FAMILY

1½". Unmistakable hairstreak. Purple above; wide black margins with few orange spots; prominent tail. Below, light gray-brown, with white-edged dark band; hindwings have blue shading along outer edge, black-centered orange spot. **HABITAT** Mtn. canyons and foothills. **FOOD PLANTS** Gambel's Oak. **SEASON** July–early Sept. **RANGE** s CO.

CORAL HAIRSTREAK
Satyrium titus
GOSSAMER-WING FAMILY

1¼". Brown above; tail-less. Below, paler brown, with row of black spots; hindwings have row of bright coral spots along rear border. **HABITAT** Permanent waterways, canyons. **FOOD PLANTS** Buds and young fruits of cherry and plum trees. **SEASON** July–Aug.

STRIPED HAIRSTREAK
Satyrium liparops
GOSSAMER-WING FAMILY

1¼". Dark brown above; 2 tails. Below, lighter brown with short, disjointed, black-edged white bands; hindwings have some orange marks, orange-capped blue spot. **HABITAT** Deciduous riparian woodlands. **FOOD PLANTS** Rose family, esp. Chokecherry, plum trees. **SEASON** July–early Aug. **RANGE** e MT south to CO.

HEDGEROW HAIRSTREAK
Satyrium saepium
GOSSAMER-WING FAMILY

1". Bright rusty brown above; very short tail (slightly longer on female). Below, dull brown with 1 faint, black, white-edged postmedian line; hindwings have small gray patch, 1 or 2 black crescents, black spot near tail. **HABITAT** Open pine forests. **FOOD PLANTS** *Ceanothus* species. **SEASON** July–Aug. **RANGE** ID to c CO.

BRAMBLE HAIRSTREAK
Callophrys dumetorum
GOSSAMER-WING FAMILY

1″. Male dark brown above; female reddish brown. Below, hindwings yellow-green to grass-green; forewings tan-brown with green at tip and base. **HABITAT** Foothills with permanent water, sagebrush grasslands. **FOOD PLANTS** Sulphur Flower. **SEASON** Mar.–July. **RANGE** Entire region, ex. e CO, e MT.

SHERIDAN'S HAIRSTREAK
Callophrys sheridani
GOSSAMER-WING FAMILY

⅞″. Plain gray above; tail-less. Below, blue-green, crossed by prominent white line edged with black. One of the earliest nonhibernating butterflies to appear. **HABITAT** Hillsides, canyons, plateaus. **FOOD PLANTS** Sulphur Flower. **SEASON** Mar.–early June. **RANGE** ID to c CO.

WESTERN PINE ELFIN
Callophrys eryphon
GOSSAMER-WING FAMILY

1″. Dark brown and unpatterned above. Below, checkered, mottled pattern of dark, medium, and light brown lines; fine white meandering line across midwing. **HABITAT** Open pine forests. **FOOD PLANTS** Lodgepole and Ponderosa Pines. **SEASON** May–June. **RANGE** Entire region, ex. e CO, ne MT.

JUNIPER HAIRSTREAK
Callophrys gryneus
GOSSAMER-WING FAMILY

1″. Brown above, with rusty wash near hindwing tails and scattered over forewings; 2 tails. Below, green crossed by prominent white line; forewings have rusty patch; hindwings have black-spotted gray-violet patch. **HABITAT** Mtn. foothills, high-elev. plains. **FOOD PLANTS** Junipers. **SEASON** May–July; in s CO: Mar.–May, July–Aug.

WESTERN TAILED-BLUE
Everes amyntula
GOSSAMER-WING FAMILY

1″. Pale blue above (female more brown), with narrow dark margins. Whitish below, with thin dark lines and spots; hindwings have orange spot over small thin tail. Low-flying. **HABITAT** Streamsides, mtn. meadows. **FOOD PLANTS** Pea family. **SEASON** Apr.–June; also Aug. in south. **RANGE** Entire region, ex. e CO, e MT.

SPRING AZURE
Celastrina ladon
GOSSAMER-WING FAMILY

1". Pale blue above; female with wide blackish borders. Below, grayish white with variable amounts of dark spots. Similar forms (later generation or different species) fly into Sept. **HABITAT** Valleys and canyons with permanent water. **FOOD PLANTS** Many, incl. Snowbrush, Cliffbush, Wild Cherry. **SEASON** Apr.–June.

ARROWHEAD BLUE
Glaucopsyche piasus
GOSSAMER-WING FAMILY

1⅛". Dark blue above, with diffuse brownish margins (very wide on female). Below, brownish gray with white-ringed black spots; whitish arrowhead marks near base of hindwings; checkered wing edges. **HABITAT** Canyons, high-elev. prairies. **FOOD PLANTS** Pea family, esp. lupines. **SEASON** May–July. **RANGE** Entire region, ex. e CO, e MT.

SILVERY BLUE
Glaucopsyche lygdamus
GOSSAMER-WING FAMILY

1¼". Brilliant silvery blue above (female darker), with blackish borders. Below, brownish gray with white-ringed black dots near margins. First blue to appear in spring. **HABITAT** Valleys, canyons, high-elev. prairies. **FOOD PLANTS** Pea family, esp. lupines. **SEASON** Mar.–July (varies with elev.).

MELISSA BLUE
Lycaeides melissa
GOSSAMER-WING FAMILY

1". Above, male blue with black and white margins; female gray-brown (occ. with blue scaling), with orange bands at edges. Below, both sexes whitish to light brown with white-ringed black spots; orange spots form band near margins. **HABITAT** Open areas. **FOOD PLANTS** Lupines, vetches, locoweeds. **SEASON** Apr.–Oct.

BOISDUVAL'S BLUE
Plebejus icarioides
GOSSAMER-WING FAMILY

1¼". Largest N. Amer. blue. Above, male blue with black borders; female brownish, occ. with blue at base. Below, light gray with white-ringed black spots. **HABITAT** Woodland openings, meadows. **FOOD PLANTS** Lupines. **SEASON** May–July; in e CO prairies: Aug.–Sept. **RANGE** Entire region, ex. ne MT.

ACMON BLUE
Plebejus acmon
GOSSAMER-WING FAMILY

⅞″. Above, male lilac blue, with thin black and white margins, black-spotted orange trailing edge; female duller, with wider orange trailing edge. Below, white with black spots; hindwings have red-orange crescents along rear edge. **HABITAT** Prairies, open areas in mtns. **FOOD PLANTS** Pea family, buckwheats. **SEASON** Mtns.: May–July; prairies: July–Sept.

GREAT SPANGLED FRITILLARY
Speyeria cybele
BRUSHFOOT FAMILY

2½″. Male orange above, brownish near body, with black dots and crescents; female straw-colored, with blackish base to wings. Below, shades of brown; hindwings reddish brown, with many silvery-white spots, wide creamy band. **HABITAT** Moist broadleaf woodlands, meadows. **FOOD PLANTS** Violets. **SEASON** June–Sept.

NORTHERN CHECKERSPOT
Chlosyne palla
BRUSHFOOT FAMILY

1½″. Above, male orange-red with black lines, checks; female blackish with whitish spots, orange-spotted margins. Below, forewings orange; hindwings orange-red with bands of creamy spots. **HABITAT** Grassy openings, foothill canyons, sagebrush grasslands. **FOOD PLANTS** Aster family, paintbrushes. **SEASON** June–July. **RANGE** South to c and w CO.

HYDASPE FRITILLARY
Speyeria hydaspe
BRUSHFOOT FAMILY

2¼″. Orange-brown above, with black spots and bars. Below, darker orange; hindwings maroon in center, with purplish wash, large black-ringed cream spots. **HABITAT** Moist mtn. meadows, roadsides; esp. near aspens. **FOOD PLANTS** Violets. **SEASON** July–Aug. **RANGE** Mainly north of CO.

CALLIPPE FRITILLARY
Speyeria callippe
BRUSHFOOT FAMILY

2⅛″. Orange above, with short black lines and spots. Below, hindwings have large silvery spots, greenish base, diffuse cream-colored band at outer margin. One of the earliest large fritillaries. **HABITAT** Hills, canyons, sagebrush grasslands. **FOOD PLANTS** Violets. **SEASON** June–Aug. **RANGE** Entire region, ex. e CO.

FIELD CRESCENT
Phyciodes campestris
BRUSHFOOT FAMILY

1¼". Blackish brown above, with rows of orange and yellow spots. Below, forewings orange with small dark patches; hindwings dull yellow and orange, with small whitish crescent in brownish trailing edge. Low-flying. Caterpillar black above with light lines and short spines. **HABITAT** Open areas below the tree line. **FOOD PLANTS** Aster family. **SEASON** May–Sept.

VARIABLE CHECKERSPOT
Euphydryas chalcedona
BRUSHFOOT FAMILY

1¾". Very variably colored. Blackish above, with creamy patches, red-orange spots along margins. Below, forewings mostly orange with tiny white spots near outer margin; hindwings have alternating orange-red and cream bands. **HABITAT** Mtn. meadows, open woodlands, clearings. **FOOD PLANTS** Snapdragon family. **SEASON** May–July.

SATYR COMMA
Polygonia satyrus
BRUSHFOOT FAMILY

2". Bright yellow-orange above, with black patches; ragged margins. Below, mottled rich brown; hindwings have white "comma" in center. Adult overwinters; flies on warm days as early as Feb. Caterpillar black with greenish yellow above. **HABITAT** Riparian canyons, woodland edges, roadsides. **FOOD PLANTS** Nettles, Hops. **SEASON** Mainly May–Sept. **RANGE** Entire region, ex. e MT.

HOARY COMMA
Polygonia gracilis
BRUSHFOOT FAMILY

1¾". Orange above, with yellow-orange submarginal crescents, black marks; ragged margins. Below, brownish gray, darker near wing bases; white "comma" mark in middle of hindwings. Caterpillar black with reddish spines near head and whitish spines at rear. **HABITAT** Streamsides in forested mtn. areas. **FOOD PLANTS** Varied, incl. currants, elms. **SEASON** Mar.–Oct.; hibernates.

PAINTED LADY
Vanessa cardui
BRUSHFOOT FAMILY

2⅛". Orange above, with black markings; forewing tips black with white spots and bar; hindwings have row of small, separate, blackish spots. Below, forewings pinkish with black, white, and olive markings; hindwings have olive-brown network with small eyespots. Caterpillar spiny, variably colored. Most widespread butterfly worldwide. Occasional mass migrations from Mexico. **HABITAT** Open areas. **FOOD PLANTS** Many, incl. mallow family, thistles, nettles. **SEASON** Mar.–Nov. **West Coast Lady** *(V. annabella)* has orange bar on front edge of forewings; occurs most often in riparian canyons.

CALIFORNIA TORTOISESHELL
Nymphalis californica
BRUSHFOOT FAMILY

2¼". Orange above, with brown near base and at margins (in flight, orange appears as wide stripe); ragged margins. Below, mottled dark brown and gray, resembling tree bark. Sometimes flies in large migratory groups. Caterpillar black with bluish spines, white dots. **HABITAT** Trails, clearings in pinewoods. **FOOD PLANTS** Buckthorns. **SEASON** Mar.–Oct.; hibernates.

MOURNING CLOAK
Nymphalis antiopa
BRUSHFOOT FAMILY

3". Mainly dark mahogany brown above, with wide creamy edges beyond blue-spotted black borders. Below, blackish brown with pale borders. Adult overwinters; one of the first butterflies to appear. Caterpillar dark purple with reddish spots on back. **HABITAT** Woodlands, parks. **FOOD PLANTS** Many, incl. willows, elms, poplars. **SEASON** Mainly Mar.–Oct.

MILBERT'S TORTOISESHELL
Nymphalis milberti
BRUSHFOOT FAMILY
2″. Dark chocolate brown above, with outer band of yellow blending to orange; dark borders. Below, dark brown with lighter band near margins. Caterpillar black with greenish-yellow sides, spines. **HABITAT** Riversides, canyons, meadows, tundra. **FOOD PLANTS** Nettles. **SEASON** Mainly Mar.–Oct.; hibernates.

RED ADMIRAL
Vanessa atalanta
BRUSHFOOT FAMILY
2″. Brownish black above, with semicircular reddish-orange band; forewing tips spotted white. Below, mottled brown, black, and blue; pale orange band on forewings. Caterpillar black with yellow spots. **HABITAT** Meadows, woodland edges, gardens. **FOOD PLANTS** Nettle family. **SEASON** Mainly June and Aug.; sometimes occurs spring–fall.

VICEROY
Limenitis archippus
BRUSHFOOT FAMILY
2¾″. Deep orange above, with bold black veining and white-spotted black borders; transverse black line crosses hindwings (line is lacking in Monarch). Below, similarly patterned but paler. **HABITAT** Meadows, riparian canyons at lower elevs. **FOOD PLANTS** Willows, poplars, cherries and other fruit trees. **SEASON** June–Aug.

WEIDEMEYER'S ADMIRAL
Limenitis weidemeyerii
BRUSHFOOT FAMILY
3″. Blackish above, with broad white band across wings; small white spots near forewing edges. Below, paler with black veins; black-bordered orange band near margins. Caterpillar gray and white, humpbacked. **HABITAT** Willow- and aspen-lined watercourses. **FOOD PLANTS** Willows aspens, cottonwoods. **SEASON** June–July.

COMMON RINGLET
Coenonympha tullia
BRUSHFOOT FAMILY

1½". Ocher above and below, with eyespot near forewing tip. Below, variable gray shading; hindwings occ. have small eyespots. Slow-flying, easily approached. **HABITAT** Grassy meadows, prairies. **FOOD PLANTS** Grasses. **SEASON** May–Sept. **RANGE** Entire region, ex. e CO.

SMALL WOOD-NYMPH
Cercyonis oetus
BRUSHFOOT FAMILY

1½". Dark brown above and below; forewings have 1–2 black eyespots, yellow-ringed below. **HABITAT** Open grassy areas in mtns.; can be abundant in sagebrush grasslands. **FOOD PLANTS** Grasses. **SEASON** June–Sept. **RANGE** Entire region, ex. e CO.

COMMON ALPINE
Erebia epipsodea
BRUSHFOOT FAMILY

1⅞". Dark brown above and below, with black-spotted orange patches near wing margins, much reduced on hindwings below. **HABITAT** Moist mtn. meadows, prairies. **FOOD PLANTS** Grasses. **SEASON** June–Aug. **RANGE** ID to c CO.

RIDINGS' SATYR
Neominois ridingsii
BRUSHFOOT FAMILY

1¾". Dark brown above, with unique light gray-brown oval patches on outer half; 2 eyespots on forewings, small black spot occ. on hindwings. Below, grayish, darker at base; cryptically patterned. **HABITAT** Grasslands, prairies. **FOOD PLANTS** Grasses. **SEASON** June–Aug. **RANGE** Entire region, ex. n ID.

CHRYXUS ARCTIC
Oeneis chryxus
BRUSHFOOT FAMILY

1⅞". Brown above, with broad, tawny outer band. Below, tawny, mottled gray, brown, black, and white. **HABITAT** Mtn. meadows, forest clearings, high-elev. grasslands, tundra. **FOOD PLANTS** Grasses. **SEASON** June–Aug.; flies annually or every other year. **RANGE** ID to c CO.

MONARCH
Danaus plexippus
BRUSHFOOT FAMILY

3¼". Orange above, with black veins, orange- and white-spotted blackish margins; male has black spot on inner vein of hindwing. Below, yellow-orange. Head and body black with white spots. Glides with wings held at an angle. Caterpillar banded black, white, and yellow. Adult and caterpillar poisonous to predators. Migrates south in fall to overwinter in coastal c CA or highlands of c Mexico. **HABITAT** Open areas. **FOOD PLANTS** Milkweeds. **SEASON** May–Oct.; migratory.

NORTHERN CLOUDYWING
Thorybes pylades
SKIPPER FAMILY

1½". Dark brown above; outer edges checkered; forewings have irregular white spots. Below, hindwings have darker mottling. Rests with wings folded or spread. **HABITAT** Woodland edges, streamsides in mtns. **FOOD PLANTS** Pea family. **SEASON** May–June. **RANGE** Entire region, ex. e CO.

DREAMY DUSKYWING
Erynnis icelus
SKIPPER FAMILY

1¼". Dark brown above; outer forewings have silvery patches, narrow dark bands; hindwings dotted with tiny pale spots. Below, lighter brown with pale spots on hindwings. Usu. seen with wings spread. **HABITAT** Woodland paths and openings, along streams. **FOOD PLANTS** Aspens, willows, poplars. **SEASON** Late Apr.–July.

SILVER-SPOTTED SKIPPER
Epargyreus clarus
SKIPPER FAMILY

2″. Chocolate brown above, with golden patches on forewings. Below, hindwings have large silver patch. Territorial; aggressively chases other butterflies away. **HABITAT** Fields, gardens, canyons. **FOOD PLANTS** Pea family. **SEASON** Late May–Aug.

ARCTIC SKIPPER
Carterocephalus palaemon
SKIPPER FAMILY

1″. Uniquely patterned; resembles a tiny fritillary. Dark brown above, with bright orange patches. Below, hindwings rusty orange with large silver spots. **HABITAT** Bogs, meadows, mtn. valleys. **FOOD PLANTS** Grasses. **SEASON** Late June–Aug. **RANGE** ID, MT, w WY.

TWO-BANDED CHECKERED-SKIPPER
Pyrgus ruralis
SKIPPER FAMILY

1″. Brown-black above, with 2 irregular bands of white spots. Below, duller; often with reddish tint on hindwings. Body stout, blackish. Rests with wings folded or spread. **HABITAT** Open meadows, mtn. openings. **FOOD PLANTS** Cinquefoils. **SEASON** May–July. **RANGE** ID to c CO.

COMMON BRANDED SKIPPER
Hesperia comma
SKIPPER FAMILY

1″. Very variably patterned. Above, tawny with dark borders; male has dark stigma (streak of scent-producing scales) across forewings. Below, greenish to ocher; hindwings with white markings that are separate or form a crooked band. **HABITAT** Open areas, streamsides in mtns.; sagebrush grasslands. **FOOD PLANTS** Grasses. **SEASON** July–Sept. **RANGE** Entire region, ex. e CO.

WOODLAND SKIPPER
Ochlodes sylvanoides
SKIPPER FAMILY

1″. Male bright orange-brown above, with dark, uneven borders; forewings have narrow black stigma that extends to border. Female duller; lacks stigma. Below, ocher to brown with yellowish spotted band. **HABITAT** Open moist areas in woodlands, parks, gardens. **FOOD PLANTS** Grasses. **SEASON** July–Aug. **RANGE** ID to c CO.

WESTERN TENT CATERPILLAR MOTH
Malacosoma californicum
TENT CATERPILLAR MOTH FAMILY

1″. Male red-brown; forewings have 2 yellow stripes. Female tan; forewings have red-brown stripes. Nocturnal. Caterpillar variable, bristly; groups build silken tents in branches; can denude trees. **HABITAT** All areas with host plants. **FOOD PLANTS** Willows, oaks, fruit trees, poplars. **SEASON** May–July.

IO MOTH
Automeris io
GIANT SILKWORM MOTH FAMILY

2½″. Forewings yellowish (male) or reddish brown (female); hindwings yellow with black eyespot; black and rusty bands near outer edge. Body yellow-brown. Nocturnal. Caterpillar green with reddish and white stripes, spines; stings. **HABITAT** Open woods. **FOOD PLANTS** Azaleas, dogwoods. **SEASON** Mar.–Nov. **RANGE** East of Rockies in CO, se WY.

GLOVER'S SILK MOTH
Hyalophora columbia gloveri
GIANT SILKWORM MOTH FAMILY

4″. Wings large, full, maroon to wine-colored near body, with wide gray marginal bands; eyespots variable, but usu. oval on forewings, pointed on hindwings. Body maroon to wine-colored; male's antennae bushier. Nocturnal. **HABITAT** Mtn. clearings. **FOOD PLANTS** Rose family, willows. **SEASON** May–June.

SHEEP MOTH
Hemileuca eglanterina
GIANT SILKWORM MOTH FAMILY

2½″. Forewings pink, hindwings orange, all with large black dots and crossbands. Body banded black and orange. Flies by day. Caterpillar brown with red stripes, whorled rows of barbed spines; causes rash if touched. **HABITAT** Sagebrush grasslands, scrubby woodland edges. **FOOD PLANTS** Bitterbrush, snowberries. **SEASON** July–early Sept.

BUMBLEBEE MOTH
Hemaris diffinis
SPHINX MOTH FAMILY

1¾″. Resembles a large bumble bee. Wings clear, mostly scaleless, with reddish black at base, veins, outer edges. Thorax fuzzy, golden brown; abdomen black with yellow band. Active by day. **HABITAT** Forest edges, meadows, gardens. **FOOD PLANTS** Honeysuckle family, esp. Mountain Snowberry. **SEASON** May–Sept.

WHITE-LINED SPHINX
Hyles lineata
SPHINX MOTH FAMILY

3″. Forewings brown with white veins, tan stripe; hindwings rose, edged with dark brown. Body brown with black and white bars. Active day and night. Caterpillar green with yellow-orange head and rear horn. **HABITAT** Meadows, gardens, roadsides. **FOOD PLANTS** Low-growing annuals, fruit trees. **SEASON** July–Sept.

EYED SPHINX
Smerinthus cerisyi
SPHINX MOTH FAMILY

2⅞″. Forewings pointed, mottled brown and gray with fine white veining. Hindwings pinkish with wide buffy margins; large blue and black eyespot with black bull's-eye. Caterpillar green with diagonal yellow stripes, yellow and green rear horn. **HABITAT** Watercourses, lowlands. **FOOD PLANTS** Mainly willows. **SEASON** May–June.

TOMATO HORNWORM MOTH
Manduca quinquemaculata
SPHINX MOTH FAMILY

4″. Forewings long, pointed, gray-brown. Hindwings light gray with black banding. Body very large, tapered, with 5–6 pairs of yellow spots on abdomen. Nocturnal. Caterpillar bright green with wavy yellow lines; green and black rear horn. **HABITAT** Gardens. **FOOD PLANTS** Tomato, tobacco, potato plants. **SEASON** June–Sept.

ACREA MOTH
Estigmene acrea
TIGER MOTH FAMILY

2¼″. Forewings white with scattered black dots; male's hindwings yellow-orange, female's white with black spots. Abdomen orange above, white below; black-barred. Nocturnal. Caterpillar covered with long red-orange hairs; large numbers on roads in fall. **HABITAT** Open areas, fields, deserts, gardens. **FOOD PLANTS** Many herbaceous plants. **SEASON** June–July.

WOOLYBEAR CATERPILLAR MOTH
Pyrrharctia isabella
TIGER MOTH FAMILY

1¾″. Forewings yellow-orange with rows of small black spots; hindwings lighter. Body rusty orange with black central stripe. Nocturnal. Caterpillar hairy, reddish brown, black at both ends; often crosses roads, paths by day. **HABITAT** Shrubby fields, roadsides, gardens. **FOOD PLANTS** Grasses, plantains, low-growing weeds. **SEASON** June–Aug.

FALL WEBWORM MOTH
Hyphantria cunea
TIGER MOTH FAMILY

1½″. Wings white, with variable amounts of brown to black spotting on forewings. Body white, sometimes spotted. Caterpillar variably colored; covered with long light hairs; lives communally in silken web at tree branch ends. **HABITAT** Areas with available food plants. **FOOD PLANTS** Over 100 species of hardwoods, incl. cherries, mulberries, willows. **SEASON** June–July.

WESTERN SPRUCE BUDWORM MOTH
Choristoneura occidentalis
TORTRICID MOTH FAMILY

1¼″. Forewings and body mottled orange and brown, sometimes grayish; hindwings gray-brown. Nocturnal. Caterpillar brown with ivory spots above, pale yellow-orange below; most destructive caterpillar in West. **HABITAT** Coniferous woods. **FOOD PLANTS** Douglas Fir, true firs, Tamarack, Engelmann Spruce. **SEASON** Late summer.

THE BRIDE
Catocala neogama
OWLET MOTH FAMILY

3″. Forewings greenish gray, mottled with black; hindwings boldly patterned, rich yellow with two broad black bands, revealed when moth takes flight. Thorax grayish, abdomen yellowish. Nocturnal. **HABITAT** Deciduous forests. **FOOD PLANTS** Walnuts, hickories. **SEASON** June–Oct.

Vertebrates

There are approximately 43,000 vertebrate species on earth. The evolution of a variety of anatomical structures has made them extraordinarily successful for half a billion years. Today vertebrates are one of the most widespread groups of animals, inhabiting every corner of the globe, from ocean depths to mountaintops, deserts, and polar regions.

Vertebrata is one of three subphyla of the phylum Chordata. All members of Chordata possess an internal stiffening rod called a notochord during their embryonic development. The sac-like marine sea squirts, salps, and their relatives (members of the subphylum Urochordata, the most primitive of the Chordata) lose the notochord completely as they develop, and in the file-shaped marine lancelets (of the subphylum Cephalochordata) the notochord remains an unsegmented rod. In vertebrates the notochord is replaced during the animal's development by a series of cartilaginous or bony disks, known as vertebrae, that run along the back.

The evolution of the vertebrates stemmed from an invertebrate sea squirt–like animal, passed through a "missing link" invertebrate-to-vertebrate stage with the lancelets, and reached the beginnings of the vertebrate stage some 500 million years ago (mya) with the appearance of the first jawless fishes. During the following 350 million years, the various classes of vertebrates evolved. The ancestors of modern fishes developed from their jawless ancestors about 400 mya; 100 million years further into vertebrate development, amphibians evolved from fishes crawling about in search of water during the droughts of the Devonian period. Reptiles first appeared about 250 mya and flourished because of their ability to reproduce on land. Mammals and birds, warm-blooded and able to successfully live in places too cold for amphibians and reptiles, spread across the world's environments, mammals beginning about 170 mya and birds about 150 mya.

Today's vertebrates share a number of characteristics that separate them from the estimated 50 million or so invertebrate species with which they share the earth. Virtually all vertebrates are bilaterally symmetrical; that is, their left and right sides are essentially mirror images of one another. The strong but flexible backbone, composed of vertebrae, protects the spinal cord and serves as the main structural component of the internal skeletal frame and the segmented muscles that attach to it.

Vertebrates are well-coordinated runners, jumpers, swimmers, and/or fliers because of this unique combination of skeletal and muscular development. Other shared characteristics of nearly all vertebrates include one pair of bony jaws (with or without teeth), one or two pairs of appendages, a ventrally located heart (protected by a rib cage), and blood contained in vessels.

The subphylum Vertebrata includes several classes: three classes of living fishes, the amphibians, the reptiles, the birds, and the mammals.

Fishes

Living fishes fall into three major groups: the primitive lampreys and hagfishes (rarely seen deepwater marine fishes), the cartilaginous fishes (sharks, skates, and rays, which are mainly marine), and the bony fishes. Aquatic, mostly cold-blooded vertebrates with fins and internal gills, fish are typically streamlined and have a muscular tail. Most move through the water by weaving movements of their bodies and tail fins, using their other fins to control direction. The skin of a fish is coated with a slimy secretion that decreases friction with the water; this secretion, along with the scales that cover most fish, provides their bodies with a nearly waterproof covering. The gills are located in passages that lead from the throat usually to a pair of openings on the side, just behind the head. With rare exceptions, fish breathe by taking water in through the mouth and forcing it past the gills and out through the gill openings; the thin-walled gills capture oxygen from the water and emit carbon dioxide.

The body shapes of fishes vary from cylindrical eels and elongated, spindle-shaped mackerels (rounded in the middle, with tapered ends) to vertically compressed (flattened) sunfishes to horizontally compressed skates and rays (mainly marine fishes). Body colors can vary within a species due to season, sex, age, individual variation, and water temperature, and the color normally fades or otherwise changes after death. Most fishes have one or more dorsal (back) fins that may be spiny or soft (a few fishes, such as trout and salmon, have an additional fleshy fin behind the dorsal fins, called an adipose fin); a tail (caudal) fin, usually with an upper and a lower lobe; and an anal fin, just in front of the tail along the edge of the ventral (belly) side. They also have a pair of pectoral fins, usually on the sides behind the head, and a pair of pelvic fins, generally under the middle of the body. Some fishes lack one or more of these fins.

The mouths and snouts of fishes may be disk-shaped, pointed, tubular, or sword-like; depending on the species, the upper jaw (the snout) projects beyond the lower, the two parts of the jaw are of equal length, or the lower jaw projects beyond the upper. Some species have sensory barbels, whisker-like projections of the skin, usually on the lower jaw, that detect objects, especially in muddy or murky water. Most fish are covered with scales, but some species lack scales altogether, and some lack scales on the head or other areas; in other species, scales have been modified into bony plates. Some fishes have a conspicuous lateral line, a sensory organ beneath the skin that responds to vibrations in the water and often looks like a thin stripe along the side.

Some fish species are solitary, some live in small groups, and others are found mainly in enormous schools, in which members respond as a unit to stimuli while feeding or migrating.

Lengths given (from tip of snout to tip of tail) are for typical adults, although, as fish grow throughout their lives, larger and smaller individuals may be seen; maximum sizes are not given.

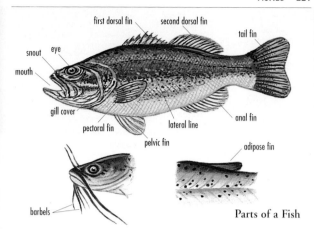

first dorsal fin
second dorsal fin
tail fin
snout
eye
mouth
gill cover
pectoral fin
pelvic fin
lateral line
anal fin
adipose fin
barbels

Parts of a Fish

Bony Fishes

Bony fishes normally have harder, less flexible bony skeletons than cartilaginous fishes (sharks, rays, skates), as well as a gas- or fat-filled swim bladder that keeps them buoyant. Most bony fishes have over-lapping scales embedded in flexible connective tissue, though some lack scales entirely. There is a single gill opening on each side protected by a hard gill cover.

Almost all living fishes are ray-finned bony fishes; a few bony fishes are classified as lobe-finned fishes (none of which occur in Rocky Mountain waters). The fins of ray-finned bony fishes consist of a web of skin supported by bony rays (either segmented soft rays or stiffer spines), each moved by a set of muscles, which makes the fins very flexible. The tail fin is typically symmetrical.

Most bony fishes reproduce by spawning: males directly fertilize eggs after the females release them from their bodies into the water. The eggs may float at mid-levels, rise to the surface, or sink to the bottom. A few fish species guard nests or incubate eggs in a pouch or the mouth. Newborn fish are called larvae; within a few weeks or months, a larva develops to resemble a miniature adult, and is called a juvenile or fry.

SHOVELNOSE STURGEON
Scaphirhynchus platorynchus
STURGEON FAMILY

20–30″. 5 lines of raised bony plates run the entire length of the body. Back and sides buffy brown; white below. Snout duck-like, up-turned, flattened; tip rounded; 4 barbels forward of small round tubular mouth; eyes tiny. Single dorsal fin set far back; tail long, narrow; upper lobe of tail fin high, thin; tapers to a thread. Slowly cruises along murky bottoms; sensitive snout and barbels locate prey by touch. **HABITAT** Channels of large rivers, often found in strong current. **RANGE** e MT, e WY.

PADDLEFISH
Polyodon spathula
PADDLEFISH FAMILY

4–6′. Body smooth, lacks scales. Back dark gray, sides pale bluish gray, belly whitish. Snout very long, paddle-shaped; tip rounded; mouth very large; tiny eyes at base of paddle, above front of mouth. Single dorsal fin set far back; tail fin forked, upper lobe longer. Filter feeder that swims with mouth open. Spawns Apr.–June below dams, over gravel shoals. Can weigh up to 200 lbs; lives up to 30 years. **HABITAT** Large rivers and lakes. **RANGE** e MT.

GOLDEYE
Hiodon alosoides
MOONEYE FAMILY

8–18″. Body deep, compressed. Bluish above; sides tan or silvery. Scales large, each edged with brown. Snout blunt; large mouth has many small teeth; eyes large, golden. Single small dorsal fin set far back above long anal fin; tail fin forked, lobes equal. Feeds on insects, fish, mollusks, crayfish. **HABITAT** Quiet river backwaters, lakes, ponds. **RANGE** e and c MT, ne WY. **Mooneye** (*H. tergisus;* 9–11″) has silver eye, rounded snout, unkeeled belly; occurs east of Rockies.

COMMON CARP
Cyprinus carpio
CARP AND MINNOW FAMILY

10–30″. Oval; back high, rounded. Dark olive-brown above, shading to yellowish gray below. 2 pairs of barbels on upper lip. Dorsal fin long, begins at high point of back, has thickened forward spine; tail fin forked, lobes rounded or pointed. All fins are bronzy brown. Scales large; some individuals have few scales. Older females may produce 2 million eggs. Introduced from Eurasia; destroys bottom plants needed by native fish as cover for eggs, fry. **HABITAT** Clear or turbid slow rivers, lakes, reservoirs; usu. shallow weedy areas.

PEAMOUTH
Mylocheilus caurinus
CARP AND MINNOW FAMILY

8–12″. Back dark gray-brown; thick black line runs from gill to tail; whitish below, with 2nd black line along forward half of body. Head and mouth small; small barbel at corner of jaw. 1 short midback dorsal fin; tail fin forked. Mature male has red lips, red stripe on gill covers and ventral fin bases. A midwater or bottom feeder; runs in schools. **HABITAT** Vegetated small rivers, deep water of larger rivers, cool lakes. **RANGE** nw and sw ID, nw MT.

NORTHERN SQUAWFISH
Ptychocheilus oregonensis
CARP AND MINNOW FAMILY

10–24". Slender; pike-like. Gray-green above; sides silver; lateral line arches downward. Head and snout long, flattened; mouth large; jaws of equal length; lacks barbels. Fins yellowish; 1 triangular dorsal fin; tail fin forked; ventral fins reddish in old males. **HABITAT** Lakes, pools, rivers. **RANGE** Snake and Columbia R. basins of n, c, and sw ID; nw MT. **Colorado Squawfish** (*P. lucius;* 3–5′) similar; endangered; occurs in flowing rivers of upper Colorado Basin.

SPECKLED DACE
Rhinichthys osculus
CARP AND MINNOW FAMILY

2–4". Back rounded, belly flattened. Body color highly variable: back dark green; sides gray, green, or yellowish mottled with dark brown spots. Snout pointed, mouth small. Fins pale, unspotted; single dorsal fin; tail fin forked, lobes equal; fins have red bases in breeding male. Important prey of trout. Tolerates very warm water. **HABITAT** Over gravel in springs, creeks, rivers, lakes. **RANGE** ID, Yellowstone NP, sw WY, w CO.

LONGNOSE SUCKER
Catostomus catostomus
SUCKER FAMILY

6–14". Cylindrical. Back brown; sides paler brown with darker speckles; belly white. Breeding males have pink stripe below lateral line. Snout long for a sucker; round protrusable mouth below. Single dorsal fin; tail fin forked, lobes equal. **HABITAT** Clear cold waters of deep lakes; spawns in late spring in nearby streams. **RANGE** n ID, MT, WY, nc CO. **Mountain Sucker** (*C. platyrhynchus;* 6–8") has blunt snout; mainly in clear mtn. streams of ID, MT, WY.

WHITE SUCKER
Catostomus commersoni
SUCKER FAMILY

8–18". Cylindrical. Color variable; back olive or brown; sides pale brown or yellow with darker speckles; belly white. Breeding males darker; pink bands on sides; fins reddish. Snout short; large protruding mouth below. Single dorsal fin; tail fin forked, lobes equal. Runs upstream in early spring; breeds in shallow gravel nests in swift water. **HABITAT** Clear streams and shallow lakes over sand, gravel, rocks. **RANGE** MT (ex. far west), WY, CO.

BLACK BULLHEAD
Ameiurus (Ictalurus) melas
BULLHEAD CATFISH FAMILY

6–12″. Robust; front heavy, compressed toward tail. Back blackish brown; sides shade to yellow brown; belly yellowish. Head wide, rounded; long black barbels on upper lip and chin. Tall thin dorsal fin and adipose fin. Feeds chiefly at night. Bullhead catfish guard their nests and protect their dense schools of fry. **HABITAT** Mud bottoms of lakes, ponds, rivers. **RANGE** wc ID, e and nw MT, n and e WY, e and sw CO.

CHANNEL CATFISH
Ictalurus punctatus
BULLHEAD CATFISH FAMILY

14–30″. Slender. Back blue-gray; sides tan or silvery blue with few scattered blackish spots; belly white; lateral line straight. Head long; upper jaw overhangs lower. 4 pairs of barbels: upper 2 black, lower ones white. Single dorsal fin short, high, rounded; adipose fin; anal fin long, with rounded outer edge; tail fin forked. **HABITAT** Clear larger rivers with sand or gravel bottoms; lakes and ponds. **RANGE** c and e MT, most of WY and CO.

NORTHERN PIKE
Esox lucius
PIKE FAMILY

15–45″. Long, cylindrical; head large; snout long, wide, rounded. Olive green, camouflaged with many large yellow spots; whitish below. Lower jaw protrudes; teeth fine. Fins pale brown with dark mottling; single rounded dorsal fin set far back on body; tail fin forked. Fast-growing; feeds on fish, frogs, leeches, ducks, aquatic mammals. Solitary, aggressive; nicknamed "waterwolf." **HABITAT** Cold lakes, reservoirs, slow rivers; winters in deep water. **RANGE** n and e MT; some introduced to lakes to the south.

GOLDEN TROUT
Oncorhynchus aguabonita
TROUT FAMILY

6–14″. Somewhat compressed. Back brown or olive with black spots; 8–10 gray patches and red stripe along lateral line; sides golden yellow; belly red or orange. Head small; mouth large. White-tipped dorsal fin, small adipose fin, and notched tail fin olive with black spots; pelvic and anal fins reddish with black and white leading edge. Gill covers reddish. Native only to Kern R. in s Sierra Nevada, CA. **HABITAT** Clear cool streams and lakes above 7,000′. **RANGE** Introduced to mtns. of ID, w MT, w WY; local in CO.

CUTTHROAT TROUT
Oncorhynchus clarki
TROUT FAMILY

8–14″. Olive above; sides olive-brown, tinged with orange or pinkish; large black spots; bright red slash mark on throat. Jaws extend behind eyes. 1 triangular dorsal fin, small adipose fin, and notched tail fin, all greenish with black spots. Golden, lightly spotted Yellowstone form makes salmon-like spawning runs from Yellowstone Lake, both downstream and upstream. **HABITAT** High elevations: gravel-bottomed rivers and streams, ponds and lakes. **RANGE** ID, w and c MT, w WY, w and c CO.

RAINBOW TROUT
Oncorhynchus mykiss
(Salmo gairdneri)
TROUT FAMILY

8–18″. Olive above; sides have wide pinkish stripe, black spotting; yellowish to white below. Head shorter and more rounded than Brown Trout and Brook Trout; mouth large; jaws extend to below eyes; lacks red on throat. 1 triangular dorsal fin, small adipose fin, and crescent-shaped tail fin, all with black spotting. **HABITAT** Gravel-bottomed rivers and streams with swift currents, deep clear lakes. **RANGE** Entire region, ex. s and e CO.

Fly-fishing in the Rockies

Western rivers run cold and clear, and they host a rich variety of aquatic insect life, providing ideal habitat for trout. Some of the world's finest trout waters are found in the Rocky Mountains, and every year anglers from around the world descend on the region to test their fly-fishing skills. Several strains of native Cutthroat Trout inhabit some rivers and lakes, but the natives have been largely supplanted by Rainbow Trout, Brown Trout, and Brook Trout.

When insects such as mayflies and caddisflies hatch in profusion on a river, they seem to pour from the surface. Hungry birds swoop through the fluttering clouds of insects, and the trout begin to rise, dimpling the surface as they feed. For anglers, this is heaven on earth: a quiet evening, sunlight upon a nearby mountain range, the cries of birds, and the rhythmic sounds of trout breaking the surface.

SOCKEYE SALMON
"Kokanee Salmon"
Oncorhynchus nerka
TROUT FAMILY

8–18″. Silvery blue above, with fine speckles; whitish below. 1 unspotted dorsal fin; small adipose fin; tail fin plain, forked. Jaws hooked. Spawning male has humped back, green head, red back and sides; spawning female grayish-red with yellow blotches. Spawns up rivers that end in lakes; native fry spend 2 years here before returning to Pacific. HABITAT Rivers; introduced to lakes. RANGE Native to c ID; introduced to rest of ID, w and c MT, w WY, c CO.

CHINOOK SALMON
"King Salmon"
Oncorhynchus tshawytscha
TROUT FAMILY

32–40″. The largest salmon. Heavy, robust. Spawning: olive green above, with heavy black spotting; sides pinkish orange; whitish below. Male back humped; jaws hooked. Head small, conical; lower jaw projects. 1 midback dorsal fin; small adipose fin; tail fin forked, lobes equal; all fins heavily black-spotted. Spawns spring and fall; travels long distances up rivers. HABITAT Rivers. RANGE Migrates between Snake R. basin of c ID and Pacific Ocean.

BROWN TROUT
Salmo trutta
TROUT FAMILY

8–18″. Head large. Brown above; sides olive brown with many or few dark brown and red spots haloed by white; belly silvery. Head spotted. Single dorsal fin and adipose fin above; tail fin squarish. Tolerates warmer, siltier rivers than other trout. Introduced from Eurasia; has reduced native fish populations. Voracious feeder; even chases water-skimming swallows. HABITAT Lakes, ponds, slower rivers; spawns in nearby clear streams. RANGE Entire region, esp. Missouri R. and Snake R.; local in WY and CO.

BULL TROUT
Salvelinus confluentus
TROUT FAMILY

15–22″. Cylindrical. Dark slaty above, without wavy lines; sides olive or gray flecked with many white or yellow spots; belly white. Head flat, broad; eyes large. Dorsal fin olive; has adipose fin; tail fin lightly forked; ventral and pectoral fins have white and black leading edges. Spawning (fall) male blackish; side spots, belly, and ventral fins reddish. Once considered a form of Dolly Varden *(S. malma)*; distinguished by knob of flesh at tip of lower jaw. HABITAT Lakes, streams; small size in headwater streams. RANGE ID, w MT.

LAKE TROUT
Salvelinus namaycush
TROUT FAMILY

12–36″. Slightly compressed. Dark green or blackish above, paler olive or gray on sides; many large creamy spots. Head and mouth large. Triangular dorsal fin, small adipose fin, and deeply forked tail fin all have creamy spots; ventral fins olive or reddish, with white leading edges. Spawns Oct.–Nov. Largest native trout in N. Amer. **HABITAT** Deep cold lakes and reservoirs; stays deep in summer. **RANGE** n, c, and e ID; nw, s, and ne MT; w WY; nc CO.

BROOK TROUT
Salvelinus fontinalis
TROUT FAMILY

6–14″. Olive-brown above, with many paler olive wavy lines; sides olive, with many large yellowish spots and few small red spots with blue halos; belly white (reddish in adult male). Jaws large. Dorsal fin spotted, triangular; tail fin squared (lightly forked in juv.); ventral fins reddish, with white and black leading edges. Native to e N. Amer; widely stocked in region. Spawns in fall. **HABITAT** Lakes, cool clear ponds, spring-fed streams in mtns. **RANGE** n and e ID, w MT, w WY, w CO.

ARCTIC GRAYLING
Thymallus arcticus
TROUT FAMILY

6–16″. Compressed. Dull purplish gray above; sides silvery, brownish, or purplish with a few black spots forward; belly paler. Head short; jaws wide, teeth fine. Dorsal fin long, greatly enlarged (19–24 rays), sail-like, rounded, spotted with white or reddish fringe; male's dorsal fin larger than female's. Has adipose fin; tail fin forked; pelvic fin striped. **HABITAT** Cold streams with pools; high lakes. **RANGE** Native in MT west of Great Falls; introduced elsewhere in MT, mtns. of ID.

LAKE WHITEFISH
Coregonus clupeaformis
TROUT FAMILY

12–20″. Compressed. Slaty blue above; sides and belly silvery, plain. Head concave behind eyes; nape may show hump; double upper lip; mouth tiny, underhung; teeth on tongue, not jaws. Fins dusky; dorsal fin triangular; has adipose fin; tail fin forked. Spends most of year in deep water. In Nov. lays eggs in shallow water over rocks in lake or in tributary stream (makes spawning runs). **HABITAT** Large rivers, lakes, and tributary streams. **RANGE** Far n ID, w and n MT.

MOUNTAIN WHITEFISH
"Rocky Mountain Whitefish"
Prosopium williamsoni
TROUT FAMILY

12–20". Cylindrical. Slaty above; sides pale silvery olive or dull brown; belly white. Head smallish; mouth overhung, very small, weak, toothless. All fins black-tipped; dorsal fin triangular; large adipose fin; tail fin forked. Feeds from surface to bottom on plankton and insects. Spawns Aug.-Nov. over gravel beds in stream riffles. **HABITAT** Cold streams, upper levels of lakes. **RANGE** ID, w and s MT, w WY.

BURBOT
Lota lota
COD FAMILY

18–30". Eel-like; in cross section, circular in front, compressed toward rear. Dark brown, with mosaic of darker and paler wavy lines and spots. Head flattened; mouth wide; barbel on chin. 1st dorsal fin short; 2nd dorsal fin and anal fin long-based, fringe rear half of body; tail fin small, rounded. Pelvic fin forward of pectoral fins; used like feet when feeding on bottom; nocturnal feeder. **HABITAT** Deep cold lakes and rivers. **RANGE** Far n ID, MT, nc WY.

MOTTLED SCULPIN
Cottus bairdi
SCULPIN FAMILY

3". Robust, elongated, cylindrical; heavier forward; deep base of tail. Back and sides brown, with camouflaging black saddles and fine white spots. Head broad, flattened. Long mottled dorsal fins above most of body; tail fin rounded; pectoral fin fan-like. All fins mottled; male's first dorsal fin is black with rufous fringe. Searches for bottom-living aquatic insects, crustaceans, and fry. **HABITAT** Over gravel or rocks in cold creeks, pools in rivers, lakes. **RANGE** ID, w and c MT, w and s WY, nc CO.

GREEN SUNFISH
Lepomis cyanellus
SUNFISH FAMILY

4–8". Oval, deep. Olive-brown above; sides paler olive green; some have 6 brown bands on sides; belly pale orange. Head and mouth large; head pale green with fine blue lines. Wide gill cover ends with reddish-edged black spot. Fins darker at base; dorsal fins continuous; tail fin notched, lobes rounded; pectoral fin rounded; anal fin has 3 short spines. Male builds nest on shallow bottom; protects young for first week of life. **HABITAT** Streams, swamps, ponds; often near brush, dense vegetation. **RANGE** CO, e WY, se MT.

BLUEGILL
Lepomis macrochirus
SUNFISH FAMILY

4–10″. Oval, deep, compressed. Olive above, with 5–9 vertical dusky green bands; breeding male orange below; female whitish below. Mouth small; jaws pale blue. Dark spot on rear base of 2nd dorsal fin; tail fin slightly forked. Lower edge of gill cover blue; gill flap black. Introduced from e U.S. Swims in schools. Can overpopulate ponds without bass. HABITAT Shallow vegetated lakeshores, stream pools. RANGE Snake R. basin of ID, c and e MT, most of lowland WY and CO.

PUMPKINSEED
Lepomis gibbosus
SUNFISH FAMILY

6–8″. Oval, compressed. Dark brown above; sides brown and pale yellow, or dark green and blue (may appear banded); belly yellow-orange. Head concave on top; some have blue stripes below eyes. Ear flap spot black with distinct red tip and white edges. Dorsal fins and round-lobed tail fin dark-spotted. Introduced from e U.S. Ponds that lack predators can have large schools of runt-sized Pumpkinseeds. HABITAT Shallow, sheltered ponds, streams, marshes. RANGE Mainly ID, MT.

SMALLMOUTH BASS
Micropterus dolomieu
SUNFISH FAMILY

6–18″. Robust. Olive-brown above; sides greenish yellow with diffuse, brownish bands (lacks lengthwise black stripe); belly silvery. Juv. paler than adult. Mouth extends to point below front of eye. 1st dorsal fin spiny; 2nd rounded; tail fin notched, lobes rounded. Introduced from e U.S. Differs from Largemouth Bass in having only faint striping on sides, and mouth does not extend to rear of eye. HABITAT Deep lakes, cool clear streams over rocks or near logs. RANGE Widespread in w ID; local in MT, WY, CO.

LARGEMOUTH BASS
Micropterus salmoides
SUNFISH FAMILY

8–18″. Head large. Dark green above; sides olive green with brownish mottling; belly whitish. Broad black lateral stripe from eye to tail. Large mouth extends to point below rear of eye; cheeks striped. 1st dorsal fin spiny; 2nd dorsal fin rounded; tail fin slightly indented. Introduced from e U.S. Feeds on other fishes and crayfish. Most widely sought freshwater game fish in U.S. HABITAT Warm shallow lakes, ponds, and slow rivers with vegetation. RANGE Local east and west of Rockies.

BLACK CRAPPIE
Pomoxis nigromaculatus
SUNFISH FAMILY

4–11″. Oval, compressed; lower jaw protrudes. Pale brown or sooty green, heavily mottled with dark brown spots. Head concave above eyes; jaws up-turned. Single dorsal fin and anal fin large, rounded, begin with 6–8 spines; tail fin forked; most fins distinctly spotted. Introduced from e U.S. **HABITAT** Ponds; clear, streams near cover. **RANGE** w and s ID, e and c MT; local in WY and CO. **White Crappie** *(P. annularis)* paler; 5–10 greenish bars on sides; mainly e MT, e CO.

YELLOW PERCH
Perca flavescens
PERCH FAMILY

4–10″. Robust, oval in cross section. Olive green, brownish, or golden, with 5–8 blackish, vertical bars on back and sides. Appears hunch-backed before 1st dorsal fin. Head small, pointed. 2 separated dorsal fins dusky; 1st dorsal fin and first 2 rays of anal fin have sharp spines. Lives in schools; in deep water by day, shallows at dawn and dusk. Introduced from e U.S. and Canada. **HABITAT** Clear streams, lakes with vegetation. **RANGE** ID, MT, WY, n CO.

SAUGER
Stizostedion canadense
PERCH FAMILY

10–24″. Cylindrical; similar to Walleye. Dull brown above; sides silvery or buffy, with 3–4 oblique blackish saddles and many tiny black spots; belly whitish. Head pointed; mouth large, well-toothed; corner of mouth extends past eye (unlike Walleye); eyes large. 2 well-separated dorsal fins and forked tail fin evenly and strongly black-spotted. Lacks white tip on lower tail lobe found in Walleye. **HABITAT** Shallow lakes, large rivers. **RANGE** n and e MT, n WY.

WALLEYE
Stizostedion vitreum
PERCH FAMILY

12–30″. Cylindrical. Olive-brown above; sides brassy greenish-yellow with random blackish blotches and many tiny black spots; belly whitish. Head pointed; mouth large, well-toothed; corner of mouth extends to front of eye only; eyes very large. 1st (spiny) dorsal fin black to rear; rear of lower lobe of forked tail fin whitish. Often plainer than Sauger. **HABITAT** Cold lakes, reservoirs, rivers. Spawns in tributaries, lake shoals in early spring. **RANGE** Native n MT to ne CO; introduced in ID, w WY, c and se CO.

Amphibians

The ancestors of today's amphibians began evolving from fish about 300 million years ago. Members of the class Amphibia typically start life in fresh water and later live primarily on land. Most undergo metamorphosis (a series of developmental stages) from aquatic, water-breathing larvae to terrestrial or partly terrestrial, air-breathing adults. The most primitive of terrestrial vertebrates, amphibians lack claws and external ear openings. They have thin, moist, scaleless skin and are cold-blooded; their body temperature varies with that of their surroundings. In winter, they burrow deep into leaf litter, soft soils, and the mud of ponds, and maintain an inactive state. Unlike reptiles, amphibians can become dehydrated in dry environments and must live near water at least part of the year and for breeding. Their eggs lack shells, and most are laid in water.

Salamanders

Salamanders (order Caudata) have blunt heads, long slender bodies, short legs, and long tails. Most lay eggs in fresh water that hatch into four-legged larvae with tufted external gills; after several months or years, the larvae typically lose their gills and go ashore. Mole salamanders burrow into soft soil. Giant salamanders, the world's largest land salamanders, start out as aquatic larvae and usually become land dwellers as adults. Adult lungless salamanders lack lungs and breathe through their thin moist skin; mostly terrestrial, they live under bark, wood, or stones, sometimes near streams. During all life stages, salamanders eat small animal life. They are generally hard to see, as they feed under wet leaves and logs; they are easiest to see at night in early spring, when they congregate to mate and lay eggs at temporary pools created by the thaw and rains (vernal pools). Inactive in winter, they reside in decaying logs, between tree roots, and in soil. Salamanders differ from lizards, which are reptiles, in having thin, moist, unscaled skin and four toes on the front feet (lizards have five), and in their lack of claws and external ear openings. Salamanders are fast declining in number worldwide, due to habitat destruction and perhaps acid rain, pesticides, and increasing ultraviolet light. The size given for salamanders is the typical length from the tip of the nose to the end of the tail.

COEUR D'ALENE SALAMANDER
Plethodon idahoensis (vandykyei)
LUNGLESS SALAMANDER FAMILY
4″. Cylindrical; toes short. Top of head, back and tail buffy yellow with scalloped borders; sides black with many fine white dots; throat yellow, belly dusky; 14–15 grooves on sides. **HABITAT** Wet wooded areas, open talus slopes, seepages and streamsides. **RANGE** n ID, far wc MT.

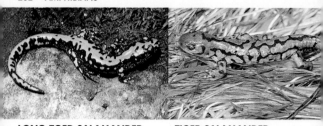

LONG-TOED SALAMANDER
Ambystoma macrodactylum
MOLE SALAMANDER FAMILY

5½". Slender; toes long; neck narrow. Top of head, back, and tail yellow, buffy yellow, or yellow-green; sides dark brown or blackish, with tiny white dots on sides; belly brownish; 12–13 grooves on sides. HABITAT Wet coniferous forests, alpine meadows, sagebrush deserts. ACTIVITY Apr.–Sept.: day and night. RANGE c and n ID, w MT.

TIGER SALAMANDER
Ambystoma tigrinum
MOLE SALAMANDER FAMILY

10". Stout; snout rounded. Northern blotched race (pictured) yellowish olive with black marbling above, black lines on sides. Utah race of sw WY, w CO gray or brown with black spots. Barred race of e CO black with yellow bars and bands. HABITAT Sagebrush deserts, dry coniferous forests, watersides. ACTIVITY Apr.–Aug.: mainly nocturnal. RANGE ID (ex. sw), MT (ex. nw), WY, CO.

IDAHO GIANT SALAMANDER
Dicamptodon aterrimus
GIANT SALAMANDER FAMILY

10". Robust; skin smooth. Brown or purplish above, with blackish brown mottling and spots; belly pale brown or gray. Tail keeled. Adults live under forest litter, but also climb trees and bushes. Once considered race of Pacific Giant Salamander *(D. ensatus).* HABITAT Wet forests near rivers. RANGE n and nc ID, far wc MT.

Frogs

Adult frogs and toads (order Anura) have large heads and eyes, and wide, usually toothless mouths; they appear neckless, and most lack tails. Many can rapidly extend a long tongue for capturing insects. They have two long muscular hindlegs and two smaller front legs. All must keep their skin moist and avoid drying out in the sun. In the Rocky Mountain states, all frogs pass the winter in a state of torpor, burying themselves in mud at the edge of a pond or crawling between the bark and trunk of a large tree. In the spring, the male vocalizes to attract the larger female, and clings to her while fertilizing eggs as she lays them, usually in water. The eggs hatch into round-bodied, long-tailed aquatic larvae called tadpoles or pollywogs, which begin life with external gills that are soon covered with skin. The tadpole generally later transforms into a tail-less ground, tree, or marsh dweller with air-breathing lungs. Males of the tailed frog family (Ascaphidae) have a tail-like copulatory organ, found only in this group. Members of the spadefoot family (Pelobatidae) have a hard spade on their hindlegs to facilitate burrowing; they breed in puddles after very heavy rains, and develop from egg to tadpole to frog in only two weeks. Toads are a family (Bufonidae) of frogs that have shorter legs and warty skin, which secretes poisons that cause irritations. They have a large, swollen paratoid gland behind each eye. In the treefrog family (Hylidae), tadpoles live in water and adults live in trees; treefrogs have disks on their toes for clinging. The true frogs (Ranidae) are large, with slim waists, long legs, pointed toes, and webs on their hindfeet; most live in or near water and are good jumpers. Like salamanders, frogs are declining in number worldwide, partially because of environmental pollution.

Frogs and toads have well-developed ears (the eardrum is the conspicuous round disk behind each eye) and good vocal capabilities. In spring or summer, most male frogs and toads announce their presence with loud vocalizations that vary from species to species. When calling, the animals rapidly inflate and deflate balloon-like vocal sacs on the center or sides of the throat that amplify the sound. Calls are primarily used during the breeding season to attract mates, some by day, some at night; other species give calls to defend feeding territories long after breeding. Most frogs in the Rocky Mountain region have rather soft voices, but the calls of Bullfrogs carry far. The size given for frogs is the typical length from the tip of the nose to the end of the body, and does not include the extended legs.

eggs

tadpole

adult

Life Cycle of a Frog

TAILED FROG
Ascaphus truei
TAILED FROG FAMILY

2″. Brown above, with irreg. blackish spots; skin covered with small warts; black line from snout past eye; yellow triangle on top of head; toes long, slender. Male has pear-shaped, tail-like copulatory organ. **VOICE** Quiet; lacks vocal sacs. **HABITAT** High elevations: cold clear streams, nearby woodland floors. **ACTIVITY** Apr.–Sept.: mainly nocturnal. **RANGE** n and c ID, nw MT.

WESTERN TOAD
Bufo boreas
TOAD FAMILY

4". Grayish green or dark brown above; blackish raised warts with red dots; yellow stripe on back from eyes to rump; whitish below with black blotches. Oval gland behind eye. Tends to walk rather than hop. Lives in burrows when not foraging. **VOICE** Weak peeps; lacks vocal sacs. **HABITAT** In and near fresh water; woods, grasslands, gardens. **ACTIVITY** Apr.–Oct.: mainly nocturnal in hot months, by day in higher mtns. **RANGE** ID, w MT, w WY, CO mtns.

GREAT PLAINS TOAD
Bufo cognatus
TOAD FAMILY

3". Skin has many small warts. Gray, olive, or brown above, with large, dark brown oval blotches, bordered in white or buff; white or buff mid-back line. Elongated paratoid glands meet over crown. Digs own burrows. **VOICE** Shrill riveting trill of 20 or more seconds; chorus loud at close range. **HABITAT** Grasslands, sagebrush deserts. Breeds in ditches, streams, temporal pools. **ACTIVITY** Apr.–Sept.: forages at night and on rainy days. **RANGE** East of Rockies in MT, WY, CO.

PACIFIC TREEFROG
"Pacific Chorus Frog"
Hyla regilla
TREEFROG FAMILY

2". Skin rough. Toes lack webbing; have suction pads. Can change color in minutes; most have dark triangle on nose and wide brown stripe behind eyes; otherwise all yellow-green, or all buffy, or brown with many dark brown blotches and spots. **VOICE** High musical *kree-eek*. **HABITAT** Near water: rocks, shrubs, grass. **ACTIVITY** Apr.–Sept.: day and night. **RANGE** n and w ID, far w MT.

WESTERN CHORUS FROG
Pseudacris triseriata
TREEFROG FAMILY

1⅛". Slender; snout pointed; skin smooth. Buffy-, olive-, or reddish-brown above, with 5 dark brown stripes from nose through eyes and along sides; belly pale brown. Legs fairly short, spotted. **VOICE** Rasping, rising 1–2 second *prreep*. **HABITAT** Marshy ponds, moist meadows. **ACTIVITY** Mar.–Nov. in lowlands; May–Sept. in mtns.; active by day if nights cool, nocturnal on hot days. **RANGE** s ID, e and c MT, WY, CO.

BULLFROG
Rana catesbeiana
TRUE FROG FAMILY

6″. Yellowish green above, sometimes with dark mottling; pale yellow below. Head large, rounded. Ridge from eye over large eardrum to forelegs, but not on sides of back. Legs long, may be dark-banded; feet mainly webbed. Tadpoles become adults in 1–3 years. Introduced; displacing native frogs. **VOICE** Resonant *jug-o-rum,* day or night. **HABITAT** Marshes, ponds, rivers. **ACTIVITY** Apr.–Oct.: day and night; feeds mainly at night. **RANGE** e CO; local in w CO, c and se WY, w MT, w ID.

NORTHERN LEOPARD FROG
Rana pipiens
TRUE FROG FAMILY

3″. Slender; snout pointed. Body and legs have large oval spots with thin yellow edges. Green with dark green spots, or light brown with dark brown spots. Raised yellow ridges flank back and run along upper jaw. Ear drum usu. plain brown. Numbers are decreasing. **VOICE** Low 3-second snore, mixed with grunts and moans. **HABITAT** Marshes, rivers, meadows. **ACTIVITY** Day and night; Mar.–Nov. in lowlands. **RANGE** Entire region, ex. c ID and se CO.

OREGON SPOTTED FROG
Rana pretiosa
TRUE FROG FAMILY

3″. Brown above, with light-centered blackish spots; yellow to orange below, with dark mottling on throat; yellowish stripe on upper jaw. Ridges on back; legs fairly short; eyes slightly upturned. Toes fully webbed. Exterminated in most areas west of Cascades by introduced Bullfrog and predatory fish. **VOICE** 6–9 short rapid croaks; calls from water. **HABITAT** Ponds, lakes, streams. **ACTIVITY** Mar.–Oct.: by day. **RANGE** n and c ID, w MT, nw WY.

PLAINS SPADEFOOT
Spea (Scaphiopus) bombifrons
SPADEFOOT FAMILY

2″. Plump toad with wedge-shaped spade under hindfeet, raised bump between bulbous eyes. Skin olive-brown with darker brown spots and raised tubercles; pale buff or gray stripe on side of back; belly white. Eyes have vertical pupil. Lives in burrows to 2′ long. **VOICE** Duck-like bleat. **HABITAT** Open prairies: wet sand or gravel areas. **ACTIVITY** May–Aug.: nocturnal. **RANGE** East of Rockies in MT, WY, CO; also sc CO.

Reptiles

Members of the class Reptilia are cold-blooded, like amphibians. Their body temperature varies with that of their surroundings, and their activities come to a halt in cold weather, when they hibernate alone or in communal dens. Reptiles are scarce in the mountains due to the cool summers there; they are more frequent in the southern lowlands and deserts. Of the four orders of living reptiles, the Rocky Mountain states have two: turtles and scaled reptiles; the latter order includes both snakes and lizards. The reptilian body is low-slung and has a long tail and, except for the snakes, four short legs. Unlike the thin-skinned amphibians, reptiles are covered with protective scales (some are modified into plates in turtles) that waterproof their bodies and help keep them from becoming dehydrated. They breathe via lungs. All breed on land and mate by internal fertilization. Their eggs have brittle or leathery shells; some snakes give birth to live young. Newborns and young are shaped like adults but may differ in color. Reptiles grow throughout their lives, though growth rates are much slower after an animal reaches maturity.

Turtles

Members of the order Testudines, turtles are the oldest living group of reptiles, dating back to the time of the earliest dinosaurs. The upper part of their characteristic bony shell is the carapace, the lower part the plastron; both parts are covered with hard plates called scutes. Some species have ridges, called keels, on the carapace and tail. Most can withdraw the head and legs inside the shell for protection. Aquatic species have flipper-like legs. Turtles are the only toothless reptiles, but their horny beaks have sharp biting edges. The exposed skin of turtles is scaly and dry. Most spend hours basking in the sun. From October or November to March or April, turtles in the Rocky Mountain states hibernate. All turtles lay eggs; most dig a hollow, lay the eggs, cover them up, and leave them alone. When the eggs hatch, the young claw their way to the surface and fend for themselves. Lengths given are for the carapace of a typical adult.

Parts of a Turtle

ORNATE BOX TURTLE
"Western Box Turtle"
Terrapene ornata
POND AND BOX TURTLE FAMILY

5″. Carapace thick, high, flat on top; black or dark brown with yellow lines radiating from 3 spots on each side; thin yellow stripe at midline of dome. Plastron black with maze of yellow lines; forward hinge lets it protect head. Eyes and foreleg scales reddish in male, yellow in female. Mainly eats large insects. **HABITAT** Grasslands, sandhills; water (rare). **ACTIVITY** Apr.–Oct.: by day in spring and fall; nocturnal on hot summer days. **RANGE** se WY, e CO.

PAINTED TURTLE
Chrysemys picta
POND AND BOX TURTLE FAMILY

8″. Carapace oval, fairly flat, smooth; 3 rows of smooth black or olive scutes edged in yellow or red; some have yellow stripe down middle; outer scutes lined with red. Plastron red; black in middle with radiating dark lines. Head, neck, legs, and tail black, with longitudinal yellow or red lines. **HABITAT** Low elevations: marshy ponds, slow streams, river backwaters; walks on land between waterways. **ACTIVITY** Mar.–Nov.: by day; groups bask on logs in water. **RANGE** n ID, MT, n and e WY, e and sw CO.

COMMON SNAPPING TURTLE
Chelydra serpentina
SNAPPING TURTLE FAMILY

15″. Carapace oval, somewhat domed; smooth or with 3 rows of keels, with central keel heavier; trailing edge jagged; black or dark brown. Plastron cross-shaped, yellowish. Head massive, neck long. Tail as long as carapace, with sawtoothed keels. Excellent swimmer; rarely leaves water except for nesting or basking. **CAUTION** Powerful jaws can give a serious bite. **HABITAT** Rivers and ponds with mucky bottoms. **ACTIVITY** Mar.–Oct.: day and night. **RANGE** e MT, e WY, e CO.

SPINY SOFTSHELL TURTLE
Apalone spinifera
SOFTSHELL TURTLE FAMILY

Female 13″; male 7″. Carapace flattish, flexible, covered in leathery skin (not scutes); rear of shell sandpapery. Olive or tan with small black spots (larger in middle); edge of carapace pale yellow-orange with black line. Plastron smooth, flat, gray. Head brown; yellow stripe through eye; snout tubular. Feet paddle-like, fully webbed. Fast-moving on land or in water. **HABITAT** Low elevations: rivers, irrigation ditches. **ACTIVITY** Apr.–Sept.: by day; floats in still waters, basks. **RANGE** e and c MT, se WY, e CO.

Lizards

Lizards (suborder Sauria of the scaled reptile order, Squamata) generally have long tails; most species have legs and are capable of running, climbing, and clinging, though in some the legs are tiny or lacking. Typical lizards resemble salamanders but can be distinguished from them by their dry scaly skin, clawed feet, and external ear openings. Lizard species vary greatly in size, shape, and color; in many, color and patterns differ among adult males, adult females,

LONG-NOSED LEOPARD LIZARD
Gambelia wislizenii
IGUANA FAMILY
12″. Brownish gray above with leopard-like spots that are blackish (when hot) or brown (when cool); thin whitish bars fade with age; paler below. Yellowish eye ring; throat gray-streaked. Fast runner, often on 2 feet; chases large insects, mice, other lizards. **CAUTION** Bites if handled. **HABITAT** Open sand and gravel areas with few bushes. **ACTIVITY** May–Aug.: by day. **RANGE** s ID, far w CO.

LESSER EARLESS LIZARD
Holbrookia maculata
IGUANA FAMILY
5″. Drab; no external ear openings; tail rather short, slender. Gray or brown above with faint blotches; pale gray stripes on midback and sides. Male has 2 black spots on sides of belly. Breeding female tinted orange. Burrows headfirst into sand. **HABITAT** Sandy streambeds, grasslands, fields. **ACTIVITY** Mar.–Oct.: by day. **RANGE** e and far sw CO.

EASTERN COLLARED LIZARD
Crotaphytus collaris
IGUANA FAMILY
12″. Head large; neck narrow with 2 white-edged black collars; tail longer than body, thin, not flattened. Male: head swollen, plain gray or yellow; brown or blue-green above, with many yellow spots; blue-gray or greenish below; throat blue-green or orange; tail gray with brown spots. Female: gray or brown with creamy spots; may show rusty barring. Runs from danger on hind legs. **HABITAT** Below 8,000′: rocky canyons, ledges, open woods, scrub. **ACTIVITY** Apr.–Oct.: by day. **RANGE** w and se CO. **Mojave Black-collared Lizard** *(C. bicinctores)* of s ID browner; male has black throat patch.

and young. Most lizards in the region are iguanids, which vary greatly in form and habits. The whiptails have very long tails and are active, nervous prowlers. Skinks have smooth, shiny bodies, small legs, and tails that break easily. Most lizards are active by day, and many are particularly active in the midday heat. Most do not swim in water. Fertilization is internal; most lay eggs rather than give birth to live young. The size given for lizards is the length from the tip of the snout to the end of the tail.

DESERT HORNED LIZARD
Phrynosoma platyrhinos
IGUANA FAMILY

4½". Body flat; brown, gray, black, or sandy, with dark wavy bands; nose blunt; crown of thin spines on nape; rows of short spines on back and sides; tail short, spiny. Eats ants. Relies on camouflage, not speed, to elude capture. **HABITAT** Desert scrub, washes. **ACTIVITY** Apr.–Sept: by day; basks on rocks. **RANGE** s ID.

SHORT-HORNED LIZARD
"Horned Toad"
Phrynosoma douglassii
IGUANA FAMILY

3". Head plain; fan of short spines behind eyes. Brown, buffy yellow, or bluish gray above (color matches soil); 2 dark blotches at back of neck; smaller spots along sides; sides and tail edged with spines. **HABITAT** Below 9,000′: rocky to sandy open areas; open juniper, pine woods. **ACTIVITY** Apr.–Oct.: by day. **RANGE** s ID, c and e MT, most of WY and CO.

SAGEBRUSH LIZARD
Sceloporus graciosus
IGUANA FAMILY

5½". Male striped brown and grayish white above; throat pale blue; belly bright blue with white line down middle; reddish-orange spot on sides. Female has faint or no blue below. Scales spiny. Only lizard in Yellowstone and Grand Teton N.P.'s. **HABITAT** Sagebrush deserts, open juniper and pine woods. **ACTIVITY** Apr.–Sept.: by day. **RANGE** c and s ID, s MT, much of WY, w CO.

WESTERN FENCE LIZARD
Sceloporus occidentalis
IGUANA FAMILY

8". Male has chevrons of light and dark brown and grayish white above; throat and belly dark blue with irreg. dark line down middle. Legs partly orange below. Female has faint or no blue on belly. Skin has coarse spiny scales. **HABITAT** Desert canyons, woods, boulders, old buildings, log piles. **ACTIVITY** May–Sept.: by day, basks in morning sun. **RANGE** sw ID.

EASTERN FENCE LIZARD
Sceloporus undulatus
IGUANA FAMILY

5″. Gray-brown. Northern prairie race (e CO, se WY; pictured): gray stripes. Red-lipped plateau race (CO, sc WY): weak striping, lips red when breeding. Northern plateau race (w CO, sw WY): wavy brown and gray bands, gray side stripe. **HABITAT** Sunny rocky areas in semi-deserts, prairies, pinewoods. **ACTIVITY** Mar.–Oct.: by day. **RANGE** s WY, CO.

TREE LIZARD
Urosaurus ornatus
IGUANA FAMILY

5½″. Slender; tail 1½ times body length. Pale gray-brown above with irreg. small dark blotches. Fold of skin at base of throat. Male has blue or orange throat, bright blue belly patches. Feeds in trees, perched upright; wary. **HABITAT** Below 9,000′: valleys with trees; buildings; rocks in arid areas. **ACTIVITY** Apr.–Oct.: by day. **RANGE** sw WY, w CO.

SIDE-BLOTCHED LIZARD
Uta stansburiana
IGUANA FAMILY

5½″. Head and body gray to brown, white-edged, dark brown spots on back and tail. Male sides and tail blue-speckled; throat blue, edged with orange. Fold of skin on neck; large black blotch on side behind forelegs. Often bobs head. **HABITAT** Cliffs, sagebrush deserts, juniper scrub. **ACTIVITY** Apr.–Oct.: by day. **RANGE** sw WY, w CO.

SIX-LINED RACERUNNER
Cnemidophorus sexlineatus
WHIPTAIL FAMILY

9″. Slender; snout wedge-shaped; tail long, thin. Head and foreparts greenish; rest of body and sides of tail dark brown, with thin golden stripes. Adult's tail mainly brown, juv.'s blue. Very fast in fleeing danger. **HABITAT** Prairie grasslands, sandhills, streambeds, rocks at bases of mtns. **ACTIVITY** Apr.–Oct.: by day; basks often. **RANGE** se WY, e CO.

WESTERN WHIPTAIL
Cnemidophorus tigris
WHIPTAIL FAMILY

10″. Slender; tail very long, thin, gray-brown (adult) or blue (young). Dark brown with 4 golden stripes above, golden spots on sides; throat white; belly may have dark spots. Digs burrows. **HABITAT** Open pinyon-juniper woods without tall grass; desert scrub. **ACTIVITY** Apr.–Oct.: by day. **RANGE** sw ID, w CO.

PLATEAU STRIPED WHIPTAIL
Cnemidophorus velox
WHIPTAIL FAMILY

9″. Slender. Unspotted dark brown above, with 6–7 yellowish stripes; tail light blue; throat and belly light blue-green or whitish. Juv. has bright blue tail. Unisexual; no mating; all can lay 3–5 eggs. **HABITAT** Pinyon-juniper woods, mtn. scrub, sagebrush, valleys. **ACTIVITY** May–Oct.: by day. **RANGE** s two-thirds of far w CO.

MANY-LINED SKINK
Eumeces multivirgatus
SKINK FAMILY

7″. Slim. Tail looks swollen; buffy brown with dark spots. Midback pale gray stripe bordered by dark and pale brown stripes or rows of spots; creamy below. In s CO may be unstriped brown above. **HABITAT** Loose sandy soils in plains; pinyon-juniper woods and rocky, scrubby areas in mtns. **ACTIVITY** Apr.–Oct.: by day. **RANGE** se WY, e and sw CO.

GREAT PLAINS SKINK
Eumeces obsoletus
SKINK FAMILY

12″. Uniformly colored; scales on sides angled forward. Adult speckled (brown scales have black edges); belly buffy. Juv. black with blue-black tail; lips speckled white. Seldom seen in open; usu. stays under rocks, logs on ground. **HABITAT** Sandhills, floodplain valleys, rocky slopes. **ACTIVITY** Apr.–Sept.: by day. **RANGE** Far ne and much of se CO.

WESTERN SKINK
Eumeces skiltonianus
SKINK FAMILY

8″. Adult brown above, with wide buff and blackish stripes from face to base of tail; gray below; tail gray-brown. Body scales smooth and shiny, small; head scales large. Juv. stripes more black and white; tail bright blue. Hides under bark, logs, rocks. **HABITAT** Grasslands, woods, rocky streamsides. **ACTIVITY** May–Sept.: by day. **RANGE** All ID, far w MT.

NORTHERN ALLIGATOR LIZARD
Elgaria coerulea
ALLIGATOR LIZARD FAMILY

11″. Brown above with black speckles; fold of skin along sides; grayish below with dark stripes. Head large; eyes dark. Scales rough. Forages in grass, leaves; rests under wood, bark, logs, and rocks. **HABITAT** Wet coniferous forest edges, talus slopes. **ACTIVITY** Apr.–Sept.: by day. **RANGE** n ID, w MT.

Snakes

Snakes (suborder Serpentes of the scaled reptile order, Squamata) have elongated scaly bodies without limbs, eyelids, or external ear openings. They grow throughout their lives, shedding their skin from snout to tail several times each year. Snakes are carnivorous, and they swallow their prey whole. The flicking, forked tongue serves as an organ of smell, collecting information on potential prey and dangers. Snakes usually mate in the fall, before their winter hibernation, which usually begins in November and ends in March or April. Most species lay eggs in June that hatch in September; a few give birth to live young in late summer. Most snakes in the Rocky Mountain states are nonpoisonous, but beware of the Western Rattlesnake, which lives mainly below 8,000′. In the accounts below, the size given is the length of a typical adult.

RUBBER BOA
Lichanura (Charina) bottae
BOA AND PYTHON FAMILY

24″. Thick; skin looks and feels rubbery; tail blunt; scales smooth, shiny. Plain brown above, yellowish below. Eyes tiny. Climbs trees; good burrower and swimmer. Feeds mainly at night and on warm overcast days; constricts mice, shrews, birds. **HABITAT** Below 9,200′: woods, grasslands, sandy watersides. **ACTIVITY** Apr.–Oct.: by night, warm cloudy days. **RANGE** All ID, w MT, nw WY.

RACER
Coluber constrictor
COLUBRID SNAKE FAMILY

3′4″. Slender. Western race: Adult slaty, brown, olive green, or grayish olive above; yellowish below. Young yellowish with black-edged rufous spots on back. Active by day; moves fast; climbs trees. Not a constrictor. **CAUTION** Bites hard, thrashes (but not poisonous). **HABITAT** Below 7,000′: woodland edges, grasslands, shrubby canyons, sagebrush deserts. **RANGE** s ID, sw and e MT, WY, e and wc CO.

WESTERN HOG-NOSED SNAKE
Heterodon nasicus
COLUBRID SNAKE FAMILY

28″. Heavy-bodied; neck broad; snout spade-like, upturned. Pale brown, buffy, or gray; large dark brown spots on back, smaller spots on sides; washed blackish below. Good burrower; can detect buried toads, lizards, other snakes by smell. **HABITAT** Sand and gravel prairie, scrub, floodplains. **ACTIVITY** Apr.–Oct.: by day. **RANGE** e MT, far e WY, e CO.

MILK SNAKE
"Milk Kingsnake"
Lampropeltis triangulum
COLUBRID SNAKE FAMILY

2″. Black rings with alternating red or orange rings and white, gray, or yellow-green rings. Head black with pale snout. In WY and MT, black rings narrower, snout orange. Constricts. **HABITAT** Woods, rocky hillsides, prairies, farms. **RANGE** c and se MT, n and e WY, e and far w CO.

NORTHERN WATER SNAKE
Nerodia (Natrix) sipedon
COLUBRID SNAKE FAMILY

3′. Front has wide dark brown and narrower buffy brown bands; rear blotched; belly has black, red, or yellow marks. Older adults appear all dark. Adept swimmer; basks on shores. **CAUTION** Bites when handled (not poisonous). **HABITAT** Streams, reservoirs, marshes. **ACTIVITY** Apr.–Oct.: day and night. **RANGE** e CO.

WESTERN TERRESTRIAL GARTER SNAKE
Thamnophis elegans
COLUBRID SNAKE FAMILY

30″. Brown above; head plain; body has squarish dark brown spots; buffy yellow stripe on nape to midback and on lower sides. Feeds in water and on land. Basks in sun. **HABITAT** Watersides, woods, grasslands, to 13,000′. **ACTIVITY** Apr.–Oct.: by day. **RANGE** Entire region, ex. far e CO.

PLAINS GARTER SNAKE
Thamnophis radix
COLUBRID SNAKE FAMILY

30″. Slender. Midback yellow or orange stripe; rest of back brownish gray or reddish with large black dots; thin pale yellow stripe on sides with row of black spots below. Often basks in sun. **HABITAT** Below 7,500′: urban areas, valleys, grasslands, ponds. **ACTIVITY** Apr.–Oct.: day and night. **RANGE** e MT, e WY, e CO.

GOPHER SNAKE
Pituophis catenifer
COLUBRID SNAKE FAMILY

5′. Head yellowish brown; dark line across top. Great Basin race (pictured): brown, with yellow bands. Bullsnake race, east of Rockies: yellowish brown, with brown blotches. **HABITAT** Below 9,000′: woods, grasslands, deserts. **ACTIVITY** Apr.–Oct.: by day, warm nights. **RANGE** Entire region, ex. n ID, nw MT.

COMMON GARTER SNAKE
Thamnophis sirtalis
COLUBRID SNAKE FAMILY

3′. Extremely variable in color and pattern. Head is wider than body; scales keeled. Red-sided race east of Rockies has a yellowish back stripe; rest of back a checkerboard of red and black spots; yellowish below, with black spots; top of head olive brown. Valley race of ID: body brownish or gray; top of head blackish; wide yellow back stripe. **CAUTION** If handled, bites and expels musk and feces (not poisonous). **ACTIVITY** Nearly year-round: by day. **HABITAT** Below 8,000′: marshes, ponds, and streamsides. **RANGE** ID, MT, n and e WY, ne CO.

Poisonous Snakes and Snakebite

The Rocky Mountain region has only one poisonous snake species—the Western Rattlesnake, found mainly below 8,000′. This rattler has retractable fangs that can deliver blood-destroying venom, but it will flee from footsteps. If you encounter one, freeze to let it withdraw, then step away. While bites sting, they are rarely fatal. However, for any poisonous snakebite the best course of action is to get to medical care as soon as possible, with the dead snake or positive identification, so the proper antivenin can be administered. Meanwhile, the victim should avoid moving, as movement helps the venom spread through the system, and keep the injured body part motionless just below heart level. The victim should be kept warm, calm, and at rest while on the way to medical care. If you are alone and on foot, start walking slowly toward help, exerting the injured area as little as possible. If you run, or if the bite has delivered a large amount of venom, you may collapse, but a snakebite seldom results in death.

WESTERN RATTLESNAKE
Crotalus viridis
PIT VIPER FAMILY

4′. Stout; head wide, triangular; long hollow fangs; rattles on tail. Prairie Rattlesnake race (pictured), east of Rockies: grayish buff with large, dark brown blotches above; spots form into faded bands toward rattles; top of head variegated; yellowish angled stripes below eye. Midget Faded Rattlesnake race of sw WY and far w CO usu. only 2′ long; pale yellow with indistinct blotches. Great Basin Rattlesnake race of s ID similar to Prairie race. Excitable and aggressive; gives warning by rattling tail and holding ground. Winters in communal dens. Feeds on ground squirrels, other rodents, rabbits; locates prey with heat sensors. **CAUTION** Poisonous; bites can be fatal. **ACTIVITY** Apr.–Oct.: day and night. **HABITAT** Grasslands, sagebrush, rocky woods, canyonsides. **RANGE** Most of region, mainly below 8,000′; rarely to 11,000′.

Birds

Members of the class Aves, birds are the only animals that have feathers, and most are capable of flight. Like their reptile ancestors, they lay eggs; like mammals, they are warm-blooded. They generally have excellent sight and hearing, but few have a good sense of smell. The bird skeleton is adapted for flight: the bones are lightweight, with a sponge-like interior. The forelimbs have become wings, with strong pectoral muscles attached to a keeled breastbone, and the hindlimbs are modified for running, grasping, or perching. Wing shapes vary among types of birds, ranging, for example, from the long, broad wings of the soaring raptors to the narrow, fast-moving wings of hummingbirds.

While all Steller's Jays in one area look the same regardless of their age or gender or the time of year, this is not the case for most birds. Plumages may vary from juvenile to immature to adult, from male to female, and from breeding to nonbreeding seasons (summer and winter, respectively). (If both sexes have a summer plumage distinct from nonbreeding plumage, we note this as "summer adult." If only the male has such a summer plumage, we note "summer male.") In some species, groups living in different geographic areas (subspecies, or races) have slightly or distinctly different plumages. Some birds within a given species have different colorations (called *morphs* or *phases*) that have nothing to do with where they live. Some birds have ornamental plumes, often developed in the breeding season. This guide describes the plumages most often seen in the Rocky Mountain states. The photograph shows the male or the adult (if adults look alike) unless otherwise noted.

Flight allows birds to migrate great distances, though some are year-round residents in one region. Many birds who spend the winter in warmer, southern climes migrate north to breed, taking advantage of the abundant animal life in the summertime Rocky Mountain states. Other birds breed to the north, in Canada or Alaska, and pass through the region only in migration. Cold and snow rarely kill birds directly but may reduce the amounts of food (insects, animals, seeds, berries) they must obtain to maintain their ideal body temperature. Many of our breeding species winter in Texas, the Southwest, Mexico, or beyond. Most individuals return to the same breeding and wintering grounds throughout their lives.

Northbound migration occurs from March to early June, southbound from July to November. Migrants often wait until the wind is at their backs before beginning the journey. In spring, warm southerly winds help migrants return from southern regions to the Rockies. In autumn, winds from the north and northwest aid southbound migrants on their journey south. For more about bird migration, see the essay on bird-watching on page 247.

In bird species that do not nest in colonies, a male who is ready to breed stakes out and defends a nesting territory from other males. The female chooses a male in part on the quality and size of his territory, the presence of a secure nest site, and the quality of his

Parts of a Bird

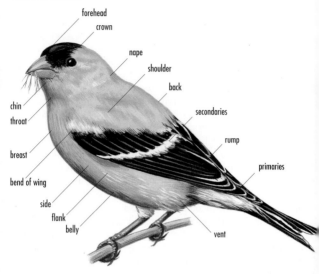

forehead
crown
nape
shoulder
back
secondaries
rump
primaries
chin
throat
breast
bend of wing
side
flank
belly
vent

plumage and song. The avian life cycle typically starts with the female laying one or more eggs in a nest, which, depending on the species, may be a scrape in the sand, a cup of rootlets and fibers, a woven basket, a stick platform, or another type of structure. After an incubation period of roughly two to four weeks, the young are hatched and fed by their parents for a period varying from a few days (shorebirds) to a few weeks (most species) to many months (raptors). Smaller birds tend to breed the year following their birth, while many larger birds remain immature for several years before breeding. During the breeding season, many male birds exhibit more colorful and elaborate plumages and courtship displays and rituals in order to attract a mate. Most species mate in solitary pairs, the males competing for breeding territories; other species nest colonially. In this section of the guide, assume a bird is a solitary nester unless the description notes that it nests in colonies. Space limitations prevent us from giving descriptions of nests and eggs.

Birds use their voices in many ways. In many species, contact and alarm call notes are given year-round by both sexes. The more musical songs, usually given only in spring and summer by the male, attract mates and define territory. Once the young are born, many birds stop singing; the region's forests, scrub, and fields are much quieter in August than in June.

This section's descriptions give the length of the bird from the tip of the beak to the end of the tail. For some large species, both length and wingspan are given.

Bird-watching

Bird-watching, or birding, as it is often termed, can be a casual activity, develop into a hobby, or become a passion. Some observers enjoy generally keeping track of birds they come across in their daily activities or while hiking, driving, or boating, while others become intent on seeing as many different types of birds as possible. It's possible to see 200 or more species a year in the Rocky Mountain region.

In breeding season, many birds tend to live in only one habitat and are active at certain times of day. Freshwater marsh birds (rails and bitterns) are most often calling and active at dawn and dusk. Until mid-morning on hot days, songbirds search woods, fields, and thickets for food; from mid-morning to late afternoon, they tend to be quiet; they forage again late in the day. Birds that live near rivers, lakes, and other aquatic habitats (herons, cormorants, ducks, sandpipers) may be active all day. Make an after-dark visit to a forest or wooded riverside to listen for owls, which may respond to taped or imitated calls and can be viewed with spotlights.

The greatest variety of birds can be seen during the migration seasons. In early spring (March and April), larger birds such as nonwintering hawks and waterfowl return to the lowlands, while winter residents begin moving northward. Most songbirds migrate north to and through the region during the latter half of April and the month of May; males arrive a week or so before females in order to stake out territories. When the landbird migration tapers off in late May, shorebirds are still flying through. While larger birds migrate by day, most species, especially smaller, insect-eating ones, fly at night, resting and feeding during the day and tend to gather in quiet places where food is easy to find. In a light woodland along a stream, where there are newly opened leaves and plenty of small insects, it is possible to see a half-dozen or more species of migrant songbirds in a single spring morning.

Fall migration is underway by July, when the first southbound Arctic-breeding shorebirds reappear; adults in these groups migrate a week to a month before their offspring. From August into October, most of the dabbling ducks and songbirds pass through. The migration of diving ducks, geese, and raptors starts in September and continues into November. During severe winters, many birds may shift farther southward.

For the serious birder, at least one good field guide is essential; many excellent ones are available, including the *National Audubon Society Field Guide to North American Birds (Western Region)*. Binoculars (7-, 8-, 9-, or 10-power) are a must; a close-focusing pair is especially helpful. Birders learn to move slowly and quietly, and to not make loud noises. Please respect local laws, do not unduly frighten birds, and take great care not to disrupt nesting or resting birds.

For suggestions on attracting birds to your yard, see page 296. In this section, the icon ⚘ denotes species that will come into a yard to a feeder. The icon ▰ indicates species that might use a nest box in a yard.

COMMON LOON
Gavia immer
LOON FAMILY

winter (left), summer (right)

32". Summer: black back with large white spots; head, neck, and bill black; white bands on neck. Winter: slaty above, white below; crown and hindneck blackish, sharply demarcated in zigzag edge from white throat and foreneck. Bill heavy, pointed. **VOICE** Quavering laughter, yodeling, mainly on spring and summer nights. **HABITAT** Summer: mtn. lakes. Migration: lakes, reservoirs. **RANGE** Apr.–May, Oct.–Nov.: entire region. May–Sept.: nw WY, nw MT.

PIED-BILLED GREBE
Podilymbus podiceps
GREBE FAMILY

13". Summer: body brown; chin black; black ring on white bill. Winter: body brown; chin white; bill yellow or gray, lacks ring. Bill short, conical. Dives frequently for small fish. **VOICE** Series of 8 *cow* notes. **HABITAT** Marshes, ponds, lakes. **RANGE** Apr.–Oct.: entire region. Nov.–Mar.: local.

HORNED GREBE
Podiceps auritus
GREBE FAMILY

14". Neck thin; bill slender; eyes red. Summer: black above; neck and underparts chestnut; head black; yellowish stripe over eye. Winter: back and hindneck slaty; crown black; throat and foreneck white. **VOICE** Croaks and chatters in summer. **HABITAT** Lakes. **RANGE** Mar.–Apr., Sept.–Oct.: entire region. Apr.–Sept.: n MT, nw WY (local).

RED-NECKED GREBE
Podiceps grisegena
GREBE FAMILY

19". Crown, back, and hindneck blackish; whitish below. Bill black above, yellow below. Summer: foreneck reddish; cheeks and throat white. Winter: foreneck gray or buffy; white crescent from throat to nape. **VOICE** Wails and trills. **HABITAT** Ponds, lakes. **RANGE** May–Aug.: n ID, nw MT (local). Apr., Sept.–Oct.: ID, MT (rare).

EARED GREBE
Podiceps nigricollis
GREBE FAMILY

13″. Slaty above, whitish below. Bill slender, black; eyes red. Summer: sides rusty; head and neck black; face streaked yellow. Winter: neck gray; head black; white throat/nape patch. **VOICE** Soft *poo-eep.* **HABITAT** Ponds, marshes. **RANGE** Apr.–May, Sept.–Nov.: entire region (widespread). May–Sept.: entire region (local).

WESTERN GREBE
Aechmophorus occidentalis
GREBE FAMILY

27″. Dark gray above, white below. Top half of head (to below eye) and hindneck black; throat and foreneck white; bill greenish yellow. Neck long, thin, snake-like; eyes red. Nests in colonies, on reed platforms in marsh. **VOICE** Rolling *kerr-rick.* **HABITAT** Summer: shallow lakes. Migration: deeper lakes. **RANGE** Mid-Mar.–Nov.: entire region.

AMERICAN WHITE PELICAN
Pelecanus erythrrorhynchos
PELICAN FAMILY

L 5′2″; WS 8′. All white at rest; bill long, with pouch. Legs short; feet wide, webbed. Flight shows black primaries. Dips bill into water for fish. Flies in V or wheels in sky on thermals. Nests in colonies. **VOICE** Grunts at nest **HABITAT** Lakes, reservoirs. **RANGE** Apr., Sept.–Oct.: entire region (local). May–Aug.: local, mainly in e ID, ne MT, nw and e WY, ne CO.

DOUBLE-CRESTED CORMORANT
Phalacrocorax auritus
CORMORANT FAMILY

33″. Black (may look greenish); back and wings brownish; breeding crest (small tufts on sides of head) hard to see. Bill hooked. Swims with bill angled up; spreads wings to dry at rest. Nests in colonies. Expanding. **VOICE** Usu. silent. **HABITAT** Lakes, rivers. **RANGE** Mid-Mar.–Apr., Sept.–Oct.: entire region. May–Aug.: most common in s ID, c and e MT, WY, e CO.

AMERICAN BITTERN
Botaurus lentiginosus
HERON FAMILY

28″. Adult brown, paler below, with brown streaks on underparts; thin white eyebrow stripe; black stripe partway down neck. Neck thick; legs greenish. Imm. lacks black neck stripe. Shy; points bill skyward if disturbed. **VOICE** Loud, pumping *uunk-KA-lunk.* **HABITAT** Marshes. **RANGE** Apr.–Oct.: entire region (local, uncommon).

SNOWY EGRET
Egretta thula
HERON FAMILY

24″. All white. Bill slender, black; lores yellow. Neck long. Legs long, black; feet yellow. During courtship, long, lacy, white plumes on back, chest, and crown. Imm. back of legs yellow-green. Nests in colonies. **VOICE** Harsh *aah*. **HABITAT** Marshes, lakesides. **RANGE** Apr.–Sept.: s ID, sw WY, w and e CO (local, uncommon). **Cattle Egret** (*Bubulcus ibis;* 20″) is white with yellow bill; Apr.–Sept.: e and s CO.

GREAT BLUE HERON
Ardea herodias
HERON FAMILY

L 4′; WS 6′. Adult back and wings blue-gray; black patches on side of breast and belly; crown black with white center; black plumes from back of head when breeding; face white; most of neck gray; underparts striped gray and white. Legs very long, dark; bill yellow. Nests in colonies. **VOICE** Deep squawk. **HABITAT** Freshwater shorelines. **RANGE** Mar.–Oct.: entire region (local but widespread breeder). Nov.–Feb.: ID, sw MT, sw WY, CO (uncommon).

BLACK-CROWNED NIGHT-HERON
Nycticorax nycticorax
HERON FAMILY

26″. Adult crown and back black; wings gray; lores and underparts white; eyes red. Neck long; legs shortish, yellow. Imm. back and wings brown, with large whitish spots; striped brown and white below. Nests in colonies. **VOICE** Low *kwock*. **HABITAT** Ponds, marshes. **RANGE** Apr.–Oct.: s ID, MT (local), s WY, CO.

WHITE-FACED IBIS
Plegadis chihi
IBIS FAMILY

24″. Summer: glossy chestnut with glossy green wings; white line encircles eye and bare red skin at base of bill. Bill long, drooping, silvery; neck long. Legs long; red when breeding. Flies with neck out; alternates flaps and glides; often in lines. Nests in colonies. **VOICE** Low grunts. **HABITAT** Marshy ponds, lakes in open country. **RANGE** Mid-Apr.–May, Sept.: entire region. June–Aug.: mainly s ID, c and e MT, WY, e CO.

Waterfowl

The waterfowl family (Anatidae) contains the huge white swans, the medium-size geese, and a wide variety of smaller ducks. All have webbed feet and thick bills designed for filtering small organisms in the water or for grasping underwater vegetation and invertebrates, often mollusks. Most waterfowl undergo lengthy migrations between northern or inland breeding areas and southern and/or coastal wintering waters. Their nests, made of grasses and lined with feathers, are usually on the ground, hidden in tall grass or reeds, and contain many eggs.

Mallard dabbling

Mallard taking off, straight up, from surface of water

Ducks may be split into two main groups. Dabbling ducks upend on the surface of fresh and brackish waters and can jump up and take flight straight out of the water; some reveal a colorful patch (speculum) on the wings near the body. Diving ducks dive deep under the surface of fresh and salt waters; in taking flight, they run and flap horizontally over the water's surface before gaining altitude. Swans and geese upend like dabbling ducks, rather than dive for food; most patter across the water to get

Canada Goose taking off by running across water

airborne. Waterfowl males are in breeding plumage from fall through early summer but in late summer develop a drab non-breeding plumage similar to that of females. Many species remain in the region until the lakes and marshes freeze. Some overwinter where hot springs, flowing rivers, or available food allow them to stay.

TRUMPETER SWAN
Cygnus buccinator
WATERFOWL FAMILY

L 6′; WS to 8′. Adult all white; bill and legs black; black facial skin envelops front of eye. Imm. grayish white; bill reddish on sides. Flies with neck outstretched. Once endangered; survived at Red Rocks Lake N.W.R. in s MT. Range and numbers gradually expanding. **VOICE** Loud deep *coo-hoo.* **HABITAT** Marshes, lakes. Winter: also farms. **RANGE** Resident in sw MT, ne ID, nw WY, esp. Yellowstone and Grand Teton N.P.'s.

TUNDRA SWAN
Cygnus columbianus
WATERFOWL FAMILY

L 4'5"; WS 7'. Adult mostly white; head and neck often stained buffy; bill thick, black, tapers to eye; small yellow spot before eye. Neck extremely long. Feet black; tail short. Imm. light brown; bill mostly pink. Flies with neck outstretched. **VOICE** Mellow, high-pitched *hoo-oo-hoo.* **HABITAT** Large lakes, marshes. **RANGE** Mar., Oct.–Nov.: entire region. A few winter locally.

SNOW GOOSE
Chen caerulescens
WATERFOWL FAMILY

28". Adult pure white, with black primaries; bill pink, with black "lips"; face often stained rusty; legs pink. Flight reveals black primaries. Imm. pale brownish-gray. "Blue" phase has white head, dark brown body. Flies in high V formation. **VOICE** High nasal honks. **HABITAT** Marshes, lakesides. **RANGE** Mar.–Apr., Oct.–Nov.: entire region (numbers increasing). Dec.–Feb.: e CO (local).

CANADA GOOSE
Branta canadensis
WATERFOWL FAMILY

common race (left), small race (right)

L 3'4"; WS 6'. Adult back and wings dark brown; head and long neck black with large white chinstrap; breast pale to dark brown; vent and rump white; tail short, black. Often flies in V formation. Many races; some races are much smaller, with short necks. **VOICE** Honking *car-uunk.* **HABITAT** Marshes, rivers, ponds, wide lawns, fallow fields, towns. **RANGE** Resident in entire region. Oct.–Apr.: migrants and winterers increase numbers.

WOOD DUCK
Aix sponsa
WATERFOWL FAMILY

19". Dabbler. Male iridescent; back dark purple (looks black); chest reddish-purple with white stripes; sides buffy. Head green; laid-back crest has white stripes; throat and 2-pronged chinstrap white; eye ring and base of bill red. Female brown, with white eye ring. **VOICE** Male: usu. quiet; high whistle when courting. Female: *oo-eek*. **HABITAT** Swamps, marshes, slow rivers. **RANGE** Feb.–Nov.: entire region (local). A few winter in CO.

GREEN-WINGED TEAL
Anas crecca
WATERFOWL FAMILY

14". Dabbler. Male body gray, with vertical white stripe behind buffy chest; head chestnut; green eye patch extends to fluffy nape; vent patch yellow; bill small, black. Female brown. Flight reveals green wing patch. Region's smallest duck. **VOICE** Male: whistled *crick-et*. **HABITAT** Marshes, ponds. **RANGE** Mar.–Nov.: entire region. Dec.–Feb.: from s ID and w MT south.

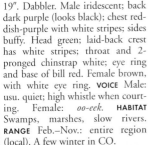

MALLARD
Anas platyrhynchos
WATERFOWL FAMILY

male (left), female (right)

24". Dabbler. Male body and wings gray; head and neck green; white ring above purplish chest; rump black; tail white; bill yellow. Female buffy, heavily mottled with brown; bill pale orange with dark saddle. Legs orange. Flight reveals blue hindwing patch, bordered with white. Region's most widespread duck. **VOICE** Male: quiet; gives *reeb* call when fighting. Female: quack. **HABITAT** Ponds, rivers, marshes, parks, towns. **RANGE** Resident in entire region (common).

NORTHERN PINTAIL
Anas acuta
WATERFOWL FAMILY

Male 28"; female 21". Dabbler. Male back, wings, and sides gray; head and hindneck brown; foreneck and belly white; tail very long, black. Female smaller, pale brown, with bronzy-brown wing patch. Neck thin; tail sharp, pointed. **VOICE** Male: wheezy *prip prip.* Female: quack. **HABITAT** Marshes, ponds. **RANGE** Mar.–Nov.: entire region. Dec.–Feb.: s ID, w MT, w and s WY, CO.

BLUE-WINGED TEAL
Anas discors
WATERFOWL FAMILY

15". Dabbler. Male body brown with black dots; head dull blue-gray with white crescent before eye; crown black. Female mottled brown; similar to female Cinnamon Teal. Bill heavier, longer than Green-winged Teal's. Flight reveals pale cerulean blue forewing patches and green wing patch. **VOICE** Male: *peep.* **HABITAT** Marshes, weedy ponds. **RANGE** Apr.–mid-Oct.: entire region.

CINNAMON TEAL
Anas cyanoptera
WATERFOWL FAMILY

15". Dabbler. Male head, neck, sides, and belly reddish chestnut; crown black; back scalloped brown; cerulean blue forewing patch visible in flight. Female mottled brown; in flight, similar to Blue-winged Teal. Bill heavy, black. **VOICE** Male: soft *chuck.* Female: soft quack. **HABITAT** Marshes, shallow lakes. **RANGE** Mar.–Oct.: entire region; sparse in far e MT, e WY.

NORTHERN SHOVELER
Anas clypeata
WATERFOWL FAMILY

18". Dabbler. Male head green; chest white; sides rusty; eyes yellow; bill black. Female brown, speckled; bill orange or yellow. Neck short; bill long, wide, held close to water. Flight reveals blue forewing patch. **VOICE** Male: low *took.* Female: quack. **HABITAT** Marshes, ponds. **RANGE** Mid-Mar.–May, Sept.–Nov.: entire region. June–Aug.: breeds in ID, MT, WY, locally in CO. A few winter in c CO.

GADWALL
Anas strepera
WATERFOWL FAMILY

20″. Dabbler. Male body and head gray; bill black; rear end black. Female brown; bill black, with orange edge. Flight reveals square white wing patch bordered in black. **VOICE** Male: croaks, whistles. Female: subdued quack. **HABITAT** Lakes, marshes. **RANGE** Mar.–Nov.: entire region. Dec.–Feb.: local from s ID and w MT south.

AMERICAN WIGEON
Anas americana
WATERFOWL FAMILY

21″. Dabbler. Both sexes brownish with dull rusty-orange sides and speckled head. Male has green patch behind eye; forehead white; vent black and white. Flight reveals white forewing patch. **VOICE** Whistled *whee whee whew.* **HABITAT** Shallow lakes, ponds, fields, park lawns. **RANGE** Mar.–Nov.: entire region. Dec.–Feb.: from s ID and w MT south (local).

CANVASBACK
Aythya valisineria
WATERFOWL FAMILY

21″. Diver. Male back and sides white; chest and tail black; head reddish brown; eyes red. Female back, wings, and sides gray; chest dark brown; head light brown, with white eye ring, dark eyes; tail blackish. Sloping forehead forms straight line with long black bill. Flight reveals plain gray wings. **VOICE** Male: *coo.* Female: quack. **HABITAT** Lakes. **RANGE** Mar.–Apr., Oct.–Nov.: entire region (local, common). May–Sept.: n MT; local in s ID, WY, CO (rare).

REDHEAD
Aythya americana
WATERFOWL FAMILY

20″. Diver. Male body gray; head rufous; chest and rear end black; eyes yellow. Female all plain brown; whitish eye ring. Forehead steep, rounded; bill blue-gray, with black tip. **VOICE** Male: cat-like *meeow* in courtship. Female: soft quack. **HABITAT** Summer: ponds, lakes. Migration and winter: lakes. **RANGE** Feb.–Apr., Oct.–Nov.: entire region. May–Sept.: common breeder in most of region. Dec.–Jan.: w MT and south (local).

RING-NECKED DUCK
Aythya collaris
WATERFOWL FAMILY

17″. Diver. Male head, chest, and back black; sides gray; white slash behind black breast; head has purple gloss. Female brown, with pale buffy wash on face. Neck ring hard to see. **VOICE** Male: loud whistle. Female: soft purring. **HABITAT** Lakes, rivers. **RANGE** Mar.–Apr., Sept.–Nov.: entire region. May–Aug.: w MT, nw WY, CO mtns. Dec.–Feb.: w MT south.

LESSER SCAUP
Aythya affinis
WATERFOWL FAMILY

17″. Diver. Male back gray; head black (dark purple gloss); sides pale gray; chest and tail area black. Female dark brown, with white face. Bill blue-gray; eyes yellow. **VOICE** Usu. silent. **HABITAT** Lakes, marshes. **RANGE** Mar.–Apr., Oct.–Nov.: entire region. May–Sept.: s ID, MT, WY, n CO (locally common). A few winter from sw MT south.

HARLEQUIN DUCK
Histrionicus histrionicus
WATERFOWL FAMILY

17″. Diver. Male slaty blue above and below, boldly marked with large white stripes and spots; sides rusty. Female dark brown; 3 white spots on head. Bill short, black. Flight reveals dark wings, white line on edge of male's back. **VOICE** Squeaks and whistles. **HABITAT** Mtn. rivers. **RANGE** Apr.–Sept.: n ID, w MT, nw WY (local, rare).

BARROW'S GOLDENEYE
Bucephala islandica
WATERFOWL FAMILY

19″. Diver. Male black above with white spots; underparts white; head black (purple gloss); white crescent on face. Female pale brown, head darker. Eyes golden. **VOICE** Male: grunts, clicks (courtship). **HABITAT** Summer: lakes. Winter: rivers, lakes. **RANGE** Oct.–Apr.: ID, w MT, w WY, c CO. May–Sept.: breeds in n and c ID, nw MT, nw WY (local).

COMMON GOLDENEYE
Bucephala clangula
WATERFOWL FAMILY

18″. Diver. Male striped black and white above; white below; head black (dark green gloss), white spot near bill. Female head dark brown; white neck ring; body paler brown. Eyes golden. **VOICE** Male: high *jee-up*. Female: low quack. **HABITAT** Summer: lakes. Migration and winter: lakes, rivers. **RANGE** Nov.–Apr.: entire region.

BUFFLEHEAD
Bucephala albeola
WATERFOWL FAMILY

14″. Diver. Male back black; underparts white; white wedge on back of head. Female brown, with white spot behind eye. Flight reveals white base of wings (male), white secondaries (female). **VOICE** Usu. silent. **HABITAT** Lakes, reservoirs. **RANGE** Oct.–Apr.: entire region (local). May–Sept.: mtn. lakes of ID, nw MT, nw WY, n CO.

HOODED MERGANSER
Lophodytes (Mergus) cucullatus
WATERFOWL FAMILY

18″. Diver. Adult male back, head, and neck black; sides rufous; head patch and chest white; eyes yellow. Female gray-brown, with fluffy brown crest. Crest fan-like. **VOICE** Low grunts. **HABITAT** Tree-fringed ponds, rivers. **RANGE** Mar.–Apr., Oct.–Nov.: entire region (uncommon). May–Sept.: breeds in n ID, w MT (local). A few winter locally.

COMMON MERGANSER
Mergus merganser
WATERFOWL FAMILY

25″. Diver. Male back black; chest and underparts white; head black (green gloss), rounded. Female body gray; head and neck rusty; chin distinctly white. Bill red, slender but with thick base. **VOICE** Usu. silent. **HABITAT** Rivers, lakes. **RANGE** Nov.–Mar.: entire region. Apr.–Oct.: n and c ID, w and c MT; local in mtns. of WY, CO.

RED-BREASTED MERGANSER
Mergus serrator
WATERFOWL FAMILY

23″. Diver. Male back black; chest buffy; sides gray; neck and belly white; head dark green. Female gray; head rusty; throat and foreneck white. Bill long, slender, red; nape crest shaggy. **VOICE** Usu. silent. **HABITAT** Winter: coastal waters. Migration: also inland waters. **RANGE** Mar.–Apr., Oct.–Nov.: entire region. A few winter locally in WY, CO.

RUDDY DUCK
Oxyura jamaicensis
WATERFOWL FAMILY

16″. Diver. Breeding male body bright ruddy; top of head black, bottom white; bill bright blue. Winter male slaty brown; bill gray. Female brown; dark line on pale cheeks. Tail black, fan-shaped, often raised. Usu. in parties of 1–3 dozen (nonbreeding). **VOICE** Usu. silent. **HABITAT** Reedy lakes. **RANGE** Apr.–Nov.: entire region. A few winter in s ID, CO.

Raptors

The word "raptor" is usually used for birds of prey that are active in the daytime (it is also sometimes used for the nocturnal owls, described on page 281). Families found in the Rocky Mountain states include the American vultures (Carthartidae), the hawks and eagles (Accipitridae), and the falcons (Falconidae). The bills of raptors are strong for tearing flesh, while the feet (usually yellow) are generally powerful (except in vultures), with curved talons for grasping prey. The carrion-feeding vultures are black, with broad wings and bare heads. Members of the hawk and eagle family are the very large eagles, with feathered legs; the large Osprey; harriers, which fly low

Flight silhouettes of raptors
(illustrations not to relative scale)

TURKEY VULTURE
Cathartes aura
AMERICAN VULTURE FAMILY

in flight (left), close-up of head (right)

L 28″; WS 6′. Adult all black, brown-tinged above; head small, naked, red; bill yellow. Imm. head naked, gray. Soars with wings held at 20 degrees above horizontal; seldom flaps wings. Long rounded tail and pale silver flight feathers can be seen from below. Gathers at nightly communal roosts in tall trees or towers. **VOICE** Grunts and hisses; usu. silent. **HABITAT** Lowland forests, grasslands. **RANGE** Apr.–Oct.: entire region, ex. parts of n ID, nw MT.

over open areas and use their superb hearing as an aid in hunting; and the hawks. There are two types of hawks: the accipiters, whose shorter wings allow them to achieve rapid twisting flight, and the broad-winged, soaring buteos. The pointed-winged falcons are fast fliers. Immature raptors, often striped below, take a year or more to reach adulthood. Females are 10 to 20 percent larger than males in most species. Some raptors migrate to warmer climes in winter (flying during the day unlike most songbirds). When feeding and during migration, they save energy by riding rising columns of air (thermals) and updrafts of wind created at the tops of ridges. Acute vision allows raptors to spot unsuspecting prey from great heights.

Sharp-shinned Hawk (Accipiter)

American Kestrel (Falcon)

Northern Harrier

Red-tailed Hawk (Buteo)

immatures (left), adult (right)

OSPREY
Pandion haliaetus
HAWK AND EAGLE FAMILY

L 23"; WS 5'6". Brown above with white crown; dark line through eye; white below. Feet gray; eyes yellow. Imm. has pale feather edges on wings and back; buffy crown. Flies with wings bent at "wrist" like flattened M; flight feathers and tail finely banded. Hovers frequently; often flies grasping fish in talons. Nest is mass of sticks topping dead tree or platform. **VOICE** Emphatic repeated *kee-uk*. **HABITAT** Rivers, lakes. **RANGE** Apr.–May, Sept.–Oct.: entire region. June-Aug.: ID, w and c MT, n WY, n CO (local).

BALD EAGLE
Haliaeetus leucocephalus
HAWK AND EAGLE FAMILY

adult and young at nest (left), adult in flight (right)

L 32″; WS 7′. Adult body, wings, and thighs dark chocolate brown (may appear black); massive head white; bill yellow, strongly hooked; eyes, feet, and massive legs yellow; tail white, somewhat rounded. Imm. all dark brown when perched; flight reveals diffuse whitish wing linings and base of tail. Flies with slow deliberate wingbeats, wings held flat, straight out, primaries spread. Perches on tall trees. Numbers increasing, with DDT ban and protection. Region has influx of Alaskan and Canadian winterers. **VOICE** Piercing scream. **HABITAT** Rivers, lakes. **RANGE** Resident in ID, w MT, nw WY, and locally south to CO. Nov.–Mar.: entire region.

NORTHERN HARRIER
Circus cyaneus
HAWK AND EAGLE FAMILY

adult male (left), immature (right)

L 22″; WS 4′. Wings and tail long, narrow; rump white; head and bill small, with owl-like facial disks. Male pearly gray; whiter below. Female brown above, dirty white with brown stripes below. Imm. brown above, rusty orange below. Flies low over open areas, wings raised at an angle, listening and watching for rodents, frogs, and baby birds; often hovers and drops. Generally perches on ground, not in trees. **VOICE** Weak *pee*. **HABITAT** Marshes, fields. **RANGE** Resident in entire region. Sept.–Apr.: more common in CO. May–Aug.: more common in MT, WY.

SHARP-SHINNED HAWK
immature (left), adult (right)
Accipiter striatus
HAWK AND EAGLE FAMILY

L 12″; WS 21″. Adult slate gray above; rusty, barred below. Tail long, narrow, square with notch in middle. Feet small, yellow. Imm. brown above, striped below. Flies with fast wingbeats followed by glides. Expert at capturing small birds. Soars during migration. **VOICE** High *kek* notes. **HABITAT** Summer: wooded areas. Migration and winter: all areas. **RANGE** Apr., Sept.–Oct.: entire region. May–Aug.: ID, w MT, WY, w and c CO. Nov.–Mar.: w MT and south.

COOPER'S HAWK
adult (left), immature (right)
Accipiter cooperii
HAWK AND EAGLE FAMILY

L 17″; WS 28″. Plumages nearly identical to Sharp-shinned Hawk but head and feet larger and tail longer, distinctly rounded; adult has black cap. Imm. belly whiter, with fewer streaks than Sharp-shinned. **VOICE** High *kek* notes. **HABITAT** Summer: forests, esp. broadleaf. Migration and winter: also open areas. **RANGE** Sept.–Apr.: entire region. May–Aug.: ID, w MT, w and c WY, c CO.

NORTHERN GOSHAWK
Accipiter gentilis
HAWK AND EAGLE FAMILY

L 23"; WS 3'7". Adult dark gray above, fine gray barring below; black crown and stripe behind eye; wide white eyebrow. Imm. heavy stripes below; wide white eyebrow. Tail long, rounded. **VOICE** Harsh *kek* notes. **HABITAT** Mixed forests, esp. coniferous. Winter: all areas. **RANGE** Nov.–Mar.: entire region. Apr.–Oct.: mtn. forests.

SWAINSON'S HAWK
Buteo swainsoni
HAWK AND EAGLE FAMILY

L 20"; WS 4'. Adult plain brown above; throat white; upper chest rufous; rest of underparts whitish. Flight reveals white underwing linings and blackish flight feathers; tail gray with fine bands. Dark-morph brown, with rufous underwings. Imm. streaked below. **VOICE** Whistled *kreee*. **HABITAT** Prairies, farms. **RANGE** Apr.–Oct.: entire region.

RED-TAILED HAWK
Buteo jamaicensis
HAWK AND EAGLE FAMILY

adult (left), immature (right)

L 22"; WS 4'2". Adult head, back, and wings dark brown; lower chest has band of heavy brown streaks; varies from whitish to dark rufous or blackish below; tail pale orange above, rufous above. Imm. similar but tail pale brown with many indistinct bands; underparts usu. white. Flight reveals mainly white underwings with dark leading edge and black crescent beyond wrist. **VOICE** Down-slurred squeal: *keee-rrr*. **HABITAT** Woodland edges, isolated trees in fields. **RANGE** Apr.–Oct.: entire region. Nov.–Mar.: ID, sw MT, WY, CO.

FERRUGINOUS HAWK
Buteo regalis
HAWK AND EAGLE FAMILY

L 24″; WS 4′8″. Adult rufous above, white below. Flight reveals white breast, flight feathers, and tail; rusty wing linings. Dark morph: body and wing linings brown. Imm. brownish above, white below. **VOICE** Descending *kree-ahh.* **HABITAT** Grasslands, sagebrush, canyons. **RANGE** Apr.–Sept.: s ID, c and e MT, WY, CO. Oct.–Mar.: sw ID, sw and e CO.

ROUGH-LEGGED HAWK
Buteo lagopus
HAWK AND EAGLE FAMILY

L 22″; WS 4′8″. Adult head and upper chest striped black and white; back and wings dark brown; black patch across lower belly; tail white, with broad black band. Dark-morph adult black, with paler flight feathers. Often hovers. **VOICE** Usu. silent. **HABITAT** Open country, riversides. **RANGE** Oct.–Apr.: entire region; rare some winters, common others.

GOLDEN EAGLE
Aquila chrysaetos
HAWK AND EAGLE FAMILY

immature (left), adult (right)

L 3′; WS 6′6″. Adult dark brown with golden nape; base of tail banded gray. Bill heavy; legs heavily feathered; feet yellow. Imm. dark brown; wide band of white at base of tail. Flight reveals white window at base of primaries, esp. in imm. Flies on wings slightly angled up. In winter, feeds on mammals up to size of Pronghorn; rest of year, prefers rabbits, large rodents. **VOICE** High *kee-kee-kee;* screams. **HABITAT** Mtns., forests, grasslands. **RANGE** Resident in entire region. Nov.–Mar.: more common in lowlands of WY and CO.

MERLIN
Falco columbarius
FALCON FAMILY

L 12″; WS 25″. Adult male gray above; pale buffy below, with brown streaks; tail has black band near tip. Female and imm. dark brown above, striped below. Thin black sideburn. Flies fast and low when chasing birds. **VOICE** High *ki ki ki ki*. **HABITAT** Forests, grasslands, marshes. **RANGE** Sept.–May: entire region. June–Aug.: breeds in n and e ID, MT, locally in WY.

PEREGRINE FALCON
Falco peregrinus
FALCON FAMILY

L 18″; WS 3′4″. Upperparts and tail dark slaty gray; underparts and underwings gray-barred. Flight reveals pointed wings, broad at base; tail tapers to square end. **VOICE** Harsh *kak kak*. **HABITAT** Coasts, marshes, cities. **RANGE** Apr.–Sept.: all region's mtns., canyons (local). Apr.–May, Sept.–Oct.: entire region (uncommon). Nov.–Mar.: entire region (rare).

AMERICAN KESTREL
Falco sparverius
FALCON FAMILY

L 11″; WS 23″. Male back rufous; wings blue-gray; chest pale buffy with black spots. Female rufous above, with fine black bars. 2 thin sideburns. In flight, pointed wings obvious. **VOICE** Shrill *killy killy*. **HABITAT** Fields, woods, towns. **RANGE** Apr.–Nov.: entire region. Dec.–Mar.: c ID and w MT south.

PRAIRIE FALCON
Falco mexicanus
FALCON FAMILY

L 18″; WS 3′6″. Adult pale brown above, whitish with brown speckles below; crown brown; eyebrow pale; throat white; 1 sideburn below eye. Imm. streaked below. Flight reveals black patch at base of wings. **VOICE** Loud *ki-ki-ki-ki*. **HABITAT** Grasslands, sagebrush, canyons. **RANGE** Resident in entire region.

GRAY PARTRIDGE
Perdix perdix
PARTRIDGE FAMILY

13″. Dull brown above; neck and chest gray; sides gray with rufous bars; eyebrows and throat rufous; tail very short, rufous. Belly white in female; large dark brown patch in male. Introduced from Eurasia. From fall to spring, in coveys of 10–30. **VOICE** Male: hoarse *keee-uck*. **HABITAT** Open farmlands. **RANGE** Resident in ID, MT, w and n WY.

CHUKAR
Alectoris chukar
PARTRIDGE FAMILY

14″. Gray upperparts and chest; belly white; sides barred chestnut and black; wings brown. Black line through eye and down neck frames white throat. Bill and legs red. Outer tail feathers rufous. Introduced from e Mediterranean. **VOICE** Loud *chuk-chuk-chukar*. **HABITAT** Rocky hills, canyons. **RANGE** Resident in s ID, MT (local), WY, w CO.

RING-NECKED PHEASANT
Phasianus colchicus
PARTRIDGE FAMILY

Male 33″; female 23″. Male head and neck iridescent dark green, with white necklace, red bare skin around eye. Rest of body rufous and bronze, with 19 black and white chevrons above. Female warm buffy, with black spots above. Tail feathers long, pointed. Flies with rapid wingbeats followed by glides. Introduced from Eurasia. **VOICE** Male: loud *kaw kawk*. **HABITAT** Farms, meadows, brush. **RANGE** Resident west and east of Rockies.

SPRUCE GROUSE
Dendragapus canadensis
PARTRIDGE FAMILY

16″. Franklin's race: male dark brown above; black below, with white scaling on chest; tail black; white spots on rump. Red wattle over eye, white cheek stripe, and black throat. Female speckled black, brown, white. Often fearless of humans. **VOICE** Male: hisses. Female with chicks: low clucks. **HABITAT** Shrubbery, roadsides in dense coniferous forests. **RANGE** Resident in n and c ID, w MT.

BLUE GROUSE
Dendragapus obscurus
PARTRIDGE FAMILY

18″. Male mainly blue-gray; wings brown; tail fairly long, black; in courtship display, neck has fried-egg-like patch, with reddish "yolk." Female brown, finely barred with black. **VOICE** Male: 5–7 deep *whoop* notes. **HABITAT** Uplands: coniferous and mixed forests, nearby brush. **RANGE** Resident in entire region.

RUFFED GROUSE
Bonasa umbellus
PARTRIDGE FAMILY

18″. Grayish to reddish brown, speckled white and black; neck patch and terminal tail band black. Head small, slightly crested; tail fairly long, gray. Hard to see until it flies up on rapid noisy wingbeats. Male "drums" on low perch in spring by thumping wings against chest, slowly at first, then faster. **VOICE** Alarm call: *quit quit*. **HABITAT** Broadleaf and riverine woods. **RANGE** Resident in n and e ID, w and sc MT, w WY.

SAGE GROUSE
Centrocercus urophasianus
PARTRIDGE FAMILY

Male 28″; female 22″. Mottled gray-brown above; belly black. Male chest white; yellow wattle over eye; black throat makes V on foreneck. Female smaller; head and chest scaled brown. In spring, male inflates 2 yellowish-orange air sacs on chest. **VOICE** When flushed: *kuk-kuk-kuk*. Courting male: weak *wom-poo;* air sacs make popping sound. **HABITAT** Sagebrush. **RANGE** Resident in s ID, s and e MT, WY, w CO.

WHITE-TAILED PTARMIGAN
Lagopus leucurus
PARTRIDGE FAMILY

summer (left), winter (right)

13″. Summer: back, chest, and head gray-brown; belly, wings, and outer tail white; small red wattle over eye. Winter: all white, ex. for black eye and bill. White feathers cover feet. When molting: irreg. gray-brown feathers on white. This well-camouflaged ground bird is hard to spot; best places to see one are in CO at Trail Ridge Rd. in Rocky Mountain N.P., Mount Evans, and Loveland Pass. **VOICE** High cackles; low clucks. **HABITAT** Alpine tundra, above tree line. **RANGE** Resident in far n ID, nw MT, sc WY, c CO, usu. above 12,000′.

WILD TURKEY
Meleagris gallopavo
PARTRIDGE FAMILY

Male 4′; female 3′. Male body dark brown, looks iridescent coppery-green; flight feathers black, banded white; tail rufous with black bands; head bare, warty, red and/or blue; black "beard" hangs from chest. Female similar, with smaller, duller head. Legs red. Feeds on ground, usu. in flocks; roosts in trees at night. Introduced from e and sw United States. **VOICE** Male: repeated gobble. **HABITAT** Broadleaf and coniferous woods in mtns; along rivercourses in plains. **RANGE** Resident in wc ID, w and s MT, e WY, e and sw CO.

SHARP-TAILED GROUSE
Tympanuchus phasianellus
PARTRIDGE FAMILY

18″. Brown, speckled black and white above. Breast scaled; lower belly and fluffy vent feathers white. Courting male has purple neck sacs. **VOICE** Cackles; low *coooo.* **HABITAT** Grasslands, scrubby forests. **RANGE** Resident in e ID, MT (ex. far w), n and e WY, w CO. **Greater Prairie-Chicken** (*T. cupido,* of ne CO sandhills) and **Lesser Prairie-Chicken** (*T. pallidicinctus,* of far se CO) are barred below, have wide tails; courting male has yellow neck sacs.

SCALED QUAIL
Callipepla squamata
NEW WORLD QUAIL FAMILY

11″. Back, wings, tail, and sides pale gray; sides have white stripes; entire neck and chest gray with black scales; head gray with white crest ("cottontop"). Large coveys outside breeding season. **VOICE** Call: *pay-cos.* **HABITAT** Arid scrub and grasslands. **RANGE** Resident in ec and se CO.

GAMBEL'S QUAIL
Callipepla gambelii
NEW WORLD QUAIL FAMILY

male (left), female (right)

11″. Head has black, forward-leaning topknot. Male chest and upperparts gray; sides chestnut with white streaks; belly yellow with large black blotch; crown rufous; face black, edged with white lines. Female head plain gray; belly yellowish. **VOICE** 4-note *chi-ca-go-go.* **HABITAT** Valleys, arid scrub. **RANGE** Resident in wc and sw CO.

CALIFORNIA QUAIL
female, male
Callipepla californica
NEW WORLD QUAIL FAMILY

10". Male pale brown above; chest gray; crown chestnut; rounded black plume on forehead; eyebrow and necklace white; throat black. White stripes on rusty sides; black scaling on white belly; chestnut patch at center of belly. Female head and chest plain pale gray; plume smaller. VOICE *chi-CAH-go.* HABITAT Pine and broadleaf woods, scrub, towns. RANGE Resident in sw ID.

MOUNTAIN QUAIL
Oreortyx pictus
NEW WORLD QUAIL FAMILY

11". Tall, thin, erect black plume on head. Back and tail gray or brown; wings brown; belly rusty with wide black and white bars. Crown, neck, and chest gray; white line from eye to foreneck frames rusty throat. VOICE Male: loud *quark;* long series of mellow *took* notes. HABITAT Dry pine and mixed woods, mtn. scrub. RANGE Resident in nc and sw ID.

VIRGINIA RAIL
Rallus limicola
RAIL FAMILY

10". Adult brown above; chest and wings rufous; sides barred black and white; cheeks gray; eyes red; bill long, thin, drooping, red with black tip. Legs dull red; toes long; tail short. Imm. has black chest. Usu. secretive. VOICE Repeated *kid ick;* grunting *oink* notes. HABITAT Marshes. RANGE Apr.–mid-Oct.: entire region. A few winter in WY, CO.

SORA
Porzana carolina
RAIL FAMILY

9". Plump; bill short, thick, yellow. Adult blackish brown above; sides of neck and chest slaty; belly barred blackish; face and foreneck black; legs olive green. Imm. chest brown; throat white. Usually secretive. VOICE Whistled *ker-wee;* descending whinny. HABITAT Marshes. RANGE Apr.–Sept.: entire region (local).

AMERICAN COOT
Fulica americana
RAIL FAMILY

15″. Body duck-shaped; feet not webbed, but toes lobed. Sooty gray; head and neck black; bill thick, white, black near tip; sides of undertail white. Swims, dives and skitters over surface to become airborne similar to a diving duck. Flocks often graze on lawns near water. **VOICE** Grating *kuk* notes. **HABITAT** Marshes, ponds, lakes. **RANGE** Apr.–Oct.: entire region. Nov.–Mar.: s ID, WY, c CO.

SANDHILL CRANE
Grus canadensis
CRANE FAMILY

L 3′4″; WS 6′. Mostly gray, often stained rusty; forecrown red; cheeks white. Neck long, thin; bill shortish, thin, straight, black; legs long, black. Flies with neck outstretched. **VOICE** Loud rattling *kar-r-r-r-o-o-o*, often given in flight. **HABITAT** Marshes, shallow lakes, fallow fields. **RANGE** Mar.–Apr., mid-Sept.–Oct.: entire region. May–Sept.: breeds in s and e ID, w MT, w WY, nc CO. San Luis Valley, in sc CO, is major spring and fall staging area.

Shorebirds

The term "shorebird" is used for certain members of the order Charadriiformes: plovers, avocets, stilts, and sandpipers, including godwits, dowitchers, yellowlegs, curlews, and small sandpipers informally known as "peeps." Most shorebirds found in the Rocky Mountain region frequent open muddy or sandy wetlands around lakes, reservoirs, and rain pools. They feed on small invertebrates.

Nearly all shorebirds have a distinct breeding plumage in late spring and early summer. Most species seen in the Rocky Mountain region travel thousands of miles yearly between their breeding grounds, often in the Arctic tundra, and wintering grounds to the south, usually between the southern United States and Tierra del Fuego, Argentina. Shorebirds are most numerous in the region in May and from August through September. They are widespread east of the Rockies, and only locally common to the west. Some species breed in the wetlands and prairies of the region; some individuals of Arctic-breeding species spend the summer here.

In the identification of shorebirds, proportion and shape, as well as behavior and voice, are frequently more important than plumage color.

BLACK-BELLIED PLOVER
Pluvialis squatarola
PLOVER FAMILY

12″. Breeding: back and wings speckled black and white; crown, hindneck, and sides of chest white; face, foreneck, and chest black Nonbreeding: grayish above, white below; back speckled; flight reveals black patch at base of underwing. Bill short, straight; eyes large, black; legs black. Usu. in flocks. **VOICE** Whistled *pee-a-wee.* **HABITAT** Open watersides, mudflats. **RANGE** May, Sept.–Oct.: entire region (local, uncommon).

MOUNTAIN PLOVER
Charadrius montanus
PLOVER FAMILY

9″. Like a Killdeer without black chest bands. Brown above; sides of chest buffy; forehead, eyeline, foreneck, and belly white. Cap rusty brown with black at front in summer; cap dull brown in winter. **VOICE** Long low whistles; high trills. **HABITAT** Open grasslands of high plains, usu. far from water. **RANGE** Apr.–Sept.: c and e MT, e and s WY, e CO.

SEMIPALMATED PLOVER
Charadrius semipalmatus
PLOVER FAMILY

7″. Upperparts dark brown; white below. Breeding: base of bill and legs yellow; black breast band. Nonbreeding and imm.: bill black; breast band brown. Appears neck-less; bill short. **VOICE** Whistled *tu-wheet.* **HABITAT** Mudflats, beaches. **RANGE** May, mid-July–Sept.: entire region (uncommon).

KILLDEER
Charadrius vociferus
PLOVER FAMILY

10″. Brown above, white below; 2 black chest bands; pied face; red eye ring; legs pinkish. Flight reveals wing stripe, orange rump. Common plover in open habitats. Parent feigns broken wing to distract intruders. **VOICE** Strident *dee dee dee;* also *kill-dee.* **HABITAT** Farms, fields, mudflats. **RANGE** Mar.–Oct.: entire region. Some winter in s ID, w MT, WY, CO.

BLACK-NECKED STILT
Himantopus mexicanus
STILT AND AVOCET FAMILY

14″. Dark above (male black, female dark brown), white below; rump and tail white. Head mainly black, with large white spot over eye; bill long, thin, black. Legs very long, red. Flight reveals wings uniformly blackish above and below. Wades up to its belly, eating aquatic insects, small fish. **VOICE** Sharp *yip yip yip.* **HABITAT** Shallow marshes, saltpans. **RANGE** Apr.–Sept.: c MT, s ID, WY (local), se CO.

AMERICAN AVOCET
Recurvirostra americana
STILT AND AVOCET FAMILY

18″. Back and wings pied black and white; white below; rump and tail white. Neck long; bill long, slender, up-turned, black. Legs long, light blue. Breeding: head and neck pale rusty orange. Nonbreeding: head and neck gray. Feeds in flocks; sweeps bill from side to side in water when feeding. Nests in colonies. **VOICE** Loud *wheep.* **HABITAT** Shallow lakeshores, mudflats. **RANGE** Mar.–Oct.: s ID, MT, WY, CO.

GREATER YELLOWLEGS
Tringa melanoleuca
SANDPIPER FAMILY

14″. Breeding: back brown-black with white dots; head, neck, and sides speckled dark brown. Nonbreeding: paler. Belly and rump white. Neck long; legs long, bright yellow; bill 1½ times longer than head, with relatively thick gray base and thin, black, slightly up-curved tip. **VOICE** Excited *tew tew tew.* **HABITAT** Mudflats, marshes. **RANGE** Apr.–May, Aug.–Oct.: entire region.

LESSER YELLOWLEGS
Tringa flavipes
SANDPIPER FAMILY

11″. Smaller version of Greater Yellowlegs (see previous species): plumages similar; legs also bright yellow; bill shorter (equal to length of head), straight, all black. Occurs in tighter flocks and is less wary than Greater Yellowlegs. **VOICE** 1–2 mellow *tu* notes. **HABITAT** Mudflats, marshes. **RANGE** Apr.–May, July–Oct.: entire region.

WILLET
Catoptrophorus semipalmatus
SANDPIPER FAMILY

nonbreeding in flight (left), on land (right)

15″. Breeding: speckled brownish gray. Nonbreeding: plain gray. Bill thick-based, fairly long, straight; legs blue-gray; tail gray. Flight reveals startling black wings with broad white central stripe. Calls from fence posts and trees near nest; performs noisy aerial displays. By midsummer, Rocky Mountain Willets have begun flight to either Pacific or Atlantic coast for winter. **VOICE** Song: *pill-will-willet*. Call: *kip, kip, kip*. **HABITAT** Shallow lakeshores, prairie marshes. **RANGE** Apr.–Aug.: s ID, c and e MT, WY, and CO (local).

SOLITARY SANDPIPER
Tringa solitaria
SANDPIPER FAMILY

9″. Dark brown above, with fine white spots; belly and eye ring white; bill fairly long, straight, paler at base; legs blackish. Flight reveals all dark wings, outer tail banded white. Usu. alone; rarely mixes with other shorebirds. **VOICE** Strident *peet weet*. **HABITAT** Wooded pondsides, mudflats. **RANGE** Apr.–May, July–Sept.: entire region.

SPOTTED SANDPIPER
Actitis macularia
SANDPIPER FAMILY

8″. Breeding: brown above; large black spots on white underparts. Nonbreeding: unspotted; brown smudge on sides of white chest. Often teeters rear end. Flies on stiff bowed wings; distinct wing stripe. Often solitary. **VOICE** *Peet-weet-weet*. **HABITAT** Riversides, ponds. **RANGE** May–Sept.: entire region.

UPLAND SANDPIPER
Bartramia longicauda
SANDPIPER FAMILY

12″. Dark brown above, with buff speckles; small head, long thin neck, and chest buffy, speckled; bill short, with slight droop; legs yellow-green; tail wedge-shaped, with pale sides. Perches on fence posts, poles. Has shallow wingbeats in flight. **VOICE** Call: rolling *pip-ip-ip-ip.* Song: drawn-out *whoo-leee, whee-looooo.* **HABITAT** Grasslands of high plains. **RANGE** May–Aug.: c and e MT, e WY, ne CO.

LONG-BILLED CURLEW
Numenius americanus
SANDPIPER FAMILY

23″. Head, neck, and upperparts brown with buffy spots; buffy below. Neck long; legs long, gray. Bill very long, down-curved, lower mandible red at base. In flight, appears uniformly buffy, with rufous wing linings. **VOICE** Loud *cur-leee;* rapid *kli-li-li-li.* **HABITAT** Open grasslands; mudflats. **RANGE** Apr.–Sept.: s ID, MT, w and s WY, e CO.

MARBLED GODWIT
Limosa fedoa
SANDPIPER FAMILY

18″. Breeding: head, neck, and upperparts brown with buffy spots; buffy below, with streaks on neck, bars on breast. Nonbreeding: clear unbarred buff below. Neck long; legs long, blackish. Bill very long, slightly up-curved, red with black tip. In flight, appears uniformly buffy, with rufous wing linings. **VOICE** Loud *god-WIT.* **HABITAT** Mudflats, beaches. **RANGE** Apr.–May, Aug.–Sept.: entire region. June–July: breeds in ne MT.

SEMIPALMATED SANDPIPER
Calidris pusilla
SANDPIPER FAMILY

6½″. Breeding: spotted dark brown above and on chest; belly white. Nonbreeding: gray-brown above; faint streaking on sides of neck. Bill short, thick, straight, black. Legs black; toes webbed at base. Usu. in flocks on mud. **VOICE** Low *jerk.* **HABITAT** Mudflats, drying marshes. **RANGE** May, Aug.–Sept.: e MT, e WY, e CO.

WESTERN SANDPIPER
Calidris mauri
SANDPIPER FAMILY

6½". Breeding: rusty above; fine black dots on foreparts. Nonbreeding: gray above, white below. Bill fairly long, black, droops at tip; legs black. Fall imm. rusty on sides of back. Usu. feeds wading in shallow water. **VOICE** High *cheep.* **HABITAT** Mudflats. **RANGE** Mid-Apr.–May, July–Sept.: entire region.

LEAST SANDPIPER
Calidris minutilla
SANDPIPER FAMILY

6". Reddish brown above; chest buffy brown, lightly spotted. Bill short, thin, slightly drooping, black. Legs greenish yellow, but often muddy, appearing blackish. **VOICE** High *kreet.* **HABITAT** Mudflats, wet short-grass meadows. **RANGE** Apr.–May (uncommon), July–Oct. (common): entire region.

BAIRD'S SANDPIPER
Calidris bairdii
SANDPIPER FAMILY

7½". Breeding: back brown with heavy black spots; head and chest pale brown with fine black dots. Bill straight, medium length; legs black; wingtips extend beyond tail. Juv. (seen in fall migration): buffy, with paler scalloping on back. Usu. feeds in short grass above beaches. **VOICE** Low raspy *kreep.* **HABITAT** Marshy pools, mudflats. **RANGE** Apr.–May (rare), July–Oct. (common): entire region.

PECTORAL SANDPIPER
Calidris melanotos
SANDPIPER FAMILY

9". Scaly dark brown above; foreneck and chest buff with fine black streaks, sharply demarcated from clear white belly. Bill slightly curved. Legs dull yellow-olive. Neck longer than those of smaller "peeps." **VOICE** *Krrip.* **HABITAT** Wet meadows, mudflats. **RANGE** Apr.–May, July–Sept.: entire region (uncommon).

LONG-BILLED DOWITCHER
Limnodromus scolopaceus
SANDPIPER FAMILY

12″. Breeding: speckled brown above, orange below; sides black-barred. Nonbreeding: gray-brown above, whitish below. Juv. brown above; breast buffy orange. Bill very long, straight; legs greenish, medium length. Flight reveals white V on lower back, narrow white bars on tail. Feeds with rapid, sewing-machine motion. **VOICE** High sharp *keek.* **HABITAT** Mudflats, pond shores. **RANGE** Apr.–May, July–Oct.: east of Rockies; west of Rockies (local).

COMMON SNIPE
Gallinago gallinago
SANDPIPER FAMILY

11″. Dark brown above, with a few white stripes. Head has 4 bold blackish stripes. Sides barred; mid-belly white; tail rusty. Legs short; bill very long, straight. Flies in erratic zigzag. In aerial courtship display, vibrating tail feathers hum. **VOICE** Hoarse *skaip.* **HABITAT** Wet meadows, marshes. **RANGE** Resident in entire region; in winter, withdraws from higher mtns. and n and e MT.

WILSON'S PHALAROPE
Phalaropus tricolor
SANDPIPER FAMILY

9″. Breeding female (pictured): back gray with reddish stripes; white below; crown and hindneck silvery; line through eye and on sides of neck black, becoming reddish; fore-. neck buffy orange. Breeding male: duller; crown and sides of neck brown; incubates eggs. Bill needle-like. Swims in circles; runs erratically on mud. **VOICE** Soft *chek-chek-chek*; nasal *wurk.* **HABITAT** Marshy ponds, ssalty lakes. **RANGE** Apr.–Sept.: entire region, ex n ID, far w MT.

RED-NECKED PHALAROPE
Phalaropus lobatus
SANDPIPER FAMILY

8″. Breeding: back black with rusty stripes; head blackish; throat and underparts white; neck rusty; chest slaty; male duller than female. Nonbreeding (pictured): gray above with white stripes; white below; crown and line behind eye black. Bill thin, black. Swims in circles. **VOICE** Low *whit.* **HABITAT** Shallow lakes. **RANGE** May, Aug.–Sept.: entire region (local).

Gulls and Terns

All members of the gull family (Laridae)—gulls, terns, and their relatives—have webbed feet and breed in the open, in colonies, on islands free of land predators; their nests are usually mere depressions on the ground. Although gulls are common near the sea (and are often called "seagulls"), many breed far inland near freshwater and saltwater lakes. Superb fliers, most adult gulls have wings with white trailing edges and fairly long, strong bills that are slightly hooked at the tip. These generalist feeders and scavengers eat living and dead animal life, and many have adapted to feed on human refuse. Gulls go through a confusing array of plumages and molts until they reach adulthood in two years (small species), three years (medium), or four years (large). For many gull species, this guide describes selected life-stage categories, including juvenile (the bird's birth summer), first winter, first summer (bird is one year old), second winter, summer adult, and winter adult. The small to medium-size terns, sleek and slender-billed, fly in a buoyant or hovering manner, diving headfirst for small fish; most have black caps (in summer) and elegant forked tails.

FRANKLIN'S GULL
Larus pipixcan
GULL AND TERN FAMILY

14″. Summer adult: back gray; wings gray, with white trailing edge, white band before black primary patch, white feather tips; underparts white; head sharply black; bill red. Winter adult: forecrown, eye ring, and throat white; rear of head blackish. Juv.: black tail band and primaries. Usu. in flocks; nests in colonies. **VOICE** Variety of *yuk* notes and cries. **HABITAT** Ponds, lakes, wet fields. **RANGE** Apr.–May, Aug.–Oct.: entire region. June–July: breeds in s ID, nc and ne MT, nw WY.

BONAPARTE'S GULL
Larus philadelphia
GULL AND TERN FAMILY

13″. Summer adult: back and wings silvery; neck, underparts, and tail white; head black; white leading edge of wing, black tips on primaries; legs red; bill short, black. Winter adult: head white; black spot behind eye. 1st winter: head white, tail black-tipped. Often hovers. **VOICE** Nasal *cher*. **HABITAT** Lakesides, rivers. **RANGE** Apr.–May, Aug.–Oct.: entire region.

HERRING GULL
Larus argentatus
GULL AND TERN FAMILY

L 25"; WS 4'10". Winter adult: back and wings silvery; wingtips black with white spots; head and underparts white, with fine spots. Bill yellow; black and red dot near tip. 2nd winter: pale brown with spots; flight feathers and tail black; bill pink with black tip. 1st winter: darker brown, with speckled back; bill black. **VOICE** Varied, incl. loud series of *kee-yow* and *gah* notes. **HABITAT** Lakes, rivers, dumps. **RANGE** Oct.–May: entire region (uncommon).

CALIFORNIA GULL
Larus californicus
GULL AND TERN FAMILY

21". Summer adult: dark gray above; head, tail, and underparts white. Winter adult: brownish streaks on head and shoulders. Bill yellow; red and black spot near tip. Flight shows black wingtips, white spot on first primary, dark gray upperwing, white tail. 1st winter: gray-brown with barring above. Nests in colonies on islets in lakes. **VOICE** High *kee-yah;* low *cow-cow-cow.* **HABITAT** Lakes, fields, towns. **RANGE** Apr.–Oct.: entire region; breeds locally.

RING-BILLED GULL
Larus delawarensis
GULL AND TERN FAMILY

summer adult (left), 1st winter (right)

L 19"; WS 4'. Summer adult: head and underparts white; back and wings silvery; wingtips black with white spots; bill yellow with black ring near tip; legs greenish yellow. Winter adult: head flecked brown. 1st winter: back gray; wing coverts speckled brown; tail whitish with black terminal band; bill pink with black tip; legs pink. Juv.: pale brown, speckled; bill black; legs pink. Nests in colonies on lakes. **VOICE** High-pitched mewing. **HABITAT** Lakes, rivers, urban parks, parking lots. **RANGE** Mar.–Nov.: entire region, Dec.–Feb.: s ID to e CO (local).

CASPIAN TERN
Sterna caspia
GULL AND TERN FAMILY

21". Summer adult: pale silvery above, white below; cap black; bill thick, red; legs black. Flight reveals short notched tail, black under primaries. **VOICE** Harsh *kra-haa*. **HABITAT** Lakes, rivers. **RANGE** May–Sept.: entire region (uncommon); breeds in s ID, e MT, nw and se WY.

COMMON TERN
Sterna hirundo
GULL AND TERN FAMILY

15". Summer adult: back and wings silvery, with blackish primaries; white below; cap and hindneck black; bill red, black-tipped; tail forked, outer streamers dusky. Winter adult: forehead white; nape black. Flight shows primaries blackish above, with wide black trailing edge below. **VOICE** Short *kip;* drawnout *keearr.* **HABITAT** Lakes. **RANGE** May, Aug.–Sept.: entire region (uncommon). June-July: breeds in n MT.

FORSTER'S TERN
Sterna forsteri
GULL AND TERN FAMILY

15". Pale silvery above, white below; primaries white; bill slender; tail forked, long. Summer adult: cap black; bill red-orange with black tip; legs red. Winter adult: crown white; long black eyemask; bill black. Imm.: back brownish; bill and eyemask black. Nests in colonies in marshes. **VOICE** Grating *kay-r-r-r;* repeated *kip.* **HABITAT** Marshes, lakes, beaches. **RANGE** May–Sept.: entire region (local, common).

BLACK TERN
Chlidonias niger
GULL AND TERN FAMILY

10". Summer adult: back, wings, and tail all gray; head and underparts black; bill and legs black; vent white. Winter adult: dark gray above; face and underparts white; nape and ear spot black. Tail short, notched. Nests in small colonies. **VOICE** Sharp *kreek.* **HABITAT** Reedy lakes, wet meadows, ponds. **RANGE** May–Sept.: entire region.

BAND-TAILED PIGEON
Columba fasciata
PIGEON AND DOVE FAMILY

15″. Back, wings, and tail slaty; head and underparts purplish gray. Flight reveals blackish tail base. Courting male flies in circles with fanned tail. Region's largest pigeon. **VOICE** Low, owl-like *hoo-hooo*. **HABITAT** Ponderosa Pine forests, oak shrublands. **RANGE** Apr.–Oct.: from w and nc CO south.

ROCK DOVE
"Rock Pigeon"
Columba livia
PIGEON AND DOVE FAMILY

13″. Typical head dark gray; coppery iridescence on neck; body and tail pale gray; 2 black bars on secondaries. Colors range from black to pale brown to white or partially white. Common city pigeon. Flight reveals pointed wings. **VOICE** Gurgling *coo-cuk-crooo*. **HABITAT** Towns, farms, cliffs. **RANGE** Resident in entire region.

MOURNING DOVE
Zenaida macroura
PIGEON AND DOVE FAMILY

12″. Back, wings, and tail dull brown; head and underparts pale buffy; black spot below eye; black and white edges on tail. Male cap and nape blue-gray. Wings whistle in flight. **VOICE** Mournful coo: *WHO-o coo, coo, coo*. **HABITAT** Fields, woods, gardens, sandy scrub. **RANGE** Resident in entire region; fewer in winter.

BLACK-BILLED CUCKOO
Coccyzus erythropthalmus
CUCKOO FAMILY

12″. Upperparts, crown, cheeks soft brown; white below; red eye ring; tail long, with thin white crescents below. **VOICE** Series of *cucucu* notes. **HABITAT** Broadleaf tree and brush areas. **RANGE** June–Sept.: c MT to e CO. **Yellow-billed Cuckoo** *(C. americanus)* has rufous primaries, large white spots under tail; summers from se MT to sw and se CO.

GREATER ROADRUNNER
Geococcyx californianus
CUCKOO FAMILY

22″. Adult buffy white with dark brown stripes, dark brown crown. Tail brown, wedge-shaped, outer tail feathers tipped white. Runs up to 15 mph after lizards, snakes, insects, small birds, mammals. **VOICE** Clucks; 6–8 dove-like, descending *coo* notes. **HABITAT** Desert brush, arid grassland. **RANGE** Resident in sc and se CO; more common May–Sept.

Owls

Owls are nocturnal birds of prey that range in size in the Rocky Mountain states from about 6 to 28 inches long. They have large heads, with large, forward-facing, yellow or brown eyes. Their eyesight and hearing are both acute. Distinct "facial disks" conceal large ear openings that provide them with keen hearing, which can pinpoint a squeak or a rustle in the grass in total darkness. The ears are asymmetrically placed on either side of the head, providing greater range of sound and better triangulation for pinpointing sources of sounds. Some owls have ornamental tufts of feathers at the corners of the head, called "ear tufts;" which look like ears or horns. The fluffy-looking bodies of owls are cryptically colored and patterned to blend with the background of their daytime nest or roost. Owls are most readily seen in winter in open areas and leafless woods. Their bills are short but strongly hooked. The legs are typically short, and the feet have sharp curved talons. Owls fly silently; their feathers are very soft and delicately fringed. Imitations and tapes of their distinctive voices, given or played at night, bring a response from an owl, which may call or fly in close to the source of the call, or both; in daytime, the same sound may bring crows, jays, and other birds, which usually mob roosting owls they discover.

Parts of an Owl

BARN OWL
Tyto alba
BARN OWL FAMILY

18". Pale orange washed with gray above; flecked white or buff below. No ear tufts; white, heart-shaped facial disk. Legs long, feathered. Superb "mouser"; hearing acute. Nocturnal; perches on poles. **VOICE** Harsh screams, hisses, clicks. **HABITAT** Old farm buildings, riversides, deserts, towns. **RANGE** Resident in sw ID, se WY, sw and e CO.

FLAMMULATED OWL
Otus flammeolus
OWL FAMILY

7". Looks like a Screech-owl with dark eyes. Gray with black streaks and bars; facial disk gray with dark fringe; ear tufts short. Strictly nocturnal; remains well hidden by day. **VOICE** Long slow series of single or double hoots. **HABITAT** Oak and Ponderosa Pine woods. **RANGE** May–Sept.: wc ID, w and c CO.

WESTERN SCREECH-OWL
Otus kennicottii
OWL FAMILY

9″. Gray, with streaks on finely barred breast. Facial disks ringed in black; white spots on sides of back. Fluffy ear tufts (can lay flat); eyes yellow; bill black; tail short. **VOICE** Low short whistles that speed up; quick hoots. **HABITAT** Broadleaf and riverine woods, towns. **RANGE** Resident in ID, w MT, w WY, w and c CO. **Eastern Screech-Owl** (*O. asio*, of se MT, e WY, ne CO) gray or reddish brown; bill pale; call a rising and falling whinny or a long trill.

GREAT HORNED OWL
Bubo virginianus
OWL FAMILY

L 23″; WS 4′7″. Dark brown with black spots above; underparts pale brown with heavy, dark brown bars; dark streaks on upper chest; facial disks rich, rusty brown, ringed in black. Head large; eyes yellow; fluffy ear tufts. Region's largest common owl. **VOICE** 5–8 deep hoots, 2nd and 3rd rapid and doubled. **HABITAT** Forests, riverine woods, cliffs in sagebrush deserts, towns. **RANGE** Resident in entire region.

SNOWY OWL
Nyctea scandiaca
OWL FAMILY

24″. Face, chest, and leg feathers snow white. Older male pure white; female and imm. crown, upperparts, and belly laced with black dots and scales. Head rounded; no ear tufts; eyes yellow. Feeds often by day; sits on exposed perches. **VOICE** Quiet in winter. **HABITAT** Farmland, marshes. **RANGE** Nov.–Mar.: e MT (uncommon; absent some winters); rarer in WY, e CO.

NORTHERN PYGMY-OWL
Glaucidium gnoma
OWL FAMILY

7″. Crown, upperparts, and chest brown or gray with fine whitish dots; breast white, striped brown or gray. Lacks ear tufts; eyes yellow; false black eyes with white eyebrows on back of head; tail long, banded dark and light brown. Feeds by day on small birds; often mobbed by them. **VOICE** Long series of even *toot* notes. **HABITAT** Coniferous forests. **RANGE** Resident in mtns. of entire region (uncommon).

BURROWING OWL
Athene (Speotyto) cunicularia
OWL FAMILY
9″. Brown above, spotted with white; white below, scaled brown. Head rounded, lacks ear tufts; facial disks light brown; eyes yellow. Legs long, grayish; tail short. Digs burrow in open field; also uses Prairie Dog towns; sentinel may stand on earthen mound by burrow in daytime. **VOICE** Mellow *coo-coo* at night; quick notes if alarmed. **HABITAT** Dry grasslands, sagebrush deserts. **RANGE** Apr.–Oct.: s ID, c and e MT, WY, e and w CO (local).

GREAT GRAY OWL
Strix nebulosa
OWL FAMILY
28″. Gray with blackish stripes and finer barring above and below; head massive, without ear tufts; face gray with concentric dark rings; eyes small, yellow; white tufts flank yellow bill; white "bow tie" on throat. **VOICE** Series of deep slow hoots. **HABITAT** Tall coniferous forests near meadows. **RANGE** Resident in n and c ID, w MT, nw WY (rare).

LONG-EARED OWL
Asio otus
OWL FAMILY
15″. Ear tufts long, close together on smallish head; eyes yellow; eye disks rufous-orange, edged in black. Speckled dark brown and blackish above; striped blackish below, over finer brown banding. Nocturnal feeder; rarely seen by day. In winter, roosts communally. **VOICE** Varied; 1 or 2 long *hoooos;* wails and screams. **HABITAT** Riverine woods, aspen parklands, planted conifer groves. **RANGE** Resident in entire region (local).

SHORT-EARED OWL
Asio flammeus
OWL FAMILY
16″. Brown above, with darker and paler brown spots; buffy below, with brown stripes; facial disks buffy with blackish "eye shadow" around yellow eyes. Head has tiny inconspicuous ear tufts. Flight reveals brown wings above, with buffy patch near bend of wing. Flies early and late in day and by night. **VOICE** Barking *wow* near nest. **HABITAT** Marshes, meadows, farms. **RANGE** Entire region; local in summer, more common in winter.

NORTHERN SAW-WHET OWL
Aegolius acadicus
OWL FAMILY

8″. Dark brown above, thick rusty stripes below; large white spots on shoulders; crown finely white-striped. Head large; lacks ear tufts; facial disk has radiating rusty stripes. **VOICE** Long rapid series of *too* notes. **HABITAT** Coniferous forests. Winter: broadleaf woods. **RANGE** Resident in mtns. of entire region. Some winter in lowlands. **Boreal Owl** (*A. funereus;* 10″) has black face fringe; resident in mtn. forests.

COMMON NIGHTHAWK
Chordeiles minor
NIGHTJAR FAMILY

10″. Dark brown, heavily gray-spotted; throat white (buff in female); legs very short. Flight reveals long, pointed, black primaries with prominent white bar; long notched tail. Flies high and erratically. Hunts at night for aerial insects. Male "booms" in courtship display. **VOICE** Nasal *peeent.* **HABITAT** Open woods, sagebrush, towns. **RANGE** Mid-May–Sept.: entire region.

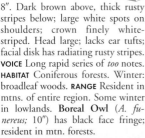

COMMON POORWILL
Phalaenoptilus nuttallii
NIGHTJAR FAMILY

8″. Adult mottled gray-brown; throat black above white half-collar. Wings rounded (no white band); tail short, corners white. Often sits on dirt roads at night; some hibernate in rocky crevices for winter. **VOICE** Loud *pour-wheeel,* given at night. **HABITAT** Desert washes, sagebrush flats, arid hills and canyons, pinyon-juniper woods. **RANGE** May–Oct.: s ID, c and e MT, s and e WY, w and c CO.

BLACK SWIFT
Cypseloides niger
SWIFT FAMILY

7″. All black above and below; may show white forehead. Flight reveals long narrow wings, slightly forked tail. Nests behind tall waterfalls. Flight fast and high; swifts do not perch on wires and branches as swallows do. **VOICE** Rarely heard *plik* notes. **HABITAT** Open sky over hills, wet cliffs in mtns. **RANGE** May–Sept.: n ID, w MT, w and c CO (very local).

VAUX'S SWIFT
Chaetura vauxi
SWIFT FAMILY

4½". Sooty gray with diffuse whitish-gray throat; bill and feet tiny; tail short, spiny. Flight reveals long pointed wings, bowed in crescent when gliding. **VOICE** High *chitter* and *chip* notes. **HABITAT** Forests, lakes, towns. **RANGE** May–Aug.: n ID, w MT. **Chimney Swift** (*C. pelagica;* 5½") has darker throat; May–Sept.: towns of e MT, e WY, e CO.

WHITE-THROATED SWIFT
Aeronautes saxatilis
SWIFT FAMILY

6½". Mainly black; white throat narrows down to midbelly; flanks and trailing edge of secondaries white; bill tiny; tail deeply notched. Flight reveals long pointed wings. Very fast flier. Does not perch; clings upright. Nests in small colonies. **VOICE** Shrill descending *ji-ji-ji-ji-ji.* **HABITAT** Cliffs, canyons, deserts. **RANGE** Apr.–Sept.: region's mountainous areas.

BLACK-CHINNED HUMMINGBIRD
Archilochus alexandri
HUMMINGBIRD FAMILY

3½". Male green above and on sides; chest crescent and midbelly stripe white; throat patch black above, violet below; tail black, notched. Female green above; throat and underparts white; tail green, with white corners. Bill long, needle-like, black. **VOICE** Loud *teeuw.* **HABITAT** Riverine woods, canyons, towns. **RANGE** May–Sept. (June–Aug. in n mtns.): ID, sw WY, CO (ex. ne).

BROAD-TAILED HUMMINGBIRD
Selasphorus platycercus
HUMMINGBIRD FAMILY

4". Male crown, back, and side patch brilliant green; throat patch reflects red; mostly white below; tail black. Female green above; throat white with fine dots; pale orange below; outer tail corners white. **VOICE** Soft *chip* notes; male has noisy wingbeat *whirr.* **HABITAT** Wooded valleys and mtns.; often near homes. **RANGE** May–Sept.: s and e ID, sw MT, w and sc WY, w and c CO.

CALLIOPE HUMMINGBIRD
Stellula calliope
HUMMINGBIRD FAMILY

female (left), male (right)

3″. Male crown and upperparts green; white below, with throat patch of red stripes; tail very short, black. Female green above, white below; washed buffy on sides; tail has white corners. Bill short, needle-like, black. Silent flier. Smallest bird in N. Amer. **VOICE** High *tsik.* **HABITAT** Dry coniferous forests, wooded canyons. **RANGE** May–Aug.: ID, w MT, nw WY. July–Aug.: also c WY, w and c CO.

RUFOUS HUMMINGBIRD
Selasphorus rufus
HUMMINGBIRD FAMILY

3½″. Male crown, upperparts, and sides rufous; chest crescent and midbelly stripe white; throat patch red; tail rufous, feathers pointed; in display flight, wings make loud staccato sounds. Female green above, white below; sides buffy; outer tail feathers rufous, black, and white. Bill needle-like, black. **VOICE** Short single notes. **HABITAT** Coniferous, broadleaf, and riverine forests, parks. **RANGE** Mid-Apr.–Aug.: n and c ID, w MT, nw WY. July–Aug.: also w and s WY, w and s CO.

BELTED KINGFISHER
Ceryle alcyon
KINGFISHER FAMILY

13″. Male blue above, with tiny white spots; throat, neck, and belly white; blue belt on chest. Female (pictured) similar; belly has 2nd (rufous) belt extending onto sides. Front-heavy; head large, with ragged fore and rear crests; bill very long, thick, pointed, black; white spot before eye. Active, calls often; dives headfirst to seize small fish. For nest, excavates tunnel 1–2′ into earthen bank, sometimes far from water. **VOICE** Loud woody rattle. **HABITAT** Rivers, streams, lakes. **RANGE** Apr.–Oct.: entire region. Nov.–Mar.: w MT and south.

Woodpeckers

Woodpeckers, which range in size from small to midsize birds, cling to the trunks and large branches of trees with their sharp claws (on short legs) and stiff, spine-tipped tails that help support them in the vertical position. Several species also feed on the ground. Their long, pointed bills are like chisels, able to bore into wood. Curled inside the woodpecker head is a narrow tongue twice the length of the bill, tipped with spear-like barbs that impale wood-boring insects. Members of this family laboriously dig out nest holes in living or dead tree trunks and limbs. The sexes are very much alike, but the red (or yellow) patches on the heads of the males are reduced or lacking in females of many species. In spring, males rapidly bang their bills against resonant wood on trees and buildings in a territorial drumming that is louder and more rapid than the tapping made while feeding.

Some species of woodpeckers exhibit regional variations. For instance the plains races of Hairy and Downy Woodpeckers have large white spots on their wings while the mountain races have tiny spots.

RED-HEADED WOODPECKER
Melanerpes erythrocephalus
WOODPECKER FAMILY

9″. Adult back and wings black, ex. for white secondaries (large, squarish, white wing patch); underparts and rump clear white; tail black. Imm. head, back, and most of wings brown. Will feed on ground for insects, nuts. **VOICE** Loud high *chuurr.* **HABITAT** Broadleaf woods, orchards, towns. **RANGE** May–Sept.: c and e MT, nc and e WY, e CO; wanders in late summer.

LEWIS'S WOODPECKER
Melanerpes lewis
WOODPECKER FAMILY

11″. Crown, back, and wings black (glossed dark green); face and cheeks dark red; chest and complete collar silvery; belly pink. Imm. all blackish, like a small crow. In flight, all dark above. Flight is crow-like, with steady wingbeats. Feeds on large insects in trees, high in air. **VOICE** Harsh *churr;* soft drum. **HABITAT** Open areas with pine, oak, cottonwood trees; farms, orchards. **RANGE** Apr.–Sept.: n and c ID, w MT, most of WY and CO. Many winter in CO, a few to the north.

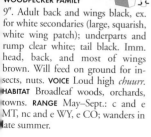

RED-NAPED SAPSUCKER
Sphyrapicus nuchalis
WOODPECKER FAMILY

8″. Adult male back and wings black, weakly barred white; white patch on wing; pale yellow below, with speckles; head pied; red forecrown and nape separated by black line; throat red. **VOICE** Slurred mewing; irreg. drum. **HABITAT** Forests. **RANGE** Apr., Sept.: entire region. May–Aug.: n and c ID, w MT, WY, w and c CO.

WILLIAMSON'S SAPSUCKER
Sphyrapicus thyroideus
WOODPECKER FAMILY

9″. Adult male black; shoulder and rump white; 2 white head stripes; throat red. Adult female barred black and buff; head brown; belly pale yellow. **VOICE** Slurred *cheer;* irreg. drum. **HABITAT** Coniferous forests. **RANGE** Apr., Sept.: s and w parts of region. May–Aug.: n and c ID, w MT, nw and c WY, w and c CO.

HAIRY WOODPECKER
Picoides villosus
WOODPECKER FAMILY

9″. Like Downy Woodpecker, head boldly pied; midback white; wings black, few white spots on primaries; underparts white. Male has small red nape patch. **VOICE** Loud rattle on one pitch; sharp *peek;* long drum. **HABITAT** Coniferous and broadleaf forests (esp. aspens). **RANGE** Resident in entire region.

DOWNY WOODPECKER
Picoides pubescens
WOODPECKER FAMILY

6½″. Like Hairy Woodpecker, head boldly pied; midback white; wings black, white-spotted; underparts white. Male has red nape patch. **VOICE** Rapid descending whinny; flat *pick;* long drum. **HABITAT** Lowland broadleaf and riverine woods, thickets, parks; a few in mtns. **RANGE** Resident in entire region.

THREE-TOED WOODPECKER
Picoides tridactylus
WOODPECKER FAMILY

9″. Back and sides barred black and white; wings black, with few white dots; midbelly white; head mainly black. Male cap yellow; female crown black. Finds beetles by tearing bark from trees killed by fire. **VOICE** Soft *teek*. **HABITAT** Coniferous forests. **RANGE** Resident in n and c ID, w MT, mtns. of WY, w and c CO.

BLACK-BACKED WOODPECKER
Picoides arcticus
WOODPECKER FAMILY

9″. Black above, white below; sides gray-barred. Head black, with white and black "mustache" lines; male has yellow crown patch. In flight, all black above, ex. for white outer tail feathers. **VOICE** Soft *pick;* long drum. **HABITAT** Coniferous forests, esp. after fires. **RANGE** Resident in n and c ID, w MT, nw WY.

NORTHERN FLICKER
Colaptes auratus
WOODPECKER FAMILY

12″. Brown, with black chest patch, bars, and spots; rump white. In plains, underwing yellow; black "mustache" in male. In mtns., underwing reddish; red "mustache" in male. **VOICE** Rapid *wic* notes; loud *klee-err.* **HABITAT** Woods, farms, towns. **RANGE** Resident in entire region; lowlands in winter.

PILEATED WOODPECKER
Dryocopus pileatus
WOODPECKER FAMILY

16″. Black; crest pointed, red; white and black stripes on face and down sides of neck. Male forehead and "mustache" red; female forehead and "mustache" black. Neck thin; bill heavy, silver. **VOICE** Rapid irreg. series of *cuk* and *wucka* notes. **HABITAT** Coniferous forests. **RANGE** Resident in n and c ID, w MT.

Songbirds (Passerines)

The birds described from here to the end of the birds section belong to a single order called Passeriformes. Known as passerines or, more commonly, perching birds or songbirds, they are the most recently evolved of the 25 bird orders. Members of this order comprise more than half the world's birds. Their sizes range from 3½-inch kinglets to 24-inch ravens, but they are generally small land birds with pleasing songs; among the finest songsters are the wrens and thrushes. Songbirds use call notes year-round, while most give their songs only during the breeding season (spring and early summer). In some species, the male has a particularly colorful summer breeding plumage that changes in winter to drabber, female-like coloration. In the spring, migrant males generally arrive in the Rocky Mountain states seven to ten days before the females and stake out breeding territories, which they defend against neighboring males. After a male shows a female around his territory, she may be satisfied (especially if the vegetation and insect life are plentiful) and stay with him, or search for another singing male whose territory is more to her liking. Most songbirds build open-topped, rounded nests of grasses, sticks, vegetable fibers, and rootlets in a tree fork, in a shrub, or tucked under tall grass. Some eat insects year-round, while others focus on seeds, grains, or fruit; all feed insects to their hatchlings. In the fall, the sexes may migrate south together, the adults often several weeks or more before the young born that year.

OLIVE-SIDED FLYCATCHER
Contopus cooperi (borealis)
TYRANT FLYCATCHER FAMILY

7½". Upperparts and crown dark olive-brown; sides olive-brown, form a vest; throat and midbelly stripe white. Bill thick; tail medium length. Perches on highest twigs of trees. **VOICE** Song: whistled *hic* then *three-beers.* Call: rapid *pip-pip-pip.* **HABITAT** Summer: coniferous forests. Migration: also broadleaf woods, parks. **RANGE** May–Sept.: ID, w MT, w and c WY, w and c CO.

WESTERN WOOD-PEWEE
Contopus sordidulus
TYRANT FLYCATCHER FAMILY

6½". Adult pale grayish brown above; 1 or 2 pale whitish wing bars; dingy whitish below; sides grayish; bill often orangy beneath. Head peaked at rear; bill thin; tail fairly long. Imm. wing bars buffy; bill black. **VOICE** Song: harsh nasal *peee-err.* **HABITAT** Broadleaf, pine, and riparian woods. **RANGE** May–Sept.: entire region.

LEAST FLYCATCHER
Empidonax minimus
TYRANT FLYCATCHER FAMILY

5″. Grayish olive-brown above; dirty white below, some with yellowish wash on belly; 2 white wing bars; bold white eye ring. Head fairly large; tail short. **VOICE** Emphatic *che-BECK*. **HABITAT** Edges of waterside woodlands in prairies; greenbelts, towns. **RANGE** May, Aug.–Sept.: east of Rockies from MT to e CO. June–July: breeds in MT (ex. far w), ne WY.

DUSKY FLYCATCHER
Empidonax oberholseri
TYRANT FLYCATCHER FAMILY

5¾″. Grayish olive above; throat white; olive wash on chest; belly pale cream; 2 wing bars and outer tail feathers whitish; white eye ring and lores. Flicks tail up. **VOICE** Song: 3-part *sillt-surrp-seet*. Call: soft *wit*. **HABITAT** Open riverine and mtn. woods, shrubby hillsides. **RANGE** May–Aug.: ID, w MT, most of WY, w and c CO.

CORDILLERAN FLYCATCHER
"Western Flycatcher"
Empidonax occidentalis
TYRANT FLYCATCHER FAMILY

5½″. Olive-brown above; chest and sides washed olive; throat and belly lemon yellow; 2 whitish wing bars; eye ring white, pointed at rear. **VOICE** Song: loud *pit-SEET*. **HABITAT** Watersides, aspen and coniferous forests, esp. shady ravines; sagebrush in migration. **RANGE** ID, w MT, most of WY, w and c CO.

ASH-THROATED FLYCATCHER
Myiarchus cinerascens
TYRANT FLYCATCHER FAMILY

8″. Crown, cheeks, and upperparts dull brown; throat and chest pale gray; belly pale yellow; 1 whitish wing bar; primaries and longish tail rusty. Head fluffy to rear; bill thin, black. **VOICE** Soft *pur-weer* and *pwit*; harsher *ka-brick*. **HABITAT** Open woods (esp. pinyon-juniper), brush. **RANGE** Apr.–Sept.: s ID, far sw WY, CO (ex. ne).

SAY'S PHOEBE
Sayornis saya
TYRANT FLYCATCHER FAMILY

7½". Crown and upperparts dull brown; throat and chest gray; belly and vent dull cinnamon; 2 faint wing bars; tail fairly long, black, wagged often. Bill thin, black. Hovers above grass and flies sorties from perch. **VOICE** Song: *pit-cedar*. Call: falling *peeurr*. **HABITAT** Shrubby grasslands, cliffs, farms. **RANGE** Apr.–Oct.: entire region, ex. high mtns.

CASSIN'S KINGBIRD
Tyrannus vociferans
TYRANT FLYCATCHER FAMILY

8½". Adult back olive; crown dark gray; throat white; chest slaty gray; belly yellow; tail blackish with pale tip. Much darker chest than on Western; lacks white outer tail feathers. **VOICE** Husky *chi-beeer* and *chi-be-be-be-be*. **HABITAT** Hillsides with scrub, grass, a few trees. **RANGE** Apr.–Sept.: se MT, e WY, CO.

WESTERN KINGBIRD
Tyrannus verticalis
TYRANT FLYCATCHER FAMILY

9". Crown and back gray; thin dark line through eye; throat and chest pale gray; belly yellow; tail black, with white outer feathers. Bill short, wide. Aggressive toward larger birds near nest. Sits on wires, other exposed perches. **VOICE** Shrill *kit* and *kit-kit-kiddledit*. **HABITAT** Riverine woods, grasslands, farms. **RANGE** Apr.–Sept.: entire region, ex. high mtns.

EASTERN KINGBIRD
Tyrannus tyrannus
TYRANT FLYCATCHER FAMILY

8". Back and wings slaty; crown and cheeks black; throat and breast white; tail black, with wide white terminal band. Often flies slowly, with quivering wings. Chases raptors and crows from territory. Perches conspicuously. **VOICE** Rapid agitated *kit-kit-kit-kittery;* nasal *tzeer*. **HABITAT** Trees near farms, fields, roads. **RANGE** May–mid-Sept.: n and c ID, MT, WY, w and e CO.

HORNED LARK
Eremophila alpestris
LARK FAMILY

7½". Brown above; white below, with black chest band. Black crown ends in 2 tiny "horns"; forehead and throat white, with black stripe in-between. Bill slender, pointed, black. Flight reveals black tail, white outer tail feathers. Imm. has plain head. **VOICE** Song: high tinkling. Call: *tsee-titi*. **HABITAT** Grasslands, farms, deserts; also alpine meadows in summer. **RANGE** Resident in entire region.

TREE SWALLOW
Tachycineta bicolor
SWALLOW FAMILY

6". Adult dark iridescent green-blue above, entirely snowy white below. 1st year female and imm. brown above. Tail notched. Slow flier; short flapping circles and a climb. **VOICE** Song: *weet-trit-weet*. Call: *cheat cheat*. **HABITAT** Wooded river valleys, forest edges, ponds, towns. **RANGE** Mar.–Sept.: entire region. **Purple Martin** (*Progne subis*; 8") male all purple, tail forked; female breast dusky; summers in w CO.

VIOLET-GREEN SWALLOW
Tachycineta thalassina
SWALLOW FAMILY

5". Crown, back, and forewing green; back of neck, flight feathers, midrump stripe, and tail dark violet; white underparts continue up behind eye; sides of rump white. Tail short, notched. Flight very fluttery. **VOICE** Thin *chip;* rapid *chit-chit-chit-weet-weet*. **HABITAT** Forest edges, towns. **RANGE** Mar.–Sept.: entire region, ex. ne MT, e CO.

NORTHERN ROUGH-WINGED SWALLOW
Stelgidopteryx serripennis
SWALLOW FAMILY

5½". Dull brown above; throat and chest pale brown; lacks neck band; breast and vent dull white. Tail notched. Tree Swallow imm. brown above, all snowy white below. Flies with slow deep wingbeats. Often in solitary pairs. **VOICE** Raspy *brit*. **HABITAT** Wetlands with earth banks. **RANGE** Apr.–Sept.: entire region.

BANK SWALLOW
Riparia riparia
SWALLOW FAMILY

5″. Dull brown above; white below, crossed by distinct brown neck band. (Northern Rough-winged Swallow has dusky brown throat; lacks neck band.) Flies with rapid wingbeats. Often in flocks, very social. Nests in burrows in riverbanks. **VOICE** Low flat *chert chert;* buzzy chatter. **HABITAT** Rivers and lakes with sandbanks. **RANGE** May–mid-Sept.: entire region.

CLIFF SWALLOW
Hirundo pyrrhonota
SWALLOW FAMILY

6″. Adult crown, back, and wings dark blue; rump buffy; throat dark chestnut; breast grayish white; forehead cream; hindneck gray; tail black, short, square. Glides in circles high in air. Nests in colonies in gullies, under bridges, eaves; builds spherical mud nest. **VOICE** Song: harsh creaking. Call: grating *syrup.* **HABITAT** Farms, waterways with cliffs. **RANGE** Late Apr.–Sept.: entire region.

BARN SWALLOW
Hirundo rustica
SWALLOW FAMILY

7″. Adult glossy blue above; forehead chestnut; throat dark orange, with thin blue necklace; rest of underparts buffy orange; outer tail streamers very long. Imm. pale buff below, with dark necklace. Fast flier. **VOICE** Song: long twittering. Calls: soft *vit vit* and *zee-zay.* **HABITAT** Fields, farms, waterways, towns. **RANGE** Apr.–Oct.: entire region.

GRAY JAY
Perisoreus canadensis
JAY AND CROW FAMILY

12″. Rocky Mountain race: adult back, wings, and tail dull, dark gray; crown, cheeks, and throat white; rear crown black; breast pale gray. Bill black; tail long, rounded. Juv. all slaty with white mustache. Bold food robber at campsites. **VOICE** Low *chuck.* **HABITAT** Wet coniferous forests, mostly in mtns. **RANGE** Resident in n and c ID, w MT, w WY, w and c CO.

WESTERN SCRUB-JAY
Aphelocoma californica
JAY AND CROW FAMILY

12″. Back gray-brown; belly gray; crown, hindneck, partial collar, wings, rump, and tail blue; throat white with faint blue streaks. No crest; bill heavy; tail long, rounded. Shy at nest but bold rest of year at picnic sites and parks. Caches acorns in ground for winter. **VOICE** Loud series of *kwesh* or *check* notes. **HABITAT** Oak and juniper woods, towns. **RANGE** Resident in far sw WY, w and e foothills of CO.

STELLER'S JAY
Cyanocitta stelleri
JAY AND CROW FAMILY

12″. All dark; bill heavy. Head and pointed crest black; thin white stripes on forehead; back and upper breast blackish (grayer to south); belly and rump plain blue; wings and tail blue with fine black barring. Brash and nearly omnivorous; visits campsites for scraps. **VOICE** Loud *shaq, kwesh,* or *whek* notes, repeated 3–4 times. **HABITAT** Coniferous forests, parks. **RANGE** Resident in ID, w and c MT, WY, w and c CO.

BLUE JAY
Cyanocitta cristata
JAY AND CROW FAMILY

12″. Crest, crown, back, rump, and tail blue; row of white spots on wing; face and throat white; black collar; belly pale gray; vent white; white corners on long tail. Usu. in small flocks; wanders westward. Aggressive at feeders. **VOICE** Harsh *jaay;* liquid *queedle;* imitates hawk screams. **HABITAT** Waterside woods, towns. **RANGE** Resident in e MT, n and e WY, e CO.

PINYON JAY
Gymnorhinus cyanocephalus
JAY AND CROW FAMILY

10″. Adult all dull blue; faint white streaks on throat. Bill black, chisel-like; tail shorter than other jays; no crest. Imm. paler with grayish underparts. Even, crow-like flight. Very social; usu. seen in large flocks. Stores pine nuts for winter and spring. **VOICE** High, descending *kra-a-a;* series of *kway* notes. **HABITAT** Stunted forests of pine, juniper; mtns. **RANGE** Resident in se ID, sc and se MT, e and s WY, w and c CO. Some winterers disperse elsewhere in region.

CLARK'S NUTCRACKER
Nucifraga columbiana
JAY AND CROW FAMILY

13". Head, back, and underparts plain silvery gray; vent white; wings black, trailing edge of secondaries white; tail fairly short, black in center, with white outer tail feathers. Bill long, pointed, black. Walks like crow on ground (jays hop); often flies high. **VOICE** Guttural *kraaah*. **HABITAT** Open coniferous forests in mtns. **RANGE** Resident in uplands of entire region.

BLACK-BILLED MAGPIE
Pica pica
JAY AND CROW FAMILY

20". Head, chest, back, rump, and vent black; belly and long shoulder patch white; wings and tail iridescent purple and green. Bill stout, black; tail very long, with wedge-shaped tip. Flight reveals mainly white primaries. Feeds on insects, fruit, baby birds, roadkills. Mobs hawks, larger birds. Uses communal roosts. **VOICE** Rapid series of *jack* notes; rising *maayg?* **HABITAT** Riverine woods, sagebrush deserts, farms. **RANGE** Resident in entire region.

Attracting Birds to Your Yard

Many people enjoy attracting birds into their yards, and supplemental feeding helps birds in winter when naturally occurring seeds are covered by snow. Once started, winter feeding should be continued into spring. Some birds will visit feeders all year. Throughout the birds section, species that will come into a yard to feed are indicated by the 🐦 icon.

Birdfeeders come in many designs. Hanging, clear seed feeders with short perch sticks are popular with goldfinches, siskins, and other finches. Window boxes and platforms on a pole are best for such medium-size birds as Evening Grosbeaks and Steller's Jays, while Mourning Doves, Dark-eyed Juncos, and many sparrows prefer to feed on the ground. Mounting a birdfeeder inevitably means an ongoing struggle with squirrels, who are endlessly resourceful at defeating devices intended to keep them out of the feeders.

Grains and seeds are the best all-purpose fare for feeders. Many species like sunflower seeds. Thistle seed is popular with goldfinches, white millet seed is a good choice for small species, and cracked corn is appreciated by large, ground-feeding birds. Many seed mixes are available at supermarkets and garden supply stores. Birds also like nuts and fruit. Suet, in a mesh holder hung from a branch or mounted on a tree trunk, attracts nuthatches and woodpeckers; it should be discontinued in summer because it spoils

COMMON RAVEN
Corvus corax
JAY AND CROW FAMILY

24″. All glossy black; bill black, very heavy; throat has long shaggy feathers. Flight reveals pointed wings, "fingered" wingtips; long, wedge-shaped tail. Usu. alone or in pairs. **VOICE** Very low *croonk*. **HABITAT** Mtns., forests, fields, farms, deserts. **RANGE** Resident in ID, w MT, w and c WY, w and c CO. **Chihuahuan Raven** (*C. cryptoleucus;* 19″) of arid se CO plains has smaller bill, but is very similar.

AMERICAN CROW
Corvus brachyrhynchos
JAY AND CROW FAMILY

18″. All glossy black; bill heavy, black. Flight reveals rounded wings, "fingered" wingtips, squarish tail with rounded corners. Bold, noisy, conspicuous. Huge night roosts in winter outside breeding season. **VOICE** Loud falling *caaw*. **HABITAT** Towns, farms, woodland edges, fields. **RANGE** Resident in entire region. Mar.–Apr., Oct.–Nov.: mainly migrant in e WY.

---

quickly and mats feathers. Hummingbirds and orioles will come to specially designed red plastic dispensers of sugar water.

Water is important, especially during periods when natural water sources dry up or freeze over. Many species are attracted to a birdbath, which should be regularly scrubbed with a brush to rid it of algae and prevent diseases from spreading.

You might want to make or purchase a nest box to attract breeding birds. The most popular—inviting to woodpeckers, chickadees, nuthatches, wrens, bluebirds, and even some owls—is an enclosed box with a square floor area 4 to 7 inches wide and deep and about twice as high as it is wide (8 to 12 inches). Specifications for such a box vary depending on the species and include floor area, the size of the entrance hole, the height from the base of the box to the hole, and proper siting of the box. Other birds will nest in open-fronted shelves placed under eaves. Information on building and siting nest boxes and feeders is available at your local Audubon Society or nature center. In the birds section, the icon 🏠 denotes species that have used nest boxes in the right habitat.

Some people argue against feeding birds at any time of year because it can help spread diseases among birds that otherwise would not come into contact with each other. Also, the abundance of plant and animal food in the warmer months makes it unnecessary to feed birds in the Rocky Mountain states from May to October.

BLACK-CAPPED CHICKADEE
Poecile (Parus) atricapillus
CHICKADEE FAMILY

5½". Back, wings, and long narrow tail gray; white below, with light buffy sides; wings edged white; cap and throat black; face white. Friendly, inquisitive; often in family groups. Acrobatic when feeding. **VOICE** Song: clear *fee-bee*. Call: *chick-a-dee-dee-dee-dee*. **HABITAT** Broadleaf and riverine woods, thickets, towns. **RANGE** Resident in region, ex. sw ID.

MOUNTAIN CHICKADEE
Poecile (Parus) gambeli
CHICKADEE FAMILY

5½". Back, wings, belly, and tail gray; crown and throat black; cheek and sides of neck white; white line over eye. Tail long, narrow. Often in flocks; acrobatic when feeding. **VOICE** Song: high whistled *fee-bee-bee*. Call: raspy *chick-a-dee-dee-dee*. **HABITAT** Coniferous forests. **RANGE** Resident in uplands of entire region.

CHESTNUT-BACKED CHICKADEE
Poecile (Parus) rufescens
CHICKADEE FAMILY

5". Back, rump, and sides chestnut; rest of underparts white; crown and throat dark brown; cheeks and sides of neck white; wings and tail gray. Tail long, narrow. Often in flocks; feeds high in trees. **VOICE** Call: high *zitta-zitta-zee*. **HABITAT** Wet coniferous forests, parks, towns. **RANGE** Resident in n and nc ID, w MT.

JUNIPER TITMOUSE
"Plain Titmouse"
Baeolophus (Parus) griseus
CHICKADEE FAMILY

5¾". Adult plain gray above, paler gray below; crest gray. Tail long. Acrobatic feeder; eats nuts, seeds, insects. **VOICE** Harsh *see-dee-dee*. **HABITAT** Pinyon-juniper woods. **RANGE** Resident in sc ID, sw WY, w and sc CO.

BUSHTIT
Psaltriparus minimus
BUSHTIT FAMILY

4". Entirely dull gray. Head small; bill tiny; tail long, narrow. Eyes dark in male, yellow in female. Acrobatic feeder; gathers in flocks of up to 30 birds when not nesting. **VOICE** Song: high trill. Call: frequently given, weak *pit*. **HABITAT** Juniper woods, thickets, towns. **RANGE** Resident in sw ID, sw WY, w and c CO.

RED-BREASTED NUTHATCH
Sitta canadensis
NUTHATCH FAMILY

4½". Male back steel blue; underparts rufous; cap black; black line through eye and white line over it. Female similar, but crown gray; buffy below. Tail short. **VOICE** High nasal *enk* series. **HABITAT** Summer: coniferous forests. Winter: also broadleaf woods. **RANGE** Resident in mtns. of entire region; in fall and winter, disperses into lowlands.

WHITE-BREASTED NUTHATCH
Sitta carolinensis
NUTHATCH FAMILY

6". Male back gray-blue; wings edged white; face and underparts white; narrow crown black; vent and sides washed rusty. Female crown gray. Creeps headfirst in all directions on tree trunks. **VOICE** Song: rapid *wer* notes. Call: loud *yank*. **HABITAT** Broadleaf woods; fewer in pines; towns. **RANGE** Resident in mtns., wooded valleys of entire region.

PYGMY NUTHATCH
Sitta pygmaea
NUTHATCH FAMILY

4". Blue-gray above, pale buffy below; crown brown; dark brown line through eye; whitish spot at back of nape; throat white. Tail short. Climbs over branches and needles, often upside down. Often in small flocks. **VOICE** High series of *peep* notes. **HABITAT** Ponderosa Pine forests. **RANGE** Resident in n and c ID, w MT, e WY, w and c CO.

BROWN CREEPER
Certhia americana
CREEPER FAMILY

5½". Brown with buff stripes above, white below; wing stripe buffy; rump rufous; eye line white; tail tips spiny. Looks like a wren; sings like a warbler; climbs trees like a woodpecker: starts at bottom of trunk, probes bark with slender bill. **VOICE** Song: high *see see see tu wee*. Call: 1–2 high *tsee* notes. **HABITAT** Summer: coniferous forests. Winter: all wooded areas. **RANGE** Resident in mtns. of entire region; winters also in plains, lowlands.

ROCK WREN
Salpinctes obsoletus
WREN FAMILY

6". Gray-brown above, speckled with buff and white; whitish below; pale buffy on sides; buffy eyebrow. Bill slender; tail fairly long. Often bobs body. **VOICE** Song: loud repeated *cha-wee*. Call: sharp *tee-keer*. **HABITAT** Canyons, rocky areas in deserts. **RANGE** Mid-Apr.–Oct.: entire region. A few winter in s CO.

CANYON WREN
Catherpes mexicanus
WREN FAMILY

5½". Back and belly rufous with black and white dots; wings and fairly long tail rufous with black banding; crown dull brown; throat and foreneck clear white; bill long, slender, drooping. **VOICE** Song: descending loud *tee-tee-tee-tew-tew-tew-tew*. Call: harsh *jeet*. **HABITAT** Cliff faces, canyons with streams. **RANGE** Mar.–Oct.: s ID, sc MT, sw WY, CO (ex. ne). Some overwinter, esp. in ID and CO.

BEWICK'S WREN
Thryomanes bewickii
WREN FAMILY

5½". Crown and upperparts brown; pale gray below; white eyebrow; faintly striped cheeks; throat white; bill slender. Tail fairly long, rounded; black dots on white outer tail feathers; tail often raised or flicked sideways. **VOICE** Song: melodious, complex. **HABITAT** Broadleaf and riverine woods, thickets, towns. **RANGE** Apr.–Sept.: sw WY, CO (ex. ne). A few winter in s CO.

HOUSE WREN
Troglodytes aedon
WREN FAMILY

5". Head and back plain dull brown; wings and tail lightly dotted or barred black; light brown below; sides finely barred. Tail often cocked. Aggressive to other nearby hole-nesters; destroys their eggs. **VOICE** Song: long, pleasing, descending gurgle. Call: *chuurr.* **HABITAT** Riverine woods, broadleaf scrub, towns. **RANGE** Mid-Apr.–mid-Oct.: entire region.

WINTER WREN
Troglodytes troglodytes
WREN FAMILY

4". Dark brown above and below; sides, wings, and tail finely black-barred; indistinct eyebrow and throat buffy. Often cocks very short tail over back. N. Amer.'s smallest wren. **VOICE** Song: beautiful long series of warbles and trills. Call: hard *kip kip.* **HABITAT** Coniferous forest ravines, brush piles. **RANGE** Apr.–Oct.: mtns. of n ID, w MT. Nov.–Mar.: uncommon from w MT to e CO.

MARSH WREN
Cistothorus palustris
WREN FAMILY

5". Back brown, with narrow white stripes; white below; wings, rump, and tail chestnut; sides buffy; white eyebrow under dark brownish crown. Tail often cocked. **VOICE** Song: gurgling rattle. Call: loud *check.* **HABITAT** Cattail and bulrush marshes. **RANGE** May–Oct.: s ID, w MT, WY, w and e CO. Nov.–Apr.: s MT and south (local).

AMERICAN DIPPER
"Water Ouzel"
Cinclus mexicanus
DIPPER FAMILY

8". Adult uniformly gray. Bill black, narrow; eyelid white; legs pale pink; tail short, often cocked like a wren's. Juv. slaty above, pale gray below; bill pinkish. Bobs on rocks in streams; flies low over water. Walks underwater to feed on large insect larvae. **VOICE** Song: loud, musical, varied; repeats phrases. Call: piercing *zeet.* **HABITAT** Rocky Mtn. streams. **RANGE** Resident in mtns. of entire region. Oct.–Apr.: disperses to lower elevs.

GOLDEN-CROWNED KINGLET
Regulus satrapa
KINGLET FAMILY

3½". Back olive; dingy olive below; wings have yellowish edging and wing bars; crown black, with center orange and yellow (male) or yellow (female); eyebrow white; black line through eye. Tail short, notched. **VOICE** Call: 3 high *tsee* notes. Song: same, then chatter. **HABITAT** Spruce and fir forests; in winter, all woods, parks. **RANGE** Resident in n and c ID, w MT, w WY, w and c CO. Oct.–Apr.: also lowlands.

RUBY-CROWNED KINGLET
Regulus calendula
KINGLET FAMILY

4". Drab olive all over, paler below; 2 white wing bars; large white eye ring. Tail has short notch. Male raises red midcrown patch when displaying; often flicks wings. **VOICE** Song: high warbles ending with 3 *look-at-me's*. Call: scolding *je-dit*. **HABITAT** Dry coniferous forests; in winter, all woods, parks. **RANGE** Apr., Oct.: entire region. May–Sept.: breeds in n and c ID, w MT, nw and sc WY, w and c CO. A few winter in s ID, s CO.

BLUE-GRAY GNATCATCHER
Polioptila caerulea
OLD WORLD WARBLER FAMILY

4½". Blue-gray above, white below; eye ring white; male has black line over eye in summer; tail black with white outer feathers. Often wags tail sideways. **VOICE** Song: thin wheezy warble. Call: inquiring *pweee*. **HABITAT** Open woods, esp. juniper; thickets. **RANGE** May–Oct.: far s ID, far sw WY, w and c CO.

EASTERN BLUEBIRD
Sialia sialis
THRUSH FAMILY

7". Male brilliant deep blue above; throat, chest, and sides rusty orange; midbelly and vent white. Female head and back blue-gray; wings and tail blue; washed rusty below. **VOICE** Song: down-slurred *cheer cheery charley*. Call: musical *chur-lee*. **HABITAT** Orchards, riverine forest edges, fields with perches. **RANGE** Mar.–Oct.: e MT, e WY, ne CO. A few winter in e CO. Increasing and expanding westward.

WESTERN BLUEBIRD
Sialia mexicana
THRUSH FAMILY

7″. Male back rusty; head, throat, wings, rump, and tail intense blue; chest and sides rusty orange; belly grayish white. Female head and back gray; wings and tail pale blue; orange wash on chest; white eye ring. Drops to ground from low perches. **VOICE** Song (varied): musical *cheer cheer-lee churr*. Call: soft *pheew*. **HABITAT** Open pines, oak woods, farms. **RANGE** Apr.–Oct.: n ID, far nw MT, w and c CO. A few winter in s CO.

MOUNTAIN BLUEBIRD
Sialia currucoides
THRUSH FAMILY

7″. Male all blue, darkest on wings, slightly paler below. Female head, back, and chest gray; wings and tail pale blue; narrow white eye ring. Wings and tail longer than Western Bluebird's; bill short, thin. Hovers over grassy areas; drops to ground from low perches. **VOICE** Song: short weak warbling. Call: low *churr*. **HABITAT** Open pines, sagebrush deserts, alpine meadows, farms. **RANGE** Mar.–Nov.: entire region, ex. e CO. Some winter in s CO.

TOWNSEND'S SOLITAIRE
Myadestes townsendi
THRUSH FAMILY

9″. Head and body gray or brownish gray; white eye ring; wings dusky with buffy patches; tail black with white outer tail feathers. Flight reveals buffy stripe at base of flight feathers. Feeds on berries in cool months, flying insects in summer. **VOICE** Song: rising and falling fluty whistles. Call: high *eeek*. **HABITAT** Summer: coniferous and mixed forests. Winter: open woods, incl. pinyon-juniper. **RANGE** Resident in uplands of entire region. Oct.–Apr.: also s ID, e MT, e WY, e CO.

VEERY
Catharus fuscescens
THRUSH FAMILY

7″. Crown, back, wings, and tail dark brown; very thin eye ring; sides of face and chest grayish, with distinct dark brown spots; midbelly and vent white. Shy, rarely seen in open. **VOICE** Song: descending spiral of flute-like notes. Call: low *pheeeuw*. **HABITAT** Streamside thickets, floors of moist woodlands. **RANGE** May–Sept.: n, c, and e ID, w and c MT, n and e WY, c CO.

SWAINSON'S THRUSH
Catharus ustulatus
THRUSH FAMILY

7". Back, head, wings, and tail grayish brown; dark brown spots on buffy throat and chest; belly white; lores and wide eye ring buffy. More arboreal than other thrushes; feeds on fruit in trees. **VOICE** Song: beautiful, breezy, up-slurred whistles. Calls: *whit* and *heep*. **HABITAT** Wet coniferous and broadleaf forests, riverine thickets. **RANGE** May–Sept.: entire region. June–Aug.: breeds in most of ID, w MT, w WY, nw and c CO.

HERMIT THRUSH
Catharus guttatus
THRUSH FAMILY

7". Head, back, and wings pale brown; sides grayish; blackish spots on throat and chest; belly and vent white; rump and tail dull rufous brown; very thin, pale eye ring. **VOICE** Song: clear, flute-like; similar phrases repeated at different pitches. Call: low *chuck*. **HABITAT** Summer: wet coniferous forests. Winter: forest edges, parks. **RANGE** Apr.–May, Sept.–Oct.: entire region. June–Aug.: breeds in most of ID, w MT, w and c WY, w and c CO.

AMERICAN ROBIN
Turdus migratorius
THRUSH FAMILY

adult (left), immature (right)

10". Male breast and sides rufous-orange; back and wings gray-brown; head blackish; partial white eye ring; throat striped; bill yellow; tail black, with tiny white corners. Female head, back duller brown. Tail fairly long. Imm. buffy white below, with heavy blackish spots; pale buffy scaling on back. In spring and summer, eats earthworms; in fall and winter, roams in berry-searching flocks and roosts communally. **VOICE** Song: prolonged, rising and falling *cheery-up cheery-me*. Calls: *tut tut tut* and *tseep*. **HABITAT** Woods, shrubs, lawns. **RANGE** Resident in entire region. In winter, withdraws from high mtns. and n MT.

VARIED THRUSH
Ixoreus naevius
THRUSH FAMILY

9". Male back, crown, rump, and tail blue-gray; cheeks and wide breast band black; line behind eye, throat, underparts, 2 wing bars, and patches on wing orange. Female similar, but slaty and black areas replaced by brown; breast band thin. **VOICE** Song: long quavering trills (louder in middle) at varied pitches. Call: soft *took*. **HABITAT** Wet coniferous forests, parks. **RANGE** Mar.–Oct.: n ID, nw MT. Nov.–Apr.: n and c ID south and east to e CO (rare).

GRAY CATBIRD
Dumetella carolinensis
MOCKINGBIRD FAMILY

9". Entirely slaty gray, ex. for black crown, rusty vent, and long, rounded, black tail. A skulker; often cocks or swings tail. **VOICE** Song: mimics other birds; doesn't repeat songs. Calls: cat-like *meeah*; sharp *check*. **HABITAT** Thickets in broadleaf and riverine woods. **RANGE** May–Sept.: entire region, ex. sw ID.

NORTHERN MOCKINGBIRD
Mimus polyglottos
MOCKINGBIRD FAMILY

10". Back, head, shoulder, rump gray; paler grayish white below; 2 slender wing bars and large wing patch white; tail blackish, with white outer tail feathers. Bill short, thin. Chases other birds; mobs cats, snakes. **VOICE** Song: mimics other birds, repeats each song 3–6 times; sings day and night. Calls: loud *chack*; softer *chair*. **HABITAT** Shrubs, fields, towns. **RANGE** Apr.–Oct.: se WY, w and e CO. A few overwinter.

SAGE THRASHER
Oreoscoptes montanus
MOCKINGBIRD FAMILY

8". Dull brownish gray above; whitish below, with dark brownish stripes; pale brownish-gray wash on chest and sides; white corners on tail. Bill thin, slightly curved; eyes yellow; tail fairly long. Runs on ground for insects and spiders in summer; feeds in fruiting bushes in winter. **VOICE** Song: clear, sweet, continuous warbling. Call: harsh *chuck*. **HABITAT** Sagebrush deserts. **RANGE** Apr.–Oct.: s ID and e MT south to sc CO.

CURVE-BILLED THRASHER
Toxostoma curvirostre
MOCKINGBIRD FAMILY

11". Dull plain gray above; faint paler wing bars; pale dusky brown below. Tail long, dark gray, tipped white. Eyes yellow; bill slender, downcurved. Imm. and winter birds have diffuse gray spots below. **VOICE** Song: varied musical phrases. Call: loud *whit-wheat,* like a "wolf" whistle. **HABITAT** Cactus-studded grasslands. **RANGE** Resident in se CO.

BROWN THRASHER
Toxostoma rufum
MOCKINGBIRD FAMILY

11½". Bright rufous-brown above; buffy white below, with dark brown stripes; white wing bars; gray cheeks around yellow-orange eyes; bill sturdy, downcurved. Tail very long, rounded. **VOICE** Song: mimics other birds, repeating each song twice. Call: loud *chack.* **HABITAT** Riverine thickets. **RANGE** Apr.–Sept.: c and e MT, e WY, e CO.

AMERICAN PIPIT
"Water Pipit"
Anthus rubescens
PIPIT FAMILY

6". Summer: brown above, buffy below. Winter: brown above; whitish below, with brown streaks. White outer tail feathers. **VOICE** In flight: series of *chwee* notes. Call: *pi-pit.* **HABITAT** Summer: alpine meadows. Migration: fields, shorelines. **RANGE** Apr.–May, Sept.–Nov.: entire region. June–Aug.: breeds in n and c ID, w MT, nw WY, c CO. **Sprague's Pipit** (*A. spraguei*) back scaly, face buffy, chest striped; May–Aug.: breeds in ne MT grasslands.

EUROPEAN STARLING
Sturnus vulgaris
STARLING FAMILY

8". Summer adult glossy green-purple; bill yellow. Winter adult blackish, heavily speckled with white; bill dark. Wings short, pointed, rusty-edged; bill sturdy, pointed; legs dull red; tail short, square. Introduced from Europe. Detrimental to native birds; takes over nest holes and birdhouses; depletes wild fruit, feeder suet. **VOICE** Song: whistles, squeals, and chuckles; mimics other birds. Calls: rising, then falling, *hoooeee;* harsh *jeer.* **HABITAT** Towns, farms, fields. **RANGE** Resident in lowlands.

CEDAR WAXWING
Bombycilla cedrorum
WAXWING FAMILY

8″. Adult back and laid-back crest brown; soft brown chest grades to yellow belly; wings gray, with waxy red tips to secondaries; black eye-mask, edged in white. Yellow band at tip of gray tail. Imm. striped brown, with white eye line. Often seen in flocks. **VOICE** Call: high thin *seee*. **HABITAT** Forests, mainly broadleaf; parks. **RANGE** Sept.–Apr.: entire region. May–Aug.: breeds in ID, MT, nw WY, c CO.

BOHEMIAN WAXWING
Bombycilla garrulus
WAXWING FAMILY

7″. Adult back, rump, and underparts gray; head brown; throat and line through eye black; white and yellow lines on black primaries; red-tipped secondaries. Bill thin; pointed crest; tail slaty with yellow tip; vent rusty. **VOICE** High buzzy *zeeee*. **HABITAT** Summer: coniferous forests. Winter: fruiting trees in all habitats. **RANGE** Nov.–Mar.: entire region; common some winters.

LOGGERHEAD SHRIKE
Lanius ludovicianus
SHRIKE FAMILY

9″. Back, crown, and rump silvery; white below; wide black eyemask; wings black, with white spot on base of primaries (smaller than Mockingbird's); tail black, edged white. Head large; bill heavy, hooked; feet short, black. Spots large insects, lizards, small birds from perches on trees and telephone wires. **VOICE** Song: repeated phrases; mockingbird-like. Call: harsh *shack*. **HABITAT** Shrubby grasslands, farms, deserts. **RANGE** Apr.–Oct.: s ID, c and e MT, WY, CO. A few winter in s CO.

NORTHERN SHRIKE
Lanius excubitor
SHRIKE FAMILY

10″. Adult back and crown gray; white below, with fine gray bars; wings black with large white spot; black eyemask; long, rounded, white-edged black tail. Imm. barred brown below; brown eyemask. Head large; bill heavy, hooked. Preys on small birds and rodents; impales surplus on thorns. **VOICE** Call: loud *chek-chek*. **HABITAT** Trees and shrubs in open country. **RANGE** Oct.–Mar.: entire region; common some winters.

PLUMBEOUS VIREO
"Solitary Vireo"
Vireo plumbeus (solitarius)
VIREO FAMILY

5½". Stocky. Head, back, and tail gray; 2 white wing bars; whitish below, sides washed gray; white "spectacles." Heavier beak than warblers. **VOICE** Song: low phrases with long pauses. Call: husky *churr*. **HABITAT** Forests. **RANGE** Late Apr.–May, Sept.: entire region. June–Aug.: breeds from n ID and w MT to c CO.

RED-EYED VIREO
Vireo olivaceus
VIREO FAMILY

6". Olive green above, white below; yellow wash on belly (fall); crown gray, bordered in black; black line through eye; white eyebrow. **VOICE** Song: monotonous *cher-eep cher-oop*, repeated up to 40 times a minute. Call: scolding *meew*. **HABITAT** Broadleaf woods. **RANGE** May, Sept.: entire region. June–Aug.: breeds in n ID, MT, e WY, nc and ne CO.

WARBLING VIREO
Vireo gilvus
VIREO FAMILY

5". Drab-looking. Pale gray above, with slight olive cast; dusky white below; no wing bars; eyebrow white, not outlined in black. Imm. sides washed yellow-green. **VOICE** Song: melodious warbling; like that of Purple Finch, but burry. Call: wheezy *twee*. **HABITAT** Aspen and riverine forests. **RANGE** May, Sept.: entire region.

Wood Warblers

Warblers native to the New World, often called wood warblers, were once dubbed subfamily Parulinae, part of the warbler, grosbeak, and sparrow family (Emberizidae), but are now considered their own family, Parulidae. Many adult males have the same plumage year-round, but some have breeding (summer) and nonbreeding (winter) plumages. Females, fall males, and immature birds often have a trace of the summer male pattern. Each species has a distinct song, while the warbler call tends to be a simple *chip*. During the summer, these birds breed in a variety of woodland and scrub habitats. Most nests are cups on small forks of branches or hidden under bushes. Warblers glean insects from leaves with their thin, unhooked bills. In early autumn, most return to more southerly regions. Other northern and eastern warblers migrate through the Rocky Mountain states or turn up as vagrants.

ORANGE-CROWNED WARBLER
Vermivora celata
WOOD WARBLER FAMILY

5″. Very plain. Adult olive green above, yellow below; orange crown patch rarely seen. Imm. grayish olive; vent yellow. **VOICE** Song: high trill, drops and tapers at end. Call: sharp *chit.* **HABITAT** Broadleaf forests, thickets, brushy fields, parks. **RANGE** May, Sept.–Oct.: entire region. June–Aug.: breeds in mtns. of ID, w MT, WY, w and c CO.

NASHVILLE WARBLER
Vermivora ruficapilla
WOOD WARBLER FAMILY

4¾″. Back, wings, and tail olive green; no wing bars; throat and underparts clear, unstriped yellow; gray head with white eye ring. **VOICE** Song: 2-part *see-it see-it see-it titititi.* **HABITAT** Open broadleaf and pine woods. **RANGE** May, Sept.: entire region (uncommon). June–Aug.: breeds in n ID, w MT.

VIRGINIA'S WARBLER
Vermivora virginiae
WOOD WARBLER FAMILY

4½″. Head, back, wings, and tail plain gray; throat, upper chest, and rump yellow; belly whitish; thin white eye ring. Forages low. **VOICE** Song: colorless *chip-chip-chip-chip-wik-wik.* Call: *chink.* **HABITAT** Brushy areas, pinyon-juniper woodlands in mtn. canyons. **RANGE** May–Sept.: s WY, w and c CO.

YELLOW WARBLER
Dendroica petechia
WOOD WARBLER FAMILY

5″. Male olive-yellow above; head, underparts, and wing and tail edging bright yellow; chestnut stripes on chest and sides. Female lacks stripes. **VOICE** Song: cheerful rapid *sweet sweet sweet I'm so sweet.* **HABITAT** Shrubby areas, woods near water, towns. **RANGE** May–Sept.: entire region.

BLACK-THROATED GRAY WARBLER
Dendroica nigrescens
WOOD WARBLER FAMILY

5″. Male back and rump gray; white below, with black streaks; head black; wide white "mustache" and line behind eye. Adult female has black necklace. **VOICE** Song: buzzy *weze-weze-weze-weze-weet.* Call: dull *tup.* **HABITAT** Pinyon-juniper woods, thickets. **RANGE** May–Sept.: far s ID, sw WY, w and sc CO.

YELLOW-RUMPED WARBLER
Audubon's race (left), Myrtle race (right)
Dendroica coronata
WOOD WARBLER FAMILY

5½". Audubon's race: rump and throat yellow; dark cheek patch. Summer male: gray above, with black streaks; chest black; belly white; yellow tuft on sides; large white wing patch; head gray with yellow crown patch, broken white eye ring. Summer female: gray-brown above; whitish below, streaked brown. Winter adults: brown, heavily striped; retains yellow rump. Myrtle race: darker cheeks, white throat; winters in lowlands. Imm. (both races) duller, variable. **VOICE** Song: warbling *seet-seet-seet-seet-turrrr*. Call: soft *check* (Audubon's); hard *check* (Myrtle). **HABITAT** Summer: coniferous forests. Winter: woods, thickets. **RANGE** Mid-Apr.–May, Sept.–Oct.: entire region (both races). June–Aug.: Audubon's race breeds in ID (ex. sw), w and c MT, mtns. of WY and CO.

TOWNSEND'S WARBLER
Dendroica townsendi
WOOD WARBLER FAMILY

5". Male greenish above, with black streaks; upper breast yellow with black streaks; belly white; crown, throat black; eyebrow, "mustache" yellow. Female throat yellow. **VOICE** Song: buzzy *zir-zir-zir-zir-see-see*. Call: soft *chip*. **HABITAT** Coniferous forests. **RANGE** May, Aug.–Sept.: ID, MT, w WY, w and c CO. June–July: breeds in n and c ID, nw MT.

GRACE'S WARBLER
Dendroica graciae
WOOD WARBLER FAMILY

5". Gray above; 2 white wing bars; eyebrow, throat, and upper chest yellow; belly white with black streaks on sides. Female paler gray above. Forages high; creeps along branches. **VOICE** Song: pleasing *che-dle chedle che-che-che-che*. **HABITAT** Pine forests, nearby broadleaf trees. **RANGE** May–Aug.: sw CO.

OVENBIRD
Seiurus aurocapillus
WOOD WARBLER FAMILY

6". Upperparts and sides of head brownish olive; white below, with black stripes; crown stripe orange, bordered by black; eye ring white; legs pink. Walks on forest floor. **VOICE** Song: *TEACH-er*, repeated 3–6 times. **HABITAT** Mixed woods with dense undergrowth. **RANGE** May–Sept.: e MT, e WY, nc and ne CO.

AMERICAN REDSTART
male (left), female (right)
Setophaga ruticilla
WOOD WARBLER FAMILY

5″. Adult male mainly black; midbelly white; large orange patches on wings, sides of chest, and basal corners of tail. Female grayish olive above, white below; yellow patches on wings, sides of chest, and basal corners of tail; head gray, with narrow white "spectacles." Often fans tail; chases flying insects. **VOICE** Songs: variable; one is *teetsa teetsa teetsa teetsa teet;* another is *zee zee zee zee tsee-o.* **HABITAT** Broadleaf woods, shrubs. **RANGE** May, Aug.–Sept.: entire region. June–July: breeds in n ID, MT, n WY.

NORTHERN WATERTHRUSH
Seiurus noveboracensis
WOOD WARBLER FAMILY

6″. Upperparts and head plain brown; underparts and eyebrow white; throat dotted; breast striped brown; legs pink. Bill long, thin. Often bobs tail. **VOICE** Song: rapid *wit wit wit sweet sweet sweet chew chew chew.* **HABITAT** Swamps, moist woods, watersides. **RANGE** May, Aug.–Sept.: entire region. June–July: breeds in n ID, w MT.

MACGILLIVRAY'S WARBLER
Oporornis tolmiei
WOOD WARBLER FAMILY

5″. Male green above, clear yellow below; head and throat slaty gray, throat scaled black. Female lacks black throat scales. Incomplete white eye ring; legs pink. **VOICE** Song: loud *chitle-chitle-chitle-cheer-cheer.* Call: loud *check.* **HABITAT** Thickets in broadleaf and riverine woods. **RANGE** May–Sept.: ID, w and c MT, w and c WY, w and c CO.

COMMON YELLOWTHROAT
Geothlypis trichas
WOOD WARBLER FAMILY

5″. Male upperparts and sides brownish olive; throat and chest yellow; midbelly white; black mask; white line over mask. Female olive-brown above; throat yellow. **VOICE** Song: rollicking *witchity-witchity-witchity-witch.* Call: flat *chep.* **HABITAT** Swamps, marshes, shrubs. **RANGE** Late Apr.–Sept.: entire region.

WILSON'S WARBLER
Wilsonia pusilla
WOOD WARBLER FAMILY

4¾". Male olive green above; underparts, forehead, and eyebrow yellow; round black cap. Imm. and many females have only trace of black cap. **VOICE** Song: rapid, thin *chi chi chi chi jet jet.* **HABITAT** Thickets in coniferous forests; alder marshes. **RANGE** May, Sept.–Oct.: entire region. June–Aug.: breeds in ID (ex. sw),   w MT, w WY, w and c CO.

YELLOW-BREASTED CHAT
Icteria virens
WOOD WARBLER FAMILY

7". Olive green above; throat and breast yellow; belly and vent grayish white; "spectacles" white; lores black in male, gray in female. Sings in low fluttering flight, day or night. Tail long. **VOICE** Song: long series of scolds, whistles, and soft, crow-like *caw* notes. Call: loud *chack.* **HABITAT** Dense thickets, riverine scrub. **RANGE** May–Sept.: s ID, c and e MT, c and e WY, CO.

WESTERN TANAGER
Piranga ludoviciana
TANAGER FAMILY

female (left), summer male (right)

7". Summer male back and tail black; collar, rump, and underparts yellow; wings black, with yellow shoulder, 1 white wing bar; head and throat red. Female and imm. back gray; head, rump, and underparts yellow; 2 whitish wing bars. Lives in treetops. **VOICE** Song: 3 slurred hoarse phrases. Call: *perdick.* **HABITAT** Coniferous and riverside broadleaf forests. **RANGE** May–Sept.: ID (ex. sw), w and c MT, WY, w and c CO.

BLACK-HEADED GROSBEAK
Pheucticus melanocephalus
GROSBEAK FAMILY

7½". Male back black; collar, chest, sides, rump rusty orange; midbelly striped rusty and white; head black. Female striped brown above, buffy orange below; cheeks and crown dark brown; eyebrow and midcrown stripe white or buffy. **VOICE** Song: sweet fast warble. Call: high *eek.* **HABITAT** Woods, thickets. **RANGE** May–Sept.: entire region.

BLUE GROSBEAK
Guiraca caerulea
GROSBEAK FAMILY

7″. Adult male dark blue above and below; black stripes on back; shoulder and wing bar chestnut. Female and imm. dull brown, with 2 buffy wing bars. Bill thick, silvery. Feeds on ground; twitches tail. **VOICE** Song: sweet warbled phrases. Call: loud *chink*. **HABITAT** Brushy pastures, thickets. **RANGE** May–Sept.: w and se CO; s WY (uncommon).

LAZULI BUNTING
Passerina amoena
GROSBEAK FAMILY

5½″. Male head and upperparts pale powdery blue; 2 white wing bars; chest pale orange; belly white. Female head and back brown; 2 buffy wing bars; buffy below; rump bluish. Forages in weeds. **VOICE** Song: series of rising and falling warbles. Call: short *pit*. **HABITAT** Riverine woods, thickets. **RANGE** May–Sept.: entire region.

DICKCISSEL
Spiza americana
GROSBEAK FAMILY

6½″. Summer male brown above; back striped; shoulder rusty; yellowish eyebrow; white chin; black throat patch; chest yellow; belly white. Female lacks black throat patch. **VOICE** Song: buzzy *dick-dick-dick-ciss-ciss*. Call: *brrzztt*. **HABITAT** Grasslands, grainfields. **RANGE** May–Sept.: e MT, far e WY, e CO.

GREEN-TAILED TOWHEE
Pipilo chlorurus
AMERICAN SPARROW FAMILY

7″. Adult back, wings, and tail olive green; face, neck, and sides gray; midbelly white; crown rufous; chin and short "mustache" white. Scratches on ground under brush. **VOICE** Song: slurred *weet-weet-churrr*. Call: catlike *meeow*. **HABITAT** Thickets, mtn. sagebrush. **RANGE** May–Sept.: s ID, sc MT, w and s WY, w and c CO.

SPOTTED TOWHEE
"Rufous-sided Towhee"
Pipilo maculatus
AMERICAN SPARROW FAMILY

8″. Male head, chest, rump, tail black; back and wings black with white spots; sides rufous; midbelly white. Female: brown replaces black of male. **VOICE** Song: long buzzy *cheweee*. Call: catlike *meee*. **HABITAT** Thickets, underbrush. **RANGE** Apr.–Oct.: n and c ID, MT, n and e WY, w and c CO. Some winter in s ID, CO.

CANYON TOWHEE
"Brown Towhee"
Pipilo fuscus
AMERICAN SPARROW FAMILY

8½". Plain brown above, pale gray below; cap rufous; throat buffy, with necklace of brown dots; large brown chest spot. Tail long, rounded, without white. Feeds on ground. **VOICE** Song: chipping trill. Call: rising *chee-up*. **HABITAT** Brushy canyons, arid scrub. **RANGE** Resident in sc and se CO.

AMERICAN TREE SPARROW
"Winter Sparrow"
Spizella arborea
AMERICAN SPARROW FAMILY

6". Rufous brown above; black stripes on back; 2 white wing bars; unstreaked pale gray below; black "ace" on chest; rufous crown and line through eye; gray eyebrow. In small flocks. Feeds on ground and in weeds. **VOICE** Call: musical *twee-dle-eet*. **HABITAT** Weedy fields and thickets. **RANGE** Oct.–Apr.: entire region.

CHIPPING SPARROW
Spizella passerina
AMERICAN SPARROW FAMILY

5½". Summer: brown above, with black streaks; clear pale gray below; white wing bars; rufous cap; white eyebrow; black eye line; narrow notched tail. **VOICE** Song: long, run-together series of about 20 dry *chip* notes. **HABITAT** Open coniferous and broadleaf woods, nearby fields, towns. **RANGE** Apr.–Oct.: entire region. Winter: few in CO.

CLAY-COLORED SPARROW
Spizella pallida
AMERICAN SPARROW FAMILY

5½". Back striped brown; rump brown; buffy wash below; crown dark brown; median crown stripe whitish; eyebrow yellowish; buffy cheek edged with brown triangle. **VOICE** Song: low *buzz-buzz-buzz,* on one pitch. **HABITAT** Prairie with thickets or scattered small trees. **RANGE** May, Sept.–Oct.: migrant in e WY, e CO. Summer: breeds in c and e MT.

BREWER'S SPARROW
Spizella breweri
AMERICAN SPARROW FAMILY

5½". Back and crown buffy brown, finely streaked with black; faint buffy wing bars; clear grayish below. Tail notched. **VOICE** Song: series of musical trills lasting up to 10 seconds. Call: soft *seep*, given in flight. **HABITAT** Sagebrush deserts. **RANGE** Mid-Apr.–Sept.: ID, MT, WY, w and c CO.

VESPER SPARROW
Pooecetes gramineus
AMERICAN SPARROW FAMILY

6″. Pale brown with fine black stripes above and below; small rusty shoulder patch; 2 buffy wing bars; white eye ring; bill and legs pink. Tail notched at tip, blackish, with white outer feathers. Feeds on ground. **VOICE** Song: melodious *slurr-slurr-slee-slee-teuw-teuw-teuw.* **HABITAT** Grasslands, sagebrush deserts. **RANGE** Apr.–Oct.: entire region.

LARK SPARROW
Chondestes grammacus
AMERICAN SPARROW FAMILY

6″. Brown above; black streaks and buffy wing bars; white below; black spot on chest; black-edged chestnut cheek and crown patches; midcrown, eyebrow, and throat white; black "mustache." **VOICE** Song: broken trills, buzzes, and notes. Call: sharp *tsip.* **HABITAT** Deserts, pinewoods, farms. **RANGE** May–Sept.: entire region, ex. mtns. of n ID, w MT.

BLACK-THROATED SPARROW
Amphispiza bilineata
AMERICAN SPARROW FAMILY

5″. Adult unstriped brown above; no wing bars. Head gray with white eyebrow and "mustache"; large black patch from chin tapers to V on chest; white below. **VOICE** Song: sweet *chit chit cheeeeeee.* **HABITAT** Desert scrub, sagebrush. **RANGE** May–Aug.: sw ID, sw and se CO.

SAGE SPARROW
Amphispiza belli
AMERICAN SPARROW FAMILY

6″. Back pale sandy brown with few streaks; whitish below, with black breast spot; sides finely streaked; head gray; throat, short eyebrow, and eye ring white; thin gray "mustache." Tail long, narrow, notched. **VOICE** Song: musical *sit-sit-soo-see-say-soo-see.* Call: soft *tinkle.* **HABITAT** Sagebrush deserts. **RANGE** Apr.–Oct.: s ID, sw WY, w CO.

LARK BUNTING
Calamospiza melanocorys
AMERICAN SPARROW FAMILY

7″. Summer male black, ex. large white wing patch. Female and winter male brown above with darker streaks; white eyeline over brown cheek; creamy wing patch; white with brown stripes below. **VOICE** Song: whistles, trills, and slurs, each repeated up to 10 times. **HABITAT** Prairie grasslands, feedlots. **RANGE** May–Sept.: east of Rockies.

SAVANNAH SPARROW
Passerculus sandwichensis
AMERICAN SPARROW FAMILY

5½". Brown-and-white-striped above and below; front of and often entire eyebrow yellow; bill and legs pink. Tail short, notched. **VOICE** Song: high buzzy *zit zit zit zeeee zaaay*. Call: light *tzip*. **HABITAT** Moist grasslands, farms. **RANGE** Apr.–Oct.: entire region.

FOX SPARROW
Passerella iliaca
AMERICAN SPARROW FAMILY

7". Head and back dull grayish brown; wings, rump and tail rufous brown; buffy white below, spotted with slaty brown; bill dark above, paler below. **VOICE** Song: a whistle, then trills and slurs. Call: sharp *chink*. **HABITAT** Shrubby hillsides, riversides, thickets. **RANGE** Mar.–Oct.: n and c ID, w MT, mtns. of WY and CO.

SONG SPARROW
Melospiza melodia
AMERICAN SPARROW FAMILY

6¼". Dark brown stripes on warm brown back; grayish eyebrow; white below, with heavy streaks; large, central, dark brown spot on chest. Tail fairly long, unpatterned, rounded. **VOICE** Song: *sweet zeet zeet zeee diddle diddle dee*. **HABITAT** Shrubs, marshes, parks, watersides. **RANGE** Resident in entire region; in winter, most withdraw from n plains.

LINCOLN'S SPARROW
Melospiza lincolnii
AMERICAN SPARROW FAMILY

5½". Brown above; black back stripes; chest and sides buffy, streaked; belly white; gray eyebrow; crown rusty, with gray stripe. **VOICE** Song: musical gurgling. Calls: flat *chup*; buzzy *zeee*. **HABITAT** Summer: bogs, ponds. Winter: thickets. **RANGE** Apr.–May, Sept.–Oct.: entire region. June–Aug.: breeds in n and c ID, w MT, mtns. of WY and CO.

WHITE-CROWNED SPARROW
Zonotrichia leucophrys
AMERICAN SPARROW FAMILY

7". Adult back brown with darker streaks; nape and underparts gray; crown striped black and white. **VOICE** Song: 1–3 notes, then a trill. Call: sharp *pink*. **HABITAT** Forests, thickets. **RANGE** Apr.–May, Sept.–Nov.: entire region. June–Aug.: breeds in mtns. of ID, w MT, WY, CO. Dec.–Mar.: s ID, CO.

DARK-EYED JUNCO
Junco hyemalis
AMERICAN SPARROW FAMILY

Oregon race (left), Gray-headed race (right)

6". Many distinct races all with white outer tail feathers; males described: Oregon race of n ID, w MT, nw WY: black hood; back and sides rufous. Pink-sided race of sc MT and nc WY: head gray; back brownish. White-winged race of ne WY: pale gray hood, back, and sides. Gray-headed race of sc WY and CO mtns.: head gray; back rusty; pale gray below. Slate-colored race of Canada winters east of Rockies: all slaty ex. white midbelly. **VOICE** Song: loose musical trills. Call: light *snack*. **HABITAT** Brushy areas, forest edges, ravines, towns. **RANGE** Resident in mtns. Oct.–Apr.: lowlands.

HARRIS'S SPARROW
Zonotrichia querula
AMERICAN SPARROW FAMILY

7½". Winter adult striped brown on back; 2 buffy wing bars; belly creamy; tail long; crown, face, and throat black (some with white "bow tie"); bill pink; cheek brown. Summer adult has gray cheek. Imm. white below, with black neck band. **VOICE** Alarm call: *wink*. **HABITAT** Open woods, brushy areas. **RANGE** Oct.–Apr.: e CO. May, Sept.–Oct.: e MT, e WY.

MCCOWN'S LONGSPUR
Calcarius mccownii
AMERICAN SPARROW FAMILY

6". White tail has inverted black T. Summer male hindneck, sides, and rump gray; back striped; shoulder rusty; crown, line below eye, and chest patch black; throat and midbelly white. Female and winter male sparrow-like. **VOICE** Song: sweet warbling on display flights. Calls: soft rattle; soft *pink*. **HABITAT** Prairie grasslands. **RANGE** Apr.–Nov.: c and e MT, e WY, ne CO.

CHESTNUT-COLLARED LONGSPUR
Calcarius ornatus
AMERICAN SPARROW FAMILY

6". White tail has inverted black V. Summer male striped brown above; chest and sides black; nape chestnut; head black and white; buffy on cheeks and throat. Female sparrow-like. **VOICE** Song: rapid warble. Calls: repeated *kittle;* high rattle; short buzz. **HABITAT** Grasslands. **RANGE** Apr.–Oct.: c and e MT, e WY, ne CO.

SNOW BUNTING
Plectrophenax nivalis
AMERICAN SPARROW FAMILY

6½". Winter: mainly white; back and wings speckled black; crown buffy. Flight reveals large white wing patch, black primaries. Found in roving flocks. **VOICE** Calls: whistled *tew;* short buzz; musical rattle. **HABITAT** Vast open farmlands, prairies. **RANGE** Oct.–Mar.: ID, MT, WY, n CO. **Lapland Longspur** *(Calcarius lapponicus;* 6½")* is sparrow-like, has black tail; male has rusty nape; winters on plains.

BOBOLINK
Dolichonyx oryzivorus
BLACKBIRD FAMILY

7". Summer male black with large, golden yellow nape patch; rump and base of wings white. Female, fall male, and imm. sparrow-like; buffy, with brown stripes on head, back, and sides. Usu. in flocks during migration. **VOICE** Song: rollicking, repeated *bob-bob-o-lincoln,* often given in flight. Call: clear *pink.* **HABITAT** Hayfields and grasslands; perches on nearby fences, shrubs, trees. **RANGE** Mid-May–Aug.: n ID, MT, WY (local), n CO.

RED-WINGED BLACKBIRD
Agelaius phoeniceus
BLACKBIRD FAMILY

male (left), female (right)

9". Male glossy black; red shoulder bordered by yellow. Female brown-streaked; crown and eye line dark brown; eyebrow buffy. In flocks (non-breeding). **VOICE** Song: gurgling *conk-a-ree.* Calls: harsh *check;* high *tee-eek.* **HABITAT** Marshes, ditches; fields and farms (winter). **RANGE** Mar.–Nov.: entire region. Dec.–Feb.: also lowlands from s MT south.

WESTERN MEADOWLARK
Sturnella neglecta
BLACKBIRD FAMILY

10". Speckled brown above; throat, breast yellow; belly, sides white; sides striped black; black V on chest; crown brown and white striped. **VOICE** Song: 4–5 flute-like whistles: *too tee too tiddleyou.* **HABITAT** Grasslands, deserts, farms. **RANGE** Mar.–Sept.: entire region; most common east of Rockies. Oct.–Feb.: w and e CO; rarer to north.

YELLOW-HEADED BLACKBIRD
Xanthocephalus xanthocephalus
BLACKBIRD FAMILY

10″. Male head and chest yellow-orange; rest of body black; white patch near bend of wing. Female dark brown above; throat, chest, and eyebrow pale yellow; belly striped black and white. Bill heavy. **VOICE** Song: gurgling *gunk-eeeeeee*, like a rusty hinge. Call: low *kruck*. **HABITAT** Marshes; fields in migration. **RANGE** Apr.–Oct.: entire region.

COMMON GRACKLE
Quiscalus quiscula
BLACKBIRD FAMILY

13″. Male often appears black, but has iridescent blue-green head, dark purple wings, bronzy green back and breast; tail long, wedge-shaped. Female very dark gray. Usu. in flocks outside breeding season. **VOICE** Song: short high *gurgle-eek*. Call: loud *shack*. **HABITAT** Farms, watersides, gardens, fields, shade trees. **RANGE** Apr.–Oct.: c and e MT, e WY, e CO.

BROWN-HEADED COWBIRD
Molothrus ater
BLACKBIRD FAMILY

male (left), female (right)

7″. Male dark, shiny, greenish black with brown head. Female uniformly dull brown. Bill medium long, black, conical. Causes great losses in numbers of native songbirds: female lays single eggs in several nests of other birds; baby cowbird pushes out other eggs and babies, is raised by foster parents. **VOICE** Song: bubbly creaking *bubble-lee come seee*. Flight call: high *weee teetee.* **HABITAT** Most open and partially wooded lowland habitats; farms in winter. **RANGE** Apr.–Oct.: entire region. Winter: local in entire region.

BREWER'S BLACKBIRD
Euphagus cyanocephalus
BLACKBIRD FAMILY

9″. Male black with iridescent purple on head, green on body; eyes yellow. Female (pictured) grayish brown; eyes dark. Bill thin. Walks on ground. In flocks outside breeding season; nests in small colonies. **VOICE** Song: creaky squeak. Call: sharp *chek*. **HABITAT** Farms, sagebrush deserts, towns. **RANGE** Apr.–Oct.: entire region. Nov.–Mar.: s ID, s WY, CO.

ORCHARD ORIOLE
Icterus spurius
BLACKBIRD FAMILY

7". Summer male head, throat, back, and tail black; sides, breast, rump, and shoulder rufous-chestnut; wings edged white. Female olive above, greenish yellow below; 2 white wing bars. Imm. male similar to female, ex. face and "bib" black. **VOICE** Song: loud, rapid, and varied whistles. Call: sharp *chuck*. **HABITAT** Wooded riversides, isolated tree stands, orchards. **RANGE** Mid-May–mid-Aug.: far e MT, far e WY, e CO.

BULLOCK'S ORIOLE
"Northern Oriole"
Icterus bullockii (galbula)
BLACKBIRD FAMILY

8". Male crown, eye line, throat stripe, back, wings, and central tail black; large white wing patch; much of head, eyebrow, underparts, and outer tail feathers orange. Female olive above; chest pale orange; belly white. Imm. like female. **VOICE** Song: 4–8 doubled whistles. Call: rapid chatter. **HABITAT** Broadleaf and riverine woods, parks, towns. **RANGE** May–mid-Sept.: entire region, ex. higher mtns.

BLACK ROSY-FINCH
Leucosticte atratus
FINCH FAMILY

6". Male back, chest, and head black, ex. pale gray patch from eye to nape; wings, rump, and belly rosy; bill black in summer, yellow in winter. Female dull slaty; pale whitish line behind eye. **VOICE** Song: descending *chu* notes. Call: House Sparrow–like *chirp*. **HABITAT** Summer: breeds above tree line, roosts on cliffs. Winter: mixed-species flocks in lowland plains. **RANGE** May–Oct.: c ID, sw MT, w WY. Nov.–Apr.: lowlands of s ID, w WY.

GRAY-CROWNED ROSY-FINCH
Leucosticte tephrocotis
FINCH FAMILY

6". Male back and chest brown; forecrown black; pale gray patch from eye to nape; wings, rump, and belly rosy; bill black in summer, yellow in winter. Female brown with gray hindcrown, usu. without rosy. **VOICE** Song: descending *chu* notes. Call: *chirp*. **HABITAT** Summer: breeds above tree line, roosts on cliffs. Winter: mixed-species flocks in lowland plains. **RANGE** May–Oct.: mtns. of n ID, w MT, n WY (Bighorns). Nov.–Apr.: all lowlands.

BROWN-CAPPED ROSY-FINCH
Leucosticte australis
FINCH FAMILY

6". Male back, breast, and head brown; forecrown blackish; no gray patch on head; wings, rump, and belly rosy; bill black in summer, yellow in winter. Female dull grayish brown, with gray hindcrown. **VOICE** Song: descending *chu* notes. Call: *chirp.* **HABITAT** Summer: breeds above tree line, roosts on cliffs. Winter: mixed-species flocks in lowland plains. **RANGE** May–Oct.: Snowy range of se WY; mtns. of w and c CO. Nov.–Apr.: nearby valleys.

PINE GROSBEAK
Pinicola enucleator
FINCH FAMILY

9". Male back black-striped; underparts, head, and rump pink; sides and belly gray; wings black, with white wing bars; tail black, long, notched. Female body gray; head rusty. Bill rather small, stubby. **VOICE** Song: musical warble. Call: whistled *tee wee tee.* **HABITAT** Summer: coniferous forests. Winter: broadleaf trees with remaining fruit. **RANGE** Resident in mtns. of ID, w MT, nw and sc WY, w and c CO. In winter, disperses into nearby lowlands.

CASSIN'S FINCH
Carpodacus cassinii
FINCH FAMILY

6". Male back and wings pale gray-brown with dark brown stripes; throat and chest rosy; belly whitish; sides lightly streaked; crown red; cheeks striped brown. Female head and body heavily brown-striped. Tail notched. **VOICE** Song: lively fluty warbling. Call: high *pwee-de-lip.* **HABITAT** Coniferous forests in mtns. and foothills. **RANGE** Mar.–Nov.: ID, w MT, w and c WY, w and c CO. Dec.–Feb.: disperses into lowlands.

RED CROSSBILL
Loxia curvirostra
FINCH FAMILY

6". Adult male head and body brick red; wings and tail blackish. Adult female head and body yellow-olive; wings and tail blackish. Tips of bill cross; tail notched. Juv. head and body olive, with brown stripes; wings and tail blackish. **VOICE** Song: *chipa-chipa-chipa-che-chee-chee.* Call: sharp repeated *kip,* often given in flight. **HABITAT** Coniferous forests. **RANGE** Resident in ID, w MT, WY, w and c CO. In some winters, wanders onto plains.

HOUSE FINCH
Carpodacus mexicanus
FINCH FAMILY

male (left), female (right)

5½". Male back, midcrown, wings, and tail brown; sides and belly whitish, streaked brown; 2 pale wing bars; wide eyebrow; throat, chest, and rump rosy red. Female upperparts and head plain dull brown; dusky below, with brown streaks. **VOICE** Song: musical warbling ending with a down-slurred *jeer*. Call: musical *chirp*. **HABITAT** Towns, farms, riverine woods. **RANGE** Resident in ID, w MT, w and s WY, CO. **Purple Finch** (*C. purpureus*; 5¾") male has striped purple back; female has darker cheek patch and heavy "mustache"; Oct.–May: plains, valleys.

COMMON REDPOLL
Carduelis flammea
FINCH FAMILY

5". Male whitish; brown stripes above and on sides; cap red; chin black; breast washed rosy; tail short, forked. Female has red cap; lacks rosy on breast. Usu. in flocks. **VOICE** Call: rising *swee-eet*. **HABITAT** Brushy and weedy areas in mtns., lowlands. **RANGE** Oct.–Apr.: entire region, esp. east of Rockies; many in some winters, few in others.

PINE SISKIN
Carduelis pinus
FINCH FAMILY

5". Sexes and plumages alike all year. Very heavily striped brown above and below; yellow stripe on wing; yellow on basal sides of notched tail. Bill thin, pointed. **VOICE** Song: wheezy trills and warbles mixed with calls. Calls: loud *clee-up*; rising *shreee*. **HABITAT** Coniferous and mixed forests, towns. **RANGE** Resident in mtns. of ID, w MT, WY, w and c CO. Nov.–May: entire region, incl. lowlands.

LESSER GOLDFINCH
Carduelis psaltria
FINCH FAMILY

4½". Adult male back, cheeks, and rump green; crown, wings, and tail black; wing has white patches; yellow below. Female greenish above, yellow below; 2 white bars on black wings. Tail short, notched. **VOICE** Song: repeated phrases; mimics other birds. Call: rising *see-ee-eep,* falling *tee-yer.* **HABITAT** Woodland edges, brushy fields, gardens. **RANGE** May–Oct.: se WY, CO (more common in s CO).

AMERICAN GOLDFINCH
Carduelis tristis
FINCH FAMILY

5". Summer male yellow; cap, wings, and tail black; rump white. Summer female olive green above; throat and chest yellow. Winter male brown above; face and shoulder yellow. Winter female grayish. White bars on black wings. **VOICE** Song: long, rising and falling twittering. Call: rising *sweee-eat.* Flight call: *per chicory.* **HABITAT** Lowland fields, forest edges, farms. **RANGE** May–Sept.: entire region. Oct.–Apr.: lowlands of ID and se MT south.

EVENING GROSBEAK
Coccothraustes vespertinus
FINCH FAMILY

8". Male back and breast brown; rump and belly yellow; head dark brown with yellow eyebrow and forehead; wings black with white secondaries. Female plain gray-brown; wings black with large white spots. Bill massive, ivory; head large; tail black, fairly short. **VOICE** Song: short warble. Call: ringing *cleeer.* **HABITAT** Coniferous and mixed forests; towns (winter). **RANGE** Nov.–Apr.: entire region. May–Oct.: n and c ID, w MT, mtns. of WY and CO.

HOUSE SPARROW
Passer domesticus
OLD WORLD SPARROW FAMILY

6". Male back and wings rufous, streaked with black; underparts, crown, cheeks, and rump gray; 1 white wing bar; throat and upper chest black (only chin black in winter); wide chestnut stripe behind eye. Female plain brown above, ex. blackish back streaks, buffy stripe above eye; pale dusky below. Abundant European import. **VOICE** Song: often-given *chireep* and *chereep* notes. Call: *chir-rup.* **HABITAT** Towns, parks, farms. **RANGE** Resident in entire region.

Mammals

Members of the vertebrate class Mammalia are warm-blooded and able to maintain a near-constant body temperature. Males generally have an external penis for direct internal fertilization of the female's eggs. Almost all mammals are born live rather than hatching from eggs (exceptions are the platypus and the echidnas of Australia). Mammary glands, unique to mammals, produce milk that is high in nutrients and fat and promotes rapid growth in the young.

Mammals have abundant skin glands, used for temperature regulation (sweating), coat maintenance, territory marking, sex and species recognition, breeding-cycle signals, and even defense, as in skunks and others that can repel predators with powerful secretions. Most mammals have well-developed eyes, ears, and noses that provide good night vision and hearing and a strong sense of smell. An insulating layer of fur allows most mammals to maintain a fairly constant body temperature independent of their surroundings. Many molt twice a year and have a noticeably thicker coat in winter. Some, such as certain weasels and hares, change colors, developing a concealing white coat in winter.

Nine mammalian orders are represented in the Rocky Mountain states, including humans (members of the primates order). Opossums (order Didelphimorphia) give birth to young in an embryonic state; they then develop in a separate fur-lined pouch on the mother's belly. The tiny energetic shrews (Insectivora), which eat insects and other invertebrates, have long snouts, short dense fur, and five toes on each foot. Bats (Chiroptera), with their enlarged, membrane-covered forelimbs, are the only mammals that truly fly.

Hares, rabbits, and pikas (Lagomorpha) resemble large rodents but have four upper incisor teeth—a large front pair and a small pair directly behind them—that grow continuously, and five toes on their front feet and five in back. Rodents (Rodentia—including chipmunks, marmots, squirrels, mice, rats, muskrats, voles, porcupines, and beavers) have two upper incisor teeth that grow continuously, and most have four toes on their front feet and five in back.

Carnivores (Carnivora)—bears, the Coyote, wolves, foxes, raccoons, weasels, and cats—have long canine teeth and sharp cheek teeth for killing and eating prey. The even-toed hoofed mammals (Artiodactyla), in the Rocky Mountain states represented by deer, goats, sheep, American Bison, and the Pronghorn, have two or four toes that form a cloven hoof. The odd-toed hoofed mammals (Perissodactyla) are represented by the Feral Horse.

In the species accounts that follow, the typical adult length given is from the tip of the nose to the end of the tail, followed by the tail length; for larger mammals, shoulder height is also given. Wingspan is given for bats.

Mammal Signs and Tracks

The evidence that a particular animal is or has been in a certain area is called its "sign." The sign can be scat (fecal matter), burrow openings, nutshells, tracks, or other evidence. Tracks are a useful aid in confirming the presence of mammal species. Impressions vary depending on the substrate and whether the animal was walking or running. Animals can leave clear tracks in mud, dirt, snow, and sand, usually larger ones in wet mud and snow. Because animals come to ponds or streams to drink or feed, tracks are likely to be found near waterways; damp mud often records tracks in fine detail, sometimes showing claws or webbing. Prints in snow may leave a less clear impression but can often be followed for a long distance and may show the pattern of the animal's stride. The track drawings below, of selected mammals that live in the Rocky Mountain region, are not to relative scale.

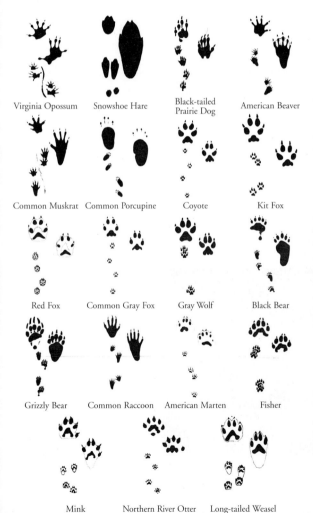

Virginia Opossum   Snowshoe Hare   Black-tailed Prairie Dog   American Beaver

Common Muskrat   Common Porcupine   Coyote   Kit Fox

Red Fox   Common Gray Fox   Gray Wolf   Black Bear

Grizzly Bear   Common Raccoon   American Marten   Fisher

Mink   Northern River Otter   Long-tailed Weasel

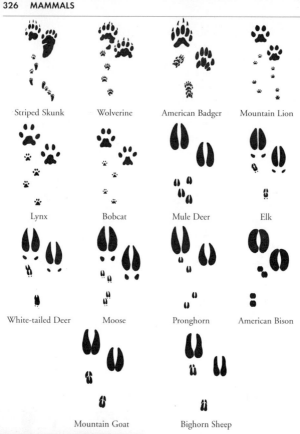

Striped Skunk
Wolverine
American Badger
Mountain Lion

Lynx
Bobcat
Mule Deer
Elk

White-tailed Deer
Moose
Pronghorn
American Bison

Mountain Goat
Bighorn Sheep

VIRGINIA OPOSSUM
Didelphis virginiana
OPOSSUM FAMILY

L 30″; T 12″. Grizzled gray, with mix of black underfur and longer white guard hairs. Head pointed; nose long; face white, with long whiskers; ears small, round, black with white tip. Legs short, black; feet have 5 digits; hindfeet have opposable, grasping inner thumbs. Tail long, tapered, naked, pink with black base. Eats fruit, nuts, bird eggs, large insects, carrion. Hangs from branches using wraparound, prehensile tail. If surprised at close range, may "play possum" (feign death). **BREEDING** 1–14 (avg. 8) pea-size young attach themselves to nipples in mother's pouch for 2 months; 1–2 litters per year. **SIGN** Tracks: 2″ hindprint, 3 middle toes close, outer toes well spread; foreprint slightly smaller, star-like. **HABITAT** Plains: riverine woods, farms, residential areas. **ACTIVITY** Nocturnal; much less active in winter. **RANGE** sw WY, e CO.

WATER SHREW
Sorex palustris
SHREW FAMILY

L 6"; T 3". Dark gray above, white below. Comb of stiff hairs on hindfeet. Swims well; runs over water surfaces. Eats insects, fish. BREEDING 2–3 litters of 6 young Mar.–Aug. HABITAT Mtns.: streams, wet meadows, bogs. ACTIVITY Very active day and night, year-round. RANGE ID, w MT, nw and se WY, w and c CO.

MASKED SHREW
Sorex cinereus
SHREW FAMILY

L 4"; T 1½". Body grayish brown; belly gray; nose conical; ears hidden; eyes tiny; tail long, brown above, buff below. Heart beats extremely fast. BREEDING 5–7 young Mar.–Oct. HABITAT Moist areas, mtn. meadows, willows. ACTIVITY Intensely active day and (esp.) night, year-round. RANGE ID (ex. sw), MT, WY, w and c CO.

VAGRANT SHREW
Sorex vagrans
SHREW FAMILY

L 4"; T 2". Reddish brown in summer, black in winter. Tail gray. Nose long, conical; eyes tiny; ears hidden on sides of head. Legs and feet short. Feeds on invertebrates and fungi in vole runways. BREEDING 2 litters of 2–9 young Mar.–May, Oct.–Nov. HABITAT Mixed forests, meadows, bogs. ACTIVITY Very active day and night, year-round. RANGE c ID, w and c MT, w and c WY, w and c CO.

Bats

Bats are the only mammals that truly fly (flying squirrels glide). The bones and muscles in the forelimbs of bats are elongated; thin, usually black wing membranes are attached to four extremely long fingers. When bats are at rest, the wings are folded along the forearm; they use their short, claw-like thumbs for crawling about. Small insectivorous bats beat their wings six to eight times a second.

Bats are mainly nocturnal, though some species are occasionally active in the early morning and late afternoon. Their slender, mouse-like bodies are well furred, and their eyesight, while not excellent, is quite adequate to detect predators and general landscape features. Most use echolocation (sonar) to locate flying insects and avoid obstacles. In flight, they emit 30 to 60 high-frequency calls per second that rebound off objects. Their large ears receive these reflected sounds, and the bats interpret them as they close in on prey or evade an obstacle. Echolocation sounds are mainly inaudible to humans, but bats also give shrill squeaks most humans can hear. By day, most bats hang upside-down from the ceilings of caves, tree hollows, barns, and attics, using one or both feet. Members of solitary species may roost alone under a branch or amid the foliage of a tall tree. In other species, large colonies gather in caves and under natural and man-made overhangs.

All bats of the Rocky Mountain region are insect-eaters. By night they pursue larger individual insects through the air or glean them from foliage. Some skim open-mouthed through swarms of mosquitoes or midges. A bat will trap a large flying insect in the membrane between its hindlegs, then seize it with its teeth. Because of the lack of insects in winter, the region's bats either hibernate here or migrate south to hibernate or feed in winter. Sheltered hibernation roosts can provide protection from extreme cold.

Watch for bats overhead on warm summer evenings, especially around water, where insects are abundant and where bats may skim the water surface to drink.

Parts of a Bat

finger — tail membrane — tail — wrist — elbow — forearm — skin — thumb

Echolocation

LITTLE BROWN MYOTIS
"Little Brown Bat"
Myotis lucifugus
VESPERTILIONID BAT FAMILY
L 3½"; WS 9". Rich glossy brown above, buffy below. Face broad, black; ears short, rounded, black. Often flies before dusk; flight erratic. Squeaks audible. One of many similar myotises in region. **BREEDING** 1 young in June in attics, barns, caves. **HABITAT** Roosts in trees, caves, mines, attics; forages widely, esp. over water. **ACTIVITY** Summer: active. Winter: hibernates in caves.

LONG-EARED MYOTIS
Myotis evotis
VESPERTILIONID BAT FAMILY
L 3½"; WS 9". Body pale brown, glossy; long-haired. Ears very long, black, tips rounded; extend beyond nose if laid forward. Face brown; nose small, pointed, black. Feeds on moths, beetles, flies. **BREEDING** 1 young born June–July in small colony. **HABITAT** Mainly open coniferous forests in mtns.; also mesas. Usu. roosts singly in buildings, under bark, caves. **ACTIVITY** Just before dusk and all night during warmer months.

SILVER-HAIRED BAT
Lasionycteris noctivagans
VESPERTILIONID BAT FAMILY

L 4″; WS 11″. Black, frosted with silvery hairs on back. Face blunt; ears fairly short, rounded, naked, black. Flies high, straight; feeds in treetops and at water surface. **BREEDING** 2 young in June in tree cavity. **HABITAT** Wooded areas; roosts under bark and in tree cavities, rarely in buildings. **ACTIVITY** Nocturnal; during warmer months.

BIG BROWN BAT
Eptesicus fuscus
VESPERTILIONID BAT FAMILY

L 4½″; WS 13″. Dark brown above, pale brown below. Wing and tail membranes furless. Face and ears broad, black. Flight straight, fast. Flies later in autumn, earlier in spring than others. Occ. seen in daytime in autumn. Region's most commonly seen bat. **BREEDING** 2 young in June. **HABITAT** Roosts and breeds in attics, barns, tree hollows, behind shutters, under bridges. **ACTIVITY** Spring–fall: active. Winter: hibernates.

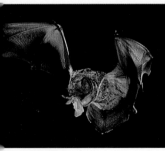

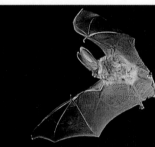

HOARY BAT
Lasiurus cinereus
VESPERTILIONID BAT FAMILY

L 5″; WS 15″. Mahogany brown above, heavily frosted with white hairs; throat buffy yellow. Ears short, rounded, with naked black rims. Nose blunt. Tail membrane heavily furred, brown. Most highly migratory bat in region; many winter in Chile and Argentina. **BREEDING** 2 young in June. **HABITAT** Coniferous and broadleaf woods; roosts in foliage. **ACTIVITY** During warmer months, emerges late in evening to feed on moths. **RANGE** Summer: entire region.

TOWNSEND'S BIG-EARED BAT
"Western Big-eared Bat"
Plecotus townsendii
VESPERTILIONID BAT FAMILY

L 4″; WS 13″. Pale gray or brown above, buffy below. Large ears (to 1½″) joined in midcrown, extend to midbody when laid back. 2 large lumps on nose. **BREEDING** Females form nursery colonies in caves, buildings; 1 young in May–June. **HABITAT** Areas with crevices for roosting, and caves for hibernation. **ACTIVITY** Feeds on moths at night during warmer months. **RANGE** ID, w MT, WY, w, c, and se CO.

AMERICAN PIKA
Ochotona princeps
PIKA FAMILY

L 8″. Fur gray-brown to buff. No visible tail. Sits on rock pile, proclaiming territory with series of high-pitched calls. **BREEDING** 2–6 young May–June; sometimes 2nd litter in Aug. **SIGN** Fresh hay in rock slides or spread out to dry in sun. Scat: small black pellets; white urine stains on rocks. **HABITAT** Mtns.: boulder-covered hillsides. **ACTIVITY** Mainly by day; eats stored hay in winter. **RANGE** n, c, and e ID, w and sc MT, nw and sc WY, w and c CO.

PYGMY RABBIT
Brachylagus idahoensis
HARE AND RABBIT FAMILY

L 11″; T 1″. Slate gray with pinkish tinge. Ears short for a rabbit (1½″), pale. Tail short, gray below. Digs own burrow system, unlike other rabbits. Scampers rather than leaps. Feeds on sagebrush leaves and grasses. Region's smallest rabbit. **BREEDING** 4–8 young June–July. **SIGN** Burrows have 2–5 entrances, each entrance 3″. **HABITAT** Deserts: in clumps of tall sagebrush. **ACTIVITY** Appears by day, but mainly nocturnal; year-round. **RANGE** sw and e ID, far sw MT.

DESERT COTTONTAIL
Sylvilagus audubonii
HARE AND RABBIT FAMILY

L 15″; T 2″. Pale gray-brown washed yellow above, white below; nape pale rusty. Tail short, white below. Runs up to 15 mph. Climbs upended logs to check for predators. **BREEDING** Several litters of 2–6 young, usu. Apr.–Aug. Cottontail young born blind and furless. **SIGN** Piles of pellets on logs, stumps. **HABITAT** Below 7,000′: grasslands, farms, deserts. **ACTIVITY** Day and night, year-round. **RANGE** c and e MT, WY, CO.

MOUNTAIN COTTONTAIL
"Nuttall's Cottontail"
Sylvilagus nuttallii
HARE AND RABBIT FAMILY

L 15″; T 2″. Pale grayish brown above, white below. Ears (2½″) black-tipped. Legs medium-length. Tail short, white below. Spends most of day resting in tall grass or rocky crevice. **BREEDING** 3–8 young Apr.–July; several litters each year. **SIGN** Tracks: foreprint round, 1″; hindprint oblong, 3½″. **HABITAT** Forest clearings, shrubby areas, sagebrush. **ACTIVITY** Mainly nocturnal. **RANGE** w and s ID, MT (ex. far nw, far se), WY (ex. far se), w and c CO.

SNOWSHOE HARE
summer (left), winter (right)
"Varying Hare"
Lepus americanus
HARE AND RABBIT FAMILY

L 19″; T 1½″. Summer: brown, grizzled with blackish; short tail dusky white below; feet sometimes white. Winter: thickly furred hindfeet serve as snowshoes; pure white ex. for black ear tips. Larger than a cottontail, with longer (4″) black-tipped ears, larger hindfeet. Usu. shy; if surprised, may thump hindfeet, then run off at up to 30 mph; if frightened, grunts, chirps, or screams. **BREEDING** 3 litters of 3 young Apr.–Aug; alert, furred, able to hop in hours. **SIGN** Packed-down trails in snow. Scat: piles of brown, lima-bean-size pellets. Tracks: hindprint 5″; toes widely spaced. **HABITAT** Coniferous and mixed forests. **ACTIVITY** Nocturnal, year-round; rests by day in nest-like "form" or hollow log. **RANGE** n, c, and e ID; w, c, and ne MT; mtns. of WY and nw and c CO.

WHITE-TAILED JACKRABBIT
summer (left), winter (right)
Lepus townsendii
HARE AND RABBIT FAMILY

L 26″; T 3½″. Hare. Summer: gray-brown above, peppered with black, paler below; ears tipped black. Winter: all white. Ears to 4⅜″ long. Legs long, thin; hindfeet to 6¾″ long. Tail white. Runs to 45 mph. Numbers diminished. **BREEDING** 1–3 litters of 1–6 young Apr.–Sept. Young born furred and able to hop within hours. **SIGN** Makes tunnels in snow. Tracks: foreprint round, 1½″; hindprint oval, 2½″; tracks 5–20′ apart. **HABITAT** Open grassy and sagebrush plains. **ACTIVITY** Mainly nocturnal, year-round. **RANGE** ID, c and e MT, WY, CO (ex. sw and se).

BLACK-TAILED JACKRABBIT
Lepus californicus
HARE AND RABBIT FAMILY

L 24″; T 4″. Hare. Buffy brown above, peppered with black; white below. Neck longer than rabbits'. Ears very long (5″), brownish with black tip. Legs long, thin, with large hindfeet (5″). Tail black above (black extends onto rump), white below. Stands up high when alert. Usu. hops rather than walks; can run 35 mph; every 5th leap higher to check for predators. Gives squeals, thumps feet when distressed. **BREEDING** 2–4 litters of 2–4 young Mar.–Oct. **SIGN** Trails in grass. Tracks: foreprint round, 1½″; hindprint oval, 2½″; 5–20′ apart, depending on speed. **HABITAT** Prairies, scrubby deserts, cultivated fields. **ACTIVITY** Day and night, year-round; avoids midday summer heat. **RANGE** s ID, sw MT, far se WY, sw and e CO.

Rodents

Rodentia is the world's largest mammalian order; more than half of all mammal species and more than half of all mammal individuals on earth are rodents. In addition to the mice and rats (a family that also

House Mouse

includes the mouse-like but chubbier voles and the muskrats), other rodent families in the Rocky Mountain region are the squirrels (including chipmunks, marmots, and prairie dogs), jumping mice, pocket mice, pocket gophers, porcupines, and beavers. Species in the Rocky Mountain states range from mice weighing roughly an ounce to the American Beaver, which may weigh up to 66 pounds, but most rodents are relatively small. They are distinguished by having only two pairs of incisors—one upper and one lower—and no canines, leaving a wide gap between incisors and molars. Rodent incisors are enameled on the front only; the working of the upper teeth against the lower ones wears away the softer inner surfaces, producing a short, chisel-like, beveled edge ideal for gnawing. The incisors grow throughout an animal's life (if they did not, they shortly would be worn away), and rodents must gnaw enough to keep the incisors from growing too long. The eyes are bulbous and placed high on the sides of the head, enabling the animals to detect danger over a wide arc. Chipmunks and ground squirrels hibernate underground for six to eight months in most of the region.

American Beaver

YELLOW-PINE CHIPMUNK
Tamias amoenus
SQUIRREL FAMILY

L 9″; T 4″. Five black stripes on back (middle 3 reach tail) enclose 2 interior gray stripes and 2 flanking white stripes; sides yellowish orange; belly whitish. White stripes above and below eye, flanked by 3 black stripes. Ears blackish in front, white behind. Steals campground food. **BREEDING** 4–7 young in May. **HABITAT** Mtns.: coniferous forest edges with fallen trees. **ACTIVITY** By day; hibernates in winter. **RANGE** ID, w and c MT, nw and wc WY.

LEAST CHIPMUNK
Tamias minimus
SQUIRREL FAMILY

L 8″; T 4″. 5 brown and 4 whitish stripes on back (reaching tail); sides yellow-gray; belly pale. 3 brown, 2 whitish stripes on each side of face. Tail light brown. **BREEDING** 4–7 young in May, in tunnel or tree hole. **HABITAT** Juniper woodlands, open meadows, sagebrush deserts. **ACTIVITY** By day; hibernates in winter. **RANGE** s and e ID, s, c, and e MT (local in nw), WY, w and c CO.

COLORADO CHIPMUNK
Tamias quadrivittatus
SQUIRREL FAMILY

L 9″; T 4″. Back has 4 gray stripes, 2 brown stripes, and median blackish stripe reaching base of tail; sides orangy rufous (more orange than Uinta Chipmunk). Head strongly striped; ears blackish in front, whitish behind; white patch behind ears. **BREEDING** 2–6 young in late spring. **HABITAT** Open shrubby foothills, mtn. forests. **ACTIVITY** By day; hibernates in winter. **RANGE** sw, c, and se CO.

RED-TAILED CHIPMUNK
Tamias ruficaudus
SQUIRREL FAMILY

L 9½″; T 4½″. Strongly colored. Bright rufous shoulders and sides; back has 4 whitish, 3 black median, and 2 brown flanking stripes. Face has 2 white and 3 brown stripes. Rump gray; tail dark rufous. Feeds high up in trees. **BREEDING** 4–6 young in early summer; makes nest in ground burrows and to 60′ up in trees. **HABITAT** Dense coniferous forests; bouldery slopes below tree line. **ACTIVITY** By day; winters underground. **RANGE** n ID, w MT.

UINTA CHIPMUNK
Tamias umbrinus
SQUIRREL FAMILY

L 8½"; T 4". Back has 4 gray stripes, 2 brown stripes; median blackish stripe reaches base of tail; sides washed tawny. Head striped; forehead brown; ears blackish in front, whitish behind; white patch behind ears. Tail black-tipped, white-bordered. BREEDING 5 young in early summer. HABITAT 6,000–11,000′: pine, juniper, scrub oaks. ACTIVITY By day; hibernates in winter. RANGE sc MT; nw WY, plus Medicine Bow and Uinta Mtns.; nc and nw CO.

WHITE-TAILED ANTELOPE SQUIRREL
Ammospermophilus leucurus
SQUIRREL FAMILY

L 9"; T 2¾". Back gray; sides and thighs orangish; 1 white stripe on side; white below. Head tan; whitish eye ring. Tail gray above, white below. Runs with tail arched over back. BREEDING 5–14 young in Apr. SIGN Burrows with pathways radiating outward. HABITAT Below 7,000′: semidesert and pinyon-juniper shrublands. ACTIVITY By day; hibernates in winter. RANGE sw ID, w CO (common).

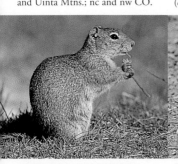

UINTA GROUND SQUIRREL
Spermophilus armatus
SQUIRREL FAMILY

L 11½"; T 3". Midback brown; rest of back, neck, and sides gray; muzzle and ears cinnamon; washed buffy on legs; belly whitish; tail mixed black and buff. Common in Grand Teton and Yellowstone N.P.s. BREEDING 4–7 young born in May. HABITAT Sagebrush, high grasslands, towns. ACTIVITY By day; adult active Apr.–July, juv. into Sept. RANGE e ID, sw MT, w WY.

COLUMBIAN GROUND SQUIRREL
Spermophilus columbianus
SQUIRREL FAMILY

L 14"; T 4". Grayish, spotted with black and buff above; belly, legs, and face rusty orange. Tail bushy, rusty orange, edged in white. VOICE Often vocal; gives high-pitched calls. BREEDING 2–7 young May–June; often colonial. SIGN Holes in ground without mounds. HABITAT Alpine and arid grasslands, clearings in coniferous forests. ACTIVITY By day; adult active Apr.–July, juv. into Sept. RANGE n and c ID, w MT.

GOLDEN-MANTLED GROUND SQUIRREL
Spermophilus lateralis
SQUIRREL FAMILY

L 11″; T 4″. Resembles oversize chipmunk without facial stripes. Back gray-brown or buff; each side has 1 white stripe bordered by heavy black stripe; belly whitish. Head and shoulders golden orange. Gray tail grizzled blackish. **BREEDING** 4–6 young in June. **HABITAT** Mtn. forests; sagebrush, meadows. **ACTIVITY** By day, Apr.–May to Sept.–Oct. **RANGE** ID (ex. s Snake R. Valley), w MT, w and s WY, w and c CO.

RICHARDSON'S GROUND SQUIRREL
Spermophilus richardsonii
SQUIRREL FAMILY

L 9″; T 3″. Crown and back smoky gray, back with fine bands of buffy speckling; pale buffy or whitish below; edges and underside of tail buffy. Stands on hindlegs like a prairie dog. **VOICE** Shrill whistle; chirps, chatters. **BREEDING** 7–8 young in May. **HABITAT** To 11,000′: sagebrush and grasslands near water. **ACTIVITY** By day, Apr.–Sept. **RANGE** sw and e ID, all MT (ex. far w and se), w and s WY, nw and nc CO.

SPOTTED GROUND SQUIRREL
Spermophilus spilosoma
SQUIRREL FAMILY

L 9″; T 2½″. Pale gray or pale brown above; distinct buffy or white spots on back and sides; ears small; belly whitish. Tail flat, thin; top has blackish spot near tip, buffy below. **BREEDING** 2 litters of 5–7 young; Apr., July–Aug. **SIGN** 2″-wide burrow under rocks or shrubs. **HABITAT** Plains: semiarid grasslands. **ACTIVITY** By day, Apr.–Sept.; in burrow during midday heat. **RANGE** se WY, e CO.

ROCK SQUIRREL
Spermophilus variegatus
SQUIRREL FAMILY

L 19″; T 8″. Region's largest ground squirrel. Gray or grayish brown above, finely mottled with black and buff; whitish eye ring; belly pale buff. Tail somewhat bushy; black near tip; fringes pale gray. Climbs bushes, trees; surveys from top of rock piles. **BREEDING** 2 litters of 3–9 young born Apr.–June, Aug.–Sept. **HABITAT** Cliffs, boulder piles, roadcuts, juniper and oaks in canyons. **ACTIVITY** By day, mostly Mar.–Oct.; also warm spells in winter. **RANGE** sw, c, and se CO.

THIRTEEN-LINED GROUND SQUIRREL
Spermophilus tridecemlineatus
SQUIRREL FAMILY

L 10"; T 4". Buffy or dull brown; nape and back have thick dark brown stripes with alternating buffy lines and rows of spots; belly whitish; tail flat, brown, fringed buffy. **BREEDING** 8–10 young in May. **SIGN** Radiating runways from burrow without mound. **HABITAT** Prairie grasslands, roadsides, lawns, towns. **ACTIVITY** By day, Mar.–Oct. **RANGE** n, c, and e MT, WY (ex. far w), CO (ex. far sw).

TOWNSEND'S GROUND SQUIRREL
Spermophilus townsendii
SQUIRREL FAMILY

L 9"; T 2". Smoky gray above, washed with pinkish buff; belly paler gray or pale buff. Head plain gray-brown; eye ring white. Tail tawny with white edge. **BREEDING** 4–10 young in Mar. **SIGN** Burrow openings rimmed with dirt piles. **HABITAT** Sagebrush deserts, dry grasslands. **ACTIVITY** By day, Feb.–July. **RANGE** s ID.

EASTERN FOX SQUIRREL
Sciurus niger
SQUIRREL FAMILY

L 24"; T 11". Most of head, back, sides, outer legs, and tail dark gray. Legs, feet, underparts, and edges of bushy tail rusty orange. Caches nuts in tree cavities. Introduced from se U.S. **VOICE** A loud *que-que-que*. **BREEDING** 2–4 young in spring; young remain in leaf nest 2 months. **SIGN** Mounds of nutshells under feeding branch; large leaf nest high in trees. **HABITAT** Riverine woodstowns. **ACTIVITY** By day, year-round. **RANGE** ne CO, MT.

ABERT'S SQUIRREL
"Tassel-eared Squirrel"
Sciurus aberti
SQUIRREL FAMILY

L 21"; T 10". Head, back, sides, and outer legs dark grizzled gray; some have rufous on midback. Black line on sides next to contrasting white underparts; long tufts ("tassels") on ears (ex. late summer); back of ears reddish. Some all black. **BREEDING** 4 young Apr.–May. **SIGN** Spherical 1'- to 3'-wide stick, grass, and bark nest in pine. **HABITAT** 7,000–8,500': Ponderosa Pine, pinyon-juniper forests. **ACTIVITY** By day, year-round; in cold weather, visits nut cache at base of tree. **RANGE** nc, c, sc, and sw CO.

RED SQUIRREL
Tamiasciurus hudsonicus
SQUIRREL FAMILY

L 13"; T 5". Underparts white; tail bushy, reddish. Summer: dark reddish gray above; black side stripe; ears rounded. Winter: pale reddish gray above; no side stripe; ears tufted. Mainly arboreal. **VOICE** Bird-like chattering; emphatic *tchick, tchick, tchick.* **BREEDING** 4–5 young Apr.–May and Aug.–Sept. in tree. **SIGN** Piles of stripped cones; nuts with ragged hole at one end. **HABITAT** Coniferous forests. **ACTIVITY** Mainly by day, year-round. **RANGE** n, c, and e ID, w and c MT, mtns. of WY and w and c CO.

NORTHERN FLYING SQUIRREL
Glaucomys sabrinus
SQUIRREL FAMILY

L 13"; T 6". Brown above, white below. Loose fold of furred skin on each side connects fore- and hindleg. Eyes large. Tail long, flattened. Glides up to 200'. Eats lichens, subterranean fungi, nuts, seeds, insects; visits bird-feeders at night. Dens in tree cavities; summer nest of bark and twigs. **BREEDING** 2–5 young Apr.–May. **SIGN** Piles of cone remnants and nutshells under dead trees with woodpecker holes. **HABITAT** Forests. **ACTIVITY** Strictly nocturnal, year-round. **RANGE** n, c, and e ID, w MT, n and wc WY.

YELLOW-BELLIED MARMOT
Marmota flaviventris
SQUIRREL FAMILY

L 24"; T 7". Coat reddish brown; belly yellow; sides of neck buffy. Head dark brown; pale brown patches on muzzle. Feet buffy or brown, strongly clawed. Tail bushy, reddish brown. Often sits on boulder above burrow. **VOICE** High, soft chirps and whistles. **BREEDING** 4–5 young in May. **SIGN** Den near large boulder. **HABITAT** Below 11,000': rocky areas in valleys, foothills, and mtns. **ACTIVITY** Mainly by day; hibernates Aug.–Mar. **RANGE** ID, w and c MT; mtns. of WY, w and c CO.

HOARY MARMOT
Marmota caligata
SQUIRREL FAMILY

L 30"; T 9". Head and most of body pale silver gray; rump brownish. Black V on forehead and shoulders. Feet black; claws strong. Tail bushy, reddish brown. **VOICE** Shrill whistle. **BREEDING** 4–5 young May–June. **SIGN** 12" burrow entrance, often under rock. **HABITAT** High elevs.: meadows and rock slides near and above tree line. **ACTIVITY** By day; hibernates Oct.–Apr. **RANGE** n and ec ID, w MT. **Woodchuck** *(M. monax)* L 21", T 5"; dark brown, grizzled gray; tail dark brown; lives in n ID.

BLACK-TAILED PRAIRIE DOG
Cynomys ludovicianus
SQUIRREL FAMILY

L 16"; T 4". Rotund. Back, sides, and legs warm buffy brown, with few black hairs; pale buffy below; terminal third of small rusty tail black. Often sits on haunches atop mound. Sociable; often seen in recognition "kissing," mutual grooming, and cooperative burrow digging. Tunnels to 14' long, with several nesting chambers and toilet chamber. Widely poisoned; competes with humans for farmland and with cattle for food. **VOICE** Highly vocal; language of about 10 calls includes bark, for which it is named. **BREEDING** 4–5 young Mar.–Apr. **SIGN** Bare mounds of earth 1–2' high; large colonies of 100–1,000 or more families. Tracks: hindprint 1¼", 5 toes print; foreprint 1", 4 toes print. **HABITAT** Shortgrass prairies. **ACTIVITY** By day; avoids midday heat and winter storms. **RANGE** c and e MT, n and e WY, e CO.

WHITE-TAILED PRAIRIE DOG
Cynomys leucurus
SQUIRREL FAMILY

L 14"; T 2". Rotund. Back, sides, and legs warm buffy brown, with few black hairs; crown and cheeks dusky; tail mainly white, with no black tip. Often sits on haunches atop mound. Colonies have just a few families. **BREEDING** 4–6 young in late spring. **SIGN** Bare mounds of earth 1–3' high and 7–10' wide, surface rougher than Black-tailed's. **HABITAT** 5,000–12,000': open sagebrush in hills, often with scattered small conifers. **ACTIVITY** By day, Mar.–Oct. **RANGE** Border of sc MT; nc, sw, and sc WY; nw and wc CO. **Gunnison's Prairie Dog** (*C. gunnisoni;* of plateaus of sw, c, and sc CO) buffy; central base of tail pale gray, tip of tail white.

AMERICAN BEAVER
Castor canadensis
BEAVER FAMILY

lodge (top left), gnawed tree (top right)

L 3'4"; T 16". Rich dark brown. Back high, rounded. Legs short; feet webbed, black; claws small. Paddle-shaped tail black, scaly, rounded, flat. Eats bark and twigs of broadleaf trees; stashes branches underwater for winter use. Swims with only head above water. Slaps tail on water to warn family of danger. Fells trees by gnawing trunk down to a "waist" that finally cannot support the tree. Dams small streams with sticks, reeds, saplings caulked with mud. In middle of pond, builds dome-like lodge up to 6' high and 20' wide; underwater tunnels reach up to dry chambers, hidden from view, above water level. Dens in banks of canals and streams in treeless areas. Ponds formed by dams promote growth of habitat (broadleaf trees) favored by beavers; dams also help form marshes for other wildlife. N. Amer.'s largest rodent. **BREEDING** Usu. 3–5 young May–June inside lodge. **SIGN** Dams, lodges, cone-shaped tree stumps; 12" territorial scent mounds of mud and grass. Tracks: 5", 5-toed hindprint covers smaller foreprint. **HABITAT** Mtns. (and less commonly) plains: ponds, rivers, adjacent woods. **ACTIVITY** Mainly at dusk and night, year-round.

NORTHERN POCKET GOPHER
Thomomys talpoides
POCKET GOPHER FAMILY

L 8″; T 2½″. Brown, yellow-brown, or gray (color matches local soil color); white marks on chin; black patch behind ears. Orange, chisel-like pair of upper and lower incisors. **BREEDING** 1–2 litters of 4–7 young. **SIGN** Fan-shaped mounds; wiggly lines of bare soil above subsurface tunnels. **HABITAT** Mtn. meadows, streamsides at mid- to high elevs. **ACTIVITY** Day and night underground. **RANGE** ID, MT, WY, w and c CO.

GREAT BASIN POCKET MOUSE
Perognathus parvus
KANGAROO RAT FAMILY

L 7″; T 3½″. Gray-brown above, white below. Ears small; fur-lined cheek pouch. Tail long, bicolored. Makes extensive burrows with chambers for sleeping, nesting, food storage. Eats seeds. **BREEDING** 2 litters of 2–8 young May–Aug. **HABITAT** Sagebrush, juniper woodlands. **ACTIVITY** Nocturnal, hibernates in winter **RANGE** s ID, sw WY.

ORD'S KANGAROO RAT
Dipodomys ordii
KANGAROO RAT FAMILY

L 10″; T 5″. Tan above, white below. White spot above eye, below ear. Tail striped black and white; dark tip. Hindfeet 2″ long; can hop to 8′. **BREEDING** 3–5 young. **SIGN** 3″ burrow openings on slopes; scooped-out dusting areas nearby. Tracks: narrow, 1½″ hindprints. **HABITAT** Below 7,000′: open deserts, grasslands with hard or sandy soils. **ACTIVITY** Nocturnal; winters in burrows. **RANGE** s ID, e MT, c and e WY, w, sc, and e CO.

WESTERN HARVEST MOUSE
Reithrodontomys megalotis
MOUSE AND RAT FAMILY

L 5½″; T 3″. Brown above; sides buffy; pale below. Ears medium-size, round. Tail dusky above, pale below. Travels in vole runways. Nimble climber. Eats insects and new growth in summer, seeds in fall and winter. **BREEDING** Several litters of 2–6 young. **SIGN** Builds 4″ globular woven nest near ground; entrance at bottom. **HABITAT** Vegetated streamsides, wet meadows. **ACTIVITY** Nocturnal, year-round. **RANGE** s ID, e MT, e and c WY, sw, sc, and e CO.

DEER MOUSE
Peromyscus maniculatus
MOUSE AND RAT FAMILY

L 7″; T 3″. Brown (adult) or gray (juv.) above, white below. Ears round, medium-size. Feet white. Tail dark above, white below. In most habitats, outnumbers all other rodents combined. Agile climber; feeds on seeds, insects, fungi. **BREEDING** 2–4 litters of 3–5 young Mar.–Oct. **HABITAT** Most habitats; not wet areas. **ACTIVITY** Nocturnal, year-round.

NORTHERN GRASSHOPPER MOUSE
Onychomys leucogaster
MOUSE AND RAT FAMILY

L 7″; T 2″. Pale cinnamon brown or pinkish cinnamon (adult; pictured) or pale gray (juv.) above, white below. Feet white. Tail short, whitish. Eats large insects. **VOICE** Vocal: sharp barks; long shrill whistles. **BREEDING** 2 litters of 1–6 young Apr.–Aug. **HABITAT** Desert valleys. **ACTIVITY** Nocturnal, year-round. **RANGE** s ID, c and e MT, WY (ex. nw), CO (ex. higher mtns.).

BUSHY-TAILED WOODRAT
Neotoma cinerea
MOUSE AND RAT FAMILY

L 17″; T 8″. Pale gray washed with buff or dark brown above, white below. Ears large. Feet white. Tail long, bushy, usu. white below. Eats foliage, seeds, fruit. **BREEDING** 1–2 litters of 2–6 young May–Sept. **SIGN** Large nest of sticks under log or in crevice; piles of leaves in autumn (pikas store grasses, herbs). **HABITAT** Rocky areas in all habitats, up to alpine zone. **ACTIVITY** Nocturnal, year-round. **RANGE** Entire region, ex. e CO.

HOUSE MOUSE
Mus musculus
MOUSE AND RAT FAMILY

L 7″; T 3″. Gray or brownish tan above, gray or buffy below. Tail long, naked, with ring-like scales. This common house pest was introduced to N. Amer. from Eurasia. **BREEDING** 2–5 litters of 3–11 young Mar.–Oct.; year-round indoors. **SIGN** Small dark droppings; musky odor; damaged materials. **HABITAT** Homes, farms, fields. **ACTIVITY** Mainly nocturnal, year-round.

BROWN RAT
"Norway Rat"
Rattus norvegicus
MOUSE AND RAT FAMILY

L 15″; T 7″. Grayish brown above; belly gray. Tail long and scaly. Excavates network of 3″-wide tunnels in ground near buildings, dumps, water. Eats insects, grain, garbage. Introduced from Eurasia. **BREEDING** Usu. 5–6 litters of 6–10 young per year. **SIGN** Dirty holes in walls; droppings; pathways to steady food supplies. Tracks: long, 5-toed hindprint forward of rounder foreprint. **HABITAT** Cities, buildings, farms. **ACTIVITY** Mostly nocturnal, year-round.

SOUTHERN RED-BACKED VOLE
Clethrionomys gapperi
MOUSE AND RAT FAMILY

L 5″; T 1½″. Bright chestnut stripe above, from nose to tail; sides buffy; belly gray. Ears small; tail short. Uses runways of other voles. Varied diet of plants and fungi. **BREEDING** Several litters of 2–8 young Mar.–Oct. **HABITAT** Moist coniferous forests, bogs. **ACTIVITY** Day and night, year-round. **RANGE** ID (ex. sw), w and n MT, mtns. of WY and CO.

MEADOW VOLE
Microtus pennsylvanicus
MOUSE AND RAT FAMILY

L 6½″; T 2″. Buffy brown in summer, grayish brown in winter. Ears small. Tail much shorter than body. Voles are major prey of owls, hawks, and small carnivores. **BREEDING** Several litters of 3–8 young. **SIGN** Summer: piles of grass cuttings along runways. Nests under old boards on ground. Tracks: hindprint ⅝″, 5 widely splayed toes. **HABITAT** Wet meadows, marshes, mtn. parklands. **ACTIVITY** Mainly moonless nights; some by day. **RANGE** n, c, and e ID, MT, w and ne WY, c and ne CO.

COMMON MUSKRAT
Ondatra zibethicus
MOUSE AND RAT FAMILY

L 23″; T 10″. Fur rich brown, dense, glossy; belly silver. Hindfeet partly webbed. Tail long, scaly, flat; tapers to point. Excellent swimmer; head, back, tail visible. Eats aquatic plants. **BREEDING** 2–3 litters of 6–7 young Apr.–Sept. **SIGN** "Lodge" of cattails, roots, mud in marsh or other water; rises to 3′ above water; burrows in stream banks. Tracks: 2–3″ narrow hindprint (5 toes print); smaller round foreprint; often with tail drag mark. **HABITAT** Marshes, ponds, rivers, lakes. **ACTIVITY** Day and night; lodge-bound on coldest days.

SAGEBRUSH VOLE
Lemmiscus curtatus
MOUSE AND RAT FAMILY

L 5″; T ¾″. Ashy gray above, silvery below. Nose and small ears buff. Feet silvery. Tail very short. Feeds on grasses in summer; bark, twigs, and roots in winter. **BREEDING** Several litters of 2–11 young Apr.–Nov. **SIGN** Colonial burrow entrances under bush clumps. **HABITAT** Sagebrush and bunchgrass flats. **ACTIVITY** Day and night, year-round. **RANGE** s and e ID, sw, c, and ne MT, WY (ex. ne), nw and nc CO.

WESTERN JUMPING MOUSE
Zapus princeps
JUMPING MOUSE FAMILY

L 10″; T 6″. Crown and back slaty; cheeks and sides yellow-brown; ears large, round; belly whitish. Tail twice as long as body, thin; dark on top, pale below. Large hind thighs; hops up to 5′. **BREEDING** 2 litters of 3–9 young. **SIGN** 1″ piles of grass with flower petals. **HABITAT** Moist meadows, streamsides, thickets with dense sedges. **ACTIVITY** Day and night, Apr.–Oct. **RANGE** ID, MT (ex. se), WY (ex. ne), w and c CO.

COMMON PORCUPINE
Erethizon dorsatum
NEW WORLD PORCUPINE FAMILY

L 33″; T 8″. Blackish. Long wiry guard hairs on front half of body; thousands of shorter, heavier quills (hairs modified into sharp, mostly hollow spines) on front of body but mainly on rump and longish rounded tail; underfur long, soft, wooly. Back high-arching; legs short. Soles of feet knobbed; claws long, curved; walks pigeon-toed on ground. Eats green plants, and twigs, buds, and bark of trees; sometimes damages wooden buildings and poles. **VOICE** Squeals and grunts. **BREEDING** 1 young Apr.–June. **SIGN** Tooth marks on bark; irreg. patches of bark stripped from tree trunks and limbs. Tracks: inward-facing, up to 3″; claw tips well forward. Scat: piles of variably shaped pellets near crevice or base of feeding tree. **HABITAT** Forests (esp. coniferous) and nearby open areas. **ACTIVITY** Mainly nocturnal, year-round.

Carnivores

Members of the order Carnivora eat meat, although many also eat fruit, berries, and vegetation. They have long canine teeth for stabbing prey, and most have sharp cheek teeth for slicing meat. None truly hibernate, but several retire to well-insulated logs and burrows to sleep soundly during colder parts of the winter. Most live on land, although otters spend most of their time in water. Most carnivores have a single yearly litter of offspring, which are born blind and receive many months to a year or more of parental care. Carnivore families in the Rocky Mountain region include bears, dogs (Coyote, Gray Wolf, and foxes), weasels (skunks, otters, badgers, martens, and the Mink), raccoons, and cats.

COYOTE
Canis latrans
DOG FAMILY

H 25″; L 4′; T 13″. Coat long, coarse; grizzled gray, buffy, and black. Muzzle long, narrow, brownish; ears rufous. Legs long; tail long, bushy, black-tipped. Runs up to 40 mph. Eats small mammals, birds, frogs, snakes. Only large carnivore to persist in heavily settled areas. **VOICE** Bark; flat howl; series of *yip* notes followed by wavering howl. **BREEDING** 4–8 pups in spring. **SIGN** 24″ den mouths on slopes. Tracks: dog-like, but in nearly straight line; foreprint larger, 2⅜″. Scat: dog-like, but usu. full of hair. **HABITAT** Plains, scrub deserts, mtns., forests, farms, urban areas. **ACTIVITY** Day and night, year-round.

KIT FOX
"Swift Fox"
Vulpes velox
DOG FAMILY

L 28″; T 10½″. Back, sides, and top of tail silvery; belly, thin legs, and underside of tail buffy yellow. Forehead and narrow muzzle gray; blackish spot on each side of snout; throat white; ears large, pointed, rusty. Tip of long bushy tail black. **VOICE** Shrill *yap,* whines. **BREEDING** 3–7 young Feb.–Apr.; mates for life. **SIGN** Den with several 8″ entrances, mound of dirt, and bones at side. Tracks: about 1½″; shows 4 toes and claws. **HABITAT** Prairies, arid grasslands. **ACTIVITY** Mainly nocturnal, year-round. **RANGE** n and e MT (rare), WY (ex. nw), n and e CO.

RED FOX
Vulpes vulpes
DOG FAMILY

H 15″; L 3′2″; T 14″. 3 color morphs: typically rusty orange with white underparts, black legs and feet (shown); a few are mostly blackish; "cross" morph is rusty gray with black cross over back and forelegs. Muzzle narrow; ears pointed, blackish. Tail long, bushy, white-tipped. Eats rodents, rabbits, birds, insects, berries, fruit. Has strong scent. **VOICE** Short *yap* and long howls. **BREEDING** 4–8 young Mar.–Apr. **SIGN** Den often a large rodent burrow on a rise, with entrance enlarged to 3′. Tracks: foreprint slightly larger, 2⅛″; 4 toe pads print. **HABITAT** Open woods, pastures, river valleys. **ACTIVITY** Mainly nocturnal, year-round. **RANGE** ID, w MT, nw and sc WY, w and c CO.

COMMON GRAY FOX
Urocyon cinereoargenteus
DOG FAMILY

H 15″; L 3′2″; T 13″. Grizzled silvery gray above; throat and midbelly white; collar, lower sides, legs, sides of tail rusty; top and tip of tail black. Eats rabbits, rodents, birds, grasshoppers, fruit, berries. Often climbs trees, unlike Red Fox and Coyote. **BREEDING** 2–7 young in summer. **SIGN** Den hidden in natural crevice in woods; snagged hair and bone scraps often near entrance. Tracks: foreprint 1½″; hindprint slightly narrower. **HABITAT** Lower slopes of mtns., wooded canyons, scrubby plains. **ACTIVITY** Mainly nocturnal, year-round. **RANGE** se WY (rare), w, c, and se CO.

GRAY WOLF   adult
Canis lupus
DOG FAMILY

H 35"; L 6'; T 18"; female smaller. Grayish; some washed buffy or with black and white mottling on back and sides; legs buffy. Tail long, bushy, black at end. Some individuals black. Compared to Coyote, has nose pad more than 1" wide, and foreprint 5" long; wider facial ruff, rounder and shorter ears, runs with tail carried high. Normally wary of humans. Was extirpated in region; a few have returned to n ID and nw MT on their own; others are being released in larger protected areas in c ID, MT, WY. **VOICE** Deep, far-carrying howl. **BREEDING** Usu. about 6 sooty-black young Apr.–May. **SIGN** Dens on hillsides; burrow entrance 20"x 24"; den up to 30' deep; open bare earth in front. Scat: like dog's, but with hair. Tracks: larger than dog's; foreprint 5" long; hindprint 4½". Stride about 30"; steps cover each other in single row (like Coyote, but unlike dog). **HABITAT** Forests and grasslands in mtns. and valleys. **ACTIVITY** Most active at night but also seen by day, year-round. **RANGE** n ID, nw MT, nw WY; may be reintroduced or allowed to spread elsewhere.

adult with young

BLACK BEAR
Ursus americanus
BEAR FAMILY

black coat

H 3′4″; L 5′; T 4″; female much smaller. Heavy, bulky. Head round; muzzle long, brownish; ears short, rounded. Legs long. Tail tiny. Black, long-haired, often with white patch on chest. Some individuals cinnamon brown. Eats more vegetation than most carnivores; eats inner layer of tree bark, berries, fruit, plants, honeycombs, insects in rotten logs, and vertebrates, incl. fish and small mammals. Powerful swimmer and climber; can run up to 30 mph. **CAUTION** Do not feed, approach, or get between one and its food or cubs; will usu. flee, but can cause serious injury. Campers must firmly seal up food and place out of reach. **BREEDING** Usu. 2 cubs, about ½ lb at birth, born in den Jan.–Feb. **SIGN** Torn-apart stumps, turned-over boulders, torn-up burrows, hair on shaggy-barked trees. Tracks: foreprint 5″ wide; hindprint up to 9″ long. Scat: dog-like. **HABITAT** Mtn. forests, swamps, brushy hillsides. **ACTIVITY** Mainly nocturnal, but often out in daytime; year-round. **RANGE** n, c, and e ID, w and c MT, w and sc WY, w and c CO.

cinnamon-brown coat

adult

GRIZZLY BEAR
"Brown Bear"
Ursus arctos
BEAR FAMILY

H 4′3″; L 7′. Dark brown, frosted (or grizzled) with silver or golden hairs; no visible tail. Differs from cinnamon phase of Black Bear by its grizzled color, raised hump at shoulder, concave muzzle, and longer front foot claws. Males usu. forages alone, female with cubs. Digs larger rodents from burrows, kills larger mammals and fish; also eats berries, herbs. Once widespread in entire region, now exterminated over vast areas. **CAUTION** Very dangerous if surprised at close range; can outrun a human. Do not approach; if attacked, climb a tall tree or roll into a tight ball and play dead. **BREEDING** 2–3 young born in underground den in Jan. Starting at age 5, females breed every 2–3 years; cubs stay with mother more than a year. **SIGN** Creates well-worn footpaths. Covers uneaten portions of ungulate corpses with sticks and brush (awaits return of appetite nearby). Large pits and overturned boulders from rodent searches. Girdled trees with marks higher than Black Bear's. Tracks like Black Bear, but hindprint 11″ long, 7½″ wide; foreprint half as long, but with longer, straighter foreclaws. **HABITAT** Mtns.: wilderness areas, meadows, brush, forests. **ACTIVITY** Day and night, spring–fall. **RANGE** nw and sc MT, may be reintroduced to c ID.

female with cub

COMMON RACCOON
Procyon lotor
RACCOON FAMILY

L 32″; T 9″. Coat long and thick, grizzled grayish brown. Black mask below white eyebrow; white sides on narrow muzzle. Legs medium-length; paws buffy; flexible toes used for climbing trees and washing food. Tail thick, banded yellow-brown and black. Swims well; can run up to 15 mph. Omnivorous; feeds in upland and aquatic habitats; raids trash bins. **BREEDING** Usu. 4 young Apr.–May. **SIGN** Den in hollow tree or crevice. Tracks: flat-footed; hindprint much longer than wide, 4″; foreprint rounded, 3″; claws show on all 5 toes. **HABITAT** Forests and scrub near water; towns. **ACTIVITY** Mainly nocturnal, but sometimes seen in daytime; dens up in winter, though active in milder periods. **RANGE** ID, MT, WY (ex. nw), lowland CO.

RINGTAIL
Bassariscus astutus
RACCOON FAMILY

L 28″; T 14″. Yellowish brown or gray above, pale buffy below. Face short, pointed; eyes large, black, ringed with whitish fur; ears large, pointed. Feet short; claws very sharp. Tail longer than head and body; black with black tip and 7–8 white bands (rings). Makes squirrel-like leaps. Eats small animals, fruit. **BREEDING** 3–4 young May–June; den hidden under boulders. **SIGN** Tracks: up to 2¾″, round; shows 5 toes but no claws. **HABITAT** Rocky areas, canyons, large trees with hollows, old buildings. **ACTIVITY** Strictly nocturnal, Apr.–Oct. **RANGE** w and sc CO; s WY (rare).

AMERICAN MARTEN
Martes americana
WEASEL FAMILY

L 24″; T 9″; female smaller. Fur soft, dense; entirely brown; throat and chest buffy orange. Snout pointed; ears small, rounded. Legs medium-length; feet heavily clawed. Tail bushy, fairly long, dark brown. Feeds on voles, squirrels, birds, berries. Active on ground and in trees. **VOICE** Vocal: variety of growls, screams, whines. **BREEDING** 2–5 young Mar.–Apr. in hollow tree or usurped burrow. **SIGN** Prints round, 1¾″. **HABITAT** Forests: spruce, fir, and hemlock. **ACTIVITY** Late afternoon to early morning, year-round. **RANGE** n, c, and e ID, w MT, w and sc WY, w and c CO.

FISHER
Martes pennanti
WEASEL FAMILY

L 3′; T 15″; female much smaller. Head broad; snout pointed; neck heavy. Tail bushy, dark brown. White-tipped hairs give frosted appearance. Hunts porcupines: attacks head, then eats through unprotected underside; rarely eats fish. **BREEDING** 1–4 young in Mar. **SIGN** Porcupine remains. Tracks: 2½″ wide in snow; wider than long. Scat: 4–6″, dark, cylindrical, often with quills. **HABITAT** Mature coniferous and mixed forests, esp. in hilly country. **ACTIVITY** Day and night, in trees and on ground, year-round. **RANGE** n and ne ID, w MT, nw WY.

MINK
Mustela vison
WEASEL FAMILY

L 21"; T 7"; female smaller. Lustrous blackish brown above and below; chin white. Muzzle pointed; ears tiny; legs short; tail fairly long, bushy. (Weasels are white below; have thinner tails.) Swims often; can dive to 15'. Feeds on fish, birds, rodents (esp. muskrat), frogs; often travels far in search of food. **BREEDING** 3–4 young Apr.–May. **SIGN** Holes in snow (where Mink has pounced on vole). 4" burrow entrances in stream bank. Tracks: round, 2", in snow. **HABITAT** Freshwater shores. **ACTIVITY** Late afternoon to early morning, year-round; dens up in coldest, stormiest periods.

NORTHERN RIVER OTTER
Lutra canadensis
WEASEL FAMILY

L 3'7"; T 16". Fur dense, dark brown, often silvery on chin and chest. Ears and eyes small. Legs short; feet webbed. Tail long, thick-based, tapering to a point. Swims rapidly, stops with head out of water. Eats fish, frogs, turtles, muskrats. Runs well on land; loves to exercise and play; wanders widely. Eliminated from many areas due to river degradation, trapping. **BREEDING** Mates in water; 2–3 young born blind but furred in Apr. **SIGN** 12" wide slides on sloping muddy riverbanks in flat areas; vegetation flattened in large patch for rolling, feeding, defecating; trails between bodies of water. Tracks: 3", toes fanned. **HABITAT** Clean rivers, wood-edged ponds and lakes. **ACTIVITY** Day and night, year-round. **RANGE** ID, w and c MT, nw and c WY, c CO.

SHORT-TAILED WEASEL
"Ermine"
Mustela erminea
WEASEL FAMILY

winter (left), summer (right)

L 11"; T 2"; female smaller. Summer: brown above; underparts, inside of legs, and feet white; tail has brown base, black tip. Winter: white, with black tail tip. Neck long; legs short; tail thin, furred. Expert mouser; also feeds on rabbits, birds, frogs, insects. Tireless, active hunter; hunts by smell and sight. **BREEDING** 4–9 young in Apr. **SIGN** Spiral scat along trails. Tracks: similar to Long-tailed Weasel's, but usu. slightly smaller. **HABITAT** Brush, fields, wetlands. **ACTIVITY** Day and night, year-round.

LONG-TAILED WEASEL
Mustela frenata
WEASEL FAMILY

winter (left), summer (right)

16"; T 5"; female smaller. Summer: brown above, white below; feet and outside of legs brown; tail thin, furred, with brown base, black tip. Winter: northern individuals white, with black tail tip. Neck long; head larger than neck. Legs short. Wraps sinewy body around prey as it kills by biting base of skull. Good swimmer and climber. **BREEDING** 6–8 young Apr.–May. **SIGN** Cache of dead rodents under log; drag marks in snow. Tracks: hindprint ¾" wide, 1' long; foreprint a bit wider, half as long. **HABITAT** Woodlands, brush, fields. **ACTIVITY** Day and night, year-round.

BLACK-FOOTED FERRET
Mustela nigripes
WEASEL FAMILY

L 22"; T 5". Crown, neck, sides, and base of tail buffy yellow in summer, whitish in winter; midback dark brown in summer, blackish in winter. Black mask surrounds eyes and joins over muzzle; rest of head white. Short legs and feet. Outer third of tail black. Eats mainly prairie dogs. Endangered due to poisoning of larger rodents. **BREEDING** 2–5 young in June. **SIGN** Untramped earth at entrance of prairie dog burrow. **HABITAT** Grasslands; esp. near prairie dog towns. **ACTIVITY** Day and (esp.) night; less active in winter. **RANGE** Spotty: mainly e WY, e MT.

WESTERN SPOTTED SKUNK
Spilogale gracilis
WEASEL FAMILY

L 16″; T 6″. Body black, with several long, wavy, white stripes. Head small, black with small white spots; ears tiny, at sides of head. Feet short, black. Tail short for a skunk, bushy, black with white tip. If threatened, stands on forepaws; can spray foul-smelling liquid to 13′. **BREEDING** 4–7 young in June. **SIGN** Lingering stench. Tracks: like Striped Skunk's, but smaller. **HABITAT** Canyon woodlands, scrub, farms. **ACTIVITY** Nocturnal; dens up during winter. **RANGE** c and s ID, MT near Missoula, sw, c, and ne WY, w, c, and se CO. **Eastern Spotted Skunk** *(S. putorius)* very similar; in riverine woods and fields of se WY, ne and ec CO.

COMMON HOG-NOSED SKUNK
Conepatus mesoleucus
WEASEL FAMILY

L 30″; T 14″. Entire crown, nape, and top half of body fluffy white; bushy tail all white; underparts and legs black. Long pointed snout naked on top. Head (ex. crown) black; no white stripe on forehead like other skunks. Tears up ground searching for insects, reptiles, small rodents, tubers, bulbs and roots; often called "Rooter." **BREEDING** 2–4 young in May. **SIGN** Rootings. Tracks: longer front foot toe prints than other skunks. **HABITAT** Oak and semidesert scrub, pinyon-juniper woodlands. **ACTIVITY** Nocturnal in summer; forages on some winter days. **RANGE** sc and se CO.

STRIPED SKUNK
Mephitis mephitis
WEASEL FAMILY

L 24″; T 9″. Coat thick, fluffy, mainly black; large white nape patch continues as 2 stripes along sides of back, usu. reaching long bushy tail; narrow white forehead stripe. Head pointed; ears and eyes small. In some individuals, most of upper back and tail white. If threatened, raises tail, backs up, may stomp ground; may emit foul-smelling, sulphurous spray that travels to 15′, stings eyes of predators, pets, humans. Eats insects, rodents, bird and turtle eggs, fruit, roadkills, garbage. **CAUTION** Can turn and spray in an instant. **BREEDING** 6–7 young in May. **SIGN** Foul odor if one has sprayed or been run over recently. Scratched-up lawns and garbage bags. Tracks: 1″ round foreprint; hindprint broader at front, flat-footed, 1½″. **HABITAT** Woodlands, fields, towns. **ACTIVITY** Dusk to dawn; dens up and sleeps much of winter.

WOLVERINE
Gulo gulo
WEASEL FAMILY

L 3′4″; T 10″. Robust, bear-like; fur shaggy. Dark brown with yellowish buff on rufous sides, base of bushy tail, and temple; chest has black-spotted creamy patch. Very strong and fearless for its size; drives bears from kill; has killed adult moose by clamping on to its throat. Lopes along at fast pace; often climbs trees and jumps on prey from trees; raids trap lines. Sprays foul musk on carcasses (to repel Mountain Lions and bears) and inside raided cabins. Very rarely seen due to vast territories, scarcity, and its acute senses of smell and hearing. **BREEDING** 2–5 young in spring, born in rock crevice. **SIGN** Tracks: footprints equal, round, 4–7″; heel and smallest of 5 toes rarely print. **HABITAT** Mtns.: forests, scrub, meadows. **ACTIVITY** Day and night, year-round. **RANGE** w and sc MT, nw WY, w CO.

AMERICAN BADGER
Taxidea taxus
WEASEL FAMILY

L 28″; T 5″. Body wide, flattish. Shaggy; gray-brown above, white below. Snout up-turned, black; white stripe from nose to midback. Legs short, black; strong claws. Tail bushy, yellowish. Moves clumsily. Digs up burrowing snakes, rodents. **CAUTION** Very capable of defending itself against humans. **BREEDING** 1–5 young in Apr. **SIGN** Burrow entrance 12″ wide; nearby mound of bones, fur, and dung. Tracks: toes point inward; prints round, 2″. **HABITAT** Grasslands, sagebrush, open juniper and pine woodlands. **ACTIVITY** Day and night, year-round.

MOUNTAIN LION
adult

"Cougar" "Puma"
Felis concolor
CAT FAMILY

H 30"; L 8'; T 30"; female smaller. Tawny reddish or grayish above, whitish below. Dark spot at base of whiskers; ears erect, blackish on back; neck fairly long. Legs long; paws wide; claws long, sharp, retractile. Tail long, blackish at end. Young longer-tailed than Bobcat; dark-spotted for first 6 months. Feeds mainly on deer and elk; also rabbits, large rodents, birds. Solitary territorial hunter, ex. for mother with older cubs and during 2-week breeding period; good climber. **CAUTION** Shy of humans, but fatal attacks have occurred. **VOICE** Screams, hisses, growls. **BREEDING** 2–4 young in July every other year. **SIGN** Scratch marks 6–10' up on tree; piles of dirt and leaves urinated on by male. Tracks: round; 4 toe prints show no claws. **HABITAT** Semiarid canyons, bouldery foothills, forests. **ACTIVITY** Mainly nocturnal, year-round. **RANGE** ID, w and c MT, w and c WY (esp. Bighorns), w and c CO.

female with cubs

LYNX
Lynx lynx (canadensis)
CAT FAMILY

H 23″; L 3′; T 4″. Coat buffy grayish with few black hairs. Facial ruff whitish with black streaks; ears have pointed black tufts. Legs long, buffy; feet very large, well furred to serve as snowshoes. Tail short, outer third black. Climbs trees to rest; pounces down on prey. Feeds mainly on Snowshoe Hare; Lynx numbers fluctuate with rise and fall of hare numbers. Rare. **BREEDING** 2–3 young May–June. **SIGN** Tracks: prints 3½″; shows 4 toes, no claws. **HABITAT** High-elev. coniferous forests with thickets. **ACTIVITY** Nocturnal, year-round. **RANGE** n and c ID (local), w MT, w and c WY, c CO.

BOBCAT
Lynx rufus
CAT FAMILY

H 20″; L 33″; T 4″. Orange-brown in summer, paler grayish in winter; black spots and bars on long legs and rear; underparts and inside of legs white. Face wide and flat; black lines radiate onto facial ruff; ears slightly tufted, backside black. Tail bobbed. Stalks and ambushes birds and small mammals. **VOICE** Yowls and screams (though mostly silent). **BREEDING** 2–3 young in May. **SIGN** Tracks in snow at scent posts and scratching trees. Tracks: like domestic cat's, but 2″ vs. 1″. **HABITAT** Forests, thickets, scrub, mtns. **ACTIVITY** Mainly nocturnal, year-round. **RANGE** ID, MT, WY, w, c, and se CO.

Hoofed Mammals

Most hoofed mammals worldwide are in the order Artiodactyla, the even-toed ungulates. (Ungulates are mammals that have hooves, an adaptation for running.) The order Perissodactyla—the odd-toed ungulates: horses, zebras, rhinos, and tapirs—has no extant native species in the United States. The Feral Horses of the Rocky Mountain region are the descendants of introduced domestic horses gone wild.

Even-toed ungulates have a split, two-part hoof (actually two modified toes) and two small dewclaws (vestigial toes) above the hoof on the rear of the leg. Their lower incisors are adapted for nipping or tearing vegetation, their molars for grinding it. Most hastily swallow their food, which is stored temporarily in the first compartment of their four-chambered stomachs before passing to the second stomach, where it is shaped into small pellets of partly digested plant fiber (the cud). While the animal is at rest, the cud is returned to the mouth, slowly chewed to pulp, and swallowed; it then passes through all four chambers of the stomach. This process allows an animal to feed quickly, reducing its exposure to predators, and afterward chew its cud in a concealed spot.

Moose in Grand Tetons

Members of the deer family (Cervidae) have paired bony antlers that grow, usually only on males, in summer, at which time they are soft and tender, and covered with a fine-haired skin ("velvet") containing a network of blood vessels that nourishes the growing bone beneath. By late summer the antlers reach full size, and the velvety skin dries up and peels off. The bare antlers then serve as sexual ornaments; rival males may use them as weapons in courtship battles in fall. As winter nears the antlers fall off. As long as an individual has an adequate diet, its antlers become larger and have more points each year. The Pronghorn, the sole species in its family (Antilocapridae), has permanent short horns, each with one broad, short prong jutting forward (larger in males); the horns develop keratin sheaths that are shed each year. Cattle, goats, and sheep (family Bovidae), including the American Bison, have permanent horns that grow continuously in both sexes.

FERAL HORSE
wild herd

"Mustang"

Equus caballus

HORSE FAMILY

H 4'10"; L 9'; T 30". Identical to its progenitor, the domestic horse. Snout and tail long; hooves large, uncloven. Colors vary: brown, black, gray, and white; mottled, pinto, or plain. Free-roaming herds mostly on Bureau of Land Management lands. Herbivorous. **VOICE** Snorts indicate danger, neighs distress; nickers are for communication and courtship; scream is aggressive call of male. **BREEDING** 1 (rarely 2) young born, usu. in late spring–early fall. **SIGN** Tracks; large semicircle with triangular notch behind. **HABITAT** Semi-desert shrublands, grassy pinyon-juniper woodlands. **ACTIVITY** Day and night, year-round. **RANGE** s ID, w and c MT, WY, w and sc CO.

female and foal

buck

MULE DEER
Odocoileus hemionus
DEER FAMILY

H 3′4″; L 7′; T 8″. Reddish brown in summer, light gray-brown in winter. White muzzle and eye ring contrast with black nose and eyes; ears large, mule-like. Legs slender, buffy. Conspicuous white rump patch around white, black-tipped tail. In summer, buck develops antlers (initially covered in velvety fur): 2 upward-angled beams fork twice into total of 4 points per beam. Juv. spotted. Runs with stiff-legged, bounding gait. In winter, forms small herds of both sexes. **BREEDING** Mates Oct.–Jan.; 1–2 young June–Aug. **SIGN** Browse marks; buck rubs. Tracks: narrow "split hearts": male's 3¼″, female's 2⅝″. **HABITAT** Forests, sagebrush meadows. **ACTIVITY** Day and night, year-round.

bucks in velvet

buck

ELK
"Wapiti"
Cervus elaphus
DEER FAMILY

H 5'; L 9'; T 6". Body pale gray, brown, or tan. Neck thick, chestnut brown; shaggy on buck. Head and muzzle brown; nose black. Summer buck develops large spreading antlers: 2 rear-projecting beams up to 5' long, with 6 upward-projecting points along each beam; sheds antlers in early winter. Legs long, brown; hooves black. Rump and very short tail white. Juv. spotted for 1st 3 months. Moves silently in woods; can run up to 35 mph. Very social; bull herds on fringes of cow/calf herds; combined herd can contain up to 400 animals. "Wapiti" is Shawnee word for "white (or pale) deer." **VOICE** Vocal: bull in fall gives low bellow followed by far-carrying whistle; cow whistles in spring. **BREEDING** Mates Sept.–Nov.; 1–2 young June–July. **SIGN** Bull thrashes saplings and polishes antlers on small tree trunks during rut. Muddy wallows that smell of urine. Tracks: 4½" "split hearts," larger than those of deer; dewclaws behind hooves often print. **HABITAT** Summer: high mtn. pastures. Rest of year: deep forests and grasslands at lower elevs. (esp. where fed). **ACTIVITY** Day and night, year-round. **RANGE** n, c, and e ID, w and sc MT, nw and sc WY, mtns. of w and c CO.

cow and calf

WHITE-TAILED DEER
Odocoileus virginianus
DEER FAMILY

buck

H 3'3"; L 6'; T 12". Rich reddish brown in summer, gray-brown in winter. Neck long; ears large; legs long; tail fairly long. Nose and hooves black. Ring around nose, eye ring, throat, midbelly, and underside of tail white. Summer male develops antlers with main beam curving out and up, points issuing from it. Fawn reddish orange, with many white spots. Top of tail dark in middle, fringed white; flees with tail erect and white underfur exposed. **BREEDING** Mates Oct.–Nov.; 1–2 fawns in late spring; nibble greens at 2–3 weeks; weaned at 4 months. **SIGN** Raggedly browsed vegetation along well-worn trails; buck rubs, where male rubs bark off with antlers; flattened beds in grass or snow. Tracks: 2–3" "split hearts," with narrow, pointed end forward, dots of dewclaws behind. Scat: ¾" cylindrical dark pellets. **HABITAT** Usu. lower country, plains: broadleaf and mixed woods and woodland edges, shrubs, fields, watersides. **ACTIVITY** Day and night, year-round. **RANGE** n, c, and e ID, MT, WY, n and e CO.

doe and fawns

male

CARIBOU
Rangifer tarandus
DEER FAMILY

H 3'8"; L 7'; T 7"; female smaller. Typical deer shape; relative of domestic reindeer of n Eurasia. Body and head brown; neck white, shaggy below; ears small. Legs mainly brown, white just above hooves. Tail short, white below (lacks broad white rump patch of Elk). Male and most females have antlers, with 3 tines per side: 1 forward over muzzle, 1 over ear, 1 backward in rising loop over neck; tines broad and flattened in male, spindly in female; all have many points. **BREEDING** 1 or 2 calves in May–June. **SIGN** Tracks: separated 5" crescents, with dewclaw marks. **HABITAT** Coniferous forests, nearby meadows. **ACTIVITY** Mainly by day, year-round. **RANGE** n ID, far nw MT; rare.

female and fawns

bull shedding velvet

MOOSE
Alces alces
DEER FAMILY

H 7'; L 9'; T 7"; female ⅔ as large as male. Coat long, dark brown; legs long, silvery tinge. Muzzle long, horse-like, with overhanging snout; ears large; large beard (dewlap) on throat (esp. male). High shoulder hump. Tail very short, dark. Summer and fall male sports massive, flattened antlers with many points; usu. 5' wide. Female lacks antlers. Eats water plants (in ponds, when open), herbs; browses leaves, bark, and twigs of broadleaf and coniferous plants. **VOICE** In breeding season (fall rut), both sexes give cow-like moo; male's shorter, rises at end. **BREEDING** 1–2 calves born in May. **SIGN** Raggedly torn shrub branches; wide bed of flattened vegetation; muddy wallows smelling of urine. Scat: oblong, 1¾" long. Tracks: 5–6" cloven hoofprints, with dewclaw print behind. **HABITAT** Spruce and other coniferous woods, broadleaf thickets, swamps, and ponds. **ACTIVITY** Day and night, mainly dawn and dusk, year-round; gather in "yards" in woods during deep snows. **RANGE** n, c, and e ID, w and sc MT, nw WY, nc CO. Some reintroductions elsewhere.

cow and calf

adults

PRONGHORN
"Antelope"
Antilocapra americana
PRONGHORN FAMILY

H 3′4″; L 4′6″; T 4″. Pale reddish tan above, white below. Neck tan with 2 partial white collars; buck has short black mane. Head tan and white; eyes large; ears pointed. Horns black, straight; doe's 3″, male's 6″. Each summer and fall, adult male grows hard sheath another 9″ high that tapers to point and has separate forward prong; is shed in winter. Legs long, tan on outside. Rump white; tail short. Can run at 30 mph for 15 miles, with spurts to 70 mph. Thanks to conservation management, the Pronghorn is more common today than in the early 1900s. **BREEDING** Mates Sept.–Oct.; 1–2 young May–June. **SIGN** Tracks: "split hearts," about 3″. **HABITAT** Lowlands and higher meadows: dry open grasslands with sagebrush and bunchgrass; also prairies east of Rockies. **ACTIVITY** Day and night, year-round. **RANGE** s ID, MT, WY, CO.

doe and fawns

AMERICAN BISON
"Buffalo"

adult

Bos (Bison) bison

CATTLE, GOAT, AND SHEEP FAMILY

H 6′; L 11′; T 18″; female smaller than male. Very heavy foreparts; mainly dark brown; high shoulders to forelegs covered with thick "blanket" of somewhat paler rufous-brown fur. Head massive, dark brown; curly "hairpiece" on crown between 2 fairly short, upward-pointing horns (both sexes); long beard on chin. Long tail has tip with large tuft. Reddish brown 1st summer. Largest surviving land mammal in N. Amer. Once lived in vast herds on plains and in mixed forest and meadow country in mtns. throughout region, ex. n ID and sw CO. Shot nearly to extinction in late 1800s; a few small herds protected by early conservationists. Descendants have been used to restock larger reserves and ranches. **BREEDING** Usu. 1 young in Apr.–May. **SIGN** 10′-wide, 1′-deep muddy or dusty wallows devoid of vegetation. Scat: like familiar "cow chip." Tracks: cloven hearts; rounder and larger than cattle's. **HABITAT** Open rolling prairies; larger mtn. meadows and nearby forests. **ACTIVITY** By day, year-round. **RANGE** Largest free-roaming herds in Yellowstone N.P.; others in protected areas in e ID, MT, WY, and CO.

herd crossing river

male

MOUNTAIN GOAT
Oreamnos americanus
CATTLE, GOAT, AND SHEEP FAMILY

H 3′6″; L 5′; T 6″. Coat entirely white or yellowish white; long and shaggy in winter, shorter in summer. Raised hump at shoulders. Head rectangular; nose wide, black; beard below muzzle; ears pointed. Horns black, thin, dagger-like, with slight backward curl; male's to 12″, female's to 8″. Legs thick; hooves black, sharp on edges, with rubbery soles for traction. Tail short. Amazingly agile in navigating narrowest cliff ledges. Introduced outside normal range (c ID and north). **BREEDING** Mates Nov.–Dec.; 1–2 young May–June. **SIGN** White hair snagged on plants and rocks. Tracks: widely splayed in front; 2½–3½″. **HABITAT** Steep rocky mountainsides; often above tree line, but moves lower in winter. **ACTIVITY** Day and night, year-round. **RANGE** n and c ID, nw MT. Introduced to Absaroka and Teton Mtns. of WY, several CO mtns.

female and young

males

BIGHORN SHEEP
"Mountain Sheep"
Ovis canadensis
CATTLE, GOAT, AND SHEEP FAMILY

H 3′4″; L 5′6″; T 5″. Coat brown; belly whitish. Muzzle whitish; ears small, rounded. Horns brown; male's extremely thick, ridged, curved backward, encircle ear; female's shorter, more slender, form half circle. Neck very thick. Legs sturdy, leading edges black; hooves black, sharp on edges, with rubbery soles for traction on rocks. Rump white; tail dark brown, short. Summer: small segregated herds of 3–5 rams, 5–15 ewes; winter: sexes join in herds of hundreds. Rams have autumn head-butting contests that last up to 20 hours, are audible for miles. **BREEDING** Mates Oct.–Dec.; 1 young May–June. **SIGN** Snagged long brown hair along steep trails. Tracks: splayed 3–3½″ hoof-prints, less pointed than deer's. **HABITAT** Rocky areas, lightly wooded canyons. **ACTIVITY** By day, year-round. **RANGE** ID, w and s MT, WY, w and c CO.

herd

Parks and Preserves

Introduction

The Rocky Mountain states of Colorado, Idaho, Montana, and Wyoming are a region of natural splendor. This vast and varied area of 432,764 square miles features the nation's highest mountains, the largest classified wilderness areas, the largest assortment of free-roaming wildlife, and, like a beating heart at the center of it all, our first and best-known national park.

The highest peaks belong to Colorado. Here, in Rocky Mountain National Park, naturalists can experience firsthand the wonders of alpine tundra, with all of its associated wildlife and flora. Idaho is the place for wild backcountry. The Frank Church River of No Return Wilderness, along with the Selway-Bitterroot Wilderness straddling the Idaho–Montana border, together encompass a remarkable 3.7 million acres of roadless lands filled with deep, rugged canyons, whitewater rivers, and abundant wildlife.

View of Targhee National Forest, Idaho

If the region's mountains offer unmatched vertical worlds, its far-flung plains feature another extreme: horizontal space. Colorado, Montana, and Wyoming all encompass large portions of the Great Plains. At the Charles M. Russell National Wildlife Refuge in Montana, visitors can wander over great tracts of short-grass prairie on high plains that abut the Wild and Scenic portion of the Missouri River; the land here has changed little since Meriwether Lewis and William Clark explored it nearly 200 years ago.

And then there's Yellowstone. Though visitors descend upon the park every year by the millions, its natural integrity remains undiminished. Every species of wildlife native to the area prior to settlement, including the Gray Wolf (a new and flourishing population), lives here today. The incredible assortment of geothermal features at Yellowstone includes more than 200 geysers and 10,000 hot springs, among them the world-famous Old Faithful.

This section of the guide provides introductions to 50 important parks, preserves and other natural areas of the Rocky Mountain region, along with annotated listings of dozens more. Mailing addresses and telephone numbers are given for all the sites (most will send brochures and other information), and driving directions are included for the 50 featured sites. Access is year-round, unless otherwise noted; keep in mind, however, that many of the remote, high-altitude areas become impassable during winter due to heavy snowfall. Because fees and exact hours of operation change frequently, they are not included in the listings.

This guide highlights many of the plants and animals known to inhabit each site, but always ask if local lists of flora and fauna are available, as these are a tremendous aid to identification.

Colorado

The Rocky Mountains zigzag through the west-central portion of Colorado's 104,247 square miles. The range upon range of soaring peaks make this one of the highest regions in North America. More than 54 of Colorado's peaks exceed 14,000 feet, and alpine tundra—a treeless world of ground-hugging mosses, lichens, and mats of wildflowers found above the timberline—is more widely distributed here than in any other state in the region. The expansive forests of Colorado include montane stands of Ponderosa Pine, Douglas Fir, and aspen; higher still are the subalpine forests, moist, dense groves of Engelmann Spruce, Subalpine Fir, and Lodgepole Pine, with wind-battered Bristlecone and Limber Pines occupying exposed ridges and outcrops. Snowfall in the high country is prolific, averaging 200 to 300 inches annually. In spring, the melting snowpack feeds the Colorado, Rio Grande, Yampa, White, and South Platte Rivers, all of which originate in Colorado's high peaks. Snowpack provides an essential water supply, not only for the rest of the state but for much of the arid Southwest as well.

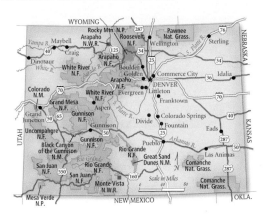

Colorado's natural riches extend far beyond mountains. To the east, in the massive rain shadow of the mountains and covering about one-third of the state, are the western edges of the Great Plains, rolling short- and mid-grass prairies, many of which are now converted to agricultural use. West of the Rockies is the Colorado Plateau—high-desert habitats of shrubs and pinyon-juniper woodlands peppered with eroded canyons and broken foothills. The Wyoming Basin in the state's extreme northwest is a semiarid landscape of sandstone cliffs and bluffs, pinyon-juniper woodlands, and Saltbush and sagebrush shrub lands. Willows and Box Elders grow along the basin's rivers and streams.

Colorado features seven national forests, four national wildlife refuges, three national parks, and 40 state parks, along with many other publicly administered lands.

ROCKY MOUNTAIN NATIONAL PARK

Estes Park

More than one-third of Rocky Mountain National Park's 265,727 acres lie above the tree line and are dominated by tundra. Access to this remote environment is unusually easy here—Trail Ridge Road, the highest paved through-route in the nation, reaches elevations of 12,183 feet and traverses about 11 miles of tundra along its 44-mile length. Pocket gophers, Snowshoe Hares, and the elusive White-tailed Ptarmigans inhabit the tundra during spring, summer, and early fall. During the brief summer, blooms of Alpine Sunflowers, phlox, Alpine Avens, and Moss Campions paint the tundra in vivid colors. Wind is a constant force in these high elevations, continually reshaping the land; gusts in winter of 170 to 200 miles per hour are not uncommon.

View into Forest Canyon from Trail Ridge Road

Sagebrush grasslands, lush meadows, dense subalpine spruce-fir forests, and montane forests of aspen, Ponderosa Pine, and Douglas Fir comprise the park's other major habitats. More than 280 bird species have been recorded, including a pair of Peregrine Falcons that return each year to nest in the northern Mummy Ridge area. Abundant mammals include Bighorn Sheep and Elk, as well as smaller high-country specialists like American Pikas and Yellow-bellied Marmots. Of the park's 147 lakes, only 50 are capable of supporting fish; the rest are rendered sterile by extreme elevations and near-perpetual ice cover. Where possible, native Cutthroat Trout have been reintroduced to streams and lakes.

There are approximately 355 miles of hiking trails, and many of them set off from major roads, making them easy to access. The Old Ute Trail (3.9 miles) begins at Upper Beaver Meadows and leads to Windy Gulch, where a massive hanging valley can be seen, formed by glaciers thousands of years ago. About 3 miles down the trail, there's an outstanding view of 14,255-foot Longs Peak, the highest summit in the park. The 2.3-mile Cub Lake Trail west of Moraine Park traverses meadows and riparian areas; the trail is well known for both its wildflower displays and its many species of birds, including MacGillivray's and Yellow-rumped Warblers, Warbling Vireos, and Western Tanagers. Yellow-bellied Marmots can also be spotted along this trail, and there is usually evidence of Elk. Keep an eye out for the beautiful and rare Wood Lily, which blooms in June and July. Near Estes Park Village, the Gem Lake Trail is a popular 2-mile hike to its namesake lake. The walk begins in aspen forests blanketed with thickets of Chokecherry, passes through pockets of juniper and mountain maple, and enters a mature Ponderosa Pine forest. The resident Abert's (or Tassel-eared) Squirrel is a striking, rabbit-eared squirrel that may be either jet black or gray and white, depending on which "phase" you encounter. Pygmy Nuthatches, Gray-headed Juncos, and Townsend's Solitaires are birds to watch for along the trail. There are also several self-guided interpretive trails, such as the Bear Lake and Sprague Lake trails.

In fall the park's immense Elk herds descend upon Horseshoe Park, Moraine Park, Upper Beaver Meadows, and other areas for their annual mating rites. The greatly agitated males, called bulls, bugle a high, eerie whistle that echoes through the forests. Each bull endeavors to collect a harem of females and to ward off the challenging bugles and displays of other bulls. This remarkable drama may be witnessed at fairly close range, as the animals seem to be oblivious to everything else. Park volunteers from local communities, called the Bugle Brigade, are on hand to direct visitors and interpret the life history of these majestic animals. Various herds totalling about 650 Bighorn Sheep also live in the park. In summer they graze at the highest, most inaccessible spots, amid steep talus slopes, cliff ledges, and cirques. Winter drives them downslope, however, and they can often be seen in the Horseshoe Park and Sheep Lakes areas into early spring.

Rocky Mountain National Park is heavily used. Since 1994, it has received an average of 3 million visitors each year—the same number as Wyoming's much larger Yellowstone National Park. Active research and monitoring of park habitats is in progress to determine, among other things, the effects of Elk browsing in areas used by songbirds for nesting cover. The Colorado Bird Observatory, which conducts bird banding and netting operations at the park during summer, encourages visitors to learn about its projects.

Lodgepole Pines and Aspen

LOCATION Estes Park (east side): north of Boulder, on Hwy. 36. Kawuneeche (west side): north of Gramby, on U.S. 34. **CONTACT** Rocky Mountain N.P., Estes Park, CO 80517; 970-586-1206. **VISITOR CENTERS** Four: headquarters, at Estes Park; Kawuneeche V.C., at Grand Lake; Alpine V.C., at the top of Trail Ridge Rd. (open June–Sept.); Lily Lake V.C., on Hwy. 7 south of Estes Park (open May–Sept.).

MESA VERDE NATIONAL PARK

Mesa Verde

Established in 1906 to preserve a series of pre-Columbian Indian dwellings and ruins, 53,000-acre Mesa Verde (Spanish for "green table") offers a breathtaking sample of the high-desert landscape—steep, twisting canyons, flat-topped mesas, and unforgettable vistas. The more than 4,000 archaeological sites tell a story that began 1,500 years ago, when agricultural people took up residence among the mesas. Their development from basket weavers and farmers to progressively more sophisticated potters,

View into Soda Canyon from Soda Canyon Trail

hunters, and builders can be witnessed in the many cliff dwellings and artifacts preserved here, including Cliff Palace, the largest dwelling. No backpacking or cross-country hiking is allowed in the park; visitors are permitted only to hike around developed areas or on the six designated trails, and access to some trails requires registering at the ranger's office. Cliff dwellings may be entered only with a ranger. All trails, with the exception of the Soda Canyon Overlook Trail, are strenuous and feature significant elevation changes.

Cliff Palace

Mesa Verde averages 12 inches of precipitation a year; average temperatures range from winter lows of –10° F to 0° F to summer highs of 100° F to 105° F. Pinyon-juniper woodland is widespread, with Gambel's Oak, Douglas Fir, and Ponderosa Pine in draws and canyons. Sagebrush, yucca, and rabbitbrush occupy the open areas. Diverse mammals reside in the park, including Desert and Mountain Cottontails, Abert's Squirrels, Ringtails, Mountain Lions, and White-tailed Prairie Dogs. The abundant rodent populations make the region attractive for Golden Eagles, Sharp-shinned Hawks, and rare Peregrine Falcons. Common songbirds include Pinyon Jays, Common Poorwills, Black-headed Grosbeaks, Western Tanagers, scrub jays, and Rufous-sided Towhees. The park's museum patio is a great spot to watch for hummingbirds. Along trails, keep an eye out for short-horned and collared lizards.

LOCATION Midway between Cortez and Mancos, on Hwy. 160. **CONTACT** Mesa Verde N.P., P.O. Box 8, Mesa Verde N.P., CO 81330; 970-529-4475. **VISITOR CENTER** Far View V.C., 15 miles past park entrance; Chapin Mesa Museum and Headquarters, 21 miles past park entrance.

ARAPAHO AND ROOSEVELT NATIONAL FORESTS

Fort Collins

These forest lands encompass north-central Colorado's portion of the Medicine Bow Mountains, as well as the Front and Gore Ranges, and total about 1.3 million acres. There are nine designated wilderness areas. Indian Peaks Wilderness straddles the Continental Divide and is easily accessed via several trails originating along the Peak-to-Peak Scenic Byway. For a motorized tour of the forests, follow the 14-mile Mount Evans Highway, the nation's highest paved road, which climbs from Echo Lake at 10,700 feet to the 14,264-foot summit of Mount Evans. Elk, Bighorn Sheep, Steller's Jays, and Clark's Nutcrackers are a few species that may be seen at any point along the drive. Visitors should be careful about where they stop to view wildlife, as this road is extremely narrow and winding. The 1.1-mile Goliath Summit Trail starts off from the highway and follows a stand of ancient Bristlecone Pines. At the top, another short trail leads along Summit Lake, where summer wildflowers bloom in profusion and American Pipits and Brown-capped

Mountain Golden Pea and aspens, Roosevelt National Forest

Rosy-finches may be sighted near the retreating snowfields. Guanella Pass, which begins in the town of Georgetown, is a 26-mile drive through alpine tundra, with its associated wildlife of American Pikas, Mountain Goats, and Yellow-bellied Marmots.

Downslope, the Laramie River Road is a highly scenic 15-mile auto tour along County Road 103. The willow thickets along the river give way to aspen groves and montane woodlands, which cover the rising slopes on the west side of the road. Pronghorn, Elk, and marmots inhabit the rocky outcrops; Moose, MacGillivray's and Wilson's Warblers, and occasional White-tailed Ptarmigans can also be spotted here. The mountains of the Rawah Wilderness are visible to the west. At its southern terminus, CO 103 meets CO 14; drive east along this

route to look at the Cache la Poudre River; farther along, stop at Big Bend Campground for a superb view of a herd of Bighorn Sheep. The herd inhabits the rugged south-facing slopes on the north side of Poudre Canyon, occasionally descending to the roadsides. Stay within the designated viewing area to avoid disturbing the animals.

White-tailed Ptarmigan

LOCATION Off I-25. **CONTACT** Arapaho and Roosevelt N.F.'s, 1311 S. College Ave., Ft. Collins, CO 80524; 970-498-2770. **VISITOR CENTER** In Ft. Collins.

ARAPAHO NATIONAL WILDLIFE REFUGE

Walden

At 8,100 feet, this is the highest-elevation national refuge in the lower 48 states. The Illinois River, bounded by willow thickets, meanders through the eastern half of the refuge. Elsewhere, irrigated meadows, natural and man-made ponds, wetlands, and sagebrush-grassland uplands sustain a diverse bird population. A half-mile interpretive trail passes through wetland areas, where shorebirds are abundant in all seasons but winter; Wilson's Phalaropes, Willets, American Avocets, Lesser Yellowlegs, and Baird's Sandpipers may be seen here. A 6-mile self-guided auto tour traverses the refuge and allows for birding from vehicles. The uplands shelter Sage Thrashers, Brewer's Sparrows, and Sage Grouse. Gadwalls are the most abundant breeding ducks on the 18,253-acre refuge, but visitors may also spot Lesser Scaups, Cinnamon Teals, American Wigeons, and a few Canvasbacks and Wood Ducks. Northern River Otters, reintroduced elsewhere, have recently moved into the refuge boundaries on the river.

LOCATION South of Walden, on Hwy. 125. **CONTACT** Arapaho N.W.R., P.O. Box 457, Walden, CO 80480; 970-723-8202. **SEASONAL ACCESS** Closed in winter.

WHITE RIVER NATIONAL FOREST

Glenwood Springs

The 2.2-million-acre White River National Forest features eight wilderness areas encompassing 750,000 acres and nearly 2,000 miles of trails. The Bailey Bird Nesting Area, within the Eagles Nest Wilderness, is a rich complex of mountain habitats that support about 43 breeding species, including several species

Hanging Lake

of finches and vireos. Dowd Junction, its steep slopes covered with mountain mahogany, serviceberry, and aspen, provides winter range for several hundred Elk. An especially beautiful sight is the emerald green water of Hanging Lake. The lake was once part of a larger, high-elevation valley, until a portion of it broke away thousands of years ago, leaving today's lake "hanging." It rests in a 500-foot bowl on the dramatic east wall of Deadhorse Creek Canyon. Yeoman Park is a glacial valley encircled by dense subalpine forest and sagebrush on the lower slopes. The area is popular with beavers: Several colonies are active and may be seen early or late in the day.

LOCATION I-70 runs east–west through the forest. **CONTACT** White River N.F., P.O. Box 948, Glenwood Springs, CO 81602; 970-945-2521. **VISITOR CENTER** Headquarters: in Glenwood Springs, on the corner of 9th and Grand.

COLORADO NATIONAL MONUMENT Fruita

Independence Monument

The grand proportions and desert colors of the American West await visitors here, along with an almost overwhelming variety of geologic wonders—towering pedestals, arches and windows, mesas, and sheer-walled canyons in desert hues of purple, gold, and red. Independence Monument is the park's largest freestanding rock formation at 450 feet. Atop the uplifts and open areas are semiarid habitats of pinyon, junipers, mountain mahoganies, and Fishhook Cactuses. This 20,450-acre area is home to some fascinating wildlife, such as Bighorn Sheep, collared lizards, Midget Faded Rattlesnakes, antelope and ground squirrels, Pinyon Jays, and Desert Cottontails. Tucked away in quiet canyons are springs, seeps, and ephemeral streams bordered by cottonwoods and willows, which provide habitat for towhees, warblers, and vireos. Several short, ½- to 2-mile trails lead from Rim Rock Drive, the main road; backcountry trails from 4 to 8½ miles traverse the interior.

LOCATION Southwest of Grand Junction, on Hwy. 340. **CONTACT** Colorado N.M., Fruita, CO 81521; 970-858-3617. **VISITOR CENTER** At park headquarters, off Rim Rock Dr., near the west entrance.

GRAND MESA, GUNNISON, AND UNCOMPAHGRE NATIONAL FORESTS Cedaredge, Delta, Mesa

These forests include in their combined 6.2 million acres more than 70 peaks above 13,000 feet, nine designated wilderness areas, and more than 130 miles of the Continental Divide National Scenic Trail. Grand Mesa is a monolithic, flat-topped mountain spangled with more than 300 alpine lakes. The Crag Crest Trail is a 10-mile loop along the spine of Grand Mesa, with great vistas, areas of geologic interest, and opportunities for sighting Golden Eagles among the cliffs and outcrops. In the Gunnison, Almont Triangle is a prime wintering site for Elk and Bighorn Sheep. In the Uncompahgre, the Montrose-Ouray scenic drive follows the cottonwood-lined Uncompahgre River, amid pinyon-juniper woodlands and ranch lands. The Telephone Trail passes through a mixture of old-growth aspens and Ponderosa Pines, attractive habitat for Red-naped and Williamson's Sapsuckers, nuthatches, and Flammulated and pygmy-owls.

Lupines, Grand Mesa

LOCATION North of Delta, off Hwy. 50; in Mesa, on Hwy. 65. **CONTACT** Grand Mesa, Uncompahgre, and Gunnison N.F.s, 2250 Hwy. 50, Delta, CO 81416; 970-874-6600. **VISITOR CENTER** In Grand Mesa N.F., on Hwy. 65 (during winter, open weekends only).

BLACK CANYON OF THE GUNNISON NATIONAL MONUMENT

Montrose

An archetypal gorge with walls rising over 2,000 feet, this jagged, site encompasses 12 miles of a 53-mile-long canyon carved over 2 million years by the relentless erosive action of the Gunnison River. The river descends an average of 95 feet per mile, making this one of the steepest gorges in North America. Shrub lands of serviceberry and Gambel's Oak are cut with side canyons forested with Douglas Fir and some aspens. There is fine birding in the area. The Warner Point Trail may yield sightings of Ruby-crowned Kinglets, Cooper's Hawks, and a soaring Golden Eagle. White-throated Swifts, Broad-tailed Hummingbirds, scrub jays, Green-tailed Towhees, and rare Peregrine Falcons make their homes here along the canyon cliffs. Mule Deer, porcupines, badgers, Bobcats, and marmots are resident mammals. Hardy individuals can obtain a backcountry permit and hike into the canyon to explore along the river.

LOCATION 15 miles east of Montrose, on U.S. 50 and CO 347. **CONTACT** Black Canyon of the Gunnison N.M., 102 Elk Creek, Gunnison, CO 81230; 970-641-2337. **VISITOR CENTER** Off South Rim Rd. at Gunnison Pt. (970-249-1914).

SAN JUAN–RIO GRANDE NATIONAL FOREST

Durango

Unparalleled high-country grandeur, and diverse opportunities for exploration make the 2-million-acre San Juan–Rio Grande National Forest a southwestern Colorado gem. The forest includes three wilderness areas and more than 1,000 miles of trails. The 55-mile Dolores River Canyon is a mixture of private and public lands; Bighorn Sheep inhabit the steep lower portions of the canyon. Priest Lakes, south of Telluride, feature a meadow-and-riparian complex of willows and sedges, with beaver ponds along the Lake Fork of the

Parry's Primroses, San Juan National Forest

San Miguel River. The San Juan Skyway is a scenic byway with magnificent vistas. The 0.7-mile Animas Overlook Interpretive Trail leads through montane and subalpine forests with views of the Animas River below. The Chimney Rock archaeological site preserves ruins of the Chacoan Anasazi culture; its more than 3,000 acres are home to a number of reptiles, including Short-horned and fence lizards.

LOCATION In Durango and Monte Vista. **CONTACT** San Juan–Rio Grande N.F., 701 Camino del Rio, Durango, CO 81301; 970-247-4874. **VISITOR CENTER** In Durango, at 701 Camino del Rio; in Monte Vista, at 1803 W. Hwy. 160.

MONTE VISTA NATIONAL WILDLIFE REFUGE

Alamosa

Whooping Crane and Sandhill Cranes

The Rio Grande meanders through the arid San Luis Valley, historically an area of Greasewoods and semiarid shrub lands and grasslands. The 14,000-acre Monte Vista National Wildlife Refuge offers the rare commodity of water, much of it in the form of man-made ponds and marshes. Fall migrations can bring as many as 35,000 ducks to Monte Vista; 20 different species have been recorded here, along with swans, egrets, songbirds, and four species of geese. In early spring, the refuge hosts migrating Sandhill Cranes, and with them, a few extremely rare Whooping Cranes. Nearby are several other notable wildlife areas. The Rio Grande State Wildlife Area's dense willow and cottonwood bottoms along the river attract swallows, creepers, warblers, and waterfowl. The San Luis Lakes State Wildlife Area is inhabited by American Bitterns, Black-crowned Night-Herons, and Snowy Plovers. At the Blanca Wildlife Habitat Area, water flows are manipulated in winter to attract Bald Eagles.

LOCATION South of Monte Vista, on Hwy. 15. **CONTACT** Monte Vista N.W.R., 9383 El Rancho La., Alamosa, CO 81101; 719-589-4021. **VISITOR CENTER** At park headquarters, on El Rancho La.

GREAT SAND DUNES NATIONAL MONUMENT

Mosca

When the Rio Grande changed its course thousands of years ago, it left behind in the old river channel vast deposits of sand and sediment. Winds blowing northeast across the San Luis Valley carried these deposits to the base of the Sangre de Cristo Mountains, forming 39 square miles of sand dunes. These are the tallest dunes in North America, rising 750 feet above the plains. As dunes go, they are very stable, because of moisture from rain and snow. While the dunes themselves support little vegetation, they are closely surrounded by a diversity of habitats, including remnant short-grass prairies, pinyon-juniper woodlands, and shrub lands of rabbitbrush. Cottonwoods and aspens line washes that come alive with spring snowmelt. Kangaroo rats, Golden-mantled Ground Squirrels, Mule Deer, and Pronghorn are common mammals. A nearby site worth visiting is the ghost forest, where Ponderosa Pines, which were interred and killed as the dunes formed, still stand today.

LOCATION Northeast of Alamosa, on Hwy. 150. **CONTACT** Great Sand Dunes N.M., 11999 Hwy. 150, Mosca, CO 81146-9798; 719-378-2312. **VISITOR CENTER** About 0.75 miles past park entrance.

PAWNEE NATIONAL GRASSLAND   Greeley

Chestnut-collared Longspur

Eastern Colorado was grassland prior to settlement by pioneers. This preserve—even though it spans more than 193,000 acres—is but a small remnant of that vast expanse. Much of the wildlife here exists at ground level or lower. Short-horned Lizards, Bullsnakes, fence lizards, and Western Rattlesnakes make their homes in underground burrows or beneath rocks. Prairie dogs, jackrabbits, and nocturnal kangaroo rats may also be seen. A first-rate birding area with more than 200 recorded species, the grassland features a 36-mile auto tour beginning at Crow Valley Recreation Area. The tour takes 3 to 4½ hours to complete, traversing open prairie and several riparian zones, including Box Elder–willow habitat at Crow Valley Campground. In the grasslands, watch for Chestnut-collared and McCown's Longspurs, Long-billed Curlews, Burrowing Owls, and beautiful Lark Buntings, Colorado's state bird. Orioles, flycatchers, and kingbirds favor the riparian areas. Pawnee Buttes, twin sentinels standing 250 feet tall, preside over this beautiful expanse.

LOCATION Northeast of Greeley, on Hwy. 14. **CONTACT** Pawnee N.G., 660 "O" St., Greeley, CO 80631; 970-353-5004.

COMANCHE NATIONAL GRASSLAND   Springfield

A visit here dispels the notion of prairie as a vast carpet of grass and little else. Comanche includes in its 435,000 acres mesas, steep canyons, marshes, and cottonwood-lined creeks and ponds, as well as short- and midgrass prairies with native Sand Sage and yucca. Approximately 235 bird species may be spotted, including Greater Roadrunners, Yellow-billed Cuckoos, Short-eared Owls, and Scaled Quails. The Lesser Prairie Chicken, a threatened species, performs its spring courtship ritual here. Males arrive in early March; their dance craze begins when the females arrive a few weeks later. There is a viewing blind, available on a reservation basis, along with parking areas for viewing from vehicles. Forty species of reptiles inhabit the grassland, as well as 60 different species of mammals, including Kit Foxes, Ord's Kangaroo Rats, and the rare Black-footed Ferrets. The area's human history is equally varied and fascinating, with Indian petroglyphs and tepee rings, and remains of old pioneer homesteads.

LOCATION South of Springfield, on Hwy. 287. **CONTACT** Comanche N.G., 27162 Hwy. 287, P.O. Box 127, Springfield, CO 81073; 719-523-6591. **VISITOR CENTER** At main entrance.

ADOBE CREEK RESERVOIR STATE WILDLIFE AREA   Las Animas

Excellent birding exists at this more than 5,000-acre preserve of shortgrass prairie and lake. Grassland species occur in the uplands; the reservoir draws Sandhill Cranes, American White Pelicans, and an occasional Peregrine Falcon. **CONTACT** Adobe Creek Reservoir S.W.A., CO Div. of Wildlife, 1204 E. Olive, Lamar, CO 81052; 719-336-4852.

BEAR CREEK REGIONAL PARK   Colorado Springs

Hike through the Gambel's Oaks, yuccas, and native grasses of this 1,235-acre park, home to Box Turtles, Goshawks, and Rock Squirrels. The nature center has interpretive exhibits and naturalists on staff. **CONTACT** Bear Creek R.P., El Paso Cty. Parks, 2002 Creek Crossing, Colorado Springs, CO 80906; 719-520-6375.

BONNY LAKE STATE PARK/SOUTH REPUBLICAN RIVER STATE WILDLIFE AREA   Idalia

These are two separate but adjoining sites encompassing more than 24,000 acres. The area hosts an impressive list of water-associated birds, including loons, Black Terns, and Tundra Swans. Deer, beavers, and muskrats inhabit the beautiful cottonwood-willow woods that surround the reservoir and river. **CONTACT** Bonny Lake S.P. and S. Republican River S.W.A., 30010 Cty. Rd. 3, Idalia, CO 80735; 970-354-7306.

Green River, Browns Park N.W.R.

BROWNS PARK NATIONAL WILDLIFE REFUGE   Maybell

This more than 13,000-acre refuge along the Green River is characterized by alluvial benches, wet meadows, numerous ponds, and steep, rocky slopes. Wildlife include many species of waterfowl, as well as Bald Eagles and prairie dogs. **CONTACT** Browns Park N.W.R., 1318 Hwy. 318, Maybell, CO 81640; 970-365-3613.

CASTLEWOOD CANYON STATE PARK   Franktown

A beautiful, steep-sided canyon carved by Cherry Creek is the main attraction at this 1,000-acre park; this is the site of a rare "dry heronry," where Great Blue Herons nest in pine trees. **CONTACT** Castlewood Canyon S.P., P.O. Box 504, Franktown, CO 80116; 303-688-5242.

CHATFIELD STATE PARK   Littleton

This 5,600-acre park is a meeting place of prairie and mountain foothills, with the South Platte River and two creeks running through the area. Mule Deer and beavers are abundant; there are blinds and spotting scopes trained on a heron rookery. **CONTACT** Chatfield S.P., 11500 N. Roxborough Park Rd., Littleton, CO 80125; 303-791-7275.

COLORADO SPRINGS STATE WILDLIFE AREA   Fountain

Visit "Woodpecker Meadow" to see five different species; a 1.75-mile nature trail with boardwalks traverses Fountain Creek. Coyotes, Red Foxes, Common Raccoons, and White-tailed Deer, as well as several raptor species, inhabit the 3,900-acre area. **CONTACT** Colorado Springs S.W.A., P.O. Box 614, Fountain, CO 80817; 719-382-5060.

DINOSAUR NATIONAL MONUMENT   Dinosaur

This 220,000-acre park spans the Colorado–Utah border. In Utah, the Dinosaur Quarry (435-789-2115) contains fossilized dinosaur bones from the late Jurassic period. On the Colorado side, the Harpers Corner Scenic Drive climbs to an elevation of 1,700 feet and provides spectacular views of the park's canyon country. **CONTACT** Dinosaur N.M., 4545 Hwy. 40, Dinosaur, CO 81610; 970-374-3000.

ELK MEADOW COUNTY PARK   Evergreen

Mountain habitats of open meadows, aspen groves, and pine woodlands shelter Elk, Mule Deer, and the captivating Abert's Squirrels. Well-marked hiking trails crisscross the 1,140-acre park. There are outstanding spring wildflower displays. **CONTACT** Jefferson Cty. Open Space, 700 Jefferson Cty. Pkwy., Suite 100, Golden, CO 80401; 303-271-5925.

GOLDEN GATE CANYON STATE PARK   Golden

This park's 14,000 acres of mountain foothills and slopes of conifers and aspens traverse elevations of 7,600 to 10,400 feet. Deer and Elk are often encountered here. Panorama Point offers scenic views that extend for nearly 100 miles along the Front Range. **CONTACT** Golden Gate Canyon S.P., 3873 Hwy. 46, Golden, CO 80403; 303-582-3707.

HAMILTON RESERVOIR   Wellington

A 500-acre site with some notable raptor and waterfowl species: Merlins, Peregrine Falcons, and Bald Eagles are the hunters; Common Loons, Clark's Grebes, Oldsquaws, and Surf and White-winged Scoters are the prey. A small herd of American Bison graze the prairie. **CONTACT** Platte River Power Authority, 2000 E. Horse Tooth Rd., Ft. Collins, CO 80525; 970-226-4000.

MESA TRAIL   Boulder, Marshall

This nearly 7-mile trail passes through a varied mix of plant communities, from thickets of hawthorns and Chokecherries, to junipers, and into Ponderosa Pine–Douglas Fir woodlands interspersed with canyons. **CONTACT** City of Boulder Open Space Dept., P.O. Box 791, Boulder, CO 80306; 303-441-3440.

MUELLER STATE PARK   Divide

There are 80 miles of hiking trails in this 12,103-acre park, with spectacular views of Pikes Peak and the Sangre de Cristo Mountains. Bighorn Sheep are commonly seen here in winter. There are ranger-led hikes and a visitor center with interpretive exhibits. **CONTACT** Mueller S.P., P.O. Box 49, Divide, CO 80814; 719-687-2366.

PUEBLO GREENWAY   Pueblo

Just outside of town, this developed site offers live animal exhibits, a nature center, and an on-duty naturalist. A paved, 3-mile path leads from the nature center along the cottonwood bottoms of the Arkansas River. **CONTACT** Greenway and Nature Center, 5200 Nature Ctr. Rd., Pueblo, CO 81003; 719-549-2414.

ROCKY MOUNTAIN ARSENAL
NATIONAL WILDLIFE REFUGE   Commerce City

This is a premier urban wildlife experience on the fringes of Denver. Access is restricted to guided tours; the 17,000 acres of ponds, lakes, and grasslands support a wide array of mammals, reptiles, amphibians, and birds. **CONTACT** Rocky Mtn. Arsenal N.W.R., Building 613, Commerce City, CO 80022; 303-289-0232.

SAND WASH BASIN   Maybell, Craig

A dramatic 100,000-acre expanse of sagebrush and salt-desert shrubs bounded by juniper-covered bluffs, this basin is inhabited by Pronghorn, Golden Eagles, and prairie dogs. County roads are passable in dry weather only. **CONTACT** Bureau of Land Management, 455 Emmerson, Craig, CO 81625; 970-826-5000.

TAMARACK RANCH STATE WILDLIFE AREA   Crook, Sterling

This 10,500-acre site includes nearly 20 miles of the South Platte River, with bottomlands, crop fields, and sandhills. Endangered Greater Prairie Chickens were recently reintroduced here. **CONTACT** Colorado Div. of Wildlife, P.O. Box 128, Brush, CO 80723; 970-842-3124.

Idaho

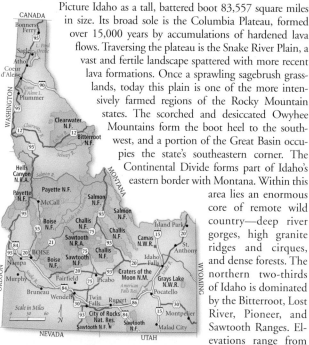

Picture Idaho as a tall, battered boot 83,557 square miles in size. Its broad sole is the Columbia Plateau, formed over 15,000 years by accumulations of hardened lava flows. Traversing the plateau is the Snake River Plain, a vast and fertile landscape spattered with more recent lava formations. Once a sprawling sagebrush grasslands, today this plain is one of the more intensively farmed regions of the Rocky Mountain states. The scorched and desiccated Owyhee Mountains form the boot heel to the southwest, and a portion of the Great Basin occupies the state's southeastern corner. The Continental Divide forms part of Idaho's eastern border with Montana. Within this area lies an enormous core of remote wild country—deep river gorges, high granite ridges and cirques, and dense forests. The northern two-thirds of Idaho is dominated by the Bitterroot, Lost River, Pioneer, and Sawtooth Ranges. Elevations range from 710 feet on the Snake River Plain near Lewiston, to 12,662 feet at the summit of Borah Peak in the Lost River Range.

Coniferous forests blanket about 45 percent of Idaho; Douglas Fir and Lodgepole and Ponderosa Pine occur in mixed or single-species stands at lower and mid-elevations, with Engelmann Spruce, Grand and Subalpine Fir, and scattered Whitebark and Limber Pine occupying elevations from 8,000 feet upward to the timberline. Dry south-facing ridges and hills are the province of bunchgrasses and shrubs; sagebrush grasslands are widespread across the valley floors and mountain foothills. A richly varied inland maritime forest blankets much of the panhandle region, fed by moist air from the Pacific Ocean.

The abundant high mountains deliver snowmelt to some of the nation's largest, wildest rivers. Portions of seven rivers in Idaho are classified as wild or scenic, or both: the Salmon, Snake, Selway, Middle Fork of the Clearwater, Rapid, Middle Fork of the Salmon, and the Lochsa. Dozens of other major rivers tumble or roar through the state as well. Several immense deep glacial lakes are found in the panhandle region, including Lake Pend Oreille and Coeur d'Alene; many thousands of crystalline alpine lakes occur throughout the high country.

Idaho has 13 national forests, seven national wildlife refuges, two major national recreation areas, and 22 state parks.

IDAHO'S NATIONAL FORESTS

National forest lands account for a whopping 38 percent of Idaho's total land mass. Central Idaho is the core of these lands, some of the wildest country remaining in the lower 48 states, including the 2.2-million-acre Frank Church River of No Return Wilderness, the largest wilderness area in the lower 48 states. This is rugged terrain—often steep and broken, with dense coniferous forests, high meadows, and jagged granite peaks. Abundant wildlife, rampaging rivers, and some of the continent's deepest, most remote canyons can be found here. The featured forests below begin in the southwestern portion of the state and zigzag northward.

Ponderosa Pines, Boise Mountains, Boise National Forest

BOISE NATIONAL FOREST   Boise

This 2.6-million-acre forest lies within an area shaped by eons of faulting, uplifting, and the crosscutting action of rivers. The Boise and Payette Rivers flow here, as well as the South and Middle Forks of the Salmon River (discussed separately below). The Trinity Recreation Area includes a 4-mile trail from Trinity Lake into Rainbow Basin, a subalpine haven at 8,500 feet, where nine cirque lakes are bounded by rugged granite headwalls and toothy ridges. The subalpine forests are interspersed with open areas of sagebrush grasslands. Numerous natural hot springs dot the area in the forest's central portion surrounding the town of Lowman, accessible by short hikes or cross-country ski treks.

LOCATION North of Boise, on Hwys. 55, 21, and 20. **CONTACT** Boise N.F., 1249 S. Vinnell Way, Suite 200, Boise, ID 93709; 208-373-4100. **VISITOR CENTER** In Boise, at 1249 S. Vinnell Way.

SAWTOOTH NATIONAL FOREST   Twin Falls

The best-known components of the 1.3-million-acre Sawtooth National Forest are the Sawtooth National Recreation Area (see entry below) and the adjacent Saw-

tooth Wilderness. This forest encompasses the Pioneer Mountains, among Idaho's tallest and most rugged mountain ranges, which includes 12,009-foot Hyndman Peak. Talus slopes, cirque basins, and high-country lakes blanket the Pioneers, along with a dense mixed coniferous forest. One-third of Idaho's Mountain Goat population resides in this national forest.

View of the Pioneer Mountains

LOCATION The forest can be accessed north of Twin Falls, on Hwys. 93 and 75; south of Twin Falls, on Hwy. 30; and northwest of Twin Falls, off I-84. **CONTACT** Sawtooth N.F., 2647 Kimberly Rd. East, Twin Falls, ID 83301; 208-737-3200. **VISITOR CENTER** Headquarters: in Twin Falls, at 2647 Kimberly Rd. East.

PAYETTE NATIONAL FOREST   McCall

The main body of this remote and rugged 2.3-million-acre forest lies within the Salmon Mountains. Powerful rivers bound the Payette on three sides: the Salmon to the north, the Snake to the west, and the Middle Fork of the Salmon to the east. Habitats range from riparian to high mountain meadows and subalpine forests. The Salmon River gorge is second only to Hells Canyon as the deepest in the lower 48 states, and the best way to experience it is by a commercial or self-guided rafting trip. The Payette administers nearly 800,000 acres of the Frank Church River of No Return Wilderness, as well as about 24,000 acres of the Hells Canyon Wilderness. In addition to these blocks of wild country, there are approximately 650,000 acres of roadless land.

LOCATION West of McCall, off Hwy. 55. **CONTACT** Payette N.F., P.O. Box 1026, McCall, ID 83638; 208-634-0400. **VISITOR CENTER** The McCall Ranger District is located at 102 West Lake Rd.

BITTERROOT NATIONAL FOREST   Hamilton, MT

The Bitterroot National Forest covers 1.6 million acres of Idaho and Montana and includes the Selway–Bitterroot Wilderness, at 1.3 million acres the second-largest wilderness in the lower 48. Careening through its heart is the Wild and Scenic Selway River, about 20 miles of which are accessible to motorists and day hikers.

Bitterroot Mountains, Selway–Bitterroot Wilderness

Elk, Moose, and Northern River Otters inhabit the fragrant cedar forests carpeted with ferns and mosses. The 1.5-mile O'Hara Interpretive Trail follows the Selway a short distance before climbing into the forest. In general, forest lands are a mixture of grasslands, with Douglas Firs and Lodgepole and Ponderosa Pines below about 6,800 feet, and larches and Subalpine Firs on moister slopes. Wildflowers are widespread and diverse; visit the Bitterroot Wildflower Area near Woodside for a terrific sampling. There are 1,600 miles of hiking trails in the forest.

LOCATION South of Missoula, on Hwy. 93. **CONTACT** Bitterroot N.F., 1801 N. First, Hamilton, MT 59840; 406-363-3131. **VISITOR CENTER** Main headquarters: in Hamilton, at 1801 N. First.

SALMON–CHALLIS NATIONAL FOREST   Salmon

Mount Borah

These forests encompass more than 4.3 million acres. Lower elevations are predominantly sagebrush grasslands, with Douglas Fir, Lodgepole Pine, and Subalpine Fir ascending the slopes. Mount Borah, Idaho's highest peak at 12,662 feet, crowns the Lost River Range in the Challis forest.

From the town of Challis, follow Highway 93 along the Salmon River to the town of North Fork, where the river swings west to enter its Wild and Scenic corridor. Forest Road 030, also called the Salmon River Road, begins in North Fork and winds 44 miles along the river, ending at Corn Creek. Bighorn Sheep, Northern River Otters, and Bald Eagles are common wildlife along this spectacular drive. The Custer Motorway Loop begins west of Challis and follows Forest Road 070 to the Yankee Fork District, where elevations climb from 1,000 to 10,000 feet through alpine lakes, cirque basins, and numerous streams. Two abandoned mining towns and the Yankee Dredge exhibit provide a glimpse of the area's human history.

LOCATION South of Salmon, on Hwy. 93. **CONTACT** Salmon–Challis N.F., R.R. 2 Box 600, Hwy. 93 South, Salmon, ID 83467; 208-756-5100. **VISITOR CENTER** Headquarters: in Salmon, on Hwy. 93.

MIDDLE FORK, SALMON RIVER — Challis

Ponderosa Pines along Middle Fork of Salmon River

The Salmon was originally named "River of No Return" by early explorers, who considered its upper reaches unnavigable. Its Middle Fork, a Wild and Scenic river for 104 miles, is every bit as treacherous and beautiful. The Middle Fork begins in the southeastern corner of the Frank Church River of No Return Wilderness, then flows north through the heart of the wilderness, joining the main Salmon River on its final run to the Snake. A 1-mile stretch of road near Dagger Falls offers the only motorized access. Rafting is the best way to experience the wildlife and scenic wonders of this river; permits are issued to qualified individuals, and a number of licensed commercial outfitters offer overnight trips. For information on rafting trips, call the North Fork Ranger District in the town of North Fork (208-865-2383).

LOCATION West of Stanley, off Bear Valley Rd. Launch site is at Boundary Creek. **CONTACT** Middle Fork Ranger District, P.O. Box 750, Hwy. 93, Challis, ID 83226; 208-879-4101.

CLEARWATER NATIONAL FOREST — Orofino

Hawthorns, Middle Fork of Clearwater River

Densely forested with cedars, hemlocks, Western Larches, and other coniferous trees, the lands in this 1.8-million-acre forest lift and plunge in a series of deep drainages and high-backed ridges. The Lochsa River, along with the Middle and North Forks of the Clearwater River, traverse the region. Follow the Lolo Motorway and the Lewis and Clark National Historic Trail, which extend for 100 miles, tracing the path used for hundreds of years by Indians, gold miners, and settlers alike. East of Potlatch, the scenic White Pine Drive passes through a remnant stand of Western White Pines, the predominant tree species in north-central Idaho before they were depleted by disease and logging. The Mallard–Larkin Pioneer area near Orofino offers 30,000 acres of superb backcountry; the Heritage Cedar Grove of ancient cedars lies at its southern edge.

LOCATION West of Orofino, on Hwy. 12. **CONTACT** Clearwater N.F., 12730 Hwy. 12, Orofino, ID 83544; 208-476-4541. **VISITOR CENTER** In Orofino, on Hwy. 12 at mile marker 40.

HELLS CANYON NATIONAL
RECREATION AREA   Riggins

Few parts of this 650,000-acre area are easily accessible to casual visitors; those who invest the time and effort required, however, are richly rewarded. The centerpiece of this dramatic and varied landscape is the Snake River, designated Wild and Scenic for 70 miles, pulsing through a gorge of approximately 8,000 vertical feet. The Oregon side of the gorge features steep walls and a series of broad, open benches; on the Idaho side the canyon walls are sheer and unyielding. Once past Hells Canyon Dam, the river flows freely for 100 miles. The drastic elevation changes create tremendous habitat diversity here, from the often-scorching canyon floor, with its riparian zones of Hackberries, White Alders, Chokecherries, and Water Birches, through mid-elevation areas of bunchgrasses and Ponderosa Pines, all the way to the alpine peaks of Seven Devils Mountains, which at more than 9,300 feet are often snowcapped into July.

Seven Devils Mountains

The 249 recorded bird species attest to this great habitat diversity. Raptors are varied and abundant—Bald Eagles congregate in the riverside trees in winter; Golden Eagles, Prairie Falcons, American Kestrels, Red-tailed Hawks, and an occasional Peregrine Falcon use the gorge for roosting or nesting, and hunt the adjacent open lands. Bighorn Sheep and numerous bat species (including the uncommon Townsend's Big-eared Bat) also inhabit the area.

A number of hiking trails wind through the Seven Devils area among 30 alpine lakes. Mountain Goats are a primary attraction in summer and early fall; brilliant wildflower displays of Indian Paintbrushes, trilliums, Trout Lilies, and Rocky Mountain Irises color the area in July. Up here it's possible to see Columbian Ground Squirrels, American Pikas, Golden Eagles, and evidence of Black Bears; the rare and secretive Lynx also inhabits the area, as does the Wolverine. Bald Eagles, Elk, Bighorn Sheep, and Mule Deer concentrate along the river in winter.

The river may be explored by foot, commercial raft trip, or jetboat tour; contact the Forest Service ranger station in Riggins (208-628-3916) for more information on boating. A trail from Pittsburg Landing follows the river for 31 miles. South of Riggins, Forest Road 517 ascends more than 6,000 feet to the popular Heaven's Gate Lookout and the Seven Devils area.

LOCATION On the south edge of Riggins, on Hwy. 95. **CONTACT** Hells Canyon N.R.A., P.O. Box 832, Riggins, ID 83549; 208-628-3916. **VISITOR CENTER** On Hwy. 95.

SAWTOOTH NATIONAL RECREATION AREA

Ketchum

Sawtooth Lake, Sawtooth Wilderness

The highly accessible Sawtooth Valley offers 756,000 acres of splendid scenery and varied natural habitats. The valley is bounded by three mountain ranges, with more than 50 of the surrounding peaks over 10,000 feet. Nestled in the high country amid open meadows and subalpine forests are more than 1,000 lakes. Approximately 750 miles of hiking trails provide many excellent day-hike possibilities. To visit, follow the Sawtooth Scenic Route, which parallels Big Wood River before climbing Galena Summit, then descends into the basin and heads north along the Salmon River. The area's recreation opportunities guide (ROG) gives detailed information about major hiking trails. Valley lands are sagebrush grasslands with beautiful early-summer wildflower displays of Fireweeds, Arrowleaf Balsam-roots, cinquefoils, and lupines; Sandhill Cranes and Savannah Sparrows occupy the meadows in spring and early summer. Bordering the valley is a mixed forest of Lodgepole Pine, Douglas Fir, and aspen, which continues into the subalpine area, interspersed with Whitebark and Limber Pines. Limited alpine habitat exists above 10,000 feet, consisting of low shrubs and dense wildflower mats. Timbered habitats shelter such birds as Cassin's Finches, Hermit Thrushes, and Black-backed and Three-toed Woodpeckers.

The area's six largest lakes are accessible by car. At Redfish Lake, a boardwalk/nature trail departs the visitor center and passes through river otter and beaver habitats, with several active dams in evidence on Redfish Lake Creek. The lake is the spawning ground for a dwindling run of the only remaining Pacific Sockeye Salmon in Idaho. Common mammals include Yellow-pine Chipmunks, marmots, and Mule Deer; seldom seen are Northern Flying Squirrels, Pine Martens, Long-tailed Weasels, Bushy-tailed Woodrats, and Wolverines.

The adjacent 217,000-acre Sawtooth Wilderness includes mountain meadows, glaciated valleys and basins, and alpine lakes.

LOCATION North of Ketchum, on Hwy. 75. **CONTACT** Sawtooth N.R.A., Star Route, Ketchum, ID 83340; 208-727-5000. **VISITOR CENTER** At entrance.

CITY OF ROCKS NATIONAL RESERVE

Almo

Twin Sisters

Fantastic spires and sheer cliffs of eroded granite soar from the valley floor of this 14,400-acre reserve, among them the Twin Sisters, a well-known landmark along the California Trail during the mid-1800s. Some of the granite dates back 2.5 billion years, making it among the oldest exposed rock on the continent. Birding is a rewarding activity here. The pinyon-juniper woodlands and sagebrush grasslands, more representative of areas farther south, offer bird species not usually found in Idaho, including Green-tailed Towhees, Pinyon Jays, and Western Scrub Jays. Watch for Pinyon Jays noisily combing the woodlands for pinyon nuts, their favorite food. Other birds here include Say's Phoebes, Black-chinned Hummingbirds, Canyon and Rock Wrens, Townsend's Solitaires, White-throated Swifts, Juniper Titmice, and Red-naped Sapsuckers.

LOCATION South of Burley, off Hwy. 77. **CONTACT** City of Rocks N.R., P.O. Box 169, Almo, ID 83312; 208-824-5519. **VISITOR CENTER** In Almo, at 3010 Elba-Almo Rd.

CRATERS OF THE MOON NATIONAL MONUMENT

Arco

Limber Pines growing on a cinder cone

Just 2,000 years ago, molten lava still flowed along the Snake River Plain. A visit to Craters of the Moon National Monument offers a close-up look at a portion of one 643-square-mile flow. The eerie volcanic landscapes, basalt formations, and lava tubes attest to the region's dynamic, often violent origins. While the newest lava flows are bereft of vegetation, scattered ancient cinder cones are blanketed in sagebrush, rabbitbrush, and bunchgrasses, with hardy Limber Pines growing in seemingly impossible areas. Visitors in June are treated to spectacular wildflower shows of desert parsleys, cinquefoils, bitterroots, and monkeyflowers. Birds such as Violet-green Swallows, Great Horned Owls, and Common Ravens have taken to nesting near the openings of lava tube caves. Numerous reptiles, including Mojave Black-collared Lizards, Sagebrush Lizards, Gopher Snakes, and Western Rattlesnakes bask on the rocky terrain. Follow the 7-mile loop road (open May to October) around the area; several foot trails lead from the road to various sites worth visiting, such as Devils Orchard, Inferno Cone, and the cave area.

LOCATION South of Arco, on Hwy. 20. **CONTACT** Craters of the Moon N.M., P.O. Box 29, Arco, ID 83213; 208-527-3257. **VISITOR CENTER** At entrance.

CAMAS NATIONAL WILDLIFE REFUGE   Hamer

This 10,578-acre refuge is a mosaic of ponds and wetlands, with up-land areas of sagebrush grasslands interspersed with stands of cottonwoods and agricultural fields. A good mixture of waterfowl, both migrant and breeding species, resides here; during peak migration periods (March to April and October to November), as many as 100,000 ducks and 3,000 geese stop over. Northern Pintails, Gadwalls, Canada Geese, teals, and scaups are a few of the species present. During summer, Mallards, Redheads, Northern Shovelers, and Cinnamon Teals raise their broods. The refuge also hosts a breeding population of rare Trumpeter Swans. Other species to watch for include White-faced Ibises, American Bitterns,

Trumpeter Swan

Snowy Egrets, and Great Blue Herons. During summer, a lucky visitor may come upon a Peregrine Falcon, reintroduced here in 1983. Look for Moose browsing the willows along Camas Creek, which flows for 8 miles through the refuge.

LOCATION North of Idaho Falls, off I-15. **CONTACT** Camas N.W.R., 2150 E. 2350 North, Hamer, ID 83425; 208-662-5423.

GRAYS LAKE NATIONAL
WILDLIFE REFUGE   Wayan

Not so much a lake as an expanse of shallow marsh with thick stands of cattail-bulrush vegetation, Grays Lake is home to the world's largest breeding population of Sandhill Cranes. The 18,300-acre refuge has also served as a reintroduction site for endangered Whooping Cranes, whose eggs are hatched by Sandhill

Crane foster parents. A gravel road circles the lake and provides the best viewing; interior areas of the refuge are closed during summer to minimize disturbance for nesting birds. Visitors should stop by refuge headquarters and climb the adjacent observation platform for an excellent view of the refuge, with 9,803-foot Caribou Mountain forming a lovely backdrop; a spotting scope and educational displays are available on the platform. The refuge hums with activity in May and June. Shorebirds such as Wilson's Phalaropes, Common Snipes, Long-billed Curlews, and Willets probe the shallow waters and mudflats for food; Franklin's Gulls nest in great raucous colonies that may number 40,000. Large numbers of Canada Geese also nest here, and visitors are treated to the sight of parents tending their downy broods.

LOCATION Northeast of Soda Springs, on Hwy. 34. **CONTACT** Grays Lake N.W.R., 74 Grays Lake Rd., Wayan, ID 83285; 208-574-2755. **SEASONAL ACCESS** Closed Nov. 16–March 31. **VISITOR CENTER** At entrance.

BEAR LAKE NATIONAL WILDLIFE REFUGE   Montpelier
This 18,000-acre refuge in the scenic Bear Valley hosts one of the nation's largest colonies of White-faced Ibises, along with numerous shorebirds and waterfowl; a large herd of Mule Deer winter along Merkley Mountain. **CONTACT** Bear Lake N.W.R., P.O. Box 9, Montpelier, ID 83254; 208-847-1757.

BRUNEAU DUNES STATE PARK   Bruneau
The tallest single-structured sand dune in North America stands here, all 470 feet of it. There are excellent interpretive exhibits and hiking trails. The Eagle Cove Environmental Education Center is on site. **CONTACT** Bruneau Dunes S.P., HC 85, Box 41, Mountain Home, ID 83647; 208-366-7919.

CAMAS PRAIRIE CENTENNIAL MARSH
WILDLIFE MANAGEMENT AREA   Fairfield
On spring mornings, this expansive wet meadow is alive with thousands of waterfowl and shorebirds; the beautiful Common Camas blooms profusely here in May, carpeting the area in rich purple. **CONTACT** Camas Prairie Centennial Marsh W.M.A., P.O. Box 428, Jerome, ID 83338; 208-324-4350.

CARIBOU NATIONAL FOREST   Pocatello
Straddling the Idaho–Wyoming border, the forest covers about 1 million acres in Idaho, more than half of which are semiarid shrub lands of Bitterbrush, sagebrush, grasses, and junipers. The Stump Creek area features about 85 miles of trails into Caribou and Webster Mountains. **CONTACT** Caribou N.F., Suite 187, Federal Bldg., 250 S. 4th Ave., Pocatello, ID 83201; 208-236-7500.

CURLEW NATIONAL GRASSLAND   Malad City
Birders visit this more than 47,000-acre site to view the many grassland species, as well as grazing Pronghorn and soaring raptors. **CONTACT** Curlew N.G., P.O. Box 146, 75 South 140 East, Malad, ID 83252; 208-766-4743.

Long-billed Curlew, Curlew National Grassland

DEER FLAT NATIONAL WILDLIFE REFUGE   Nampa
Two major attractions here are 9,500-acre Lake Lowell and the more than 86 small islands scattered through the Snake River. The refuge provides habitat for abundant and highly varied bird species, as well as for many small mammals. **CONTACT** Deer Flat N.W.R., 13751 Upper Embankment Rd., Nampa, ID 83686; 208-467-9278.

FARRAGUT STATE PARK   Athol
There is great mountain scenery on the shore of Lake Pend Oreille, and good winter viewing of Bald Eagles. Trails wind through the coniferous forests, where songbirds and small mammals abound; look for signs of Mountain Lions and Bobcats. **CONTACT** Farragut S.P., 13400 Ranger Rd., Athol, ID 83801; 208-683-2425.

HARRIMAN STATE PARK   Island Park
Harriman is a stunning place, with the Henry's Fork gliding through lush marshes and wet meadows bounded by Lodgepole Pine forests. There are 10 miles of trails. Trumpeter Swans breed here in summer. **CONTACT** Harriman S.P., HC 66, Box 500, Island Park, ID 83429; 208-558-7368.

HEYBURN STATE PARK   Plummer
This park's extensive marshes and shallow lakes on the south shore of Lake Chatcolet provide excellent songbird habitat. There are more than 20 miles of trails, one of which leads to a grove of 400-year-old Ponderosa Pines. **CONTACT** Heyburn S.P., Rte. 1, Box 139, Plummer, ID 83851; 208-686-1308.

IDAHO PANHANDLE NATIONAL FOREST · Coeur d'Alene
Extending 150 miles south from the Canadian border, this is a highly diverse inland maritime forest of spruces, firs, pines, hemlocks, and larches, with dense understories of herbaceous plants and shrubs. **CONTACT** Idaho Panhandle N.F., 3815 Schreiber Way, Coeur d'Alene, ID 83815-8363; 208-765-7223.

KOOTENAI NATIONAL WILDLIFE REFUGE · Bonners Ferry
This lovely refuge is situated along the Kootenai River, with a small portion ascending into the heavily forested Selkirk Mountains. Follow the self-guided auto tour or hiking trails to explore the meadows and wetlands. **CONTACT** Kootenai N.W.R., HCR 60, Box 283, Westside Rd., Bonners Ferry, ID 83805; 208-267-3888.

MINIDOKA NATIONAL WILDLIFE REFUGE · Rupert
Rolling hills and lava ledges characterize the 20,000-acre refuge along the Snake River and Lake Walcott, an important stopover for waterfowl on the Pacific Flyway. Walk the shore or go boating on the lake. **CONTACT** Minidoka N.W.R., 961 E. Minidoka Dam, Rupert, ID 83350; 208-436-3589.

OWYHEE MOUNTAINS · Murphy
These are the wildest mountains you'll ever visit—arid, rugged, remote, and teeming with mammals and birds. A high-clearance vehicle is recommended to explore the region. **CONTACT** Boise Bureau of Land Management, 3948 Development Ave., Boise, ID 83705; 208-384-3300.

PONDEROSA STATE PARK · McCall
This park situated on Payette Lake is known for its beautiful wildflowers, ancient Ponderosa Pines, and widely varied habitats, from steep cliffs and wetlands to dense coniferous forests. Look for Pacific Treefrogs, Long-toed Salamanders, and many species of woodland songbirds. Be sure to stop by the visitor center. **CONTACT** Ponderosa S.P., P.O. Box A, McCall, ID 83638; 208-634-2164.

ROUND LAKE STATE PARK · Sagle
Round Lake is a glacial pothole lake bounded by a rich inland maritime forest. There are a self-guided botanical trail and a 2-mile trail that circles the lake and crosses Cocolalla Creek; Red Squirrels and Steller's Jays occupy the forest. **CONTACT** Round Lake S.P., P.O. Box 170, Sagle, ID 83860; 208-263-3489.

SILVER CREEK PRESERVE · Picabo
This is a gorgeous spring creek surrounded by sagebrush grasslands. Orange-crowned and Yellow-rumped warblers are abundant. Hiking, kayaking, and canoeing are popular activities here. **CONTACT** Silver Creek Pres., P.O. Box 624, Picabo, ID 83348; 208-788-2203.

SNAKE RIVER BIRDS OF PREY NATIONAL CONSERVATION AREA · Boise
The towering cliffs along 80 miles of southwestern Idaho's Snake River provide a wealth of nesting sites for the 15 raptor species that breed here, as well as nine other species that stop over during migration. A 56-mile loop tour of the area takes about four hours. **CONTACT** Bureau of Land Management, Boise District Office, 3948 Development Ave., Boise, ID 83705; 208-384-3300.

TARGHEE NATIONAL FOREST · St. Anthony
This forest's 1.8 million acres in Idaho and Wyoming adjoin the wild country of Yellowstone and Grand Teton National Parks. There are hundreds of miles of trails, and much of the forest is easily accessed by car. **CONTACT** Targhee N.F., P.O. Box 208, St. Anthony, ID 83445; 208-624-3151.

THOUSAND SPRINGS PRESERVE · Wendell
Visit the last remaining unaltered canyon-wall spring, a spectacular sight, with spring water bursting forth through fissures in steep walls of lava rock. **CONTACT** Thousand Springs Pres., 1205 Thousand Springs Grade, Wendell, ID 83355; 208-536-6797.

Montana

The Continental Divide separates Montana's 147,046 square miles into a forested, mountainous western section, with a great expanse of northern prairie to the east.

Forests cover about 23 percent of Montana. In the northwest reaches of the state, moisture-laden Pacific air nurtures a varied, inland "maritime" forest community that includes larches, cedars, and hemlocks. The most widespread forest types, however, feature mixed- or single-species stands of Ponderosa and Lodgepole Pines and Douglas Fir. Higher-elevation subalpine forests have Engelmann Spruce, Subalpine Fir, and Limber and Whitebark Pines.

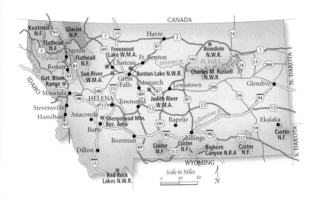

Born in the high southwest mountains are the great rivers: the Clark Fork, the Missouri, and the Yellowstone. These waters meander through spacious valleys of sagebrush grasslands, with lowland deciduous forests of willow, alder, and cottonwood trees; the valleys today are the province of agriculture, ranching, and, increasingly, residential areas. Flathead Lake, a large glacial lake in northwestern Montana, is the largest natural freshwater lake west of the Mississippi River.

Across the sparsely populated eastern two-thirds of the state, the northern Great Plains unroll as a semiarid expanse of shortgrass and sagebrush, dissected by deep breaks and rocky ridges; juniper, Ponderosa Pine, and scattered Colorado Pinyon and Douglas Fir grow in these broken areas. Mountains persist here as well; in the north-central portion of the state are the Big Snowy and Judith Mountains, and scattered "island" ranges, such as the Bearpaw and Little Rocky Mountains. Once home for millions of American Bison, this region is now occupied to a significant degree by wheat farming and cattle grazing.

Within Montana's vast borders is a commensurately large and diverse list of parks and preserves where virtually every type of natural community may be explored—20 national wildlife refuges, 10 national forests, 45 state parks, and Glacier National Park, where the Great Divide exits the United States on a glorious note.

NATIONAL BISON RANGE   Moiese

American Bison once ranked among the most widespread and abundant wildlife in North America—and certainly the largest. With a range spanning two-thirds of the continent and a population estimated at 40 to 60 million, it was unthinkable that bison might vanish. And yet they nearly did; by 1900 the wild population hovered near 100 and thoughts had turned to conserving the few remaining animals. In 1908, the National Bison Range was established with 41 captive bison on 19,000 acres of rolling prairie hills, narrow canyons, and forested creek bottoms. The herd has done well; today it is managed for an optimum size of 400, with surplus animals sold off every year. Other large grazers and browsers make use of the site, including Elk, Pronghorn, White-tailed and Mule Deer, Bighorn Sheep, and occasional Mountain Goats.

The rangeland is composed of now rare Palouse Prairie Bunchgrass. Mission Creek flows down from the hills and through richly forested bottoms of aspens, junipers, birches, and cottonwoods. Blue Grouse inhabit the woodlands, along with Yellow-breasted Chats and Lazuli Buntings, among others. Start your tour at the visitor center, which has some fine interpretive displays. Viewing out on the range is limited primarily to roads: A 19-mile loop road is open summer through early fall and takes about two hours to complete. There is also a half-hour tour route, open year-round. Bison are active grazers, and they steadily cover ground as they feed; this means the herds seldom stay in the same area for long. Bear in mind that this is a wild preserve, not a theme park, and locating most of the larger animals requires patience and a pair of binoculars. An 800-pound bull Elk bedded down amid sagebrush will become all but invisible save for his antlers poking above the shrubs. Newborn bison calves are a sight to behold from mid-April through May, and Bighorn Sheep visit the grasslands in summer. Birdlife is abundant everywhere; watch for Grasshopper Sparrows in the grasslands, and Lewis's Woodpeckers and Clark's Nutcrackers in the upper forested areas. The rugged Mission Mountains form a spectacular backdrop to the grasslands.

LOCATION North of Missoula, on Hwy. 212. **CONTACT** National Bison Range, 132 Bison Range Rd., Moiese, MT 59824; 406-644-2211. **VISITOR CENTER** 1 mile from main entrance.

GLACIER NATIONAL PARK   **West Glacier**

Glacier National Park encompasses 1 million pristine acres of natural beauty. It's a rugged area made delicate by the clean, bracing air, the almost surreal clarity of the lakes and streams, and the magnificent vistas of emerald green forests, that appear on steep, distant mountainsides.

Glacier's mountainscape formed through the sequence of faulting, upthrusts, and glaciation that carved much of the Rockies. A more recent generation of glaciers appeared about 3,000 years ago; 50 of these, diminutive as glaciers go, continue to chisel their way through high valleys and cirques. Snowfields remain on the alpine meadows well into summer and further alter the landscape, feeding the numerous tumbling streams that pull boulders and sediment downslope.

Grinnell Lake, in Many Glacier area

The park's topography is greatly varied and hosts a diverse assortment of flora and fauna. At lower elevations, meadows covered with prairie grasses and thick patches of wildflowers are interrupted by lush riparian belts of cottonwoods, willows, and buffaloberry; aspen stands border the streams and lakes. Spruce, fir, and Lodgepole Pine forests blanket the middle elevations, especially on the eastern side of the park or in areas previously disturbed by wildfire; west of the Divide, moist Pacific air enables cedars, larches, and hemlocks to grow over a rich understory of shrubs. Subalpine forests of Engelmann Spruce, Douglas Fir, and Subalpine Fir are the most widespread forest type in the park, beginning at elevations of about 6,500 feet and continuing to the tree line. On the high meadows, Subalpine Firs grow in gnarled, often stunted "islands"; the stands consist of a prolific parent tree that clones offspring through its root system.

Everywhere, at every elevation, there are wildflowers: sweeping meadows of Glacier Lilies, stands of Beargrass blooming on boulder-strewn hillsides, shooting stars, lupines, Indian Paintbrushes, phlox, pasqueflowers, and globeflowers, among many others. A visual feast for us, the

Wildflowers near Logan Pass

flowers and grasses are a dietary staple for the wildlife, including Elk, deer, and many rodents. The 60 mammal species recorded in the park include Grizzly Bears, Wolverines, Mountain Goats, and American Pikas; more than 200 bird species have been listed.

Just about any road through Glacier features numerous turnouts, all of which invite short walks and yield something wondrous. No visit, however, is complete without a drive along Going-to-the-Sun Road, a narrow, sinuous paved route connecting West Glacier with Saint Mary on the park's eastern boundary. Cut into sheer mountainsides, traversing streams, lakes, and boulder fields, the route crests the Continental Divide at Logan Pass, probably the park's most heavily used area, though still worth a visit. The visitor center here has interpretive displays as well as tips on where to go and what to see. A number of trails depart from Logan Pass, including the easy and popular Hidden Lake Trail, which offers remarkable mountain views, alpine meadows, and ample opportunities for sighting high-country wildlife, including American Pikas, Yellow-bellied Marmots, Mountain Goats, Columbian Ground Squirrels, rosy-finches, and American Pipits. The Highline Trail is a longer hike of 7.6 miles that leads to the Granite Park Chalet, with outstanding panoramas the entire way; the Chalet terrace is considered one of the best places in the park from which to safely observe Grizzly Bears.

East of Logan Pass, the Many Glacier area is another wildlife-rich and accessible stop. Bald Eagles may be seen along Sherburne Reservoir, and Common Loons ply the waters. Several trails originate near the Many Glacier Hotel, including the Cracker Lake Trail, a 6-mile hike through aspens, grasslands, and old-growth conifers. Hikers should note, however, that this area is heavily used by Grizzly Bears. The rare diurnal Northern Hawk Owl may be spotted here, perched in spruces, as well as Rufous and Calliope Hummingbirds and Olive-sided Flycatchers. Higher up, the steep slopes of Allen Mountain are a favored haunt of Bighorn Sheep. Outside of Saint Mary, the trail to Red Eagle Lake passes through old-growth spruce forests, cottonwood groves, grasslands, and ponds; those who travel the 7 miles to the lake may spot beavers, loons, Moose, or Mountain Goats on nearby Red Eagle Mountain.

LOCATION On Rte. 2. **CONTACT** Glacier N.P., West Glacier, MT 59936; 406-888-7800. **VISITOR CENTERS** In Apgar, on west side of park; in St. Mary, on east side of park.

CHARLES M. RUSSELL NATIONAL WILDLIFE REFUGE

Lewistown

Larger and less visited than Glacier National Park, the Charles M. Russell National Wildlife Refuge might be more appropriately considered a northern plains wilderness. The Missouri River flows through the 1.1-million-acre refuge's southern section, passing amid stands of stately cottonwoods, willows, dogwoods, and scattered Green Ashes. The final 149-mile stretch above the Fred Robinson Bridge, about 9 miles of which lies within the refuge, is designated a Wild and Scenic corridor and is as close to pristine as any area on the river today, allowing visitors to experience it as explorers Lewis and Clark did in the early 1800s. Upslope, the refuge lands are a mixture of sagebrush grasslands with scattered copses of Ponderosa Pine and juniper, along with smaller areas of Chokecherry and snowberry shrubs and Douglas Fir. The western side of the refuge supports more forested areas, while grasslands and shrub lands hold sway toward the east. This is Missouri Breaks country, where the land falls away into a labyrinth of steeply eroded draws, drainages, and coulees; it's like a mountain range turned

Missouri River

upside down. Pines, sagebrush, and junipers cloak the slopes and bottoms to create ideal travelways for the abundant Mule Deer population. There's no better place in the West to see an intact shortgrass prairie system. Prairie dog towns, the nucleus of prairie life, supply prey for many predators, especially the airborne variety—Ferruginous and Swainson's Hawks, Golden Eagles, Prairie Falcons, and Northern Harriers. A historic predator closely tied to prairie dogs, Black-footed Ferrets were wiped out locally long ago and are one of the nation's most endangered mammals today. The refuge began reintroducing them in 1994 and has been releasing more every year since. Refuge officials say it's still too early to know whether a self-sustaining population will develop.

Roads are hard to come by here. The gravel auto tour route, which begins and ends on Highway 191, provides one of the better ways to get a glimpse of the refuge's 3,000-head Elk herd; another good place to view Elk is just downriver from the Fred Robinson Bridge on Highway 191. Jeep trails crisscross the area; these are best negotiated with a four-wheel-drive or high-clearance vehicle. All unimproved roads are clay; if it looks like rain, by all means leave the area; even the stoutest four-wheel-drive vehicle is useless in the muck known locally as "gumbo."

LOCATION On Hwys. 24 (east end of reserve) and 191 (west end). **CONTACT** Charles M. Russell N.W.R., P.O. Box 110, Lewistown, MT 59457; 406-538-8706.

KOOTENAI NATIONAL FOREST   Libby

Kootenai River

Because of the influence of Pacific air, Kootenai's 2,245,793 acres experience a wetter, milder climate than elsewhere in the state; the resulting inland "maritime" forest includes trees more typical of the Northwest. The 6-mile Vinal Creek Trail, near the town of Yaak, offers a fine sampling, passing through a stand of massive, 300-year-old Western Larches and, at the creek crossing, ancient Western Red Cedars, some more than 25 feet in diameter. Woodland bird species are abundant along the creek, and Moose may also be sighted. The sprawling Kootenai River in the central portion of the forest attracts a wide variety of birds, including migrating Bald Eagles in fall. As many as 160 eagles loaf in snag trees along the river below Libby Dam, gorging on the carcasses of spawned-out Kokanee Salmon. Look for rare Harlequin Ducks along the Kootenai, and breeding birds near Kootenai Falls in April and May. The Ten Lakes Scenic Area northeast of Eureka features abundant wildflowers, Bighorn Sheep, and gorgeous alpine lakes in a rugged mountain setting.

LOCATION In Libby, on Hwys. 2, 37, and 56. **CONTACT** Kootenai N.F., 506 Hwy. 2 West, Libby, MT 59923; 406-293-6211. **VISITOR CENTER** In Libby.

FLATHEAD NATIONAL FOREST   Kalispell

A large and diverse forest, the Flathead extends for 130 miles south from the Canadian border; it encompasses nearly 1 million wilderness acres in the Bob Marshall–Great Bear complex, which borders Glacier National Park. Summertime use of "the Bob" has grown substantially, and solitude here may be reaching the threatened status of the resident

Grizzly Bear. The area is a supremely beautiful mosaic of rivers and creeks, extensive meadows, high-country forests, and geologic wonders; the Chinese Wall is a spectacular multihued ridge of eroded stone. The Wild and Scenic Flathead River and its three forks thrash through sheer-walled canyons topped with dense coniferous forests, home to Moose, wolves, Grizzlies, Elk, and Mountain Lions. Guide services in West Glacier offer river rafting adventures in appropriate seasons. The Jewell Basin Hiking Area is popular with families and others seeking modest day hikes or short camping trips; its 27 lakes are set amid subalpine forests, park-like meadows deep in wildflowers, tumbling streams, and high, craggy peaks.

LOCATION Off Hwy. 93. **CONTACT** Flathead N.F., 1935 3rd Ave. East, Kalispell, MT 59901; 406-755-5401. **VISITOR CENTER** In Kalispell, at 1935 3rd Ave. East.

BIGHORN CANYON
NATIONAL RECREATION AREA   **Fort Smith**

The meandering, steep-sided river gorge and 71-mile-long Bighorn Lake are the main attractions at this 120,000-acre reserve, located in both Montana and Wyoming. The Pryor Mountain Wild Horse Range is here, with a sizable herd of about 140 wild horses. Other mammals to look out for are Coyotes, White-tailed Deer, Black Bears, Beavers, Common Porcupines, and along the canyon, Bighorn Sheep. More than 200 species of birds have been spotted in the park, including Bald Eagles, American Pelicans, and Wild Turkeys. The 3-mile Om-ne-a Trail to Bighorn Lake starts off from the visitor center and follows the rim of Bighorn Canyon. Water sports on the lake include boating, waterskiing, fishing, and swimming. There are a number of campsites located below the dam.

LOCATION South of Billings, on Hwy. 313. **CONTACT** Bighorn Canyon N.R.A., P.O. Box 7458, Ft. Smith, MT 59035; 406-666-2412. **VISITOR CENTER** In Ft. Smith.

RED ROCK LAKES NATIONAL
WILDLIFE REFUGE   **Lakeview**

Located in the Centennial Valley and bounded on the south by the dramatic Centennial Mountains, this has been called the nation's most scenic refuge. Visitors should bring along a spare tire and plenty of insect repellent; the gravel roads are notorious for eating tires, and the 13,000 acres of wetlands ensure plenty of mosquitoes on hand to bite you. Roads traverse the sagebrush grasslands, wet meadows, and marshes; canoeing is another terrific way to explore. One of the largest breeding populations of Trumpeter Swans, estimated at 100 to 300, resides here. The area is also noted for its raptors: Swainson's and Ferruginous Hawks, Golden Eagles, and a few Peregrine Falcons. In addition to 258 recorded bird species, visitors are likely to encounter Pronghorn, marmots, and ground squirrels; Red Foxes, American Badgers, Short- and Long-tailed Weasels, and Moose are also present but harder to find. Wildflowers such as Sticky Geraniums, shooting stars, and lupines are abundant in midsummer. Two small campgrounds with 11 sites are located on the refuge.

LOCATION South of Lima, off I-15. **CONTACT** Red Rock Lakes N.W.R., Monida Star Rte., Box 15, Lima, MT 59739; 406-276-3536. **VISITOR CENTER** At refuge headquarters.

BENTON LAKE NATIONAL WILDLIFE RESERVE

Great Falls

This 12,383-acre reserve is a premier site for observing waterfowl and shorebirds. The "lake," today more a shallow, marshy expanse, is an ancient glacial bed fed by Lake Creek. During peak migration periods, March through April and September through October, great flocks of as many as 100,000 ducks, 4,000 Tundra Swans, and 40,000 Snow Geese visit the area. It's an awesome, noisy spectacle easily observed with binoculars. The refuge is recognized by the Western Hemisphere Shorebird Reserve Network as a critical area for migrating and nesting shorebirds. Species include American Avocets, Long-billed Dowitchers, Marbled Godwits, Lesser Yellowlegs, Soras, Black-crowned Night-Herons, and three species of terns; upland birds include Burrowing Owls, Chestnut-collared Longspurs, Savannah Sparrows, and Horned Larks. The 9-mile Prairie Marsh Drive has numbered signs that correspond to an interpretive brochure available at the information kiosk.

LOCATION North of Great Falls, off 15th St. **CONTACT** Benton Lake N.W.R., 922 Bootlegger Trail, Great Falls, MT 59404; 406-727-7400. **VISITOR CENTER** At reserve, about 1½ miles from entrance.

FREEZEOUT LAKE WILDLIFE MANAGEMENT AREA

Fairfield

Freezeout Lake Wildlife Management Area, part of an ancient glacial lake bed, is bird heaven. The area provides 5,000 acres of open water, 2,500 acres of thriving marshlands, and adjacent uplands. During peak migration periods, as many as 1 million birds visit Freezeout, with raucous flocks of Snow Geese and Tundra Swans blanketing the lake in white. Snow Geese number as many as 300,000 during the first weeks of April and November; up to 10,000 Tundra Swans arrive in the third week of March and first week of November. Serious birders make it a point to catch the spring shorebird migrations, when some unusual species for the region, including Whimbrels, may be seen. Other birds of interest include Great Egrets, Black-crowned Night-Herons, and Black-necked Stilts. Winter brings Rough-legged Hawks, Bald Eagles, and rare Gyrfalcons. Common upland species include Gray Partridges, pheasants, and Sharp-tailed Grouse.

Sunrise at Freezeout Lake

LOCATION Northwest of Great Falls, on Hwy 89. **CONTACT** Freezeout Lake W.M.A., P.O. Box 488, Fairfield, MT 59436; 406-467-3234.

SUN RIVER WILDLIFE MANAGEMENT AREA

Augusta

This is a place of dramatic contrasts, where the northern Great Plains halt abruptly, striking the steep cliffs and soaring peaks of the Rocky Mountain Front. The Sun River flows out of the mountains and high meadows of the adjacent Scapegoat Wilderness through a stunning canyon. The wildest animals on the continent thrive on the 20,000-acre site—Elk, Mule Deer, Grizzly and Black Bears, Mountain Lions, and occasional wolves. One of the continent's largest herds of Bighorn Sheep, numbering between 800 and 1,000, engage in their fall mating rites here, when mature rams face off and charge each other; the jolting collisions can be heard a mile away. An interpretive area about the sheep is located on Sun Canyon Road, about 2 miles west of the national forest boundary. Explore the grasslands for Pronghorn, Long-billed Curlews, raptors, and waterfowl. Early-season wildflower displays are tremendous, owing to the site's alignment with the chinook belt, a corridor of warm wind that often roars along the Front Range.

LOCATION Northwest of Augusta, on Gibson Reservoir Rd.; follow road's left fork to entrance. **CONTACT** Sun River W.M.A., P.O. Box 6610, Great Falls, MT 59406; 406-454-5840. **SEASONAL ACCESS** Closed Dec. 1–May 15.

JUDITH RIVER WILDLIFE MANAGEMENT AREA

Utica

The 5,000-acre Judith River Wildlife Management Area offers wildlife and habitats typical of north-central Montana. Rolling grasslands and Ponderosa Pine forests are bounded by steep, forested canyons and rocky cliffs. This site provides important winter range for Elk and Mule

Judith River

and White-tailed Deer from the nearby Big Belt Mountains. Other mammals include Bobcats, Long-tailed Weasels, American Badgers, Coyotes, and Red Foxes. Birds are also abundant, with numerous raptor species—Golden Eagles, Swainson's Hawks, and Northern Goshawks—as well as such songbirds as Western Tanagers, Mountain Bluebirds, warblers, and vireos. Hiking is allowed throughout the area in summer and fall; from December 1 through May 14, visitors must limit their activities to the roadsides.

LOCATION Near Windham, southwest of Utica, off Hwy. 87; from Utica, follow signs to the area. **CONTACT** Montana Fish, Wildlife, and Parks, Region 4 Headquarters, 4600 Giant Springs Rd., P.O. Box 6610, Great Falls, MT 59406; 406-454-5840. **SEASONAL ACCESS** Closed Dec. 1–May 14.

CUSTER NATIONAL FOREST   Billings

Custer National Forest's 1.1 million acres include a sizable portion of the Beartooth Wilderness, part of the rugged Beartooth Plateau, and feature spectacular wildflower and alpine plant life, hundreds of lakes, steep cliffs, and Montana's highest mountains. Jimmy Joe Campground, near East Rosebud Lake, boasts a remarkable concentration of more than 20 butterfly and skipper species; Black

Bears and Moose favor the campground's surrounding dense coniferous forests. Forest Road 3085 leads from the town of Bridger into the Pryor Mountains, a land of limestone hills, open meadows, dense forests, and spectacular cliffs, canyons, and caves. The route follows Sage Creek, crossing into and then back out of Crow Indian Reservation lands; visitors must obtain a permit to explore tribal lands on foot. Along the creek and in the canyons are Sage Thrashers, Rock Wrens, and Ruby-crowned Kinglets; bats roost along the limestone walls near Big Ice Cave.

Beartooth Wilderness

LOCATION From Billings, follow I-90 west to Laurel, then Hwy. 212 to Red Lodge. **CONTACT** Custer N.F., 1310 Main St., P.O. Box 50760, Billings, MT 59105; 406-248-9885. **VISITOR CENTERS** At main headquarters, and in Red Lodge, at the Beartooth Ranger District.

BOWDOIN NATIONAL WILDLIFE REFUGE   Malta

Deep in the heart of eastern Montana's "big empty" prairie-lands, this 15,550-acre refuge is both a nesting area for prairie- and water-associated birds, and a stop along the Central Flyway for migrating ducks and geese. The marshes, pothole lakes, and native prairie attract more than 230 species of birds. Colonial nesters like Black-crowned

American White Pelicans

Night-Herons and White-faced Ibises rear their young in the bulrush marshes, while Double-crested Cormorants, California and Ring-billed Gulls, and thousands of American White Pelicans nest on the islands of Lake Bowdoin, the refuge's largest lake. During April and May, Sharp-tailed Grouse perform their courtship dances on Big Island (actually a peninsula). The numerous grassland residents include Sprague's Pipits, Baird's Sparrows, Rufous-sided Towhees, and Brown Thrashers. Mammals include Pronghorn, Coyotes, White-tailed Jackrabbits, and Mountain Cottontails.

LOCATION East of Malta, on old Hwy. 2. **CONTACT** Bowdoin N.W.R., HC 65, Box 5700, Malta, MT 59538; 406-654-2863. **VISITOR CENTER** At park entrance.

BEAVER CREEK COUNTY PARK   Havre
At 10,000 acres, this is one of the largest county parks in the nation. Follow the main road through pine, aspen, and cottonwood groves bounded by rocky cliffs and small lakes. **CONTACT** Beaver Creek C.P., Shambo Rte., Box 368, Havre, MT 59501; 406-395-4565.

BEAVERHEAD–DEERLODGE NATIONAL FOREST   Dillon
Several major mountain ranges make up this forest, including the Anacondas and Madisons; they feed some of the state's largest, most beautiful rivers—the Big Hole, Madison, Jefferson, and Ruby. **CONTACT** Beaverhead N.F., 420 Barrett St., Dillon, MT 59725; 406-683-3900.

BITTERROOT NATIONAL FOREST   Hamilton
The Bitterroot's 1.1 million acres include substantial wilderness areas and adjoin the large block of national forest lands spilling over into central Idaho. The high country is rugged and glorious. **CONTACT** Bitterroot N.F., 1801 N. First St., Hamilton, MT 59840; 406-363-3131.

CANYON FERRY WILDLIFE MANAGEMENT AREA   Townsend
This area on the southern end of Canyon Ferry Reservoir, a large impoundment of the Missouri River, features dense riparian thickets interspersed with open grasslands. **CONTACT** Canyon Ferry W.M.A., Montana Fish, Wildlife, and Parks, P.O. Box 998, Townsend, MT 59644; 406-266-3367.

GALLATIN NATIONAL FOREST
Bozeman

This popular forest is bounded on the south by Yellowstone National Park and on the north by the Gallatin Valley and Bozeman, Montana. The Hyalite Peaks offer fine hiking and scenery. **CONTACT** Gallatin N.F., P.O. Box 130, Bozeman, MT 59771; 406-587-6701.

Gallatin National Forest

HAILSTONE NATIONAL WILDLIFE REFUGE   Rapelje
A large alkaline lake surrounded by expansive prairie lands, the refuge hosts a sizable prairie dog town, with Burrowing Owls, Coyotes, and Golden Eagles also in evidence; numerous species of waterfowl ply the lake. **CONTACT** Hailstone N.W.R., P.O. Box 110, Lewistown, MT 59457; 406-538-8706.

HELENA NATIONAL FOREST   Helena
The small but rugged mountains that flank the city of Helena, Montana's state capital, are densely forested, with some open park-like meadows. The Helena Ridge Walk offers a good forest experience near town. **CONTACT** Helena N.F., 2880 Skyway Dr., Helena, MT 59601; 406-449-5201.

LEE METCALF NATIONAL WILDLIFE REFUGE   Stevensville
This small and accessible refuge on the Bitterroot River floodplain has ponds, wetlands, and a mature lowland cottonwood forest. Ospreys, woodpeckers, and songbirds are abundant. **CONTACT** Lee Metcalf N.W.R., P.O. Box 247, Stevensville, MT 59870; 406-777-5552.

LEWIS AND CLARK NATIONAL FOREST   Monarch
This forest encompasses much of the beautiful Rocky Mountain Front, where the northern plains meet the mountains. Wildlife is abundant and includes many large mammals, such as Elk, Mountain Lions, Pronghorn, and Grizzly Bears. **CONTACT** Lewis and Clark N.F., P.O. Box 869, Great Falls, MT 59403; 406-791-7700.

LOLO NATIONAL FOREST   Missoula
Many gorgeous sites are scattered throughout this large forest, including the Clearwater Canoe Trail, the easily accessible Rattlesnake Wilderness, and Rock Creek. **CONTACT** Lolo N.F., Bldg. 24, Ft. Missoula, Missoula, MT 59804; 406-329-3750.

LOST CREEK STATE PARK   Anaconda

A beautiful trail winds through the park, along a tumbling mountain stream lined with dense willow riparian areas. Beavers inhabit the stream, and Bighorn Sheep can be seen along the 1,200-foot canyon that looms above. **CONTACT** Lost Creek S.P., 3201 Spurgin Rd., Missoula, MT 59804; 406-542-5500.

MAKOSHIKA STATE PARK   Glendive

A desolate badlands beauty, this park's buttes, pinnacles, and eroded spires support a wide variety of species, from grassland songbirds and raptors to horned lizards and Prairie Rattlesnakes. Several self-guided trails traverse the park; brochures are available at the visitor center. **CONTACT** Makoshika S.P., P.O. Box 1242, Glendive, MT 59330; 406-365-6256.

MEDICINE ROCKS STATE PARK   Ekalaka

Sandstone formation, Medicine Rocks S.P.

The fantastic sandstone monuments of this park are set amid rolling grasslands and stands of Ponderosa Pine. Ferruginous Hawks, Merlins, and Prairie Falcons nest on the sandstone cliffs. **CONTACT** Medicine Rocks S.P., MT Dept. of Fish, Wildlife, and Parks, P.O. Box 1630, Miles City, MT 59301; 406-232-0900.

NINEPIPE AND PABLO NATIONAL WILDLIFE REFUGES   Ronan

In the shadow of the glorious Mission Mountains, these refuges encompass more than 800 glacial potholes, along with wetlands, upland areas, and a 1,770-acre reservoir. **CONTACT** Ninepipe and Pablo N.W.R.s, Refuge Manager, National Bison Range, 132 Bison Range Rd., Moiese, MT 59824; 406-644-2211.

PINE BUTTE SWAMP PRESERVE   Choteau

This holding on the Rocky Mountain Front, owned by the Nature Conservancy, maintains unique plant communities. The pristine wildlands are roamed by Grizzly Bears, itinerant wolves, and other large mammals. A.B. Guthrie Memorial Trail affords beautiful views of the Front. Egg Mountain is located here, the site of 80-million-year-old dinosaur fossils. **CONTACT** Pine Butte Swamp Pres., HC 58, Box 34B, Choteau, MT 59422; 406-466-5526.

Upper Missouri Wild and Scenic River

UPPER MISSOURI WILD AND SCENIC RIVER   Fort Benton

Part of Lewis and Clark's original route, this river corridor stretches for 149 miles, with fairly easy paddling through beautiful, wildlife-rich lands and waters. **CONTACT** Bureau of Land Management, River Manager, P.O. Box 1160, Lewistown, MT 59457; 406-538-7461.

WILD HORSE ISLAND STATE PARK   Dayton

Access to this undeveloped island park on Flathead Lake is via tour boat or private watercraft. Visitors will see rocky, forested slopes, abundant wildflowers, Bighorn Sheep—and perhaps a few wild horses. **CONTACT** Wild Horse Is. S.P., MT Dept. of Fish, Wildlife, and Parks, 490 N. Meridian Rd., Kalispell, MT 59901; 406-752-5501.

Wyoming

The Continental Divide enters southern Wyoming west of the Snowy Range, then splits into two "divides" near the town of Rawlins. Looping away from one another, these features form the boundary of the Great Divide Basin, a sprawling desert, before joining again to plunge in a northwesterly direction through the heart of Wyoming's splendid high country—the Wind River and Salt River Ranges, the Tetons, the Absarokas, and the Beartooths. Coniferous forests of Lodgepole Pine, Douglas Fir, Engelmann Spruce, Subalpine Fir, and aspen blanket the mountainsides. At the heart of the high country is the Yellowstone Plateau, perched on a massive hot spot below the earth's crust; its restless volcanic energies fuel the geysers and sputtering mudpots of the world's first national park.

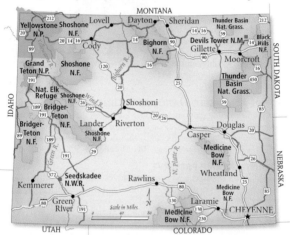

Wyoming covers 97,914 square miles, with an average elevation at 6,700 feet. Even when the mountainous areas are excluded, the average elevation in the southern half of the state is well over 6,000 feet. The highest point is 13,804-foot Gannett Peak in the Wind River Range; the lowest is 3,124 feet, located in the state's northeastern corner.

The real story of Wyoming, though, is sagebrush grasslands, spread over the state's vast allotment of the Great Plains. More sagebrush-grasslands exist here than in any other place on earth, and Wyoming is home to two-thirds of the world's Pronghorn and Sage Grouse populations, both of which depend upon sagebrush for food and shelter to survive the bitter winters. These lands are arid, with less than 12 inches of annual precipitation; and they are cool, existing at elevations above 6,000 feet. They feature the deep soils needed for the sagebrush plant's massive taproot.

Wyoming features seven national forests, three national wildlife refuges, two national parks, two national recreation areas, 12 state parks, and many thousands of acres of additional publicly administered lands.

DEVILS TOWER NATIONAL MONUMENT

Devils Tower

The striking focal point of this 1,347-acre preserve is Devils Tower, a monolithic, flat-topped core of rock rising 847 feet, with a 1.5-acre summit. The tower is the core of an ancient volcano, formed more than 60 million years ago when molten magma pushed its way upward through layers of sedimentary rock, collected in a great mass, and then cooled, forming a hard rock known as phonolite porphyry. The cooling process shattered the rock into the multifaceted columns seen today on the tower face. The ancient Belle Fourche River, still concealed beneath the surface, then went to work on the sedimentary rock layers, slowly washing them away to expose the tower.

While it takes just a half-hour to tour the base and get a sense of this unique formation, there are enough wildlife attractions to warrant a lengthier visit. The tower itself provides habitat for a number of birds and small mammals, especially on the summit. Prairie Falcons use it as a base of operation for their hunting sorties over the grasslands. Western Rattlesnakes, Least Chipmunks, and Bushy-tailed Woodrats find ample food and cover among the grasses and rocks. A Ponderosa Pine forest surrounds the tower base, home to White-tailed Deer, chipmunks, and bands of Wild Turkeys. The valley surrounding the tower features expansive meadows, where a variety of burrowers, including shrews, Northern Pocket Gophers, and Black-tailed Prairie Dogs, are found in abundance. These animals form a healthy prey base for the area's predators: Red Foxes, Long-tailed Weasels, Coyotes, American Badgers, Red-tailed Hawks, and Bobcats. The monument's South Trail passes near a thriving prairie dog town, and it is always enjoyable to spend some time observing their activities. Along the swift-flowing Belle Fourche River are mature cottonwoods, including snag trees, which provide cavities for nesting Wood Ducks and Red-headed Woodpeckers. Western Flycatchers, Yellow-rumped Warblers, and Mountain Bluebirds may also be seen in the area, a few of the 90 recorded bird species.

LOCATION Northwest of Gillette, off I-90. **CONTACT** Devils Tower N.M., P.O. Box 10, Devils Tower, WY 82714; 307-467-5283. **VISITOR CENTER** 3 miles from entrance (closed Nov.–Mar.).

YELLOWSTONE NATIONAL PARK   Yellowstone

Yellowstone, established in 1872 as the world's first national park, links us to the values of an earlier generation of Americans, to their vision of how natural and human worlds might coexist, and to the belief that we are better off with nature in our lives. These values inform the literature, interpretive displays, and even the architecture of the park's old lodges and hotels.. The burdens of upholding this legacy are considerable, but Yellowstone and its leaders—whether educating the nation on the benefits of wildfire or embracing the so-

cial and political dilemmas of wolf reintroduction—seldom shy away from the task. With the new millennium, Yellowstone faces more burdens than ever: staggering visitor numbers, inadequate funds, development along park boundaries, and the as-yet unsolved problem of American Bison and their winter migration outside the

Lower Falls, Grand Canyon of the Yellowstone River

park (see page 53). One expects that Yellowstone, like its forests and wildlife in the wake of the 1988 fires, will endure.

Wildlife and Natural Communities

Yellowstone's 3,472 square miles encompass semiarid sagebrush grasslands, expansive wet and dry meadows, subalpine forests, riparian habitats, and small areas of alpine tundra. Approximately 80 percent of the park is forested, the majority of it in Lodgepole Pine; of the remaining land, 15 percent is meadow and range, and the rest is water. Precipitation varies from 10 inches annually at the northern boundary to 80 inches in the southwestern corner.

The largest concentration of free-roaming wildlife in the world's temperate zone is found in Yellowstone. With the reintroduction of the Gray Wolf in 1995, all wild species that inhabited the region in the 1800s survive here today. Substantial numbers of American Bison, Elk, Bighorn Sheep, Pronghorn, and Mule Deer move through the park's various habitats in accordance with the seasons. Several hundred threatened Grizzly Bears live here, and Black Bears are common. Among the 50 other mammal species that live here are American Marten, Lynx, Wolverine, and nearly 300 bird species.

WOLF EAT WOLF The first order of business in reintroducing wolves was organizing packs, raising pups, and managing Coyote populations. With that work complete, Yellowstone's newly thriving wolf packs are on to more serious duties—fighting with one another. In February of 1998, the eight-member Soda Butte pack ventured into an area near Yellowstone Lake claimed by the Thoroughfare pack, also eight wolves strong. A battle ensued, and the trespassers won, killing the alpha male of the defending group and claiming the territory. The long-term impact of wolves on the park's Elk and deer herds—their chief food sources—won't be known for some time, though biologists already have noted that wolves make a healthy living off newborn Elk calves in spring.

Yellowstone Geology

Grand Geyser, Upper Geyser Basin

Yellowstone Park's geologic story centers on volcanic activity. Catastrophic eruptions occurred beginning 2 million years ago; the most recent, about 600,000 years ago, blew out nearly 240 cubic miles of debris. What is now the center of the park collapsed in the wake of that eruption, forming a caldera, or basin, 28 by 47 miles in size. The restless energies of the earth's molten core are very much in evidence today, powering the park's 10,000 thermal features—its mudpots, fumaroles, hot springs, and 200 to 250 active geysers. Mammoth Hot Springs and the Upper Geyser Basin area are two of many notable sites to visit.

THERMOPHILES ON LOAN Yellowstone's geothermal wonders support thermophilic (heat-loving) bacteria. Researchers "bio-prospecting" in mudpots and geyser basins continue to uncover new life-forms, many of which have applications for health and technology. An enzyme discovered here, named *Thermus aquaticus*, has enabled medical researchers to develop more accurate HIV tests, and has also revolutionized DNA "fingerprinting" techniques.

Getting the Most out of Your Visit

There is far too much to experience here in a day or even two. Most visitors cruise the park's 370 miles of roads trying to get a sense of things, and depart with little more than scenic images. A better strategy is to select a specific area—a river drainage, a valley, or a mountain—and get acquainted with it firsthand. The sites below are good places to start.

SEVEN MILE BRIDGE, located 7 miles east of the western entrance, is the best spot in Yellowstone for seeing Trumpeter Swans. In early summer, the birds are nesting and may be seen and heard (they aren't called trumpeters by accident) on the Madison River. Other swans congregate here during the winter, along with Bald Eagles. In early autumn, the meadows bordering the river are transformed by rutting bull Elk into a series of chessboards, as the males bugle, bluff-charge, and chase each other away from their harems of cows. Late September through early October is the peak of the rut; pull-offs along the road provide excellent viewing sites.

LAMAR VALLEY, about 25 miles east of the Tower-Roosevelt area, is beautiful in late spring and early summer, when great herds of American Bison, Elk, Mule Deer, and Pronghorn graze the new grasses, their fawns and calves in tow. Coyotes, Grizzlies, and possibly wolves may appear on the edges of the herds, tracking their movements or just passing through; it's the North American equivalent of Africa's Serengeti, a primeval scene on a grand scale.

GARDNER CANYON, on the northern boundary of the park, is an important wintering area for deer and Elk, and also offers excellent year-round viewing of Bighorn Sheep and Pronghorn. In summer some of the park's most colorful songbirds are here, including Lazuli Buntings, Western Tanagers, and Green-tailed Towhees, along with such raptors as Golden Eagles and Prairie Falcons. Check the waters of the Gardner River for the American Dipper, a tiny gray bird that hops and bobs along the water's edge before diving in to pursue aquatic insects.

ANTELOPE CREEK, located a few miles south of Tower Falls, is among the most reliable places from which Grizzly Bears may be observed at a safe distance. A good pair of binoculars or a spotting scope is necessary; best viewing hours are at dawn and dusk. In June the Grizzlies are on the lookout for unwary Elk calves; at other times they may be digging up roots and bulbs, or excavating a ground-squirrel snack.

MOUNT WASHBURN provides panoramic views of the park lands, the Grand Canyon of the Yellowstone, and surrounding high country. The hike to the summit is fairly arduous—the 6-mile round-trip takes 3 hours and climbs 1,400 feet—but it offers a good sampling of Yellowstone's subalpine forest and alpine tundra communities. Visitors will see Whitebark Pines, whose nutritious cones and nuts are a major draw for Red Squirrels, Clark's Nutcrackers, and Gray Jays; Grizzlies also feast on these nuts in the fall in advance of hibernation, sniffing out and raiding caches stored by Red Squirrels. At the summit, it's possible to spot a Peregrine Falcon. The summit hike is accessible from two points along the Tower-Canyon road. Either park at the Dunraven Picnic Area or drive 1 mile down the old Chittenden Road to the parking area there.

HAYDEN VALLEY, located along the road between Fishing Bridge and Canyon Village, is another of the park's expansive meadows. It is a

GUIDELINES FOR VIEWING PARK WILDLIFE

Maintain a distance of at least 50 yards from all large animals. American Bison, Moose, Elk, and bears all have the potential for aggressive behavior. If an animal stops feeding, appears distracted, or alters its route of travel, you are too close and should move off.

Do not feed park wildlife. Coyotes in recent years have become assertive roadside beggars. Feeding chipmunks, ground squirrels, deer, and Elk may cause them to lose their fear of people and make them too dependent on unnatural foods. Feeding wildlife will also get you a $50 fine.

Use binoculars and spotting scopes to observe wild animals without disrupting them. Vehicles are perfect observation blinds; park animals are accustomed to seeing them along the roads.

Never leave food or garbage unattended. Bears inhabit virtually every section of the park. If car camping, store food in the trunk of a vehicle or suspend it from the branch of a tree, 10 feet up and 4 feet out from the trunk.

Lamar Valley

favorite springtime haunt of Grizzly Bears, American Bison are present here almost any time of year, and Elk gather in autumn for their mating ritual. Alum Creek attracts a number of shorebirds in spring and fall, including Long-billed Dowitchers, Greater Yellowlegs, and Western Sandpipers. The Yellowstone River traverses the valley and supports Sandhill Cranes, American White Pelicans, Barrow's Goldeneyes, and other waterfowl.

YELLOWSTONE LAKE has the feel of a primordial inland sea. A one-hour boat tour of the lake includes a pass by Stevenson Island, a solid bet for great views of Bald Eagles. Beavers, Northern River Otters, muskrats, and a variety of waterfowl forage along the lakeshore, and Moose may be spotted browsing in the riparian areas. The main body of the lake is open to motorized boats, but the South and Southeast Arms are not, offering paddlers a wonderful opportunity for quiet exploration. Small boats should always remain close to shore, as the lake is subject to sudden, turbulent winds.

The lake's clear, frigid waters are patrolled by native Cutthroat Trout and a nonnative intruder, the Lake Trout. Lake Trout, which were introduced deliberately or by accident about 20 years ago, are voracious predators of other fish. The thriving Lake Trout population that now exists in Yellowstone Lake poses a serious threat to indigenous Cutthroat Trout and the many species that feed on them. Biologists say there is almost no chance the intruders can be extirpated. Costly removal efforts such as netting are now employed to mitigate the impact on native fish. Park officials believe that if long-term funding can be found for ongoing control, the loss of Cutthroats might be held to less than 30 percent over the next 20 years. Grizzly Bears, American White Pelicans, Northern River Otters, and Osprey are a few of the species that include Cutthroat Trout in their diets.

LOCATION Off Hwys. 89, 191, 16, and 212. **CONTACT** Yellowstone N.P., Visitor Services Office, Box 168, Yellowstone N.P., WY 82190; 307-344-7381. **SEASONAL ACCESS** Closed Nov.–mid-Dec. and mid-Mar.–mid-Apr.; call for exact dates. **VISITOR CENTERS** Two are open summer and winter: Mammoth Hot Springs and Old Faithful; several others are open summer only.

GRAND TETON NATIONAL PARK   Moose

Snake River and Teton Range

In contrast to the quiet, seemingly endless splendor of its northern neighbor Yellowstone, Grand Teton features great drama within its much smaller 310,000 acres. Topography supplies the spectacle. The basin, or valley, of the Snake River, known as Jackson Hole, extends north and south at an elevation of 6,750 feet. Along the western edge of the valley, and all at once, the Tetons soar skyward, a 40-mile-long range with eight peaks higher than 12,000 feet; the Grand Teton is highest, reaching 13,770 feet. Today's scene is the handiwork of successive earthquakes, which jolted the mountains upward while the valley swung downward like a trapdoor. Wind, water, and glaciers took it from there, scouring away sedimentary layers from the central peaks to expose core granite nearly as old as the earth itself. A dozen small glaciers survive at high elevations, dripping meltwater along the sheer walls, cirques, and jagged ridges sculpted by their ancestors.

A full complement of intact habitats offers superb and diverse wildlife viewing. In the valley north of Jackson, U.S. 191 passes through extensive sagebrush grasslands atop a series of benches overlooking the Snake River and its bottomlands. Mule Deer, Elk, a small Bison herd, Moose, and Pronghorn graze here spring through fall. The Snake River, meandering for 27 miles through the park, nourishes a lush riparian community of willows, alders, Dwarf Maples, and cottonwoods. Beavers do their part to further diversify these habitats, damming small creeks and side channels to create ponds and pools of slow-moving water. Oxbow Bend, a slow-moving segment about a mile east of Jackson Lake Junction, is home to a Great Blue Heron rookery, American White Pelicans, Moose, and Northern River Otters. The road south from here to Jenny Lake offers a lesson in wildlife and habitat: Much of the area burned in 1980, opening up the dense Lodgepole Pine forest and allowing shrubs, forbs, and grasses a foothold; the burned area, including standing dead trees favored by cavity-nesting birds, now supports a higher concentration of wildlife than the living stands of Lodgepole Pines nearby. West of Jenny Lake, Cascade Canyon is a portal to the high country, with boulder fields and subalpine forests of fir, Engelmann Spruce, and Limber and Whitebark Pines; Golden-mantled Ground Squirrels, American Pikas, and Yellow-bellied Marmots may be seen in the area. Higher still is alpine country, with its talus slopes, glaciers, and blooms of globeflowers, Glacier Lilies, and Alpine Forget-me-nots, the park flower.

More than 200 miles of trails wind through the valley and into the backcountry, accessing lakes, streams, canyons, and camping areas. The Teton Crest Trail runs from the park's southern boundary to Paintbrush Canyon. Other popular trails include those through Granite, Death, and Cascade Canyons; these also connect the Teton Crest Trail to the Valley Trail. Self-guided trails offer shorter, less strenuous access to park flora and fauna; the 2-mile-long Colter Bay Nature Trail and the ½-mile Menor's Ferry and Cunningham Cabin Trails are popular. Trailhead locations appear on the park's map.

Fall aspens and cottonwoods in front of Teton Range

Beginning in the grasslands in early spring and progressing upward into subalpine and alpine zones through summer is one of the Rockies' most spectacular wildflower shows. A visit in late June will usually coincide with peak blooms of lupine, Arrowleaf Balsamroot, Scarlet Gilia, and Wild Buckwheat in blues, reds, whites, yellows, and purples. The broad-shouldered Tetons in the background are still capped with snow, their crags mirrored in the calm waters of numerous lakes against a pure blue sky. Warblers sing from the willows along the Snake River; a cow Moose and her calf browse the new growth. Springtime in the Rockies.

LOCATION North of Jackson, on Hwy. 89. **CONTACT** Grand Teton N.P., P.O. Box 170, Moose, WY 83012; 307-739-3399. **VISITOR CENTERS** In the towns of Moose and Colter Bay.

NATIONAL ELK REFUGE — Jackson

By the early 1900s, nearly 75 percent of the historic Elk winter range in Wyoming's Jackson Valley had been converted to ranch lands or other uses, and the southern Yellowstone herd was in trouble. In 1910, with a $5,000 allocation from the Wyoming legislature, the practice of feeding Elk began, and the 24,700-acre refuge was established two years later.

Wintering Elk herd

Weighing up to 1,000 pounds, with impressive, gnarled antlers, Elk are easy to admire. They descend from Yellowstone, Grand Teton, and adjacent national forests in herds as large as 200, with many thousands converging upon the refuge with the approach of winter. From January through March or April, each animal is fed 8 pounds of alfalfa per day. Production of feed has been increased over the years through prescribed burning and irrigation.

Along with Elk, large herds of Mule Deer and Pronghorn may be seen year-round; a visitor center, open in winter only, offers sleigh rides, a long-time tradition on the refuge. At other times of the year, visitors can explore via the refuge road.

Today the refuge faces a new quandary, brought about by its unmitigated success—the Jackson Elk herd is bursting at the seams with an estimated 17,000 animals. The heavy concentration of Elk has raised concerns about transmission of diseases such as brucellosis, pasteurellosis, and even tuberculosis. Also, the aspen forests are heavily browsed, which could lead to a future reduction in mature trees, to the detriment of many bird species. Some biologists say the herd has outstripped the area's winter carrying capacity; others have called for an end to supplemental feeding. Wildlife managers are already discussing the choices they could face if the herd must be culled.

LOCATION North of Jackson, on Hwy. 191. **CONTACT** National Elk R., P.O. Box C, Jackson, WY 83001; 307-733-9212. **VISITOR CENTER** On Hwy. 191, at northern edge of Jackson.

SHOSHONE NATIONAL FOREST   Cody

Much of Shoshone National Forest's 2.4 million acres abut Yellowstone's eastern boundary, providing a critical extension of the area's ecosystem, with similar habitats for Elk, Grizzly Bears, wolves, Mountain Lions, Mountain Goats, Moose, and other large, free-roaming species. Included in the forest is a string of wilderness areas: To the north are the Washakie, Absaroka–Beartooth, and North Absaroka Wildernesses; the Popo Agie and Fitzpatrick Wildernesses lie respectively on the south and east flanks of the Wind River Range. The area is richly forested to about 10,000 feet, with alpine communities of mosses and herbaceous plants above the tree line. The Wild and Scenic Clark's Fork of the Yellowstone tumbles through a beautiful gorge in the forest's northern reaches; other rivers to explore include the Wind, and the North and South Forks of the Shoshone Roads

View of Pilot Peak, Absaroka Range

here provide access to some of the high country, and there are many opportunities for hiking, camping, and wildlife viewing.

For scenic driving, there is nothing quite like a tour of the Beartooth Scenic Byway. The route begins in Red Lodge, Montana, at about 5,500 feet, and ascends rapidly skyward to the Beartooth Plateau, much of which lies above 10,000 feet. Great effort is made to clear the road of its massive snowdrifts by June; it then remains open as long as warm weather persists, usually closing in September. The Whiskey Mountain–Whiskey Basin area, on the flanks of the Wind River Range, offers unmatched opportunities to see and learn about Bighorn Sheep, as the world's largest population of them lives here. Visitors should stop at the National Bighorn Sheep Interpretive Center in Dubois, where guided tours can be arranged in season. For the independent-minded, the area may be explored year-round by car, though the roads are narrow and cruel. Good viewing areas are found along the stretch of road between Trail Lake and the Whiskey Mountain Wildlife Conservation Camp (Audubon Camp in the Rockies), with mornings and evenings the prime viewing hours. During winter, the animals are readily seen right along the roadsides almost any time of day. Bring a camera with a telephoto lens and stay in your vehicle to avoid disturbing them.

LOCATION From Cody, follow Hwy. 14/16/20. **CONTACT** Shoshone N.F., 808 Meadow La., Cody, WY 82414-4516; 307-527-6241. **VISITOR CENTERS** The following ranger districts offer maps and information year-round: Wapiti Ranger District in Cody, at 203A Yellowstone; Wind River Ranger District in Dubois, at 1403 W. Ramshorn; Washakie Ranger District in Lander, at 333 E. Main St.

BRIDGER-TETON NATIONAL FOREST   Jackson

Bridger-Teton is the largest national forest outside Alaska, its 3.4 million acres encompassing both the Salt River and Wind River Ranges. The Wind River Range features more than a dozen peaks above 13,000 feet and seven of the ten largest remaining glaciers in the lower 48 states. A drive through the Green River Lakes area offers a good sam-

Summer Ice Lake, Wind River Range

ple of the wonderful Winds, ending in the upper Green River Valley with an imposing view of Squaretop Mountain standing sentinel over steep-sided lakes. The Bridger Wilderness Area, also in the Winds, features an estimated one thousand alpine lakes. The Thoroughfare Trail at Bridger Lake follows the Yellowstone River all the way to Yellowstone Lake, traversing lush meadows and Lodgepole Pine forests, home to Grizzlies. The Salt River Range, with its numerous steep, narrow canyons, is less visited and has fewer roads. Many spring creeks dissect the river and its floodplain, and there is a good chance to see nesting Trumpeter Swans and Sandhill Cranes in the wet meadows. The river is accessible via a number of public access points.

LOCATION North of Jackson, off Hwy. 89/26. CONTACT Bridger–Teton N.F., P.O. Box 1888, Jackson, WY 83001; 307-739-5500. VISITOR CENTER In Jackson.

SEEDSKADEE NATIONAL WILDLIFE REFUGE   Green River

This 23,000-acre corridor of wet meadows, oxbows, sloughs, and cottonwood-willow habitats along the Green River is bounded by salt-desert shrub lands and sagebrush. Seedskadee is a Shoshone word meaning "river of the prairie hen," which refers to the striking native Sage Grouse, present here in signif-

Cottonwoods on Green River

icant numbers. Birds are a major attraction. Look for Great Blue Heron rookeries atop the taller cottonwoods. Merlins, Common Mergansers, and Sharp-shinned Hawks nest among the cottonwoods and along the river's cliffs and clay banks. April and May are peak migration months. Breeding waterfowl include Redheads, Ruddy Ducks, Canvasbacks, Canada Geese, Ring-billed Ducks, and Lesser Scaups; shorebirds include Spotted and Stilt Sandpipers, Long-Billed Dowitchers, Marbled Godwits, and Wilson's Phalaropes. Five species of swallow are abundant on the river ledges and banks: Violet-green, Cliff, Bank, Barn, and Tree. Common mammals include beavers, river otters, Moose, and Mule and White-tailed Deer.

LOCATION North of Green River, on Hwy. 372. CONTACT Seedskadee N.W.R., P.O. Box 700, Green River, WY 82935; 307-875-2187. VISITOR CENTER At refuge, 2½ miles from entrance.

BIGHORN NATIONAL FOREST Dayton

The Bighorn Mountains of north-central Wyoming are an isolated range surrounded by great rolling plains, and almost entirely contained within the 1.1 million acres of Bighorn National Forest. Their snowy ramparts stand as a portal to the Rockies for visitors traveling west from the Dakotas or Nebraska. More than half the range is forested, with Lodgepole Pine the dominant species and mosaics of aspen forest appearing throughout. The exposed granite peaks of the core range are topped by 13,165-foot Cloud Peak. Its namesake 200,000-acre wilderness area features hundreds of alpine lakes, several glaciers, and alpine meadows of dwarfed shrubs, sedges, and wildflowers. The Little Bighorn and Tongue Rivers drain the mountains through scenic canyons; hiking trails parallel these waters before leading into the high country. There are about 276 recorded bird species. Elk, Moose, Wolverines, Fishers, Pine Martens, Northern Flying Squirrels, Northern River Otters, and Lynx are a few of the 54 known mammal species.

LOCATION Northwest of Sheridan, off Hwy. 14. **CONTACT** Bighorn N.F., 1969 S. Sheridan Ave., Sheridan, WY 82801; 307-672-0751. **VISITOR CENTER** Burgess V.C., at north end of forest, on Hwy. 14.

BLACK HILLS NATIONAL FOREST Custer, SD

Most of the scenic Black Hills National Forest, sacred lands for the Lakota Sioux and Cheyenne Indians, lies in South Dakota, but about 175,000 acres spill into eastern Wyoming. The region's steep, forested ridges, numerous streams and waterfalls, small lakes, caves, and unusual rock formations provide a varied and fascinating area for naturalists. Forest Road 863 follows Sand Creek to the stream's headwaters, passing through cottonwoods and willow bottoms along the creek, semiarid shrub lands of mountain mahoganies and sagebrush, and rich forests of Ponderosa Pines and aspens. Wild Turkeys are common here and may be seen early or late in the day in open forest or along the road. White-tailed Deer, Ruffed and Sharp-tailed Grouse, and Elk may also be seen. Sand Creek is Wyoming's most prolific trout fishery, producing more fish per mile than any other stream in the state. Yellow-billed Cuckoos and Lewis's Woodpeckers are two birds here that are seldom seen elsewhere in Wyoming.

LOCATION Off Rte. 385. **CONTACT** Black Hills N.F., Rte. 2, Box 200, Custer, SD 57730; 605-673-2251. **VISITOR CENTER** At Pactola Reservoir, SD, on Rte. 385 (closed in winter).

THUNDER BASIN NATIONAL GRASSLAND

Douglas

Thunder Basin National Grassland encompasses about 1.5 million publicly and privately owned acres of rolling, wide-open prairie. Much of the range was depleted during the early 1900s through poor farming and ranching practices and severe drought. In the late 1930s, the federal government began buying up failed ranches, reseeding native prairie grasses, and installing windbreaks and ponds. Today, the range has regained its health. Native bunchgrasses such as Blue Grama, Western Wheatgrass, and Needlegrass are interspersed with sagebrush and prickly-pear cactus. Cottonwoods line the streams, and Ponderosa Pines on the ridges and slopes stand against the vast sky. The 200 recorded bird species include Greater and Lesser Yellowlegs, White-faced Ibises, American White Pelicans, Baird's Sandpipers, and 13 species of sparrows. Wyoming supports two-thirds of the world's Pronghorn population, and Thunder Basin is home to the state's largest herd. Watch them run—a Pronghorn in full stride appears to float over the prairie, its back level, its neck at rest.

LOCATION Hwys. 59 and 450 run through the grassland. **CONTACT** Thunder Basin N.G., 2250 E. Richards St., Douglas, WY 82633; 307-358-4690.

MEDICINE BOW NATIONAL FOREST

Laramie

This 1,093,618-acre forest encompasses southeastern Wyoming's Sierra Madre, Laramie, and Medicine Bow Mountains. The lower elevations are heavily forested in Lodgepole Pine and aspen, with the higher subalpine meadows and lakes bordered by Engelmann Spruce and stunted Subalpine Fir. There are four wilderness areas totaling about 80,000 acres. Ayres Natural Bridge, in the foothills of the Laramies, is a gorgeous limestone arch spanning La Prele Creek. The

Battle Highway leads through the Sierra Madres, which support the most extensive aspen forests in Wyoming, along with a thriving community of warblers, woodpeckers, Northern Goshawks, and Northern Saw-whet Owls. The Snowy Range Highway is a national scenic byway through the Medicine Bows, known

Libby Flats

locally as the Snowy Mountains; it climbs from semiarid grasslands up to 12,013-foot Medicine Bow Peak and its alpine world of low-growing shrubs, abundant wildflowers, ptarmigans, and Bighorn Sheep. An observation point at nearby Libby Flats provides panoramic views of the entire forest.

LOCATION West of Laramie, on Hwys. 130 and 230. **CONTACT** Medicine Bow N.F., 2468 Jackson St., Laramie, WY 82070; 307-745-2300. **VISITOR CENTERS** In Centennial, on Hwy. 130; in Brushcreek, on Hwy. 130 (summer only).

AMSDEN CREEK WILDLIFE UNIT   Dayton
This 4,000-acre site provides winter range for a large Elk herd; visitors also come just to savor the beautiful Tongue River canyon, accessible via an all-weather road. **CONTACT** Amsden Creek W.U., Wyoming Game and Fish, Sheridan Regional Office, P.O. Box 6249, Sheridan, WY 82801; 307-672-7418.

BIGHORN CANYON NATIONAL RECREATION AREA   Lovell
The narrow, steep-walled Bighorn River canyon resides over this semidesert landscape of terra-cotta hues. Travel is primarily via the river and reservoir; ask rangers about hikes and wildlife sightings (see also page 400). **CONTACT** Bighorn Canyon N.R.A., 20 Hwy. 14A East, Lovell, WY 82431; 307-548-2251.

Pronghorn female and young

BOYSEN STATE PARK   Shoshoni
These park lands surround a 19,885-acre impoundment on the Wind River. Picnicking, boating, and fishing are popular activities here. Watch for Bighorn Sheep, Mule Deer, Pronghorn, Sage Grouse, and waterfowl. **CONTACT** Boysen S.P., 15 Ash Boysen Route, Shoshoni, WY 82649; 307-876-2796.

FOSSIL BUTTE NATIONAL MONUMENT   Kemmerer
This uncrowded park preserves a section of the Green River Formation, the site of three ancient great lakes, and is filled with geologic wonders—fossil fishes, mammals, reptiles, and other fauna. Colorful eroded badlands terrace the base of the butte. There is a visitor center and a ranger on duty. **CONTACT** Fossil Butte N.M., P.O. Box 592, Kemmerer, WY 83101; 307-877-4455.

HUTTON LAKE NATIONAL WILDLIFE REFUGE   Laramie
Wading birds and shorebirds, as well as waterfowl, prairie dogs, Meadow Jumping Mice, and Desert Cottontails, are plentiful at this small refuge of ponds amid the rolling Laramie Plains. **CONTACT** Hutton Lake N.W.R., P.O. Box 457, Walden, CO 80480-0457; 970-723-8202.

KEYHOLE STATE PARK   Moorcroft
Park lands adjoin the 8-mile-long impoundment on the Belle Fourche River, the only large body of water within a hundred miles. Water sports and camping are the main activities here. **CONTACT** Keyhole S.P., 353 McKean Rd., Moorcroft, WY 82721; 307-756-3596.

OCEAN LAKE WILDLIFE HABITAT AREA   Riverton
The area consists of more than 12,000 acres of extensive wetlands, open water, and sagebrush-grassland uplands. A resident flock of 200 to 400 Canada Geese nest here. **CONTACT** Ocean Lake W.H.A., Wyoming Dept. of Game and Fish, 260 Buena Vista, Lander, WY 82520; 307-332-2688.

SYBILLE WILDLIFE RESEARCH AND
EDUCATION CENTER   Wheatland
A breeding and research program here benefits the Black-footed Ferret, one of the world's rarest mammals. There are on-duty naturalists, and tours of the center can be arranged. **CONTACT** Sybille Wildlife Research and Education Ctr., 2362 Hwy. 34, Wheatland, WY 82201; 307-322-2784.

The Authors

Peter Alden, principal author of this series, is a birder, naturalist, author, and lecturer. He has led nature tours to over 100 countries for the Massachusetts Audubon Society, Lindblad Travel, Friends of the Harvard Museum of Natural History, and cruises on all the world's oceans. Author of books on North American, Latin American, and African wildlife, Peter organized an event called Biodiversity Day in his hometown of Concord, Massachusetts.

Brian Cassie co-wrote the invertebrates section of this guide. He writes and teaches about natural history and is the co-author of the *National Audubon Society Field Guide to New England.* Brian lives with his family in Foxboro, Massachusetts.

John Grassy, author of the habitats, conservation and ecology, and parks and preserves sections of this book, is an educator, conservationist, and writer. John co-wrote the *National Audubon Society First Field Guide: Mammals.* He lives with his family in Three Forks, Montana.

Jonathan D. W. Kahl, Ph.D., co-wrote the weather section of this book. He teaches and researches meteorology, air pollution, and climate at the University of Wisconsin in Milwaukee. Jon has published professional articles and children's books on atmospheric science and weather, including the *National Audubon Society First Field Guide: Weather.*

Amy Leventer, Ph.D., author of the topography and geology section of this guide, is a visiting assistant professor at Colgate University's Geology Department. She has published many articles on geology and also co-authored the *National Audubon Society Pocket Guide to Earth from Space.*

Daniel Mathews wrote the flora section of this guide. He is a naturalist writer and photographer who has published books, articles, and poetry on nature. Mathews lives in Portland, Oregon.

Wendy B. Zomlefer, Ph.D., wrote the introductions in the flora section of this guide. She is a post-doctoral associate in the botany department at the University of Florida in Gainesville and courtesy assistant curator of the University of Florida Herbarium.

Acknowledgments

The authors collectively thank the thousands of botanists, zoologists, and naturalists we have worked with over the years and whose books and papers provided a wealth of information for this book. The staff and members of the following organizations were most helpful: National Audubon Society and its chapters, Massachusetts Audubon Society, Harvard Museum of Natural History, Nature Conservancy, Denver Museum of Natural History, Sierra Club, American Birding Association, and North American Butterfly Association. We also thank the staffs of the many federal and state land, game, and fish departments.

We thank the following experts for their help in writing the text and reviewing the text and photos of various sections of this guide: Rudolf Arndt (fishes); John L. Behler (amphibians and reptiles); Richard Hurley (invertebrates); Richard Keene (weather and night sky); Gary Mechler (weather and night sky); Stephen Sharnoff and Sylvia Sharnoff (lichens); Susan Spackman (flora); Ernie Brodo, Jonathan Dey, Elizabeth Kneiper, and Bruce Ryan (lichens selections); W. P. McCafferty, Blair Nikula, Dennis Paulson, W. D. Winter, Jr., and Michael Ivie (invertebrates). Hank Fischer, the regional consultant, reviewed most sections of this guide. The Idaho Cooperative Fish and Wildlife Research Units' Landscape Dynamics Laboratory developed the habitats map. We also thank Jeff Stone of Chic Simple Design for initial editorial and design consultation.

Special thanks go to Richard Carey, Rick Cech, Sidney Dunkle, John Flicker, the late Richard Forster, Frank Gill, Karsten Hartel, Fred Heath, Boris Kondratieff, Vernon Laux, Paul Opler, Simon Perkins, Wayne Petersen, the late Roger Tory Peterson, Virginia Peterson, Noble Proctor, Judy Schwenk, Richard Walton, and Edward O. Wilson.

We are grateful to Andrew Stewart for his vision of a regional field guide encompassing the vast mosaic of the Rocky Mountain region's topography, habitats, and wildlife, and to the staff of Chanticleer Press for producing a book of such excellence. Editor-in-chief Amy Hughes provided fundamental conceptual guidance as well as constant encouragement and supervision. The success of the book is due largely to the considerable skills and expertise of project editor Pamela Nelson and series editor Patricia Fogarty. Senior editor Miriam Harris and editor Holly Thompson thoroughly examined and refined the flora section. Managing editor George Scott shepherded the book through the editorial process. Associate editor Michelle Bredeson meticulously fact checked, copyedited, and proofread the book through all stages. Assistant editor Elizabeth Wright and editorial interns Samten Chhosphel, Abby Gordon, and Morisa Kessler-Zacharias offered much assistance and support. Editorial freelancers Jennifer Dixon, Lisa Leventer, Lisa Lester, and Mike Stanzilis (aka Mike Taylor) made many valuable contributions.

Art director Drew Stevens and designers Vincent Mejia and Anthony Liptak took 1,500 images and tens of thousands of words of text and created a book that is both visually beautiful and eminently usable. Patricia Harris assisted in the layout of the book. Howard S. Friedman created the beautiful and informative color illustrations. Wil Tirion produced the stunning night sky maps. Ortelius Design made the detailed maps that appear throughout the book, and the mammal tracks illustrations were contributed by Dot Barlowe.

Photo director Zan Carter and her staff sifted through thousands of photographs from hundreds of photographers in their search for the stunning images that contribute so much to the beauty and usefulness of this guide. They carefully chose the images that best represented each subject and worked patiently with the authors, consultants, natural history experts, and the editorial, design, and production teams. Photo editors Jennifer McClanaghan and Christine Heslin researched and edited the photos used in the parks and preserves and overview sections, respectively. The team from Artemis Picture Research Group, Inc.—Linda Patterson Eger and Lois Safrani—brought considerable skills and experience to the task of researching and editing many of the species photographs. Permissions manager Alyssa Sachar facilitated the acquisition of photographs and ensured that all records and photo credits were accurate. Photo editor Ruth Jeyaveeran and photo assistants Karin Murphy, Leslie Fink, and Marie Buendia offered endless support. Dan Hugos's database helped keep track of the hundreds of photographers and thousands of photographs.

Director of production Alicia Mills and production manager Philip Pfeifer saw the book through the complicated production and printing processes. They worked closely with Dai Nippon Printing to ensure the excellent printing quality of these books. Office manager Raquel Penzo offered much support.

In addition, we thank all of the photographers who gathered and submitted the gorgeous pictures that make this book a delight to view.

—Peter Alden, Brian Cassie,
John Grassy, Jonathan D. W. Kahl,
Amy Leventer, Daniel Mathews, Wendy B. Zomlefer

Picture Credits

The credits are listed alphabetically by photographer. Each photograph is listed by the number of the page on which it appears, followed by a letter indicating its position on the page (the letters follow a sequence from top left to bottom right).

136c, 143b, 165e, 169c, 172d
Karen McClymonds 354a
Joe McDonald 328a, 341a, 349a, 363b
Charles W. Melton 35b, 98f, 110c, 111c & d, 195d, 199b, 274a, 314a, 333c
Brian K. Miller 45a
C. Allan Morgan 98g, 99c, 284c, 296b
Arthur Morris/BIRDS AS ART 248c, 252b, 254b, 259b, 261d, 263b, 270a, 272d, 278c, 279c, 280b & c, 292b, 314e, 320a
NASA/JPL/Caltech 63b & c, 65c
National Audubon Society Collection, Photo Researchers, Inc. 376b
Franz Bagyi/ OKAPIA 56
N. E. Beck, Jr. 195c
Edna Bennett 61d
H. Berthoule/Jacana 227a
Bob & Elsie Boggs 286a
John Bova 62a, 217d, 218e
Tom Branch 82a, 160c
Scott Camazine 102a, 190e
Alan Carey 39a, 41b, 281b
Ted Clutter 10a
Ray Coleman 193c
Joseph T. Collins 232a, 233
Steve Coombs 266a
Stephen Dalton 337b
Kent & Donna Dannen 143a, 144b, 156d
Tim Davis 53
E. R. Degginger 28c
Betty Derig 119c
Joe DiStefano 188b
Phil A. Dotson 352a, 360a

R. J. Erwin 95c, 206b, 212d, 216a, 224a, 228a, 340b, 342b
James R. Fisher 357
David R. Frazier 47b, 48b, 61a
S. C. Fried 298d, 317b, 321a
Michael P. Gadomski 158d, 235a
Michael Giannechini 162e
Francois Gohier 21b, 29a
Patrick W. Grace 131e
Gilbert S. Grant 192c, 196a
Dan Guravich 81b
Robert C. Hermes 147e
David Hosking 337c, 412
Joyce Photographics 25b, 30a
G. C. Kelley 348a
L. & D. Klein 117a
Paolo Koch 26a
Stephen J. Krasemann 323c, 402a
Calvin Larsen 11c
Angelina Lax 142b
Jess R. Lee 260c
Tom & Pat Leeson 99b, 136b, 260a, 262a, 330a, 336c, 345a, 347a, 348b, 351b, 358b, 359b, 361a, 367b
Jeff Lepore 203a, 251, 346a, 356b
Craig K. Lorenz 366a
Alexander Lowry 49a
Michael Lustbader 134a
David Macias 48a, 360b
Charles W. Mann 314b
Steve Maslowski 280d, 323b
Steve & Dave Maslowski 262d, 295a, 313c

Tom McHugh 146d, 264b, 332b, 341d, 342c, 343a & b
Tom McHugh/ Denver Museum of Natural History 25c
Anthony Mercieca 211b, 261c, 281a, 286b, 300d, 308a
Kathy Merrifield 156b
William H. Mullins 46b, 51a, 105a, 223a
William Munoz 50
Paul W. Nesbit 142a
Charlie Ott 100c, 334b
Richard Parker 121d, 175d
Pekka Parviainen 62b
Rod Planck 77a, 102b, 238c, 304c, 315e, 318e, 330c, 331b
Noah Poritz 197a
Andrew Rakoczy 37a
Gary Retherford 217e
A. H. Rider 155d
Leonard Lee Rue III 252d, 267b, 282a
Jerry Schad 65b
Gregory K. Scott 23b, 237b, 266c
M. H. Sharp 202a, b, c, d, e & f
James Simon 241b
Hugh Spencer 217c
Jim Steinberg 19a, 22a, 132a, 138f
Dan Sudia 61c
USGS/SPL 63b
R. Van Nostrand 262c
L. West 82c, 198a
Jeanne White 354b
Charles D. Winters 26c
Jim Zipp 261a
National Park Service, WY 51b
Blair Nikula 184b & c, 186b & d
David Nunnallee 205e, 207b, 208b

Frank Oberle 59a,
61b, 139b, 142c,
146b, 155c, 166a,
167d, 260b, 391b,
403b

Jack Olson 374b,
375a, 417b

Paul Opler 95f, 189b
& c, 201d, 204c,
205d, 209a & d,
215d

Rob Outlaw Photography 400a

Londie G. Padelsky
136d

James F. Parnell 228c,
229a, 327c, 329b

Dennis Paulson 185a

Jerry Pavia 91c, 96a,
107e, 118c, 119e,
132d, 139c, 142d,
148d, 149c, 150e,
159a, 164d, 177b & c

Joanne Pavia 90b,
97c, 104e, 114b &
d, 130a, 137c & d,
160e, 165d

Carroll Perkins 335b

B. Moose Peterson/
WRP 224d, 225a,
327a, 328b, 340d

Rod Planck 40b,
151b, 257c,
288d, 338a, 344a,
419

Rick Poley 43b

Robert & Jean
Pollock 333b

ProPhoto
Mark Giovanetti
226b
Doug Stamm 224b
& c, 226c

Betty Randall 152c,
160d, 320b, 341c,
352b

David Ransaw 131a,
140c

Paul Rezendes 85a,
135d

Jeffrey Rich 272b, 300c

Ken K. Ringer 59b

James H. Robinson
98c, 111a, 174b,
187c, 190a, 194a,
200d, 218c, 306b,
335d

Jim Roetzel 167c,
181c, 276d, 283d,
295c, 318d, 319d

Eda Rogers 96b, 112c,
114e & f, 173b

Root Resources
Jim Flynn 257b
Anthony Mercieca
294b, 315b & c,
334d, 353a
Alan G. Nelson
265a

Edward S. Ross 31d,
179a & c, 180,
181b, 184a, 186e,
187d, 189a, 190b,
191a, b & c, 192b
& d, 194b, 195e,
196b, 197c, 198c,
200b & c, 203e,
207d, 209c, 210b,
211a & c, 213c,
214a, 217b

Phillip Roullard 200e

Larry Sansone 208e,
210c, 344c

Kevin Schafer 349c

David M. Schleser/
Nature's Images,
Inc 116d, 181e,
196c

John Serrao 36a, 130e

Perry Shankle, Jr.
353b

Stephen Sharnoff 84a
& c, 85c & d, 86a,
b, c & d

Sylvia Duran Sharnoff
84b & d, 85b

John Shaw 11a, 23a,
163b, 192a

Allen Blake Sheldon
218a, 243d, 244a

Rob & Ann Simpson
77b, 79b, 81c, 88a,
109a, 110a, 112a,
182a, 223b, 230a &
b, 260d, 285c,
286d, 294a, 304d,
322c, 334a

Brian E. Small 250b,
255b, 263a, 264d,
275c, 277a, 287b,
291c, 292c, 293c,
296a, 298b, 302c,
304b, 305d, 306d,
308c, 309a, b, d &

e, 310c & e, 311a, c,
& d, 312a, b, & d,
316d, 317e, 320c,
322d, 323a, 380a

Hugh P. Smith, Jr.
261b, 265b, 269a,
275a, 280a, 286c

Mark Smith 179b

Michael M. Smith/
View Two Plus
149c

Scott T. Smith 11b,
12b, 79a, 95g, 98a,
104d, 105c, 128b,
141d, 146a, 307b,
372, 373, 381, 390a,
398, 400b, 416b

Sherm Spoelstra 41a

Ira & Bob Spring 175b

Joy Spurr 33c, 80d,
81a & d, 83a & b,
87a, 91a, 94a, 95d &
e, 96d & e, 96f, 97a,
100b, 104a, 106b,
107a, b, c, & d, 109b,
112d, 114a, 115a, e
& f, 116a & c, 117b
& d, 120c & d, 126b
& d, 129e, 133a &
d, 135b, c & e, 138b,
139d & e, 140a & d,
144a, d & e, 147b,
148b, 149d, 150a, b
& d, 151a & c, 153c,
d & e, 155a, 157c,
158a & c, 159c & e,
161e, 162a, 164a &
e, 165a, 166b & d,
167e, 168b, 170c,
171c, 172a, 174a,
176d

Steven M. Still 103c

Joseph G. Strauch, Jr.
119b, 126e, 128c &
e, 129a, 175c

Charles G. Summers,
Jr. 352c, 355a

Rita Summers 343c,
346b

Karl H. Switak 234c,
242b

Ronald J. Taylor 33a,
97f, 99f, 113e, 114c,
116b, 117c, 127a,
130b & d, 131b &
d, 133c, 134b, 135a,
141a, 145a, 148a,

149a, 156c, 163e,
172b, 175a, 176a,
177a & d
**Ronald J. Taylor/
Mark Sheehan** 96c
Tom Till 377a & b,
379b
Jeffrey L. Torretta
388, 389, 396
Mark Turner 100d,
106c, 113a, 120e,
134c, 151d, 154a,
163a, 167a, 169a,
171a, 316c
**Merlin D. Tuttle/Bat
Conservation Inter-
national** 329a, c & d
Tom J. Ulrich 250d,
263c, 276a, 284d,
289a & b, 292a,
306a, 310a, 312c,
313b, 317d, 319b,
321c, 333a, 334c,
337d, 339a, 350a
**University of Wiscon-
sin** 121c
R. W. Van Devender
232c, 240e
Jeff Vanuga 239c,
352e
Tom Vezo 42b, 249c
& e, 250a, 254a &
d, 256b & c, 264c,
271c, 272a & c,
274d, 275b, 278a,
284b, 291a, 298a,
299c, 301b & c,
305c, 313d, 316a,
318b, 322a
Visuals Unlimited
David Cavagnaro 49b
**Kevin & Betty
Collins** 90c
John Gerlach 249d
Mark E. Gibson 22b
Mack Henley 333d
**Daniel D. Lam-
oreux** 44b, 47a
Ken Lucas 227c
Maslowski 229c
Martin G. Miller 24a
Richard Norman 24b
Glen M. Oliver 88b
Hugh Rose 52a
Jim Schollmeyer
183a & b
John Sohlden 61f

Doug Sokell 100a
Richard Thom 29b
Wolfgang Vogt 26b
Harry M. Walker
319c, 331a, 362a,
363a
Mark F. Wallner
257c, 273c & d,
276b, 293a, 332c,
336a, 339c, 342d,
361b, 399a
**B. Walsh, J. Beckett,
& M. Carruthers**
(Samples courtesy of
the American Mu-
seum of Natural
History, NY) 29d
Jan L. Wassink 327c
Sally Weigand 106a,
118d
Art Wolfe 362b
George Wuerthner
20a, 43a, 370, 384,
385b, 386a & b,
387a & b, 390b,
403a, 417a
**Dale & Marian Zim-
merman** 263d,
290a, 291b, 303c,
340c
H. Zirlin 208c, 213d,
216d
Tim Zurowski 253c
& d, 265c, 269d,
271a, 277b, 278b,
282d, 288a, 293b,
294c, 295d, 298c,
299a, 305a, 306c,
313e, 317a, 319e,
321d, 322b

* *The Caddisfly Hand-
book: An Orvis Guide.*
The Lyons Press, New
York, NY, 1999.

**From *A Field Manual
of Ferns and Fern Allies
of the United States and
Canada* by D. B.
Lellinger. Smithsonian
Institution Press, Wash-
ington, DC, 1985.

Front Cover: Grand
Teton Range, Grand
Teton National Park,
Wyoming, by Jeff Foott

Spine: Devil's Tower,
Devil's Tower Na-
tional Monument,
Wyoming, by Jeff
Foott

Back Cover: Jerry
Schad/Photo Re-
searchers, Inc.(a),
Londie G. Padelsky (b),
Michael Francis (c),
Jeffrey L. Torretta (d)

Table of Contents:
Howard S. Friedman
(6a, 7a, 7c), Ed
Cooper Photo (6b),
John Bova/Photo
Researchers, Inc. (6c),
Ron Austing (7b),
Tom Till (7d)

Title Page: Snake
River Canyon, Idaho,
by Charles Gurche

Pages 8–9: Maroon
Lake, White River Na-
tional Forest, Col-
orado, by Tom Till

Pages 74–75: Elk,
Mammoth Hot
Springs, Yellowstone
National Park,
Wyoming, by Jeff
Foott

Pages 368–369:
Thousand Springs
along Snake River,
Idaho, by Charles
Gurche

All original illustra-
tions by Howard
S. Friedman, except
mammals tracks (pp.
325–326), by Dot
Barlow

Maps by Ortelius
Design

Night sky maps by
Wil Tirion

Index

Converting to Metric

Limited space makes it impossible for us to give measurements expressed as metrics. Here is a simplified chart for converting standard measurements to their metric equivalents:

	MULTIPLY BY
inches to millimeters	25
inches to centimeters	2.5
feet to meters	0.3
yards to meters	0.9
miles to kilometers	1.6
square miles to square kilometers	2.6
acres to hectares	.40
ounces to grams	28.3
pounds to kilograms	.45
Fahrenheit to Centigrade	subtract 32 and multiply by .55

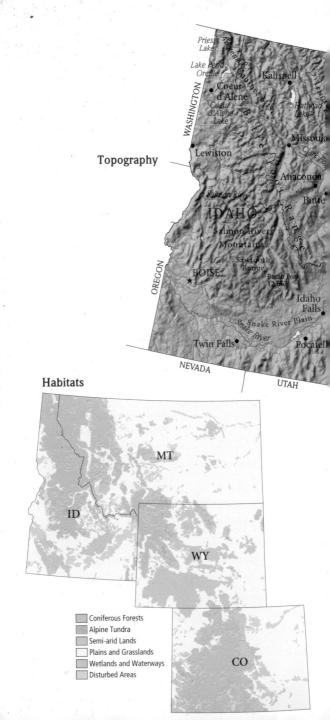

Topography

Priest Lake
Lake Pend Oreille
Coeur d'Alene
Coeur d'Alene Lake
Kalispell
Flathead Lake
Missoula
Lewiston
Anaconda
Butte
Salmon River
IDAHO
Salmon River Mountains
Sawtooth Range
BOISE
Borah Peak 12,662
Idaho Falls
Snake River Plain
Snake River
Twin Falls
Pocatell

WASHINGTON
OREGON
NEVADA
UTAH

Habitats

MT
ID
WY
CO

Coniferous Forests
Alpine Tundra
Semi-arid Lands
Plains and Grasslands
Wetlands and Waterways
Disturbed Areas